Research Companion to Working Time and Work Addiction

NEW HORIZONS IN MANAGEMENT

Series Editor: Cary L. Cooper, CBE, *Professor of Organizational Psychology and Health, Lancaster University Management School, Lancaster University, UK*

This important series makes a significant contribution to the development of management thought. This field has expanded dramatically in recent years and the series provides an invaluable forum for the publication of high quality work in management science, human resource management, organizational behaviour, marketing, management information systems, operations management, business ethics, strategic management and international management.

The main emphasis of the series is on the development and application of new original ideas. International in its approach, it will include some of the best theoretical and empirical work from both well-established researchers and the new generation of scholars.

Titles in the series include:

Research Companion to Working Time and Work Addiction

Edited by

Ronald J. Burke

Professor of Organizational Behavior, Schulich School of Business, York University, Canada

NEW HORIZONS IN MANAGEMENT

Edward Elgar
Cheltenham, UK • Northampton, MA, USA

Published by
Edward Elgar Publishing Limited
Glensanda House
Montpellier Parade
Cheltenham
Glos GL50 1UA
UK

Edward Elgar Publishing, Inc.
William Pratt House
9 Dewey Court
Northampton
Massachusetts 01060
USA

A catalogue record for this book
is available from the British Library

Library of Congress Cataloging in Publication Data
Burke, Ronald J.
   Research companion to working time and work addiction / Ronald J. Burke.
       p. cm. — (New horizons in management series)
   Includes bibliographical references and index.
   1. Work. 2. Work—Psychological aspects. 3. Work—Social aspects. 4. Quality
   of work life. 5. Work and family. 6. Workaholism. I. Title. II. Series: New
   horizons in management

   HD4854.B84 2006   2006008416

ISBN-13: 978 1 84542 408 4
ISBN-10: 1 84542 408 5

Printed and bound in Great Britain by MPG Books Ltd, Bodmin, Cornwall

Contents

v

Contributors

Arnold B. Bakker, Department of Social and Organizational Psychology, Utrecht University, Utrecht, the Netherlands

Michelle L. Buck, Kellogg Graduate School of Management, Northwestern University, Evanston, Illinois, USA

Ronald J. Burke, Professor of Organizational Behavior, Schulich School of Business, York University, Toronto, Canada

Charles P. Chen, Ph.D., Associate Professor of Counselling Psychology and Canada Research Chair in Life Career Development, Ontario Institute for Studies in Education, University of Toronto, (OISE/UT), Toronto, Ontario

Louis W. Fry, Tarleton State University, Central Texas, Killeen, Texas, USA

Lonnie Golden, Professor of Economics and Labor Studies, Pennsylvania State University, Abington College, USA

Robert A. Herring III, School of Business and Economics, Winston-Salem State University, Winston-Salem, North Carolina, USA

Atsuko Kanai, Professor, Graduate School of Education and Human Development, Nagoya University, Nagoya, Japan

Fahri Karakas, Desautels Faculty of Management, McGill University, Montreal, Quebec, Canada

Dr Barbara Killinger, Private Practice, Toronto, Ontario, Canada

Ellen Ernst Kossek, School of Labor and Industrial Relations, Michigan State University, East Lansing, Michigan, USA

Mary Dean Lee, Desautels Faculty of Management, McGill University, Montreal, Quebec, Canada

Pamela Lirio, Desautels Faculty of Management, McGill University, Montreal, Quebec, Canada

Graeme MacDermid, Lecturer, Schulich School of Business, York University, Toronto, Ontario

Shelley M. MacDermid, Center for Families, Purdue University, West Lafayette, Indiana, USA

Laura L. Matherly, Tarleton State University, Central Texas, Killeen, Texas, USA

Teal McAteer-Early, Professor of Human Resources Management, DeGroote School of Business, McMaster University, Hamilton, Ontario, Canada

Lynley H.W. McMillan, Simply Strategic, Tauranga, New Zealand

Jon C. Messenger, Conditions of Work and Employment Programme, ILO, Geneva, Switzerland

Peter E. Mudrack, Department of Management, College of Business Administration, Kansas State University, Manhattan, Kansas, USA

Michael P. O'Driscoll, Department of Psychology, University of Waikato, Waikato, New Zealand

Gayle Porter, School of Business, Rutgers, The State University of New Jersey, Camden, New Jersey, USA

Wilmar B. Schaufeli, Department of Social and Organizational Psychology, Utrecht University, Utrecht, the Netherlands

Toon W. Taris, Department of Work and Organizational Psychology, Radboud University, Nijmegen, the Netherlands

Steve Vitucci, Tarleton State University, Central Texas, Killeen, Texas, USA

Acknowledgments

This volume has a long history. Much of my research and writing over the past 40 years has examined the ways in which work experiences influence individual well-being, a thread that ties this body of scholarship together. I have worked for almost 55 years, starting with a summer job when I was thirteen, working 35 hours a week and earning 50 cents an hour. In fact, it was my early work experiences that got me interested in studying organizational psychology. Work has provided many positive experiences and feelings for me along with the inevitable negative ones. Althought I have now achieved a satisfying integration of work with my other life interests, there were times, particularly in my early career, when I probably worked too hard. Hopefully this collection will help others 'get it' sooner than I did.

I owe a debt of gratitude to several people for their contributions to and assistance with my work in this area. These include Janet Spence, Zena Burgess, Stig Matthiesen, Mustafa Koyuncu, Eddy Ng, Astrid Richardsen, Graeme MacDermid and Lisa Fiksenbaum. Lisa participated in data analysis for most of my research projects on work addiction. I also express my ongoing appreciation to my family: Susan, Sharon, Rachel and Jeff. With them, life has meaning and joy.

This is my second book with Edward Elgar, with a third being developed as this was being written. Their staff have always been helpful, efficient and professional. I thank my international contributors for sharing their thinking on this important topic. Finally, preparation of this volume was supported in part by the Schulich School of Business.

Ronald Burke

Preface

This collection reflects the culmination of a forty-year personal and professional journey. I first became interested in work, health and well-being in the 1960s while a graduate student in the Organizational Psychology Program at the University of Michigan. Jack French, Floyd Mann, Sid Cobb, among others, had begun a number of research projects to examine these issues. Since then, I have conducted and reported several projects studying job demands and psychological well-being. In addition, I became interested in Type A or coronary-prone behavior and also examined its role in work and well-being. About ten years ago I became aware of pioneering research on workaholism started by Janet Spence and her colleagues and began to include their measures of workaholism components in a number of international projects.

As an ambitious, hard-working academic pursuing a career, I undertook these initiatives while simultaneously being a husband, father, son, brother and citizen, which brought into bold relief concerns about work and family, working hours and friendships, working hours and leisure, trade-offs and choices, and, as I became older and wiser, the importance of integration and balance in one's life.

My interest in workaholism or work addiction – the terms are used interchangeably – has caused me to consider why people work hard and why so many people work so many hours. This question is always raised for me when I leave North America and visit countries such as France, Italy and Spain where people seem to be enjoying their lives as much as we do and yet work fewer hours. One of my daughters, Rachel, lives and works in Munich and manages to get her job done and do well at her employer in spite of having six weeks of mandated vacation time. As a consequence, I have become familiar with a body of writing on working hours that existed quite separately from the writing on work addiction.

We know a lot about the effects of work addiction, that there are probably different types of workaholics, with some seeming to be satisfied and productive while others seem to be in distress, and that work can have many positive consequences. Unfortunately we know much less about the antecedents or causes of work addiction. Not surprisingly, we also do not know much about treating or reducing work addiction. Until we know more about the causes of work addiction and we develop and validate a theory (or theories) of work addiction, we will have few things to say about its reduction.

It also seemed important to put work addiction into a broader societal context. There are dramatic occupational and societal differences in hours worked. It appeared likely that an understanding of factors in the wider societal environment in which people live, and work significantly longer hours, might help us to understand and explain work addiction as well. It also seemed likely that, although work addiction is a stable individual difference characteristic, it may well have its roots in a broader social and societal environment.

I have come to believe that bringing together these two bodies of research and writing – working hours and work addiction – will enrich both. I also hope that this book will generate further research and debate.

This volume is an edited collection of 15 conceptual and empirical chapters, written by distinguished academics and independent practitioners from six countries (Canada, Japan, the Netherlands, New Zealand, Switzerland, the USA). The volume is divided into four parts. In Part I, 'Introduction', Ronald Burke first provides an overview of work hours and why people work hard, setting the stage for the more narrowly-focused chapters that follow. Then Lonnie Golden explores the distinction between long hours, overwork and overemployment to help in understanding workaholism. People work long hours because of structural, economic, social and behavioral factors, with not enough attention paid to social or behavioral factors. The four chapters in Part II, 'Definition and consequences of workaholism', examine definitions of workaholism or work addiction and what is known about their consequences. Barbara Killinger, on the basis of her considerable clinical and counseling experience, focuses on what she terms the breakdown syndrome. Lynley McMillan and Michael O'Driscoll develop an integrated definition of workaholism based on their own and others' research. Peter Mudrack defines workaholism in terms of specific behavioral tendencies such as engaging in non-required work and desiring to control others.

The chapters in Part III, 'Antecedents and types of workaholics', consider both the antecedents of workaholism and working long hours, as well as comparing different types of workaholics. Graeme MacDermid, on the basis of his qualitative research, highlights the subtle ways in which organizational expectations and culture increase one's work hours. Atsuko Kanai presents findings from Japan that link tougher economic conditions faced by organizations and increasing work hours and workaholism. The chapters by Ronald Burke and by Wilmar Schaufeli, Toon Taris and Arnold Bakker show that different types of workaholics exist, some faring well while others are in distress. One's motivations for working long hours as well as one's behavior at work emerge as critical distinguishing factors between those who fare better and those who fare worse. Working long hours can be a satisfying experience for some.

Part IV, 'Addressing work hours and workaholism', covers various 'solutions' to long work hours and workaholism. Jon Messenger stresses the need to balance the needs of workers and employees. Gayle Porter and Robert Herring suggest, however, that reaching this balance may be difficult to achieve, given the needs of some employees and some organizations. Ronald Burke and Teal McAteer-Early also address the balance issue, this time in terms of one's career and one's personal life, career success and personal failure often characterizing those unable to find this balance. Mary Dean Lee and her colleagues, using both qualitative and quantitative data, report that professionals who choose to work part-time are both satisfied and effective in the workplace. Charles Chen shows how the use of rational emotive behavior therapy (REBT) can be effective in lessening work–life balance concerns and ameliorating the effects of workaholism. Finally, Louis Fry and his colleagues show that spiritual leadership theory may offer a vehicle for reducing workaholism.

PART I

Introduction

1. Work hours and work addiction[1]

Ronald J. Burke

We make a living by what we get, we make a life by what we give. (Winston Churchill)

INTRODUCTION

This chapter introduces the topic of work hours and work addiction, setting the stage for the remainder of the collection. Work and working is a mixed blessing. Work provides many benefits such as income, social contacts, opportunity to acquire and use skills, feelings of accomplishment, a sense of purpose and meaning. Work also has some costs such as fatigue, time away from friends and family, and, in some cases, psychological and physical health problems.

Working long hours suggests commitment, productivity and involvement. Sloth suggests a slacker, a person lacking in motivation. Hours worked is observable; it is a proxy for things that cannot be seen. For example, work motivation cannot be seen; one infers work motivation by hours worked. Some have even suggested (Hochschild, 1997) that work is more satisfying for some than home life.

There are also wide country differences in average hours or total hours worked per year. It is not clear how directly this is tied to country productivity, however (Rifkin, 2004). In addition, there are historical differences in hours worked. Finally, there is evidence that people in some industrialized countries are working more hours now than earlier (Schor, 2003).

I remember that in the 1960s, with the advent of automation, writers were suggesting a 20-hour work week and that there would not be enough work to go around for everyone. This projection did not materialize. But blue-collar workers now tend to be working fewer hours, while white-collar professionals and managers are working more hours (Golden and Figart, 2000a). There are also some people having to work more hours, often holding more than one job (Ehrenreich, 2003), to make ends meet. These individuals are typically at lower socio-economic levels.

Jacobs and Gerson (1998) note three trends in working time in the US over the last 30 years. First, there have been increases in the number of people working both longer and shorter hours. They report that highly educated managers and professionals are now working more. Australia and the US have the highest proportion of men working 50 or more hours per week (about 23 per cent). More employees are now working 50 hours a week or more in the US than anywhere else. Second, those working long hours want to work fewer hours, while those working shorter hours want to work more hours. Third, the sense of being overworked is associated more with demographic shifts in the labor force (more dual-earner couples and single parents) than with changes in the average work time.

But can one work too hard? Concerns about hours worked have spurred interest in work addiction and workaholism (Burke, 2000). The effects of these show up in job performance, work relationships, family relationships, children and community (McMillan et al., 2003). Long hours on the job are leading to errors, unhappiness, distress and inefficiencies. Doctors' offices are full of people showing symptoms of stress such as headaches, insomnia, hypertension and burnout (Menzies, 2005).

This chapter considers the following wide-ranging questions. Have work hours changed over time? Why do people work hard? Do one's motives for working hard matter? Can one work too hard? Can money, one of the rewards for hard work, buy happiness? And since most people would like to work fewer hours, how can this be realized? It has been shown that 50 per cent of men and 46 per cent of women wanted to work less: 5.5 hours per week less for men and 4.9 hours per week for women.

HISTORICAL VIEWS ON TIME AND HOURS WORKED

> Instant gratification takes too long. (Carrie Fisher, American actress and author)

Adam (1993) identifies important themes and issues related to time. Time is a central part of our lives but the meaning of time is rarely thought about. Our lives seem to go on without our having to think about time. Work time has become particularly important since work has come to occupy so much of our lives.

Work today has become time oriented (Honore, 2004). Work begins and ends at certain times for many. Significant numbers of workers are also paid an hourly rate. Time has become a currency, a medium of exchange. Time becomes a resource to be used and spent with care. Workers are paid by the hour, by the week or by the month. Some work overtime. Labor costs are based on man-hours. People work to deadlines. Time is sold and controlled. We never have enough time to do all we would like. Other perspectives of time, less linked to 'time is money', are accorded lower status. Although we do not think much about time, it is in our lives every day and is a complex subject (Adam, 1993).

Weber (1989) quotes Benjamin Franklin as stating that 'time is money' and 'money can begat money'. The growth of industrialism and capitalism in the late 17th century strengthened the time orientation towards work, with an emphasis on using, scheduling and budgeting time. Time is money; 'we spend it, waste it, invest it, budget it and save it. We equate it, in other words, with money' (Adam, 1993, p. 166).

Speed became increasingly important when time became quantifiable, which happened as paid employment and the link of money–efficiency–profit became entrenched (Glick, 1999). Speed became a value in Western culture particularly. Time is an investment; doing things faster therefore provides – in theory at least – a better return on this investment. This also makes an individual or organization more competitive. These notions share a purely quantitative view of time.

Frederick Taylor's time-and-motion studies in the early 1900s fostered the cult of efficiency (Taylor, 1967). This later spawned increased use of flexible working hours, initially positioned as a benefit to workers but also providing employers with increased efficiency. Employers were now able to make increasing use of weekend work, night shifts, split-shift arrangements, and part-time and contingent workers. Some of these arrangements turned out to be at odds with workers' needs for time (Galinsky et al., 2005).

North Americans continue to increase their working hours, while working hours are declining in other industrialized nations (Greenhouse, 2001). Americans worked 1979 hours in 2000, up 36 hours from 1990. Americans work 137 hours (about three and a half weeks) more a year than Japanese workers, 260 hours (almost six and a half weeks) more a year than British workers and 499 hours (about twelve and a half weeks) more than German workers.

These numbers reflect, in part, the American economic boom of the 1990s. Both boom and bust seem to result in Americans working longer hours (Hunnicutt, 2003). In the boom times, companies expect their employees to work longer; in the best times, downsizing results in fewer people working but more work for those that remain (Fisher, 1992).

Cartwright (2000) reviews research and workplace surveys in the UK and EU showing an increase in the prevalence of psychosocial illnesses and stress-related conditions. The UK was the only member of the EU where the number of hours worked had increased over the last ten years; in all other EU states it decreased (also see Green, 2001). In the UK, they talk of increases in the Americanization of their workplaces – the American disease. The UK has increasingly embraced the American model of a 24-hour society (Kreitzman, 1999).

WORK HOURS IN NORTH AMERICA VERSUS EUROPE

There appears to be a divide between the European countries, many of which have placed the issue of shorter work hours on their political agendas, and North America, where the issue of a shorter work week has been a non-starter for over 70 years. But concerns about long work hours have surfaced among managers and professionals in both Western Europe and North America (Rifkin, 2004).

According to economists, Americans work more hours than do Europeans because lower taxes in the US allow them to keep more of their money than is the case in Europe. But it may be that Europeans are not working too little but Americans are working too hard. Americans choose more income, rather than more leisure, to keep up with the Joneses. Higher taxes in Europe encourage workers to choose more leisure rather than work longer hours. Using GDP, Americans may be richer than Europeans based on economic performance. But GDP is an imperfect measure of even economic well-being. Happiness depends on both leisure and material consumption. Americans may be richer than Europeans but not necessarily happier (Rifkin, 2004).

The American Dream

One hundred years ago, Americans believed that with hard work they could better themselves – the betterment usually couched in economic terms. In addition, one was responsible for whatever success that occurred. The phrase 'American Dream' first appeared in 1931 (Rifkin, 2004, p. 13). Enthusiasm, optimism and hope were important qualities among Americans. They embraced the notion that, through one's efforts, consistent improvement could take place; they could go from rags to riches, as reflected in the Horatio Alger story. The work ethic was highly valued, discipline and hard work being extolled. Sayings such as 'Idle hands are the Devil's workshop', 'A stitch in time saves nine', 'Never put off till tomorrow what can be done today' reflected these values.

But the American Dream may have lost some of its lustre, no longer being admired as much as it was previously. Young Americans are persuaded by the media to seek instant gratification (Lasch, 1979). They are now less interested in working hard and postponing gratification for later rewards. As a result more Americans buy now and pay later, more being in debt (Schor, 1998; 2004). More buy lottery tickets; more gamble. Most Americans under 30 believe they will become rich, but by luck, not as the result of hard work. Putnam (2000) observed a decline in the rate of American participation in voluntary activities. He attributed this to increased time and money pressures and the pursuit of personal pleasure, and less interest in giving time to others. Americans seem to be increasingly looking out for number one (Frank, 1999).

Two hundred years ago, America was seen as the land of opportunity. Upward mobility was central to the American Dream. But upward mobility in the US has slowed considerably over the past thirty years (Rifkin, 2004). America has among the highest levels of income inequality in the world (Milanovic, 2005). Income growth in terms of compensation ranks the US near the bottom of the industrialized world. Rifkin believes Americans are not pursuing the American Dream but the American Daydream.

The American Dream – Daydream or Nightmare?

America has some of the highest levels of poverty among the developed nations. The US also spends a smaller proportion of its GDP to redistribute income through transfers and other social benefits than almost any other developed country. The US minimum wage is a smaller percentage of the average country wage than in almost all other developed countries. The US is one of only a few countries that does not legally require maternity and paternity benefits. Finally the productivity gap between the US and other developed countries has shrunk considerably (Rifkin, 2004).

Although Americans and Europeans are similar in terms of productivity, per capita income in Europe is about three-quarters of that in the US. A significant factor in explaining this difference is that workers in Europe work fewer hours. Europeans have chosen more leisure rather than longer work hours and higher incomes (Hayden, 2003). France has legislated a 35-hour work week. The average vacation time in Europe is six weeks. US employers are not required by law to provide vacation time but two weeks' vacation has become the norm in most sectors.

What is the point of making more money if you don't have the time to enjoy it? Americans are now working more hours as workers in other countries work fewer hours (Rifkin, 2004). American parents complain they do not have time with their children, always feel rushed, and rarely have any free time. A survey of 5000 UK workers in 2005 showed that 60 per cent would not use their full vacation time. Americans do not use 20 per cent of their paid time off. American executives do not take all their vacation time

(Robinson, 2003). Does 25 per cent more income bring greater happiness to compensate for giving up time for family and leisure?

The American Dream is based too much on personal material advancement and too little on concern with more universal human welfare. The European Dream, though newly emerging, values quality of life ahead of accumulating wealth, and sustainable development over unfettered growth.

CHANGES IN THE WORKPLACE

A survey by the Institute of Management chronicled the changing workplace in the UK (Worrall and Cooper, 1999). Questioning over 1200 UK managers from 1997 to 1999, it found that the pace of change increased over these three years. In 1997 57 per cent of managers were affected by change, in 1998 this figure had risen to 62 per cent and by 1999 it was 67 per cent. Managers see their jobs as more complex and fragmented. Eighty-five per cent of managers in the 1999 survey indicated that they now had to deal with more information. Seventy-one per cent reported having to acquire a wider range of skills and one-third now managed more staff.

Hours Worked and Health

These changes in the nature of work are also associated with increased ill health. In a UK study of organizations employing over a million white-collar workers (Austin Knight, 1995), more that half of those surveyed reported physical health problems because of the stress of their working long hours. Worrall and Cooper (1999) found that 76 per cent of managers reported that they felt that the number of hours they worked was having a negative effect on their health. In Japan they even have a word, 'Karoshi', for death by overwork. In 2001 143 people were victims of Karoshi. Others say that Japan's death toll from overwork is really in the thousands. Working long hours also has been found to impact managers' social life and ability to engage in physical exercise on a regular basis. Our work also leaves little time and energy for exercising, leading to increasing levels of obesity.

Sparks et al. (1997) undertook a quantitative and qualitative review of existing literature on working hours and health. They reported small but significant correlations between hours worked and overall health symptoms, and psychological and physical health symptoms. They reviewed research showing that working long hours increases health and safety problems, workplace injuries and errors.

When work is psychologically and physically demanding, do people burn out? People working longer hours have more ill health (Sparks et al., 1997).

A survey of UK executives (Worrall and Cooper, 1999) found that 68 per cent believed that working long hours adversely affected their productivity, 79 per cent thought that long hours affected their relationships with their partners, and 89 per cent of those with children believed working long hours negatively affected their relationships with their children.

Hours Worked and the Family

Galinsky (1999) asked children their one wish to improve how their mother's and father's work affected their lives and reported that most wished that their mothers and fathers would be less tired and less stressed.

Crouter et al. (2001) examined the relationship of men's long work hours and role overload on the quality of their relationships with their wives and first- and second-born children in a sample of 190 dual-earner families. Controlling for men's occupational self-direction and education, long hours were associated with less time spent with their wives, but were unrelated to spouses' love, perspective taking or conflict. Role overload, however, consistently predicted less positive marital relationships. The combination of long hours and high role overload was also consistently related to less positive father–adolescent relationships regardless of the children's gender or age.

Studies have shown that fathers' reports of work stress are associated with more conflict with their adolescent children (Crouter et al., 1999; Galambos et al., 1995).

Clarkberg and Moen (2001) considered the time squeeze at the household or couple level. Data were collected in interviews with 4554 couples. They found a considerable gap between couples' preferences for their joint work hours and their actual behavior. Most couples worked more hours than they desired. They attributed this to the nature of work and career paths in organizations, both demanding long hours as an indication of commitment, productivity and motivation for advancement.

Becker and Moen (1995), in interviews with 100 people in middle-class, dual-earner couples in upstate New York, found that the majority were engaged in 'scaling back' strategies that reduce and restructure the couple's commitment to paid work over the life course, limiting the impact of work on family life. Scaling back strategies involved placing limits on the number of hours worked and lowering expectations for career advancement to have more time for family; having a one-job, one-career marriage, with women typically holding the job; and making trade-offs so both individuals would share more equally in the scaling back strategies (for example, husband works fewer hours, partner increases her work commitments).

Work for almost all in the sample was accorded a higher priority than family. Time management principles were applied to manage at home (for example, concepts such as team work, partnership, fairness were commonly mentioned). None saw work as a refuge from home demands, though they all enjoyed their work. Most felt work squeezed family time.

Scaling back resulted from a conscious decision to have more time for family and as a way to deal with an increasing workload so as to have some semblance of family life (McDonnell, 2001). Flexibility at home and at work was critical.

Work Hours and Sleep

Many people (particularly North Americans) are now sleeping less and waking up earlier to deal with their workloads, gain a competitive advantage or squeeze in exercise. The *New York Times* coined the phrase 'competitive waking'; waking 'when the rooster crows' means simply running with the pack. As Donald Trump, who goes to bed at 1.00 a.m. and rises at 5.00 a.m., wrote (Trump, 2004), 'It gives me a competitive edge. I have friends who are successful and sleep ten hours a night, and I ask them, "How can you compete against people like me if I sleep only four hours?" It rarely can be done. No matter how brilliant you are, there's not enough time in the day.' People believe that working long hours gives them a competitive edge or at least gets them noticed. Others are embarrassed at sending e-mails or leaving voice mail messages at 4.00 a.m.

The average healthy adult requires about eight and a half hours of sleep a night. Most people thought seven hours was optimal and obtained only six. It has been estimated that sleeplessness costs North America up to US$ 100 billion annually in health care costs, accidents and lost productivity. Inadequate sleep has also been linked to weakened immune systems. It is clear that we are not sleeping enough. The average American gets 90 minutes less sleep today than they did a century ago. The afternoon siesta, so common in Southern Europe, has all but disappeared as well.

WHY DO PEOPLE WORK HARD?

There are several answers to this important question. These include economic necessity, organizational demands – explicit or subtle – because of greater competitive pressures, a greater workload, fewer staff as a result of downsizing and restructuring and greater job insecurity, occupational and professional norms, greater consumption and consumerism, taking advantage of opportunities that are present, and being afraid to work less and lose these opportunities: 'If I don't work these hours someone else will.'

Technology now makes it possible to work longer hours and from any-where – e-mail, blackberries, the Internet, laptops, mobile phones.

Striving for Mastery

Kofodimos (1993) observed that career-oriented women and men were having increasing difficulty balancing their professional and personal lives. Balance

> refers to a satisfying, healthy, and productive life that includes work, play and love; that integrates a range of life activities with attention to self and to personal and spiritual development; and that expresses a person's unique wishes, interests, and values. It contrasts with the imbalance of a life dominated by work, focused on satisfying external requirements at the expense of inner development, and in conflict with a person's true desires. (ibid., p. xiii)

Kofodimos sees imbalance as the product of individual character or personality and organizational and social factors. Imbalance reflects the American character, which places work first and values mastery. Imbalance is deeply rooted in placing work before personal life. It is easy to blame the organization for imbalance. While organizational pressures contribute to imbalance, they are not the only source. Internal forces – one's needs, wants and drives – also lead to imbalance. Kofodimos equates imbalance with workaholism and work addiction.

> Striving for mastery is characterized by emphasis on task accomplishment, by perception of their people as work roles, human assets or instruments for getting the work done; and by reliance on rational analyzing in making decisions. Avoidance of intimacy is characterized by a relative lack of empathy and compassion, inattention to our own and others' feelings, reluctance to experience and express vulnerability and self-doubt, and discomfort in being playful and spontaneous. (ibid., pp. 3–4)

These attitudes and behaviors make individuals more comfortable with the workplace. Striving for mastery and avoiding intimacy also bolsters one's identity and self-esteem. Managers, particularly male managers, feel self-esteem when they behave in masterful ways.

Kofodimos sees three interrelated factors leading to imbalance: devoting time, energy and commitment to work over other activities, the dominance of the mastery-orientation and intimacy avoidance approaches, and efforts to live up to an idealized masterful self-image.

The striving for mastery and the association of mastery with self-esteem begins early in life. Boys and girls are rewarded by parents and teachers for achievement, competence and performance. There are few rewards for empathy, compassion, helpfulness and playfulness (Kofodimos, 1993). Individuals become imbalanced as a result and organizations foster this imbalance. The pursuit of mastery and the resulting imbalance can have serious consequences for one's life, work and family.

The time/energy imbalance involves putting work first. Managers devote most of their time, energy and commitment to work. This results from new technologies making it possible to work anywhere and any time, global interactions across several time zones extending the workday, competitive pressures making it important to be always on, organizational evaluations and rewards, the emphasis on work in Western cultures, the polarization of work and family as competing spheres, and a love of work – work can be a source of incredible satisfaction.

Major et al. (2002) note that relatively few studies have examined work time and its antecedents and correlates. Work time has been shown to have effects on work interference with family and work–family conflict. They collected data from 513 employees from two units of a Fortune 500 company; union employees were excluded. Work time was measured by three items: hours worked in an average week, including time spent doing job-related work at home; hours worked on the last regular work day, including time spent doing job-related work at home; and hours spent on a second job in an average week if the respondent held more than one job. The authors found the following to be significant predictors of work time: career identity salience, work overload, organizational expectations, non-job responsibilities (negatively), organizational rewards (negatively) and perceived financial need. Parental demands were unrelated to work time. Work time was significantly related to work interference with family, which in turn was significantly related to psychological distress.

Gaining Rewards

Wallace (1995, 1997) studied work hours among lawyers, a profession noted for working long hours. Surveys of lawyers (Brainbridge, 1989; Dart, 1988) have found that time demands/difficulties in balancing work and family life are the biggest sources of dissatisfaction in the legal profession. Wallace included both hours worked and work spillover in her study. Hours worked could be affected by work commitment, professional commitment (both comprise elements of work salience); promotional opportunity, the social value of one's work (these serve as motivators for long hours); emphasis on profits, competitiveness with colleagues, and work overload (these comprise negative and coercive pressures); gender, marital status, whether the respondent was in a dual-career relationship, number of pre-school-aged children (domestic situation). These were hypothesized to have a direct relationship with hours worked; some would be related to workload spillover, while others would not.

Why do lawyers work as hard as they do? Significant predictors were work commitment, work overload, and not having pre-school children. Shorter professional tenure, pay and working in larger firms (control variables) also had significant relationships with hours worked.

Why do lawyers feel that their work is invading their non-work life (work spillover)? Actual hours worked made no difference. Promotional opportunity and social value of the work (both negative) and profit drive and work overload (both positive) predicted work spillover. Work spillover was really a measure of work interference with family and personal life.

Lawyers work long hours because of an internal factor (work commitment) and an external factor (work overload). These are different from those factors thought to motivate professionals: promotion, professional commitment, competitiveness among colleagues. It seems that coercive factors, more than non-coercive factors, explain hours worked.

O'Reilly and Chatman (1994) studied the effects of cognitive ability and motivation on career success in a longitudinal study of MBA graduates. Respondents provided data in the first year of their two-year full-time MBA program and three and a half to four years following graduation. Motivation included items such as ambitious, energetic, industrious, initiative, reliable and responsible. Early career success measures included job offers received at graduation, job offers received in ratio to the number of interviews attended, current salary, salary increment, and number of promotions. In addition, respondents indicated the number of hours they would like to work per week following graduation (desired hours). The authors' results suggested that both cognitive abilities and motivations were necessary to explain early career success, causing them to advocate working both smarter and harder.

Brett and Stroh (2003) defined extreme work hours as working 61 hours or more a week. They considered four theoretical explanations for working 61 or more hours a week in a sample of 471 male and 86 female MBA graduates of the same university. Of these, 170 males and 33 females worked 61 hours per week or more. Brett and Stroh developed four hypotheses to explain over-work.

1. The work–leisure trade-off: the more hours managers work, the fewer hours they will spend in leisure activities; and the more money managers earn, the fewer hours they will spend in leisure activities.
2. Social contagion: people will work 61 hours or more if their colleagues at work also do this – probably in response to the norms of the particular organization or industry (for example, financial services managers are noted for working long hours).

3. Work as an emotional respite from home: managers who work the
    longest hours are the most stressed and dissatisfied with their home life.
4. The rewards of work: managers working the longest hours will be
    more satisfied with their work and the most psychologically involved
    with work.

In the sample of male managers, the best explanation for why some
worked 61 hours or more per week were financial and psychological
rewards. There was no support for the notion that male managers who work
long hours seek relief at work from pressures at home. In the small sample
of female managers, working 61 hours a week or more was consistent with
the work–leisure trade-off theory, the social contagion theory, and the work
as its own reward theory.

Among males, hours worked and leisure hours were not correlated. The
correlation between income and leisure hours was also not significant.
There was also no support for the contagion hypothesis. Hours men worked
had no relationship to time spent on childcare or housework. Male managers working the longest hours received the most compensation. And male
managers working 61 hours or more were more job involved and reported
more intrinsic satisfaction, and more family stress.

Female managers earning more money had less leisure time – supporting the work–leisure trade-off. There was also support for social contagion
in that more women worked 61 hours a week or more if others in their
industry did. Females working more hours also earned more money, but
did not benefit psychologically in terms of intrinsic satisfaction.

Schor (1991) believes that employees get trapped in a work and spend
cycle: workers work more hours to obtain more income to acquire more
possessions in order to feel successful. In addition, organizations fare better
when employees work longer hours; as a result they expect this from
employees. Increasing levels of job insecurity also make it difficult for managers and professionals to say no.

Keeping Up

Golden (1998) writes that actual work hour behavior is a function of three
interacting factors: hours desired by the worker, hours demanded by the
employing organization and the wider institutional environment in
which hours decisions are made (legal constraints, common practice, economic conditions). George (1997) believes that workers are increasingly
influenced by marketers of goods and services to choose income over
leisure and work longer hours as a result. Employers over-value long hours,
particularly when other objective measures of productivity are not readily

available. Employees respond as individuals who prefer working long hours to look good to their managers. Employers respond by demanding even longer hours, creating what Rebitzer and Taylor (1995) term a rat race. Landers et al. (1996), in a study of two law firms, found that promoted associates worked very hard, their track record of billable hours being very important in promotion decisions. When organizations use willingness to work hours as an indicator of valuable characteristics it leads to a 'rat race' mentality.

Brown and Benson (2005), in a sample of 2399 public sector employees, found that participation in setting performance objectives, difficult objectives and higher performance ratings were associated with higher levels of work overload. Trust in one's supervisor was associated with lower levels of work overload. Performance appraisal systems have been touted as an important element in an effective human resource management (HRM) system. Brown and Benson's findings suggest that characteristics of appraisal systems may have negative effects on employees (overload, stress) and for their organizations. The greater stress on evaluating individual contributions in the appraisal process is one source of work intensification (Newton and Findlay, 1996).

Materialism

Marketers define materialism as an individual difference factor related to the belief that income, wealth and material possessions are important in achieving happiness in life (Sirgy, 1998, p. 244). Materialists have achieving and maintaining a certain standard of living as an important, perhaps the most important, life goal (Belk, 1985).

Sirgy (1998) proposes a theory of materialism and overall life satisfaction. Life satisfaction is partly determined by one's satisfaction with one's standard of living. Satisfaction with one's standard of living is determined by one's actual standard of living compared with a set goal. Materialists place high value on material possessions, wealth and income. Materialists experience a greater dissatisfaction with their standard of living than do non-materialists, which in turn lowers their satisfaction with life. Materialists experience greater dissatisfaction with their standard of living because their standard of living goals are unrealistically high. These goals are influenced by perceptions of wealth, income and material possessions of others who have more (upward social comparisons). Materialists also compare their own standard of living with others as regards income and work effort and conclude that others have more income and work no harder than they do. These comparisons lead to feelings of unfairness, envy and anger. Materialists may also spend more money than they earn, with debt ensuing as a result. There has not surprisingly been a steady increase in materialism as displayed in magazine advertising over the 80 years surveyed by Belk and Pollay (1985).

Materialism (Sirgy, 1998) is a condition in which the material life domain is given priority over other life domains. Several studies have reported a negative correlation between materialism and happiness (Dawson and Bamossy, 1991; Richins and Dawson, 1992; Wright and Larson, 1993).

Why should there be a negative relationship between materialism and happiness? Sirgy (1998) suggested that materialists indicate dissatisfaction with their standard of living because they set unrealistically high material goals which they cannot reach. Since they cannot reach these goals, they are dissatisfied with their current standard of living, which then spills over to their life in general.

Kasser and Kanner (2003), in an edited collection drawing on a diverse body of writing, show that consumerism and its wider culture have powerful and often negative effects on individuals, families and societies. Advertising, consumerism, materialism and capitalism itself contribute to these wide-ranging effects.

Kasser (2002) reviews the scientific evidence relating materialism and happiness. The pursuit of wealth not only does not lead to happiness but actually makes many people unhappy, even when they are successful in achieving wealth. Kasser believes that materialism does not directly cause unhappiness but instead both reinforce each other. Unhappy people are often the most materialistic. He argues that insecurity leads to materialism and that the pursuit of materialistic goals not only does not increase happiness but also diminishes close relationships, health, and the happiness of others in one's close relationships.

Kasser makes an important distinction between extrinsic and intrinsic aspirations. Extrinsic aspirations include wealth, fame and image; intrinsic aspirations include meaningful relationships, personal growth and community contributions. Research has shown that having relatively strong aspirations for extrinsic outcomes was associated with poorer mental health outcomes (Kasser, 2004). Having a stronger preference for intrinsic outcomes was associated with positive mental health. Self-reported attainment of intrinsic aspirations was associated with well-being; attainment of extrinsic aspirations was not.

People with strong materialistic values tend to have less close interpersonal relationships and connection with others. They are also less interested in supporting their communities and bettering the world. Instead, they see others as objects to be used. In addition, such individuals feel more pressure and stress in their lives and report a stronger sense of being controlled.

Richins and Dawson (1992) developed a measure of materialism having three components: acquisition centrality, acquisition as the pursuit of happiness, and possessions-defined success. High scorers desired a higher level of income, placed greater emphasis on financial security and less on interpersonal relationships, preferred to spend more on themselves and less on others, engaged in fewer voluntary simplicity behaviors, and were less satisfied with their lives.

While materialism generally has negative connotations, not all aspects of materialism are bad. The desire for goods may cause employees to work harder or longer, increasing their incomes and standard of living (a strong motive to succeed and be self-sufficient). High levels of consumption by individuals can increase the profitability of organizations, leading them to invest more heavily in new technology and research and development, which in turn leads to higher levels of productivity and new products and ultimately to higher living standards.

Materialists place possessions and obtaining them at the center of their lives. They pursue a lifestyle in which high levels of material consumption become their goal. Materialism provides them with meaning in life and activities for their daily living. Materialists worship things. Materialists view possessions and their acquisition as critical to their happiness, satisfaction and well-being. Materialism is the pursuit of happiness through acquisition. Materialists judge their own and others' success by the number and quality of their possessions, their consuming lifestyles, the money things cost rather than the satisfaction they bring. Material well-being is evidence of success; possessions confer status and project a desired self-image.

Richins and Dawson (1992, p. 307) define materialism as

> a value that guides people's choices and conduct in a variety of situations includ-
> ing, but not limited to, consumption arenas. With respect to consumption, mat-
> erialism will influence the type and quantity of goods purchased. Beyond
> consumption, materialism will influence the allocation of a variety of resources,
> including time. A materialist, for instance, might choose to work longer hours
> and earn more money instead of using that time for leisure activities.

They found the following results.

1. Respondents high on materialism felt they need more income to satisfy their needs than those low on materialism.
2. Respondents high on materialism rated 'financial security' higher and 'warm relationships with others' and 'a sense of accomplishment' lower.
3. Respondents high on materialism would spend more of an unexpected $20 000 windfall on themselves and less of this windfall on charitable causes, friends and family and travel than those low on materialism.
4. Those high on materialism scored higher on a non-generosity scale than those low on materialism.

5.   Those high on materialism were less likely to support a voluntary sim-
     plicity lifestyle.
6.   Those high on materialism were less satisfied with their lives (measured
     by four facets of life satisfaction and a global assessment).
7.   Those high on materialism scored lower on a measure of self-esteem.

Individuals high on materialism value possessions that are related to
appearance and status rather than ones more instrumental in nature.
Individuals low on materialism value possessions that have a symbolic
interpersonal nature. High materialists are bound to be less satisfied with
family and friends and have less fun and enjoyment as a consequence (Ryan
et al., 1996). Belk (1984) views it as valuing material possessions and being
envious of others who have a material object that you do not. These
definitions downplay the spiritual dimensions of human existence (Richins
and Dawson, 1992), the non-material (values such as character, friendship
and romantic love). Focusing on the material may even reduce the pleasure
one might get from making money by diminishing the link between the
material and the spiritual or non-material (Lane, 2000; Myers, 2000, 2003;
Needleman, 1991, 1998).

Money by itself is not harmful; in fact it is beneficial in satisfying a
variety of needs and values. Money is harmful if it is used to fill needs it
cannot fill. Money cannot buy happiness, love or character. Money cannot
reduce self-doubt, because a lack of money is not the cause of self-doubt
or low self-esteem (Locke et al., 1996).

Kasser and Ryan (1993) report the results of three studies showing that
placing a higher value and expectancy on wealth and money over other self-
relevant values and expectancies was associated with lower levels of adjustment and well-being.

Financial success is the core of the American Dream; people come to
believe that money leads to happiness and success. But some suggest a dark
side to this dream; pursuing wealth comes to be seen as empty or shallow
and limiting relationships with family, friends, community and one's self-
actualization (Fromm, 1976). Fromm makes the distinction between
'having' – a consumption orientation – and 'being' – an experiential orientation to life. Money is an external incentive for behavior that is contin-
gently given; this limits self-actualization, resulting in greater distress. Deci
and Ryan (1991) reported that personal strivings for power (desire to
control, impress or manipulate others) were associated with more negative
affect and greater distress.

Kasser and Ryan (1996) replicated and extended their earlier findings
(1993) in two other studies. In one, they found that the relative importance
and efficacy of extrinsic aspirations (financial success, social recognition,

appearance) were associated with lower vitality and self-actualization and more physical health symptoms. The relative importance of intrinsic aspirations (self-acceptance, friendship, sense of community, physical health) were associated with greater vitality and self-actualization and fewer physical health symptoms. In the second study, intrinsic aspirations were found to be associated with lower levels of narcissism and greater daily positive affect, whereas extrinsic aspirations were associated with higher levels of narcissism and less positive daily affect.

They offered three reasons why extrinsic aspirations were negatively related to well-being. First, extrinsic aspirations suggest a more general neuroticism and emotional insecurity. Kasser et al. (1995) report that students who valued financial success had parents who were less nurturing and more controlling. In addition, students from less advantaged backgrounds placed a higher value on financial success. Thus financial aspirations seem to be a compensation for feelings of insecurity developed early in life causing one to seek external rewards (praise, recognition, money) to gain a sense of self-worth and approval. Second, extrinsic aspirations lead to activities that distract one from behaviors associated with self-actualization and happiness. Third, people will generally fall short in achieving their extrinsic aspirations, resulting in frustration, stress and psychological distress.

Affluenza

De Graaf et al. (2000) use the term 'affluenza' to capture a disease resulting from over-consumption that has reached (to them) epidemic proportions in many developed countries. They define it as follows: 'Affluenza. n. a painful, contagious, socially transmitted condition of overload, debt, anxiety and waste resulting from the dogged pursuit of more' (ibid., p. 2).

Affluenza is widespread in North America and is now being spread to other parts of the world. Affluenza influences levels of personal debt, friendships, families, communities and the environment. We become addicted to stuff, spending and buying much more than we need. We become very materialistic, greedy and selfish – values that diminish family friendships and generosity (Schor, 1998).

More North Americans are now filing for bankruptcy. They are working more hours per year than any other country. They are building shopping centers at an increasing rate, now having more shopping malls than schools. Solid waste production continues to increase. The majority of workers would like to spend more time with their families. American CEOs now earn 400 times as much as the average worker, a tenfold increase since 1980 (De Graaf et al., 2000).

Symptoms of affluenza include a passion for shopping best described as a spending binge, increasing use of credit cards resulting in increases in both consumer debt and personal bankruptcies, an increase in having stuff, individuals with higher material expectations, greed fueled by a 'keeping up with the Joneses' mentality compounded by always higher expectations, congestion – both inside and outside the home, possession overload and time famine, sleep deprivation, the undermining of family life and weakened marriages, marketing to children, a decline in citizen and community participation and volunteerism, feelings of emptiness and boredom and a hunger for meaning, an increasing gap between rich and poor and stigmatizing of the have-nots, a depletion of the earth's resources, pollution of the environment, increases in a variety of addictions and higher levels of dissatisfaction.

Affluenza spread as a result of planned obsolescence. De Graaf and his associates (2000) believe that affluenza, while not a new disease, has been spreading faster than before over the past 50 years following World War II. This spawned planned obsolescence, mass consumption, instant and easy access to money through loans and credit cards, expansion of shopping malls and marketing through television spurred by the advertising industry.

What can be done to reduce affluenza? There are some signs that millions of people are attempting to simplify their lives through downshifting (Segal, 1999). More people are knowledgeable about environmental damage and the costs of this and are beginning to share this concern with others. Efforts are underway to increase citizen participation in local and national governance. Recycling efforts have increased, together with spreading the voluntary simplicity program through marketing and advertising, encouraging government to pass simplicity-friendly legislation (for example, reduced working hours, graduated retirement options) and using broader indicators of societal well-being (such as perceived quality of life, voter participation rates, number of children living in poverty) as well as costs (such as those of crime, air pollution and family breakdown).

CAN MONEY BUY HAPPINESS?

The psychology of money has been a neglected topic. Money is a taboo subject (Furnham and Argyle, 1998). Yet the dream of becoming rich is surprisingly common. Money brings security, freedom, a sense of power, and is a sign of success. There are two different themes in the literature about money. One is that money is the fruit of one's labor and should be enjoyed and used to benefit others. The other is that the relentless pursuit of money leaves the pursuer alone and unhappy. Money has many definitions, meanings and uses. Children have money and learn about money at an early age. We need some money for possessions. Yet many of our most valued possessions have little monetary value. Some possessions are necessities, in some cases to survive (food, housing) and in other cases to make life more comfortable (telephone, washing machines). Some possessions indicate status (jewelery, paintings). Some possessions are luxuries. Things that were once luxuries (TV sets) can become necessities. Many believe that their possessions will make them happy but this is often not true (Easterbrook, 2004). Possessions serve as a way to maintain life, as a way to enhance life and as symbols.

Here are some things we know about money (Diener et al., 1999):

1. People in wealthier nations are happier than people in poorer nations.
2. Increases in national wealth within developed countries have not, over recent decades, been associated with increases in happiness.
3. Within-nation differences in wealth show only small positive correlations with happiness.
4. Increases in personal wealth do not typically result in increased happiness.
5. People who strongly desire wealth and money are less happy than those who do not. Thus, avoiding poverty, living in a rich country and emphasizing goals other than wealth are associated with higher levels of happiness.

There is only a very small correlation, generally around .15 to .20, between income and satisfaction. Several hypotheses have been offered to explain this low relationship. These include the following: adaptation – we get used to the income very quickly; comparison – there is always someone richer than you are; alternatives – as one gets more money, other things (leisure, family) seem more valuable. There are other important sources of happiness than money – family, friends, leisure, health; and there is Worry. Now that one has money, one can worry about other things. There is, however, a strong relationship between income and happiness among those with lower incomes. For this group, money buys the things they need or want.

Why don't rising incomes make everybody happier? Though standards of living have increased over the past fifty years, people do not report greater satisfaction (Diener and Seligman, 2004). This is somewhat surprising, since rich people are generally more satisfied than poor people. One might therefore expect that, as a country grows richer, both rich and poor would be happier (Easterlin, 1995). This presents a paradox: an individual who becomes richer becomes happier but when a country becomes richer no one seems happier. One reason is habituation. People quickly adjust to changes in standard of living; short-term improvements in happiness fade quickly. What was considered to be a luxury a while back is now seen as essential. A second reason is that people tend to compare their situation with that of others – a 'keeping up with (or ahead of) the Joneses' phenomenon. People like to feel better off than others – their income relative to others, as opposed to their absolute income. Thus efforts by people to become happier by working harder to earn and spend more are self-defeating; they make more money but, since others do too, they are not any happier (Diener and Biswas-Diener, 2002).

While money may be associated with happiness, if one wants to stay happy it is better to compare oneself with others who are poorer. People tend to compare themselves with others (peers) of the same age. Their happiness depends on the relative success of this group, leading to a 'keeping up with the Joneses' mentality and a need to continually increase their income. This suggests that continued income growth in rich countries is irrelevant to how happy people are. In fact, continued income growth is more likely to lead simply to increases in consumption.

In addition, working harder to be able to afford more material goods can even make people unhappy if they do not have enough leisure time. People value their income in comparison with that of others but value leisure time even more absolutely. In developed countries, people tend to work too hard to consume more material goods but in the process consume too little leisure.

Another way to view money is to consider the gap between the high and low income earners within and across countries and over time. Economic theorists have suggested that, over time, capitalism would reduce the gap between the rich and the poor. Milanovic (2005), using enormous amounts of data, shows convincingly that the opposite has in fact happened; the income or inequality gap has widened. He reports that in 2001 about 1.1 billion people – almost one-fifth of the world's population – lived on less than two US dollars per day. In 2004, 852 million people faced chronic hunger, up 15 million from the previous year. And in 2004, one billion children – nearly half the children in the world – were deprived. More than 100 million children did not have adequate shelter and 4000 children died daily as a result of poor sanitation and contaminated water.

On the other hand, in 2004 there were 587 billionaires having combined wealth of 1.9 trillion dollars, representing about one-fifth of the annual economic output of the US. These individuals could hire the poorest third of the world's workforce – a billion workers – for one year on this money.

Milanovic draws five central conclusions. First, the gap or inequality between incomes in poor countries and in rich countries has widened. Second, there were fewer rich non-Western countries in 2000 than in 1960. Third, once countries joined the poor group, it was virtually impossible to move out of this group. Fourth, income inequality between individuals has stayed constant and high, tending in fact to increase modestly over the past 20 years. Fifth, the middle class has shrunk dramatically. More than 77 per cent of the world's people are poor, 16 per cent rich, leaving only 7 per cent in the middle. Globalization has probably made more people feel deprived by raising the reference point upward.

The decline of the middle class is particularly worrisome as it suggests the possibility of increased instability in the world order. It would appear that reducing income inequalities should be an important item on the world's agenda.

Do Motives for Money Matter?

Both what you want and why you want it are important predictors of well-being (Carver and Baird, 1998; Kasser et al., 2004). Srivastava et al. (2001) considered whether people's reasons for making money affected their psychological well-being. First, they developed a scale to measure people's motives for making money, identifying ten such motives. These were security, family support, market worth, pride, leisure, freedom, satisfying impulses, charity, social comparisons and overcoming self-doubt.

In two other studies of employed professionals and managers and employed entrepreneurs, after controlling for gender and actual income, people who placed a higher importance on money as compared with other goals, such as a satisfying family life or doing work one enjoys, were more likely to report lower subjective well-being. Only individuals who valued money but had negative motives for making it (for example, social comparison, overcoming self-doubt) reported lower well-being, however. This was not the case for those wanting to make money for positive reasons (such as supporting one's family).

Malka and Chatman (2003) were intrigued by the finding that income was only weakly associated with both subjective well-being or happiness and job satisfaction in the United States. This seemed surprising given the great importance placed on income in capitalist countries. They examined intrinsic and extrinsic work orientations as potential moderators of the effects of income on happiness and job satisfaction. One hundred and twenty-four MBA students completed measures of work orientation and four to nine years later indicated their salaries, happiness and job satisfaction. Individuals high in extrinsic orientation indicated greater happiness and job satisfaction to the degree they earned more money, whereas those high in intrinsic orientation were less happy at higher income levels.

Individuals high in intrinsic orientation value intellectual fulfillment, creative self-expression, and the pleasure they derive from mastery of the job.

Individuals high on extrinsic orientation value money and see work as mainly a way to earn money.

Income was weakly and positively associated with job satisfaction but not related to happiness. Intrinsic and extrinsic orientations were also weakly and positively related. Intrinsic orientation was positively and significantly related to happiness but uncorrelated with job satisfaction. Extrinsic orientation was uncorrelated with both happiness and job satisfaction. Intrinsic and extrinsic orientations were both uncorrelated with annual income. Finally happiness and job satisfaction were strongly positively correlated.

Why should individuals higher on intrinsic orientation show negative effects of money on happiness? Individuals higher on intrinsic orientation may be more affected by the negative effects of rewards. High income might also imply that the individual has ignored intrinsic factors in choosing their job. Highly paid individuals may think they are spending more time at work and not enough time at non-work pursuits.

Time Affluence

Kasser and Sheldon (unpublished manuscript) proposed that time affluence was likely to be a more important contributor to happiness or well-being than material affluence. Time, like money, is a limited resource. Time can be saved, spent or wasted. Some people seem to have lots of time, while others are always short of time. And people in some countries have more time (that is, they work less) than people in other countries.

Why should time affluence increase happiness or well-being? First, it takes time to undertake and participate in activities and events that are satisfying (Lyubomirsky et al., 2005). Second, time is needed for activities that lead to personal growth, the development of meaningful relationships and contributing to one's community and wider world (Kasser, 2002). Third, shortage of time can reduce the experience of flow (Csikscentmihalyi, 1999) and mindfulness (Brown and Ryan, 2003), both of which have been shown to increase happiness.

Kasser and Sheldon (unpublished manuscript) review the results of three studies that support a relationship between time affluence and happiness. Kasser and Brown (2003) found that work hours were negatively correlated with life satisfaction in a sample of adults, while income had no relationship with happiness. Van Boven and Gilovich (2003) reported that people were happier with things or activities they did than with things they had bought, the former taking time to pursue. Finally, Diener et al. (1995) concluded that the happiest countries were those with relatively low work hours.

Kasser and Sheldon (unpublished manuscript) developed measures of material affluence and time affluence, then considered the relationship of these to indicators of job and family satisfaction in a series of studies. In their first study, time affluence predicted both job and family satisfaction after controlling for material affluence (income). In a second study, they reported that short-term changes in well-being were related to changes in time affluence (about a month lag), controlling for changes in material affluence. In their two further studies, both mindfulness and need satisfaction (operationalized as autonomy, competence and relatedness) partially mediated the relationship between time affluence and well-being.

Time affluence is likely to be related to the quality of one's social and family relationships, participation in leisure and personal development activities, engaging in lifestyle behaviors likely to contribute to one's physical health and contributing to the improvement of one's wider community.

There are also some national policy implications that follow from this research. Since economic and material factors are only weak predictors of happiness or well-being, countries might consider policies that promote time off work. These might include increasing the number of holidays or vacation days as many European countries have done (Segal, 1999; Hayden, 2003), increasing the minimum wage so fewer people have to do two jobs (Ehrenreich, 2003; Reich, 2000) and reducing mandatory overtime options of employers (Golden, 2003).

COMING TO GRIPS WITH WORK HOURS

For fast acting relief from stress, try slowing down. (Lily Tomlin, American actress and comedienne)

Individual Change

Kofodimos (1993) lays out a change program for individuals choosing personal balance. It begins with self-assessment of one's current structure of time, energy and commitment allocation, one's current approach to living and one's current aspirations for oneself and their origin. It then moves to the development of visions for one's personal aspirations, values and purpose, one's approach to living, and one's central life priorities. The final phase identifies concrete change strategies for structuring one's life in accordance with one's key priorities, for implementing both mastery- and intimacy-oriented approaches and for living consistently with one's life values and goals on an ongoing basis. She provides structured exercises and frameworks to help one work one's way through this process.

Kofodimos also provides a tool for assessing the costs of imbalance for organizations; there are both benefits (such as high goals, decisiveness) and costs (such as stress, controlling and manipulating others). Mastery-oriented managers have difficulty adapting to change; mastery-oriented organizations are likely to be bureaucratic in nature and characterized by mistrust, anger and overly competitive behaviors. Kofodimos believes that a blended leadership that combines mastery- and intimacy-oriented behaviors is both preferable and achievable.

Kofodimos concludes her book by laying out a program for creating the balanced organization. Balanced organizations are more likely to create an environment that supports individuals in their desire for balanced lives; balanced organizations are also more likely to be adaptive and effective. She again starts with an assessment phase, including the current expectations of time and energy commitment to work, the current profile of mastery- and intimacy-oriented skills that are valued in executives, and current assumptions and objectives for individual development. The next phase involves developing visions for the integration of organizational aspirations and individual growth, for the desired leadership culture and for the role of work and the organization in the individual's balanced life. The final phase develops specific change strategies for encouraging managers to balance work with other important commitments, for supporting a balance of mastery- and intimacy-oriented leadership and for building an organization that is adaptive and effective because it believes in and supports balance.

The demand for instant and almost constant communication is increasing workplace stress. This results from both communication intrusion and communication overload. Workers can be addicted to checking email and text messages during meetings, at night and at weekends. Multi-tasking, as a solution, implies that the individual is not doing well at any of them, leading to reduced effectiveness.

Some suggested solutions to these issues include selecting one communication tool and sticking with it, checking your messages at set times during the day, doing only one thing at a time, communicating more clearly (use shorter sentences, point form) and taking a few minutes periodically during the day for relaxation and meditation.

Cartwright (2000) offers these suggestions for breaking out of the long working hours culture.

1. Schedule meetings only during core hours – no breakfast meetings or meetings after 5.00 p.m.
2. Take regular breaks. Take a short walk. Do not work through lunch.
3. Take your full vacation time. Plan your work around your holidays, not your holidays around your work.

4. Do not take work home on a regular basis.
5. Say no to unrealistic deadlines. It is better to under-promise but over-deliver than to over-promise but under-deliver.
6. Do not work late because others are doing so.
7. Monitor the hours you and your staff work. Use this information to make the case for more resources.

Clemens and Dalrymple (2005) propose different aspects of time, suggesting a difference between time management – trying to squeeze in as much as you can in a work day – and time leadership – using time well on the most important things. Individuals need to have a long-term view. In addition, responding flexibly, as needed, instead of rigidly following a schedule is advised. It also takes time for maturity to take place – it cannot be rushed. Individuals are also encouraged to develop a rhythm in their use of time that works best for them in their unique circumstances.

Organizational Change

The most common organizational initiatives to address work hour problems are work–family programs. Work–family programs emerged in response to some real and pressing organizational issues: reducing barriers to productivity such as absenteeism and turnover; growing public relations and recruitment advantages; meeting the needs of women, single parents and dual-career couples; and responding to government legislation regarding equality, daycare and parental leave.

Kofodimos (1995) believes that work–family programs, though well intentioned, are not working very well. Most are not widely used and their presence often creates indifference and resentment among some employees. Kofodimos thinks these programs address the symptoms rather than the fundamental causes of work–personal life conflict.

Work and family programs encounter difficulties: there is a lack of top management support; they are not used by career-oriented employees and others are afraid to use them or when using them become marginalized; there is a resistance on the part of supervisors to use them; there is a perception that the programs are costly and have few performance benefits; and there is little or no evidence that women who use them benefit from their use.

Why don't work–family programs work? Kofodimos sees them as self-defeating because they do not address factors that cause the conflict; these are cultural values that equate self-worth with hard work, confidence and career success. Work–family programs in fact reflect these values and maintain work–personal life conflict. Kofodimos refers to these values as the 'mastery orientation'. This involves investing time and energy in work, a competitive and control approach to management and work behaviors (goal achievement, action-orientation) and a masterful image that is esteemed by others, including employers. Kofodimos concludes that work–family programs are consistent with the mastery orientation. That is, they help employees focus their energy and time on work, they are implemented from the top of the organization down, and they address barriers that keep employees from being effective at work (a masterful image).

The mastery orientation explains why work–family programs do not work well. The mastery orientation produces negative attitudes towards these programs, a preference for those who work long and hard, a belief in the importance of treating all employees alike, continuing to define personal success in terms of mastery criteria, and continuing to see women more committed to personal life than to their careers, with the result that organizational cultures are resistant and unlikely to change.

The mastery orientation, even with the presence of work–family programs, leads to burnout, stress and overwork, careerism, demoralized staff and a quiet and unexpressed dissent.

Organizations instead need to support work–personal life balance (Golden and Figart, 2000b). This involves employees addressing and changing their mastery orientation. The goal for organizations is to support and enhance life balance (Nussbaum et al., 2003). This includes changing the time and energy devoted to work, adopting collaborative and caring leadership and valuing personal development as much as organizational contribution.

Kofodimos describes a variety of interventions useful in changing to a balance-supportive culture. These include assessing the level of mastery orientation in the organization and the individual and organizational costs of this, developing a statement of purpose and vision for achieving balance, providing coaching for mastery-oriented managers, and ensuring that organizational policies and practices support balance (see Bond et al., 2004, for examples of flexible work hours).

Societal Change

Work and family issues are best seen as a societal concern (Lewis and Cooper, 2005). Many women and men in all industrialized countries experience work–personal life integration difficulties and dissatisfaction. Although various countries have made different levels of progress and employed varied approaches, new thinking is needed here to move forward (Segal, 2003). This will, of necessity, involve challenging the priority of profits over people, the powerlessness that many individuals feel, the search for quick-fix solutions and lack of collaboration among key stakeholders (governments, organizations, trade unions and professional associations, communities, families and individuals).

More people today want a life beyond work. Employees can work more effectively if they can integrate their work, families and personal lives in more satisfying ways. This becomes a win–win situation for all involved (Friedman et al., 1998).

Globalization and technology have now interconnected much of the world's work. The increasing search for efficiency has intensified the experience of work, often also increasing working hours. The global economy has also heightened consumerism and pressures for conspicuous consumption. More people want the trappings of consumption, which also contributes to working longer hours. Many people now have more money but less time to enjoy it.

This raises some key questions. Are there alternatives to market economies? Can relationships between men and women change to become more egalitarian? Can organizations come to value those who care about their families? Will organizations undertake efforts to change their work cultures that require expending resources and a long time frame? What change processes are likely to be successful in transforming the workplace into a more supportive environment?

Lewis and Cooper (2005) suggest interventions at multiple levels simultaneously if headway on work hours is to be made:

1. government-level actions
   - levels of minimum wage, reducing the need to hold two jobs
   - legislation on maternity and paternity leaves
   - legislation on working hours
2. workplace actions
   - tackling the outdated value of face-time (being seen, hours spent in the office)
   - supporting those who pursue family policies
   - implementing more effective human resources management practices
   - incorporating work–personal life balance as a core cultural value and having the top management team practice this and recognize this as important
3. trade union actions
   - making hours a collective bargaining issue
4. community-level actions
   - revitalizing communities to make them more attractive places to spend family time in skills exchanges
5. family-level actions

- minimizing gender inequalities
- valuing care, leisure, health
- shared care programs
6. individual-level actions
    - living a more simple life – less materialistic
    - rejecting the long work hours demands of employers
    - downshifting – exchanging 'a high-pressure, high-earning, high tempo lifestyle for a more relaxed, less consumerist existence' (Honore, 2004, p. 47).

What is life for? Most believe that work is good for us. Work can be enjoyable, even uplifting. At work one can socialize with others, learn new things and meet challenges. But we should not let work take over our lives (Meiskins and Whalley, 2002). There are too many other important things that also need time, such as family, friends, hobbies and rest (Korten, 2003). As Senator Paul Tsongas said during his treatment for cancer, 'No one on their death bed says they regret not spending enough time at their job.'

NOTE

1. Preparation of this chapter was supported in part by the Schulich School of Business, York University. Sherry Kang assisted with the literature review; Louise Coutu prepared the manuscript.

REFERENCES

Adam, B. (1993), 'Within and beyond the time economy of employment relations: conceptual issues pertinent to research on time and work', *Social Science Information*, **32**, 163–84.

Austin Knight (1995), *Long Hours Culture*, London: Austin Knight.

Becker, P.E. and Moen, P. (1995), 'Scaling back: dual-earner couples' work–family strategies', *Journal of Marriage and the Family*, **61**, 995–1007.

Belk, R.W. (1984), 'Three scales to measure constructs related to materialism: reliability, validity, and relationships to measures of happiness', in T.C. Kinnear (ed.) *Advances in Consumer Research*, Vol. 11, Provo, UT: Association for Consumer Research, pp. 291–7.

Belk, R.W. (1985), 'Materialism: trait aspects of living in a materialistic world', *Journal of Consumer Research*, **12**, 265–80.

Belk, R.W. and Pollay, R. (1985), 'Images of ourselves: the good life in twentieth century advertising', *Journal of Consumer Research*, **11**, 887–97.

Bond, J.T., Galinsky, E. and Hill, E.J. (2004), *When Work Works: Flexibility, a Critical Ingredient in Creating an Effective Workplace*, New York: Families and Work Institute.

Brainbridge, J.S. (1989), 'Dissatisfaction?', *Maryland Bar Journal*, **22**, 28–31.

Brett, J.M. and Stroh, L.K. (2003), 'Working 61 plus hours a week: why do managers do it?', *Journal of Applied Psychology*, **88**, 67–78.

Brown, K.W. and Ryan, R.M. (2003), 'The benefits of being present: mindfulness and its role in well-being', *Journal of Personality and Social Psychology*, **84**, 822–48.

Brown, M. and Benson, J. (2005), 'Managing to overload? Work overload and performance appraisal processes', *Group and Organization Management*, **30**, 99–124.

Burke, R.J. (2000), 'Workaholism in organizations: concepts, results and future directions', *International Journal of Management Reviews*, **2**, 1–19.

Cartwright, S. (2000), 'Taking the pulse of executive health in the U.K.', *Academy of Management Executive*, **14**, 16–23.

Carver, C.S. and Baird, E. (1998), 'The American dream revisited: is it what you want or why you want it that matters?', *Psychological Science*, **9**, 289–92.

Clarkberg, M. and Moen, P. (2001), 'The time squeeze: is the increase in working time due to employer demands or employee preferences?', *American Behavioral Scientist*, **44**, 1115–36.

Clemens, J. and Dalrymple, S. (2005), *Time Mastery*, New York: AMACOM.

Crouter, A.C., Bumpus, M.F., Maguire, M.C. and McHale, S.M. (1999), 'Working parents, work pressures and adolescents' well-being: insights into dynamics in dual career families', *Developmental Psychology*, **25**, 1453–61.

Crouter, A.C., Bumpus, M.F., Head, M.R. and McHale, S.M. (2001), 'Implications of overwork and overload for the quality of men's family relationships', *Journal of Marriage and Family*, **63**, 404–16.

Csikscentmihalyi, M. (1999), 'If we are so rich, why aren't we happy?', *American Psychologist*, **54**, 821–7.

Dart, N.C. (1988), 'Career satisfaction', *Michigan Bar Journal*, **67**, 840–3.

Dawson, S. and Bamossy, G. (1991), 'If "We are what we have", what are we when we don't have? To have possessions: a handbook of ownership and property', *Journal of Social Behavior and Personality*, **6**, 363–84.

De Graaf, J., Wann, D. and Naylor, T.H. (2000), *Affluenza: the All-consuming Epidemic*, San Francisco: Berrett-Koehler.

Deci, E. and Ryan, R.M. (1991), 'A motivational approach to self: integration in personality', in R. Dienstbier (ed.), *Nebraska Symposium on Motivation*, Lincoln: University of Nebraska Press, Vol. 38, pp. 237–88.

Diener, E. and Biswas-Diener, R. (2002), 'Will money increase subjective well-being?', *Social Indicators Research*, **57**, 119–69.

Diener, E. and Seligman, M.E.P. (2004), 'Beyond money: towards an economy of well-being', *Psychology in the Public Interest*, **5**, 1–31.

Diener, E., Diener, M. and Diener, C. (1995), 'Factors predicting the subjective well-being of nations', *Journal of Personality and Social Psychology*, **69**, 851–64.

Diener, E., Suh, E.M., Lucas, R.E. and Smith, H.L. (1999), 'Subjective well-being: three decades of progress', *Psychological Bulletin*, **125**, 276–302.

Easterbrook, G. (2004), *The Progress Paradox: How Life Gets Better while People Feel Worse*, New York: Random House.

Easterlin, R.A. (1995), 'Will raising the incomes of all increase the happiness of all?', *Journal of Economic Behavior and Organization*, **27**, 35–44.

Ehrenreich, B. (2003), *Nickel and Dimed: On not Getting by in America*, New York: Metropolitan Books.

Fisher, A.B. (1992), 'Welcome to the age of overwork', *Fortune*, **126**, 64–71, 30 November.

Frank, R.H. (1999), *Luxury Fever: Why Money Fails to Satisfy in an Era of Excess*, New York: The Free Press.

Friedman, S.D., Christensen, P. and DeGroot, J. (1998), 'Work and life: the end of the zero-sum game', *Harvard Business Review*, **76**, 119–29.

Fromm, E. (1976), *To have or to be?*, New York: Harper and Row.

Furnham, A. and Argyle, M. (1998), *The Psychology of Money*, London, UK: Routledge.

Galambos, N.L., Sears, H.A., Almeida, D.M. and Kolaric, G. (1995), 'Parents' work overload and problem behavior in young adolescents', *Journal of Research on Adolescence*, **5**, 201–23.

Galinsky, E. (1999), *Ask the Children: What America's Children really Think about Working Parents*, New York: William Morrow.

Galinsky, E., Bond, J.T., Kim, S.S., Bachon, L., Brownfield, E. and Sakal, K. (2005), *Overwork in America: When the Way we Work Becomes Too Much*, New York: Families and Work Institute.

George, D. (1997), 'Working longer hours: pressure from the boss or pressure from the marketers?', *Review of Social Economy*, **60**, 33–65.

Glick, J. (1999), *Faster: The Acceleration of Almost Everything*, New York: Random House.

Golden, L. (1998), 'Work time and the impact of policy institutions: reforming the overtime hours law and regulation', *Review of Social Economy*, **55**, 33–65.

Golden, L. (2003), 'Forced overtime in the land of the free', in J. de Graaf (ed.), *Take Back your Time: Fighting Overwork and Time Poverty in America*, San Francisco: Berrett-Koehler, pp. 28–36.

Golden, L. and Figart, D.M. (2000a), *Working Time: International Trends, Theory and Policy Perspectives*, London: Routledge.

Golden, L. and Figart, D. (2000b), 'Doing something about long hours', *Challenge*, **43**, 15–35.

Green, F. (2001), 'It's been a hard day's night: the concentration and intensification of work in late twentieth-century Britain', *British Journal of Industrial Relations*, **39**, 53–80.

Greenhouse, S. (2001), 'Report shows Americans have more "Labor Days"', *New York Times*, p. A6, 1 September.

Hayden, A. (2003), 'Europe's work-time alternatives', in J. de Graaf (ed.), *Take Back your Time: Fighting Overwork and Time Poverty in America*, San Francisco: Berrett-Koehler, pp. 202–10.

Hochschild, A. (1997), *The Time Bind*, New York: Henry Holt and Company.

Honore, C. (2004), *In Praise of Slow*, Toronto: Alfred Knopf.

Hunnicutt, B. (2003), 'When we had the time', in J. de Graaf (ed.), *Take Back your Time: Fighting Overwork and Time Poverty in America*, San Francisco: Berrett-Koehler, pp. 114–22.

Jacobs, J.A. and Gerson, K. (1998), 'Who are the overworked Americans?', *Review of Social Economy*, **56**, 442–59.

Kasser, T. (2002), *The High Price of Materialism*, Cambridge, MA: MIT Press.

Kasser, T. (2004), 'The good life or the goods life? Positive psychology and personal well-being in the culture of consumption', in P.A. Linley and S. Joseph (eds) *Positive Psychology in Practice*, New York: Wiley, pp. 55–67.

Kasser, T. and Brown, K.W. (2003), 'On time, happiness, and ecological footprints', in J. de Graaf (ed.), *Take Back Your Time: Fighting Overwork and Time Poverty in America*. San Francisco: Berrett-Koehler, pp. 107–112.

Kasser, T. and Kanner, A.D. (2003), *Psychology and Consumer Culture: The Struggle for a Good Life in a Materialistic World*, Washington, DC: APA Books.

Kasser, T. and Ryan, R.M. (1993), 'A dark side of the American dream: Correlates of financial success as a central life aspiration', *Journal of Personality and Social Psychology*, **65**, 410–22.

Kasser, T. and Ryan, R.M. (1996), 'Further examining the American dream: Differential correlates of intrinsic and extrinsic goals', *Personality and Social Psychology Bulletin*, **22**, 280–87.

Kasser, T. and Sheldon, K.M. (unpublished manuscript), 'Material and time affluence as predictors of subjective well-being'.

Kasser, T., Ryan, R.M., Zax, M. and Sameroff, A.J. (1995), 'The relations of maternal and social environments to late adolescents' materialistic and prosocial values', *Developmental Psychology*, **31**, 907–14.

Kasser, T., Sheldon, K.M., Ryan, R.M. and Deci, E.L. (2004), 'The independent effects of goal contents and motives on well-being: it's both what you do and why you do it', *Personality and Social Psychology Bulletin*, **30**, 475–86.

Kofodimos, J. (1993), *Balancing Act*, San Francisco: Jossey-Bass.

Kofodimos, J.R. (1995), *Beyond Work–family Programs: Confronting and Resolving the Underlying Causes of Work–personal Life Conflict*, Greeensboro, NC: Center for Creative Leadership.

Korten, D. (2003), 'What's an economy for?', in J. de Graaf (ed.), *Take Back your Time: Fighting Overwork and Time Poverty in America*, San Francisco: Berrett-Koehler, pp. 219–26.

Kreitzman, L. (1999), *The 24-hour Society*, London: Profile Books.

Landers, R.M., Rebitzer, J.B. and Taylor, L.J. (1996), 'Rat race redux: adverse selection in the determination on work hours in law firms', *American Economic Review*, **86**, 329–48.

Lane, R.E. (2000), *The Loss of Happiness in Market Democracies*, New Haven, CT: Yale University Press.

Lasch, C. (1979), *The Culture of Narcissism: American Life in an Age of Diminishing Expectations*, New York: Norton.

Lewis, S. and Cooper, C.L. (2005), *Work-life Integration*, Chichester, UK: John Wiley.

Locke, E., McClear, K. and Knight, D. (1996), 'Self esteem and work', in C. Cooper and I. Robertson (eds), *International Review of Industrial and Organizational Psychology*, New York: Wiley, pp. 1–32.

Lyubomirsky, S., Sheldon, K.M. and Schkade, D. (2005), 'Pursuing happiness: the architecture of sustainable change', *Review of General Psychology*, in press.

Major, V.S., Klein, K.J. and Ehrhart, M.G. (2002), 'Work time, work interference with family, and psychological distress', *Journal of Applied Psychology*, **87**, 427–36.

Malka, A. and Chatman, J.A. (2003), 'Intrinsic and extrinsic work orientations as moderators of the effect of current income on subjective well-being: a longitudinal study', *Personality and Social Psychology Bulletin*, **29**, 737–46.

McDonnell, K. (2001), *Honey, we Lost the Kids: Rethinking Childhood in the Multimedia Age*, Toronto: Second Story Press.

McMillan, L., O'Driscoll, M.P. and Burke, R.J. (2003), 'Workaholism: a review of theory, research and future directions', in C.L. Cooper and I.T. Robertson (eds), *International Review of Industrial and Organizational Psychology*, London: Blackwell Publishers, pp. 167–90.

Meiskins, P. and Whalley, P. (2002), *Putting Work in its Place: A Quiet Revolution*, Ithaca, NY: Cornell University Press.

Menzies, H. (2005), *No Time: Stress and the Crisis of Modern Life*, Toronto: Douglas and McIntyre.

Milanovic, B. (2005), *Worlds Apart: Measuring International Global Inequality*, Princeton, NJ: Princeton University Press.

Myers, D.G. (2000), *The American Paradox: Spiritual Hunger in an Age of Plenty*, New Haven, CT: Yale University Press.

Myers, D.G. (2003), 'The social psychology of sustainability', *World Futures: The Journal of General Evolution*, **59**, 201–11.

Needleman, J. (1991), *Money and the Meaning of Life*, New York: Doubleday/ Currency.

Needleman, J. (1998), *Time and the Soul: Where has All the Meaningful Time Gone – and Can we Get it Back?*, San Francisco: Berrett-Koehler.

Newton, T. and Findlay, P. (1996), 'Playing God? The performance of appraisal', *Human Resource Management Journal*, **6**, 42–58.

Nussbaum, K., Owens, C. and Eickert, C. (2003), 'America needs a break', in J. de Graaf (ed.), *Take Back your Time: Fighting Overwork and Time Poverty in America*, San Francisco: Berrett-Koehler, pp. 172–7.

O'Reilly, C. and Chatman, J.A. (1994), 'Working smarter and harder: a longitudinal study of managerial success', *Administrative Science Quarterly*, **39**, 603–27.

Putnam, R.D. (2000), *Bowling Alone: The Collapse and Revival of American Community*, New York: Simon and Schuster.

Rebitzer, J. and Taylor, L. (1995), 'Do labor markets provide enough short-hours jobs? An analysis of work hours and work incentives', *Economic Inquiry*, **33**, 257–73.

Reich, R.R. (2000), *The Future of Success*, New York: Knopf.

Richins, M.L. and Dawson, S. (1992), 'A consumer value orientation for materialism and its measurement: scale development and validation', *Journal of Consumer Research*, **19**, 303–16.

Rifkin, J. (2004), *The European Dream*, New York: Tarcher/Penguin.

Robinson, J. (2003), 'The incredible shrinking vacation', in J. de Graaf (ed.) *Take Back your Time: Fighting Overwork and Time Poverty in America*, San Francisco: Berrett-Koehler, pp. 20–27.

Ryan, R.M., Sheldon, K.M., Kasser, T. and Deci, E.I. (1996), 'All goals are not created equal: an organismic perspective on the nature of goals and their regulation', in P.M. Gollwitzer and I.A. Bargh (eds), *The Psychology of Action*, New York: Guilford Press, pp. 7–26.

Schor, J. (1991), *The Overworked American: The Unexpected Decline of Leisure*, New York: Basic Books.

Schor, J. (1998), *The Overspent American*, New York: Basic Books.

Schor, J. (2003), 'The (even more) overworked American', in J. de Graaf (ed.), *Take Back your Time: Fighting Overwork and Time Poverty in America*, San Francisco: Berrett-Koehler, pp. 6–11.

Schor, J.B. (2004), *Born to Buy: The Commercialized Child and the New Consumer Culture*, New York: Simon and Schuster.

Segal, J.M. (1999), *Graceful Simplicity: The Philosophy and Politics of the Alternative American Dream*, Berkeley, CA: University of California Press.

Segal, J. (2003), 'A policy agenda for taking back time', in J. de Graaf (ed.), *Take Back your Time: Fighting Overwork and Time Poverty in America*, San Francisco: Berrett-Koehler, pp. 211–18.

Sirgy, M.J. (1998), 'Materialism and quality of life', *Social Indicators Research*, **43**, 227–60.

Sparks, K., Cooper, C., Fried, Y. and Shirom, A. (1997), 'The effects of hours of work on health: a meta-analytic review', *Journal of Occupational and Organizational Psychology*, **70**, 391–409.

Srivastava, A., Locke, E.A. and Bartol, K.M. (2001), 'Money and subjective well-being: it's not the money, it's the motives', *Journal of Personality and Social Psychology*, **80**, 959–71.

Taylor, F.W. (1967), *Principles of Scientific Management*, New York: Norton.

Trump, D. (2004), *Think Like a Billionaire*, New York: HarperCollins.

Van Boven, L. and Gilovich, T. (2003), 'To do or to have? That is the question', *Journal of Personality and Social Psychology*, **85**, 1193–202.

Wallace, J.E. (1995), 'Corporatist control and organizational commitment among professionals: the case of lawyers working in law firms', *Social Forces*, **73**, 811–39.

Wallace, J.E. (1997), 'It's about time: a study of hours worked and work spillover among law firm lawyers', *Journal of Vocational Behavior*, **50**, 227–48.

Weber, M. (1989), *The Protestant Ethic and the Spirit of Capitalism*, London: Allen and Unwin.

Worrall, L. and Cooper, C.L. (1999), *Quality of Work Life Survey*, London: Institute of Management.

Wright, N. and Larson, V. (1993), 'Materialism and life satisfaction: a meta-analysis', *Journal of Consumer Satisfaction, Dissatisfaction, and Complaining Behavior*, **6**, 158–65.

2. How long? The historical, economic and cultural factors behind working hours and overwork

Lonnie Golden

OVERVIEW

How long are hours of work and how many work hours are too many? The aims of this chapter are to address the following questions. What is the historical trend of hours of work per worker – are they getting longer, shorter or staying the same? When and among whom have they been rising? What forces and counterforces generally determine the length of individuals' work hours – economic, social-psychological-cultural, political-regulatory and institutional? How much of the trend in work hours is attributable to incentives and behavior of employers relative to employees? When do longer hours of work generate symptoms of overwork for workers? How might overemployment (being employed beyond one's initially preferred number of hours) eventually lead to either overwork or workaholism – an unforced addiction to work activity? Finally, how might we apply these key underlying determinants of work hours to address work addiction with potential policy levers, to regulate the (over)flow of work hours or minimize the incidence or conditions that might lead to workaholic behavior that results in negative social consequences?

This chapter aims to refine the discussion of trends and patterns in work hours by delineating and distinguishing the related notions of long hours, overwork and overemployment and their potential implications for better understanding workaholism in the present. The first part of the chapter traces trends in the history of the length and distribution of working hours. The second develops a comprehensive approach to understanding the economic and other sources of these patterns. The third focuses on the distinct concepts of long hours, overwork and overemployment, and suggests how they may interact. The final section explores the implications of the determination of work hours for the most promising directions for future research on the nature and consequences of long hours of work.

Workaholism is typically defined as an extensive or excessive and sustained allocation of time to work-related activities that is not derived directly from necessity or other external motivations such as pressures from the workplace (Snir and Harpaz, 2004). It is characterized by a tendency to over-commit to time at work (or thinking about work) at the expense of family and social time, to a greater extent than is necessary or expected, either organizationally or financially (Scott et al., 1997; Buelens and Poelmans, 2004). Work becomes an addiction or compulsion that grows more severe as one's career progresses (Hamermesh and Slemrod, 2005). This suggests that there must be some relationship between the extent or degree of workaholism and the length of work hours per worker in a country or sector of the economy. Indeed, the first generation models of workaholism identify work involvement, as reflected in long working hours, as one of its key, measurable components (Spence and Robbins, 1992; Scott et al., 1997; Burke, 1999).

However, documenting a clear association between the extent of workaholism and the number of working hours has proven elusive. This is because both workaholism and long working hours have not only negative connotations, such as adverse health consequences, but also positive implications, such as signaling commitment (Buelens and Poelmans, 2004). About 30 per cent of employees in the US and in Canada self-identify as workaholic (Kemeny, 2002). However, the rate is 53 per cent among those who report working an average of 60 or more hours per week. It is highest among the higher income earners (Hamermesh and Slemrod, 2005). Nevertheless, there is not a strong, direct correlation between working hours and different measures of workaholism (McMillan et al., 2002). Long hours may yield a variety of consequences, only some of which are detrimental forms of workaholism (Burke, 1999). Alternatively, long hours may be just a symptom within an individual's overall relationship to work (Porter, 2005). Thus, there simply may be too many elements associated with workaholism to arrive at a precise definition. There may be personality-based and organization-based causal sources, as well as perceived positive consequences that motivate longer work hours, such as improved equity (Peiperl and Jones, 2001).

THE LONG-RUN HISTORICAL TREND OF HOURS OF WORK

Most scholars begin the quest for identifying the secular trends and patterns in work hours with the onset of the industrial revolution (Thompson, 1967; Bienefeld, 1972; Hopkins, 1982; Cross, 1988). There are essentially three identifiable stages of development in the duration of weekly or annual hours worked since the 1800s: gradual reduction, stabilization, and then, more recently, polarization. In the first wave, during the initial transformation from agricultural to industrial type jobs and workplaces, many workers in the US were working as long as 70 hours per week or more (Whaples, 2001). Most of the increase in hours occurred on an annual basis, with an increase in the length of the work year and disappearance of seasonal down time. Daily hours appear to have peaked by 1830 in the US and actually declined somewhat during the rest of the century as employers accommodated workers' calls for a shorter workday. The accommodation was facilitated by technology and mechanization that made it possible for employers to maintain original output levels even while shortening daily hours (Atack et al., 2003). The decline in hours spread with the advent of the shorter hours movements in the last quarter of the 19th century. Labor strikes to limit or shorten work hours began as early as 1791 in the US and even earlier in Britain (Brody, 1989; Roediger and Foner, 1989; Martorana and Hirsch, 2001). They eventually bore fruit, albeit gradually and many decades later.

The long run trend decline in the workweek length has tended to be non-linear or cyclical. Historically, declines in the 'standard' workweek have occurred during growth periods following periods of economic stagnation. Demand for shorter work time became pent-up during down times and could only be exercised when workers gained sufficient leverage to negotiate for shorter hours (Bienefeld, 1972; Roche, 1987). This was not sustainable without the establishment of new institutions such as labor unions, the labor movement and favorable labor protection laws, particularly in the early twentieth-century developed economies (Whaples, 2001; Martorana and Hirsch, 2001; Huberman, 2004). Otherwise, hours might have continued increasing even when wage levels were rising. The highly competitive, unregulated market for labor in the nineteenth century contributed to long hours of work per week that left workers' desire for a shorter workday more often than not unfulfilled (Altman, 1999; Bourdieu and Reynaud, 2001; Atack et al., 2003).

By the 1920s in the US, the average workweek was down to about 48 hours per worker. In the first years of the Great Depression, workweeks dropped precipitously. Work-sharing practices were fairly widespread at the time, where employers reduced operating days per week or shift lengths, which was actively encouraged by Federal government policies (Nemirow, 1984; Hunnicutt, 1988; Golden, 1990; Linder, 2002). Legislation was eventually passed in 1938 that instituted a standard workweek, enforced by the now familiar time-and-a-half premium requirement for 'overtime' hours beyond 40 in a given one-week period for workers covered by the Fair

Labor Standards Act (FLSA). The primary reasons were to alleviate unemployment and to prevent the workweek from rising back up toward 48 hours once the economy recovered. However, the shorter hours movement largely dissipated thereafter, with greater interest among workers for reaping the rewards for productivity gains through pay increases rather than shortened hours (Hunnicutt, 1988). Consumption took off and quite abruptly became more favored, particularly when labor markets tightened during and after World War II. Workers' interest regarding hours became more in stabilizing the workweek through the business cycle, to keep income predictable. Indeed, the workweek showed remarkable stability for decades thereafter (Kniesner, 1976; Bernanke and Powell, 1986; Owen, 1989; Golden, 1990). Technological progress, particularly advances in the supervisory activity, have brought about shorter workweeks (Ueberfeldt, 2005). Ever higher levels of education among workers and rising real wages among women were preventing weekly work hours from falling, even while annual hours were declining owing to more vacation and holiday time (Kniesner, 1976). It appeared that forces had taken hold that would forever restrain the workweek.

Trends began to change, however, about 1970 or soon thereafter. What has occurred since then has been controversial and not yet completely settled. The stir was created largely by evidence that average annual hours in the US reversed course and started rising (Leete and Schor, 1994). The overall average length of weekly hours is clearly not the ideal indicator of work time trends because the average may be suppressed if there is a growing percentage of the labor force working in less than full-time or year-round employment, such as voluntary and particularly involuntary part-time and contingent jobs. The latter group forms a large part of the 'underemployed', those who might prefer to work longer hours but are constrained from attaining them (Nollen, 1989; Golden, 2005). The trend in weekly hours among only full-time workers has exhibited a slight increase since the early 1970s. It has escalated among those employed in managerial, professional, transportation and sales occupations (Rones et al., 1997) and among the middle and highest wage-earners (Costa, 1998; Drago, 2000; Bernstein and Kornbluh, 2005). Trends vary depending on samples and methodology used to estimate work hours. For example, the above refer to household data. However, data from establishments tell a similar story. Analysis of average weekly hours of work in the manufacturing sectors, for instance, reinforces the findings from households (Hetrick, 2000). Of course, there are dissenters who observe no increase in hours at all over time (Northrup and Greis, 1983; Rupert and Roberts, 1995; McGrattan and Rogerson, 2004; Greenwood and Vandenbroucke, 2005; Ueberfeldt, 2005).

Even if the overall weekly average is rising only modestly or even not at all, what is clear is that, for many if not all sectors of the economy or segments of the workforce, average hours are longer than they were a few decades ago and no longer decreasing. There is evidence that, at least among the most educated in the workforce and white men, average hours have lengthened in recent years (Coleman and Pencavel, 1993a, b). The share of employed men working 50 or more hours per week has been substantial among highly-educated, high-wage, salaried and older-aged workers (Jacobs and Gerson, 2004; Epstein and Kalleberg, 2004; Drago et al., 2005; Kuhn and Lozano, 2005). Currently, just short of 19 per cent of the US workforce reports working 50 or more hours per week, and almost one-third of the workforce works longer than 40 hours per week. Indeed, the last few decades may be more accurately characterized as a period of polarization of work hours or a time-divide (Bluestone and Rose, 1998; Drago, 2000; Jacobs and Gerson, 2004). There are historically greater proportions working very long or at least longer than standard hours at the same time that there has been growth in the shorter hours tail of the hours distribution. Moreover, while fewer workers worked five-day workweeks in 1991 than in 1973, the proportion working seven days rose by 70 per cent for men and virtually doubled for women (Hamermesh, 1999). Table 2.1 summarizes several key studies of work hours in the United States through the 1990s.

In contrast to the trends in the US, starting about the same time, 1970, annual and weekly hours in continental Western Europe declined, at least through the 1980s (Burgoon and Baxandall, 2004; Huberman and Minns, 2005). This decline occurred at different rates and in diverse forms in the various EU countries. Several social and institutional factors account for the cross-country differences, including statutory and collectively bargained restrictions on standard and overtime hours in the EU countries (Bell and Freeman, 1995; Di Martino, 1995; Bosch, 1999; Contensou and Vranceanu, 2000; Stier and Lewin-Epstein, 2003; Reynolds, 2004; Huberman, 2004; Rubery et al., 2005; Alesina et al., 2005). For example, from 1960 to 1985 the Netherlands, Belgium and West Germany experienced a reduction in annual hours. The trend toward shorter hours has slowed in the last decade or two (Blyton, 1989; Owen, 1989; Hinrichs et al., 1991; Bosch et al., 1993; Messenger, 2004). Employers and governments have pursued greater flexibility in working time, such as annualization of hours, in large part to compensate employers for the required reduction in the standard. As in the US, there is an increasing diversity of work patterns in Europe since the 1970s, across sectors, industries and even individual workers. Yet, US workweeks remain considerably longer than elsewhere, particularly the non-English speaking countries. Americans average 25

Table 2.1   Trends in work hours

Period	Change in work hours	Sample	Data	Sources
1979–2000	16% increase in annual hours (490)	Married couples	Current population survey (CPS)	Bernstein and Kornbluh (2005)
1979–2002	50% increase in annual hours (466)	Wives in married couples		
1976–93	2.4% increase: 1 hour weekly, 100 hours annually	Wage and salary employed men	CPS	Rones et al. (1997)
	5.9% increase: 2 hours weekly, 233 hours annually	Women, age 16+		
1967–89	3.3% increase (66 hours) in average annual hours	All employed	Panel Survey of income dynamics (PSID), CPS	Bluestone and Rose (1998)
	140 avg. annual hours	Prime-age (25–54) workers		
1982–95	600 avg. annual hours	Working couples		
1969–89	Increase of 7% (86) in annual hours	Average worker	CPS	Leete and Schor (1994)
	16% increase in annual hours	Working family		
1969–87	Increases of 163, 98 and 305 annual hours respectively	Average employed, Men, Women	CPS	Schor (1992)
1976–88	Increase of 3.0 hours per week	Married couples: wife works	PSID	Rupert and Roberts (1995)
	Decrease of 0.4 hours per week	wife does not work		
1960–88	Decreases of 2.1% and 4.7 % (99), and 2% and 3% (56)	Men: white, black	Census, CPS	Coleman and Pencavel (1993a, b)
	Decreases of 3.5%, 1.7% (27); increases of 7.2% and 10.7% (159)	Women: white, black		

Source: Golden and Figart (2001).

working hours per person of working age and 46 weeks per year in contrast to the German average of less than 19 hours and the French average of 40 weeks per year. The evidence suggests that most of the discrepancy between the continents is explained by labor market regulations that limit hours or extend vacation time, promoted by strong labor unions and adopted by governments to cope with declining industries, and has less to do with differential tax rates or innate cultural differences (Altonji and Oldham, 2003; Ueberfeldt, 2005; Alesina et al., 2005).

EXPLANATIONS OF LONG HOURS: STRUCTURAL, ECONOMIC, SOCIAL AND BEHAVIORAL FACTORS

What explains this growing proportion of the workforce working more or longer hours, at least in some countries and among certain types of workers? Is there a set of contributing factors that can be applied consistently across time and countries? The answer is 'yes', but the factors vary across disciplines considering the question. Economic studies look first at the traditional, underlying structural economic factors. The same factors that economic historians have identified as the drivers in the preceding century may now be at work in the opposite direction. When hours rose, in historical periods, it was associated with structural factors such as a higher capital–labor ratio, larger enterprise size and greater pool of immigrants and agricultural workers (Whaples, 2001). There was a supporting role for wage trends, protective labor legislation, union power and other factors associated with the characteristics of workers in the workforce at the time. There are important counterforces that suppress any further escalation of work hours, such as the rise in real wage rates and decline in price of many key leisure goods that enhance the value of non-market time (Greenwood and Vandenbroucke, 2005; Drago et al., 2005). However, it is not clear that these same factors remain as relevant as before 1970.

Microeconomic Conceptions of Work Hours Determination

Generally, why do people work as much as they do? What causes their hours of work to climb or recede or stay the same over time? Conventional economic analysis portrays the determination of working time as the result of the interaction between two wholly separate entities – optimizing agents supplying and agents demanding labor services. On the labor supply side, workers' hours of labor supply are assumed to reflect a combination of innate 'preferences', their own unique, inherent taste or distaste for work or leisure, and voluntary responses to external incentives in the labor market.

The conventional model of labor–leisure choice suggests that once participation in the workforce is decided, individuals set and adjust their hours of labor supply toward their preferred number per week, in order to maximize their 'utility' (overall well-being) level. Utility depends on two opposing goals – more income and more free time. The model assumes that workers' preferred number of work hours depends on their innate preferences, their available wage rate and income from non-labor sources. Workers can maximize their utility by adjusting their hours to the unique point where the relative preference for an hour of leisure vis-à-vis work exactly equals the equilibrium market wage rate. In virtually all textbook treatments of labor supply, the focus is placed mainly on the opposing income and substitution effects of wage rate changes. The net effect reveals whether workers increase or decrease, on balance, their preferred hours of labor supply when wage rates increase (or decrease).

The conventional microeconomic model of labor supply provides a parsimonious yet powerful foundational starting point to understand the relationship between hours of work, preferences and subsequent individual well-being. The long-run trend in average worktime is connected at least in part to factors directly affecting labor supply decisions. These include the female or youth composition of the workforce, real wage rates, non-wage income, education levels, household production technology and a shift in the composition of consumption toward services. But such models focus on rational individual or household choice as determining both the long-run trend and short-run adjustment in worktime. Thus, they provide no more than a starting point, particularly when in search of understanding longer term trends and cross-sectional variation in work hours over time and among individuals. Workers' preferred hours are also influenced by the cultural characteristics of their household (in perceived social roles other than 'employee'), which may place constraints at various stages in their life cycle (for example, as a parent, provider, student, transitioning to or from retirement). They are also influenced by the characteristics of their job and social values placed on working.

Potential Influences Promoting Longer Desired Hours of Labor Supply

Applying behavioral economic perspectives may illuminate further why people work for pay as many hours as they do (for example, Wolfe, 1997; Kelloway et al., 2004). By expanding the conventional economic model of hours of labor to incorporate various psychological, social and cultural sources of workers' preferences, constraints and preference adaptation, we may arrive at a deeper understanding of the root sources of overall trends in the number of hours people devote to work. Specifically, a model of labor hours should entail a dynamic setting whereby preferences may be adaptable under social influences and inflexibility in the workplace may often prevent individuals from getting a reduced number of hours.

The comprehensive value of work to the one who performs it is equal to the sum of the compensation rewards, net social outcomes, and intrinsic value of the work itself and its content. Clearly, generating income to reach some desired material standard of living is the primary motivation for working. However, once individuals reach some physiologically and socially acceptable minimum standard of living, 'needs' tend to become more complex, perhaps moving up the Maslow's pyramid toward the higher-order needs. Individuals may be motivated by a need to mold the social institutions or by the inherent value of labor conferred through the transformative act of working per se. It may grant one an identity, social status and sense of purpose in life. Nevertheless, the reward of work has arguably become largely the monetary compensation payoff. The once venerable alternative of working more in order to earn more time off work has become a quaint notion. Perhaps that is why, Americans are taking ever shorter vacations and leaving ever more available vacation time on the table (Galinsky et al., 2005).

By focusing on work hour preferences primarily as a reflection of changes in monetary compensation that generate opposing income and substitution effects, the conventional model of labor supply has paid insufficient attention to the importance of preference formation under the influence of social, cultural and workplace conditions (Nyland, 1989; Philip et al., 2005). The conventional labor supply model is too limited in scope to explain sufficiently the level and timing of changes in the average hours per worker over the twentieth century (Altman, 2001).The recent run-up of hours in the US cannot be attributed to changes in the demographic composition of the labor force, changes in the mix of occupations and industries or a simple reallocation of labor supply within workers' life cycles (toward middle years). Nor is it attributable to changes in the *level* of real average hourly earnings (Kuhn and Lozano, 2005). Rather, compensation practices that spread among firms raised the incentive to supply work hours beyond 40 per week. There is now greater variation in earnings within each occupational classification (ibid.).

Relative positioning in the workplace and workforce
The compensation incentives present in workplaces, occupations and the labor market appear to have heightened the motivation to strive for promotion and pay raises. Working longer hours becomes a visible way to signal promotability to employers, to the extent that they interpret such 'presenteeism' as an indication of an employee's level of effort and commitment.

A growing dispersion of earnings among occupations and industries, as well, has incentivized workers to work longer hours. The wider the gap between pay grades in an occupation or country, the larger is the motivation to engage in such positive signaling tactics. This may lead workers to attempt to equal or perhaps exceed the hours worked by their co-workers or the tacit norm in the workplace (Bell and Freeman, 1995; Drago et al., 2005; Bowles and Park, 2005). Among those who expect to be in managerial positions, there is a clear positive empirical relationship between the number of work hours they prefer and the actual work hours of their co-workers (Eastman, 1998; Feldman, 2002; Brett and Stroh, 2003). Similarly, there are negative signaling effects for workers requesting shorter hours (Rebitzer and Taylor, 1995). Those expressing a wish to reduce work hours may be passed over for hiring. There is a rising presence of professions, such as law and consulting, which reward and valorize long hours, promoting a 'rat race' with all workers increasing their own work hours for reasons of long-term relative status (Landers et al., 1996; Haight, 1997). The converse case suggests that in a climate of rising job or income insecurity workers may alter their preferences toward longer hours, in part as a means of building up savings to serve as a buffer against the risk of expected future job or income losses. Also, if workers believe their employer is screening before a downsizing or reorganization, they may view longer hours as an inoculation against the risk of future job loss, income loss or demotion (Landers et al., 1996; Bluestone and Rose, 1998).

A perhaps more innocuous motivation for preferring longer work hours may be the rising amenities of the workplace relative to household work. The workplace or career may offer a more stimulating and less stressful environment, and thus more allure, relative to time spent in the household (Hochschild, 1997). More amenable working conditions, which make jobs less hazardous or unpleasant, may reduce the resistance to long hours, particularly among the more highly educated (Gramm, 1987; LaJeunesse, 2004). If work activity is becoming more intrinsically rewarding, safe, discretionary and autonomous than alternative uses of time, then this implies something very different from what is implied if work is becoming more stress- or anxiety-producing, onerous, routinized and alienating. Work time might be yielding less disutility than it did historically (Wisman, 1989).

Relative positioning in consumption

Individuals may also seek and compete for higher social status by acquiring or accumulating status-conferring goods and services. Individuals may seek to emulate the consumption patterns of the rich in order to enhance their own relative status (Schor, 1999). Under the dual pressures of employers and consumerism, people easily get into a 'squirrel cage', 'trapped by the cycle of work-and-spend' (Schor, 1992). In the context of well-documented escalation of income inequality over the last three decades, this requires that relatively less well-off individuals work more hours in order to gain income to sustain their relative position in consumption levels (Rima, 1984; Schor, 1992; Bowles and Park, 2005). To the extent that individuals engage in income-targeting, they will seek more paid market work sufficient to support their pre-established goals regarding unsatisfied consumption wants, even at the expense of non-market time (Altman, 2001).

Moreover, intensified marketing and advertising arguably create tastes for more and more market goods and services. Wants may escalate over time, as they have over the past centuries, moving the income target ever further out, so that it is never actually reached or reachable. Workers may start with initial preferences for a shorter working time, but the cumulative effects of intensifying promotional efforts for products eventually lead workers to prefer more income to purchase these now familiar products or services (George, 1997; Fraser and Paton, 2003). Bandwagon effects suggest that individuals derive satisfaction from consuming goods and services that others are consuming (Altman, 2001). As new commodities are introduced, new bandwagon effects are triggered, and what was once considered a luxury or amenity item gradually becomes a necessity, a new want to satisfy.

In addition, decisions to work more hours may be motivated by keeping pace with particular reference groups such as family or siblings (for example, Neumark and Postlewaite, 1998). Moreover, the steady increase in debt-financed consumption makes longer work hours an option to avoid high-interest balances or risk of personal bankruptcy. Indeed, those who work overtime hours even when it is not mandatory tend to be from higher rather than lower income households (Golden and Wiens-Tuers, 2005). Rising consumerism is the primary force behind a rising proportion of workers engaged in very long hours of work (for Australia, see Drago et al., 2005).

Overemployment: Incorporating the Role of Employers and Demand for Work Hours

In the conventional economic model, the demand side is often considered a relatively passive force, accommodating workers' preferences. In the long run, workers and employers are assumed to sort themselves in ways that match up desired and required hours of work. A compensating pay premium is assumed to be created for workers whose jobs entail the adverse working condition of undesirable or inflexible hours. At the other end of the methodological spectrum, the traditional Marxian analysis presumes that employers can dictate the length of the working day. Employers set limits on hours only because they confront the physical and mental limitations of humans (and potential backlash) as constraints (Nyland, 1989; Burkett, 2001). Consequently, the diverse working times are arranged less according to employee preferences or domestic constraints and more as part of rigorous competition to attract customers (Horrell and Rubery, 1991). Worktime determination may be characterized as a tug-of-war between employer and worker, seeking their own objectives regarding worktime, won by the side with greater bargaining power at the time (Golden, 1996; Philip et al., 2005).

In the vast middle ground lie models that identify the motivations for employers to establish a level of work hours or lengthen hours demanded, regardless of workers' preferences. The demand side may impose constraints on some employees to work hours that exceed their preferred number of work hours per week or per year. The conventional employer demand for hours model assumes that continuous production technology necessarily creates multiple shifts of fixed lengths (Contensou and Vranceanu, 2000; Hart, 2004). There are always present 'fixed costs' of adding employees, such as the costs of hiring and training new employees. There are also fixed costs of contributions to employee benefit programs. Largely because of idiosyncrasies in the contribution systems of social and private insurance plans in the US, such contributions are affixed to the number of employees rather than overall payroll size. Thus, any increase in such costs encourages employers to lengthen hours rather than hire new employees and to lay off workers rather than implement temporary hour reductions (work-sharing) during downturns. Likewise, a steady increase may be occurring in hiring and training costs to the extent that there is skill-upgrading in many jobs, similarly driving up hours demanded from existing employees. The observed polarization of hours occurs because at the lower end of the job spectrum, to avoid paying employee benefits, firms offer more short-hour, part-time jobs. Furthermore, the impact of labor-saving technological advance such as computerization has been neutral on the length of hours. If computerization 'upskills' jobs in a way that raises fixed costs, this reinforces a growing demand for hours per worker, while at the same time such upskilling may soften worker resistance to longer work hours.

Overemployment and Adaptive Preferences for Hours

To the extent that employer demand for hours will hold sway, many if not most workers will face a restricted range of options, lacking the free choice over a continually flexible range of hours implied by the conventional labor supply model (Rebitzer and Taylor, 1995). If workers lack discretion over the number of work hours in a day, week or year, they may work some hours involuntarily. An individual's actual hours worked can exceed desired hours if, for example, there is unwelcome but mandatory overtime, no opportunity to cut back hours to part-time, or inadequate vacation time in a job. Any worker who is employed beyond their initially desired number of hours of work and is willing to sacrifice either income or imminent raises for reduced hours, but cannot at the current job, is considered overemployed. Workers may quite rationally settle for a longer than optimal workweek. Such settling may occur because switching to a shorter-hours job is too costly, either in terms of a transition to a new career or because compensation losses associated with part-time status, such as less benefit coverage, are considerably more than proportional to the hours reduction. Thus, a sizable segment of the workforce may not be able to obtain their optimally desired shorter hours (Lang and Kahn, 2001; Altonji and Oldham, 2003; Jacobs and Gerson, 2004; Reynolds, 2004; Messenger, 2004; Golden, 2005). Economic historians have recognized that in the nineteenth century the long hours of work per week left workers' desire for a shorter workday unfulfilled, despite the adverse side effects on workers' well-being and even employers' own long-term viability (Altman, 1999; Bourdieu and Reynaud, 2001; Burawoy et al., 2001; Atack et al., 2003). Estimates of the overemployment rate range widely, not only between countries but within the United States, from as little as 6 per cent to as much as 50 per cent (Schor, 1999; Lang and Kahn, 2001; Stier and Lewin-Epstein, 2003; Reynolds, 2004; Golden, 2005).

Under the assumption that preference formation may be adaptive rather than static, one possible response of overemployed workers is to eventually adjust upward their number of preferred hours of work. This suppresses the observed rate of overemployment in any country. A greater aversion to income *loss* relative to the perceived benefit from an equivalent income *gain* is partly responsible for the bias against hours reduction (Dunn, 1996). Indeed, surveys reveal a much stronger preference for hours reduction in the more distant future than in the current period (Golden, 2005). However, there may be a more potent explanation, that there is a dynamic process by which an individual may start out being overemployed and later no longer prefer shorter work hours despite no reduction in their hours. This would explain not only lengthening work hours but also the rise and fall of overemployment over time. Suppose hours demanded by the employer rise above those preferred by an individual, creating a spell of overemployment. This creates a feeling of time scarcity in the household. This in turn will lead a household to change its preferences from self-produced goods and services to those that are more market-produced. The household may also shift from time-*using* goods and services toward the more time-*saving* type. Both shifts require more income. In addition, households are likely to shift preferences from time-intensive to income-intensive leisure activities.

Together, all these effects ratchet upward individuals' targeted consumption levels and gradually dissipate the initial desire for shorter work hours (Rothschild, 1982). In sum, individuals may eventually choose to work longer than initially preferred, not only because their own real wage, non-wage income or constraints have changed, but because their hours preferences are influenced by their social reference groups or workplace incentives. A dynamic process is then triggered whereby an individual may start out involuntarily working long hours and later begin to do so voluntarily. Certain types of workers appear to be more prone to overemployment, such as women, whites, parents of pre-school children, managerial and professional groups and workers with long weekly hours (Golden, 2005; Drago et al., 2005). However, other types of workers, such as men and racial minorities, may tend more to adjust upward their desired hours in the face of unfulfilled preferences.

CONSEQUENCES OF LONG HOURS, OVERWORK AND OVEREMPLOYMENT

The length of hours may be detrimental socially and also individually, even when the long or excessive hours are 'preferred'. Adam Smith witnessed as far back as 1776 that 'the innate human desire to improve ones lot is strong enough to make workmen apt to overwork themselves and ruin their health and constitution in a few years.' The concept of overwork has been more precisely defined two centuries later as

> working beyond one's endurance and recuperative capacities, [which] may be a hazard in certain personality types engaged in open-ended occupations . . . which ignore the commonplace signs that inform one of their need for rest or recreation. If they are engaged in occupations that do not have a finite workday, they may at times exceed their bodies' ability to recover . . . and [not be] aware of or make provision for one's physical and emotional needs. (Rhoads, 1977)

Current estimates of the 'overworked' find almost 3 in 10 workers report recently 'feeling overworked' and about half of workers feeling so sometime in the past three months at work (Galinsky et al., 2005). The precise point at which work becomes overwork varies, of course, by the pacing and physical and mental demands of the job, workplace and occupation. It also varies by individual, depending on the demands they face during non-market work time. 'Overwork' may be thought of as occurring when the length of work hours begins to adversely affect the health and safety of individuals, families, organizations or the public, even if workers themselves voluntarily work excess hours. There is much overlap but also some

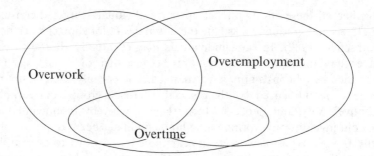

Figure 2.1   Venn diagram of overemployment, overwork (and overtime)

independence between overwork and overemployment (see Figure 2.1). More recently, overworkers have been considered more narrowly, as individuals who work to excess, not because of perceived returns from the organization but rather despite a perceived lack of such returns (Peiperl and Jones, 2001).

The adverse welfare effects stemming from long hours of work per se, such as those on psychological health, physical health and self-esteem, are becoming fairly well documented (for example, Sparks and Cooper, 1997; Burawoy et al., 2001; Van der Hulst and Guerts, 2003; Spurgeon, 2003; Caruso et al., 2004). For similar reasons of fatigue and stress, there are related heightened risks for injury or accident (Dembe et al., 2005; Loomis, 2005). The adverse symptoms generated by longer work hours tend to be exacerbated by a worker's lack of control over the volume and scheduling of work hours (Maume and Bellas, 2001; Spurgeon, 2003; Berg et al., 2004; Golden and Wiens-Tuers, 2005). Some of the adverse effects such as fatigue and stress thus may be traceable to the conditions of work more than the behavior leading to long number of hours worked (Buelens and Poelmans, 2004). Nevertheless, those who experience higher levels of overwork report a higher scale of stress and depressive symptoms and that their health and self-care are not good (Galinsky et al., 2005). In addition, extended hours dampen worker productivity (Shepard and Clifton, 2000). Thus, there may not be a strict linear relation between overwork effects and overtime hours or overemployment. However, there is a clearly positive association in certain contexts.

SUMMARY AND IMPLICATIONS FOR FUTURE RESEARCH

This chapter has traced the historical trends in work hours and its recent relationship to the detrimental outcomes associated with overemployment (beyond one's preferred work hours) and overwork (work beyond one's capacity for sustainable well-being). Work hours over time are determined by a myriad of interacting economic, social, psychological and institutional forces and counter-forces. The most salient recent trend is the growing proportion of the workforce that works very long hours, particularly in the English speaking countries and in the skilled, professional and managerial occupations. New forces, economic and cultural, have arisen to counter and perhaps even reverse the past, historical march toward a less burdensome number of work hours. Evidence exists that, even when voluntary or self-imposed, long work hours create spillover social costs (Hamermesh and Slemrod, 2005). Longer hours may become embedded if the risks of overwork are discounted or unrecognized and individuals eventually adjust upward their preferred hours to meet hours demanded of them by employers.

A potentially enlightening direction for future research would be to explore in more detail the dynamic process by which workers decide and often adapt their preferred hours of work according to external incentives in the workplace and culture. This would help to distinguish whether the drive to work to excess is motivated more by organizational values, personal disengagement or other contexts of excessive working behavior (Burke, 2000). It would also point to the potential policy levers, ranging from innovations in the regulation of overtime work, advertising and consumer credit to income tax rate reform. Only a multi-pronged series of institutional changes would counter an existing climate of ostensibly 'voluntary' increases in work hours among large segments of the workforce, who even knowingly risk adverse individual and social consequences. If the incidence or severity of work addiction is truly growing and socially costly, then research should seek to pinpoint the places and times where a healthy work ethic turns into a counterproductive addiction, and suggest appropriate interventions at those precise points.

REFERENCES

Alesina, A., E. Glaeser and B. Sacerdote (2005), 'Work and leisure in the U.S. and Europe: why so different?', *NBER Macroeconomic Annual*, 2005.

Altman, M. (1999), 'New estimates of hours of work and real income in Canada from the 1880s to 1930: long-run trends and workers' preferences', *Review of Income and Wealth*, **45** (3), 353–72.

Altman, M. (2001), 'Preferences and labor supply: casting some light into the black box of income–leisure choice', *Journal of Socio-Economics*, **30**, 199–219.

Altonji, J.G. and J. Oldham (2003), 'Vacation laws and annual work hours', Federal Reserve Bank of Chicago *Economic Perspectives*, **27** (Third Quarter), 19–29.

Atack, J., F. Bateman and R. Margo (2003), 'Productivity in manufacturing and the length of the working day: evidence from the 1880 Census of Manufacturers', *Explorations in Economic History*, **40** (2), 170–94.

Bell, L. and R.B. Freeman (1995), 'Why do Americans and Germans work different hours?', in F. Butler, W. Franz, R. Shettkat and D. Soskice (eds), *Institutional Frameworks and Labor Market Performance: Comparative Views on the US and German Economies*, London and New York: Routledge, pp. 101–31.

Berg, P., E. Appelbaum, T. Bailey and A. Kalleberg (2004), 'Contesting time: international comparisons of employee control of working time', *Industrial and Labor Relations Review*, **5** (3), 331–49.

Bernanke, B. and J. Powell (1986), 'The cyclical behavior of industrial labor markets: a comparison of the pre-war and post-war eras', in R.J. Gordon (ed.), *The American Business Cycle: Continuity and Change*, Chicago: University of Chicago Press, pp. 583–737.

Bernstein, J. and K. Kornbluh (2005), 'Running faster to stay in place: the growth of family work hours and incomes', New America Foundation, Work and Family Program, June.

Bienefeld, M. (1972), *Working Hours in British Industry: An Economic History*, London: Weidenfeld and Nicholson.

Bluestone, B. and S. Rose (1998), 'The macroeconomics of work time', *Review of Social Economy*, **56**, 425–41.

Blyton, P. (1989), 'Work time reductions and the European work-sharing debate', in A. Gladstone (ed.), *Current Issues in Labour Relations: An International Perspective*, New York: Walter de Gruyter.

Bosch, G. (1999), 'Working time: tendencies and emerging issues', *International Labour Review* **138** (2), 131–49.

Bosch, G., P. Dawkins and F. Michon (eds) (1993), *Times Are Changing: Working Time in 14 Industrialised Countries*, Geneva: International Institute for Labour Studies, pp. 289–311.

Bourdieu, J. and B. Reynaud (2001), 'Externalities and institutions: the decrease in working hours in nineteenth century France', Laboratoire d'Economie Appliquee, Research Unit Working Paper 00–01, Paris.

Bowles, S. and Y. Park (2005), 'Emulation, inequality, and work hours: was Thorsten Veblen right?', *The Economic Journal*, **115** (507), F397–F412.

Brett, J.M. and L.K. Stroh (2003), 'Working 61 plus hours a week: why do managers do it?', *Journal of Applied Psychology*, **89** (1), 67–78.

Brody, D. (1989), 'Time and work during early American industrialism', *Labour History*, **30** (winter), 5–46.

Buelens, M. and S. Poelmans (2004), 'Enriching the Spence and Robbins' typology of workaholism: demographic, motivational and organizational correlates', *Journal of Organizational Change Management*, **17** (5), 440–58.

Burawoy, M., N. Fligstein, A. Hochschild, J. Schor and K. Voss (2001), 'Roundtable discussion: overwork: causes and consequences of rising work hours', *Berkeley Journal of Sociology*, **45**, 180–96.

Burgoon, B. and P. Baxandal (2004), 'Three worlds of working time: the partisan and welfare politics of work hours in industrialized countries', *Politics and Society*, **32** (4), 439–73.

Burke, R. (1999), 'It's not how hard you work but how you work hard: evaluating workaholism', *International Journal of Stress Management*, **6** (4), 225–39.

Burke, R.J. (2000), 'Workaholism among women managers: personal and work-place correlates', *Journal of Managerial Psychology*, **15** (6), 520–34.

Burkett, P. (2001), 'Natural, social, and political limits to work time: the contemporary relevance of Marx's analysis', in L. Golden and D. Figart (eds), *Working Time: International Trends, Theory and Policy Perspectives*, Advances in Social Economics, London and New York: Routledge, pp. 143–58.

Caruso, C., E. Hitchcock, R. Dick, J. Russo and J. Schmit (2004), *Overtime and Extended Work Shifts: Recent Findings on Illnesses, Injuries and Health Behaviors*, Cincinnatti, OH: National Institute for Occupational Safety and Health.

Coleman, M.T. and J. Pencavel (1993a), 'Changes in work hours of male employees, 1940–1988', *Industrial and Labor Relations Review*, **46** (2), 262–83.

Coleman, M.T. and J. Pencavel (1993b), 'Changes in work hours of female employees, 1940–1988', *Industrial and Labor Relations Review*, **46** (4), 653–76.

Contensou, F. and R. Vranceanu (2000), *Working Time: Theory and Policy Implications*, Cheltenham, UK and Northampton, MA, USA: Edward Elgar.

Costa, D.L. (1998), 'The unequal work day: a long-term view', *American Economic Review*, **88** (2), 330–34.

Cross, G. (1988), 'Worktime in international discontinuity, 1886–1940', in Gary Cross (ed.), *Worktime and Industrialization: An International History*, Philadelphia: University of Pennsylvania Press.

Dembe, A., J.B. Erickson, R.G. Delbos and S.M. Banks (2005), 'The impact of overtime and long work hours on occupational injuries and illnesses: new evidence from the United States', *Occupational Environment Medicine*, **62**, 588–97.

Di Martino, V. (1995), 'Megatrends in working time', *Journal of European Social Policy*, **5** (3), 235–49.

Drago, R. (2000), 'Trends in working time in the US: a policy perspective', *Labor Law Journal*, **51** (4), 212–18.

Drago, R., D. Black and M. Wooden (2005), 'The existence and persistence of long work hours', IZA Discussion Paper No. 1720, August.

Dunn, L.F. (1996), 'Loss aversion and adaptation in the labor market: empirical indifference functions and labor supply', *Review of Economics and Statistics*, **78**, 441–50.

Eastman, W. (1998), 'Working for position: women, men, and managerial work hours', *Industrial Relations*, **37**, 51–66.

Epstein, C.F. and Arne Kalleberg (eds) (2004), *Fighting for Time: Shifting Boundaries of Work and Social Life*, New York: Russell Sage Foundation.

Feldman, D. (2002), 'Managers' propensity to work longer hours: a multilevel analysis', *Human Resource Management Review*, **12**, 339–57.

Fraser, S. and D. Paton (2003), 'Does advertising increase labour supply? Time series evidence from the UK', *Applied Economics*, **35** (11), 1357–68.

Galinsky, E., J.T. Bond, S. Kim, L. Backon, E. Brownfield and K. Sakai (2005), *Overwork in America: When the Way we Work Becomes Too Much*, New York: Families and Work Institute.

George, D. (1997), 'Working longer hours: pressure from the boss or from marketers?', *Review of Social Economy*, **55** (1), 33–65.

Golden, L. (1990), 'The insensitive workweek: trends and determinants of average hours in U.S. Manufacturing, 1929–1987', *Journal of Post Keynesian Economics*, **13** (1), 79–110.

Golden, L. (1996), 'The economics of worktime length, adjustment and flexibility: contributions of three competing paradigms', *Review of Social Economy*, **54**, 1–44.

Golden, L. (2005), 'Overemployment in the US: which workers face downward constrained hours?', in Y. Boulin, M. Lallement, J. Messenger and F. Michon (eds), *Decent Working Time: New Trends, New Issues*, Geneva: International Labor Organization, Chapter 8.

Golden, L. and D. Figart (eds) (2001), 'Introduction and overview: understanding working time around the world', in *Working Time: International Trends, Theory and Policy Perspectives*, Advances in Social Economics, London and New York: Routledge, pp. 1–17.

Golden, L. and B. Wiens-Tuers (2005), 'Mandatory overtime work: who, what and where?', *Labor Studies Journal*, **30** (1), 1–23.

Gramm, W. (1987), 'Labor, work and leisure', *Journal of Economic Issues*, **21**, 167–88.

Greenwood, J. and G. Vandenbroucke (2005), 'Hours worked: long-run trends', in L. Blume and S. Durlauf (eds), *New Palgrave Dictionary of Economics*, 2nd edn, London: Palgrave Macmillan.

Haight, A.D. (1997), 'Padded prowess: a Veblenian interpretation of the long hours of salaried workers', *Journal of Economic Issues*, **31**, 29–38.

Hamermesh, D. (1999), 'The timing of work over time', *Economic Journal*, **109** (452), 37–66.

Hamermesh, D. and J. Slemrod (2005), 'The economics of workaholism: why we should not have written this paper', National Bureau of Economic Research, Working Paper 11566.

Hart, R.A. (2004), *The Economics of Overtime Working*, Cambridge, UK: Cambridge University Press.

Hetrick, R. (2000), 'Analyzing the upward surge in overtime hours', *Monthly Labor Review* (February), 30–33.

Hinrichs, K., W. Roche and C. Sirianni (eds) (1991), *Working Time in Transition: The Political Economy of Working Hours in Industrial Nations*, Philadelphia: Temple University Press.

Hochschild, A.R. (1997), *The Time Bind: When Work Becomes Home and Home Becomes Work*, New York: Metropolitan Books.

Hopkins, E. (1982), 'Working hours and conditions during the industrial revolution: a re-appraisal', *Economic History Review*, **35**, 52–66.

Horrell, S. and J. Rubery (1991), 'Gender and working time', *Cambridge Journal of Economics*, **15**, 373–91.

Huberman, M. (2004), 'Working hours of the world unite? New international evidence of worktime, 1870–1913', *Journal of Economic History*, **64** (4), 964–1001.

Huberman, M. and C. Minns (2005), 'Hours of Work in Old and New Worlds: The Long View, 1870–2000', The Institute for International Integration Studies Discussion Paper, iiisdp 95, August.

Hunnicutt, B.K. (1988), *Work Without End: Abandoning Shorter Hours for the Right to Work*, Philadelphia: Temple University Press.

Jacobs, J. and K. Gerson (2001), 'Who are the overworked Americans?', in L. Golden and D. Figart (eds), *Working Time: International Trends, Theory, and Policy Perspectives*, New York: Routledge, pp. 89–105.

Jacobs, J. and K. Gerson (2004), *The Time Divide: Work, Family, and Gender Inequality*, Family and Public Policy series, Cambridge and London: Harvard University Press.

Kelloway, K., D. Gallagher and J. Barling (2004), 'Work, employment and the individual', in B. Kaufman (ed.), *Theoretical Perspectives on Work and the*

Employment Relationship, Urbana IL: Industrial Relations Research Association Series.

Kemeny, A. (2002), 'Driven to excel: a portrait of Canada's workaholics', *Canadian Social Trends*, Spring Statistics Canada – Catalogue No. 11-008.

Kniesner, T.J. (1976), 'The full-time workweek in the United States, 1900–1970', *Industrial and Labor Relations Review*, **30** (1), 3–15.

Kuhn, P. and F. Lozano (2005), 'The expanding workweek? Understanding trends in long work hours among U.S. men, 1979–2002', University of California, Santa Barbara, Economics Department, March.

Landers, R., J. Rebitzer and L. Taylor (1996), 'Rat race redux: adverse selection in the determination of work hours in law firms', *American Economic Review*, **86**, 3229–48.

Lang, K. and S. Kahn (2001), 'Hours constraints: theory, evidence and policy implications', in G. Wong and G. Picot (eds), *Working Time in a Comparative Perspective, Vol. 1*, Kalamazoo, MI: Upjohn Institute for Employment Research.

LaJeunesse, R. (2004), 'An institutionalist approach to work time', in D. Champlin and J. Knoedler (eds), *The Institutionalist Tradition in Labor Economics*, Armonk, NY: M.E. Sharpe, pp. 159–74.

Leete, L. and J. Schor, (1994), 'Assessing the time-squeeze hypothesis: hours worked in the United States, 1969–89', *Industrial Relations*, **33** (1), 25–43.

Linder, M. (2002), *The Autocratically Flexible Workplace: A History of Overtime Regulation in the United States*, Iowa City: Fanpihua Publishers.

Loomis, D. (2005), 'Long work hours and occupational injuries: new evidence on upstream causes', *Occupational Environmental Medicine*, **62** (9), 585.

Martorana, P.V. and P.M. Hirsch (2001), 'The Social Construction of "Overtime"', *The Transformation of Work*, **10**, 165–87.

Maume, D. and M. Bellas (2001), 'The overworked American or the time bind? Assessing competing explanations for time spent in paid labor', *The American Behavioral Scientist*, **44** (7), 1137–57.

McGratten, E.R. and R. Rogerson, (2004), 'Changes in hours worked, 1950–2000', *Federal Bank of Minneapolis Quarterly Review*, **28** (July): 14–33.

McMillan, L.H.W. and E.C. Brady et al. (2002), 'A multifaceted validation study of Spence and Robbins' (1992) workaholism battery', *Journal of Occupational and Organizational Psychology*, **75**, 357–68.

Messenger, J. (ed.) (2004), *Working Time and Workers' Preferences in Industrialized Countries: Finding the Balance*, Geneva: ILO Conditions of Work and Employment Programme.

Nemirow, M. (1984), 'Work-sharing approaches: past and present', *Monthly Labor Review*, **107** (September): 34–9.

Neumark, D. and A. Postlewaite (1998), 'Relative income concerns and the rise in married women's employment', *Journal of Public Economics*, **70**, 157–83.

Nollen, S.D. (1989), 'Changes in work time in the United States', in A. Gladstone (ed.), *Current Issues in Labour Relations: An International Perspective*, New York: Walter de Gruyter.

Northrup, H. and T.D. Greis (1983), 'The decline in average annual hours worked in the U.S., 1947–1979', *Journal of Labor Research*, **4** (2): 95–113.

Nyland, C. (1989), *Reduced Working Time and the Management of Production*, Cambridge, UK: Cambridge University Press.

Owen, J.D. (1989), *Reduced Working Hours: Cure for Unemployment or Economic Burden?*, Baltimore: Johns Hopkins University Press.

Peiperl, M. and B. Jones (2001), 'Workaholics and overworkers: productivity or pathology?', *Group and Organization Management*, **26** (3), 369–94.

Philip, B., G. Slater, and D. Harvie (2005), 'Preferences, power, and the determination of working hours', *Journal of Economic Issues*, **39** (1), 75–91.

Porter, G. (2005), 'Workaholism, A Sloan Work and Family Encyclopedia entry', Sloan Work and Family Research Network, http://wfnetwork.bc.edu/encyclopedia_entry.php?id=1191.

Rebitzer, J. and L. Taylor (1995), 'Do labor markets provide enough short-hour jobs? An analysis of work hours and work incentives', *Economic Inquiry*, **33**, 257–73.

Reynolds, J. (2004), 'When too much is not enough: overwork and underwork in the U.S. and abroad', *Sociological Forum*, **19**, 89–120.

Rhoads, J.M. (1977), 'Overwork', *Journal of American Medical Association*, **237** (24), 2615–18.

Rima, I. (1984), 'Involuntary unemployment and the re-specified labor supply curve', *Journal of Post Keynesian Economics*, **6**, 540–50.

Roche, W.K. (1987), 'Leisure, insecurity and union policy in Britain: a critical extension of Bienefeld's theory of hours rounds', *British Journal of Industrial Relations*, **25** (1), 1–17.

Roediger, D.R. and P.S. Foner (1989), *Our Own Time: A History of American Labor and the Working Day*, London: Verso.

Rones, P.L., R.E. Ilg and J.M. Gardner (1997), 'Trends in hours of work since the mid-1970s', *Monthly Labor Review*, **120** (4), 3–14.

Rothschild, K. (1982), 'A note on some economic and welfare aspects of working time regulation', *Australian Economic Papers*, **21**, 214–18.

Rubery, J., K. Ward, D. Grimshaw and H. Beynon (2005), 'Working time, industrial relations and the employment relationship, *Time and Society*, **14**, 89–111.

Rupert, P. and K. Roberts (1995), 'The myth of the overworked American', *Economic Commentary* (Federal Reserve Bank of Cleveland), 15 January, 1–4.

Scacciati, F. (2004), 'Erosion of purchasing power and labor supply', *Journal of Socio-Economics*, **33**, 725–44.

Schor, J.B. (1992), *The Overworked American*, New York: Basic Books.

Schor, J.B. (1999), *The Overspent American: Upscaling, Downshifting and the New Consumer*, New York: Basic Books.

Scott, K.S., K.S. Moore and M.P. Miceli (1997), 'An exploration of the meaning and consequences of workaholism', *Human Relations*, **50**, 287–314.

Shepard, E. and T. Clifton (2000), 'Are longer hours reducing productivity in manufacturing?', *International Journal of Manpower*, **21** (7), 540–53.

Snir, R. and I. Harpaz (2004), 'Attitudinal and demographic antecedents of workaholism', *Journal of Organizational Change Management*, **17**, 520–36.

Sparks, K. and C. Cooper (1997), 'The effects of hours of work on health: a meta-analytic review', *Journal of Occupational and Organizational Psychology*, **70**, 391–408.

Spence, J.T. and A.S. Robbins (1992), 'Workaholism: definition, measurement, and preliminary results', *Journal of Personality Assessment*, **58**, 160–78.

Spurgeon, A. (2003), *Working Time: Its Impact on Safety and Health*, Seoul: International Labor Organization and Korean Occupational Safety and Health Research Institute.

Stier, H. and N. Lewin-Epstein (2003), 'Time to work: a comparative analysis of preferences for working hours', *Work and Occupations*, **30** (3), 302.

Thompson, E.P. (1967), 'Time, work-discipline, and industrial capitalism', *Past and Present*, **38**, 56–97.

Ueberfeldt, A. (2005), 'Working time over the 20th century', University of Minnesota and Federal Reserve Bank of Minneapolis, 30 January.

Van der Hulst, M. and S. Guerts (2003), 'Long workhours and health', *Scandinavian Journal of Work, Environment and Health*, **29**, 171–88.

Whaples, R. (ed.) (2001), 'Hours of work in U.S. history', EH.Net Encyclopedia, 15 August, http://eh.net/encyclopedia/article/whaples.work.hours.us

Wisman, J. (1989), 'Straightening out the backward bending supply curve of labour: from overt to covert compulsion and beyond', *Review of Political Economy*, **1**, 94–112.

Wolfe, A. (1997), 'The moral meaning of work', *Journal of Socio-Economics*, **26** (6), 559.

PART II

Definition and consequences of workaholism

3. The workaholic breakdown syndrome

Dr Barbara Killinger

INTRODUCTION

Workaholism is a soul-destroying addiction that changes people's personalities and the values they live by. It distorts the reality of each family member, threatens family security and often leads to family break-up. Tragically, workaholics eventually suffer the loss of personal and professional integrity.

The key to understanding workaholism is to fully appreciate what happens to an individual's personality and behavior when the Feeling function no longer informs judgment. The emphasis too often is placed on the excessive hours that these people work, yet this is but one of a series of symptoms. Our focus will be on the highly predictable breakdown syndrome that this dangerous addiction follows.

A workaholic is a work-obsessed individual who has gradually become emotionally crippled and addicted to power and control. Caught up in a compulsive drive to gain personal approval and public recognition of their success, these driven men and women live a gerbil-wheel, adrenalin-pumping existence rushing from point A to point B, narrowly fixated on the next desired goal or accomplishment. Eventually, nothing or no one else really matters.

WHO ARE THESE PEOPLE?

Workaholism has become part of everyday life and language since Wayne Oates first coined the term (Oates, 1971). This American minister and professor of the psychology of religion told of his personal awakening to the realization of his own compulsion to overwork after his young son asked for an appointment at his office to talk about something that was bothering him.

Work is essential for our well-being and integral to our identity. As we develop our strengths and skills, we build self-esteem and a sense of accomplishment and take our responsible place in society. Our personalities suffer profound emotional distress when we lose a job or cannot do our work for whatever reason. The alarming number of employees on prolonged stress leave is evidence that physical and psychological health do break down when workaholic bosses or organizations place unreasonable demands on their staff. One does not even have to have a paid job. Many perfectionistic homemakers and students suffer from this serious affliction.

'What is the difference between a hard worker and a workaholic?' is a frequently asked question. A hard worker who is emotionally there for all family members and friends and manages to maintain a healthy balance between work and personal responsibility is not a workaholic.

Periodic bursts of overworking in order to meet an important deadline, or to handle an emergency situation, need to be purposefully followed by a reduced schedule or days off to restore depleted resources and engage in positive interactions with family and friends. Making a resolution to save at least twenty-five per cent of your energy to bring home every night and 'putting a fence' around your weekends to protect yourself from temptation are both good ideas!

Workaholics, in contrast, lack this wisdom. They are obsessed with their work performance and hooked on an adrenalin high. Bent on self-aggrandizement, these ego-driven folks reach one goal and immediately set another more ambitious one. Staying at the same level of accomplishment is considered a failure.

Workaholics walk fast, talk fast, eat fast, and single-mindedly rush and over-schedule. While still relatively healthy they can multi-task, but their diversionary tactics and lack of focus often signal performance-anxiety as growing internal chaos causes them to try to control every action and everyone around them. They must do things their way, and they refuse to delegate because 'others will not do as good a job'.

Most of my clients have become overly responsible early on in life. Many come from workaholic families where there is a doing–performance oriented value system. A conditional love is granted if the child exceeds expectations and makes the family proud. Acts of kindness or generosity may go unrewarded or unacknowledged. After a talk in Vancouver, two physicians told me that after reading my book, *Workaholics: The Respectable Addicts*, they realized that they rewarded their kids for their accomplishments, but had no language to praise the sensitive, caring and thoughtful side of their children. This deficit of feeling language and behavior creates many of the problems commonly found in these families.

Situational circumstances such as a parent's illness, a death in the family or the separation of the parents sometimes force a child too quickly into adult responsibilities. It may be the 'good kid' in the family who does well at school, excels at sports and does not cause much trouble who steps in to assume more responsibility. Although workaholics rarely acknowledge their own angry outburst at the time, when the awareness of a deep anger does surface to consciousness, one of its sources is reported to be the fact that these overly-responsible ambitious adults never had a carefree childhood.

Some go on to become the Mr Nice Guy or Ms Nice Gal, the passive–aggressive Pleaser workaholics who cannot say No, who desperately want to be admired and liked, who will do almost anything to gain accolades from the boss and fellow workers. Their persona, how they want to be viewed by others, is carefully crafted, but ego boundaries are hopelessly blurred because the Self, the being–feeling side of their personality, is seriously repressed. Wishing to take ownership of only their positive attributes, Pleasers project unwanted faults and see these same flaws in other people.

The Controller type of workaholic is someone who craves the kind of power that allows him or her to be always in control. These independent and proud individuals are often arrogant and intense, but can be most charming, witty and appear sociable when it serves their purpose. Controllers can be impatient, impulsive and demanding, and tend to be strong Thinking-type personalities who are usually found in top management positions or work for themselves. Some Controllers, comfortable in goal-directed activities but less so in social situations, find personal friendships hard to maintain. They often have many business-related acquaintances but few close friends.

Similar, yet quite different, are the Narcissistic Controllers who absolutely *must* be right, have to do things their own way, and can only see their own point of view. They are persuasive in their manipulations and relentlessly drive through their particular agenda, regardless of the consequences. They can jeopardize the welfare of others and show an alarming disregard for ethics and morality. Rules and regulations are their own. Sadly, these driven people have little or no insight into what they do to others because their repressed Feeling function lacks the necessary sensitivity.

Both Pleasers and Controllers are energetic, competitive people who rarely relax because they must stay busy and seemingly need little sleep. They are bright, intelligent people who have got caught up in the seductive, persona-enhancing perks that the workaholic lifestyle offers. Unfortunately, when the Feeling function shuts down, these same people lose the insight and wisdom necessary to be aware of their own decreasing capabilities.

PERFECTIONISM/OBSESSION/NARCISSISM

Perfectionism leads to obsession; and, in turn, obsession leads to increasing levels of narcissism.

Perfectionists believe or are made to view themselves as different, highly intelligent, even superior beings capable of great accomplishments. Often arrogant, competitive and demanding of themselves and others, these seemingly self-sufficient and independent people require the admiration of others, and demand obedience in order to get their own way.

Work becomes the adrenalin-pumping 'fix' that frees perfectionists up from experiencing the dark side of their character and/or the repressed emotional pain that a dependency on external approval creates when love has been conditional. Things go well and they rarely experience anything but success, as long as they measure up to their own and others' high expectations.

When setbacks do occur, or they fail at something that threatens a career-path, the ensuing shame and humiliation can be devastating. At such times, if others dare to challenge their expertise or derail a project, some perfectionists will erupt in a fury, while others retreat further into a protective shell of denial and secrecy. No one must know! Some just try harder, senselessly repeating old patterns that no longer work.

When the pursuit of perfection and excellence turns obsessional, the personality fails to develop normally, and chronic fears can immobilize psychological growth. The proud workaholic, torn between arrogance and growing insecurity, solves the dilemma by consciously identifying only with those positive attributes that project an idealized public image. Defense mechanisms such as denial, rationalization, projection of blame, compartmentalization and dissociation must work overtime to keep repressed anxious self-doubt and despair at bay.

Narcissism is the real evil of workaholism. As obsessional thoughts dominate and feelings grow increasingly numb and flat, self-serving narcissistic traits become more pronounced.

Narcissistic people have an idealized, inflated view of themselves. These self-aggrandizing individuals consider themselves unique and superior, yet there is ever present an extreme and anxious concern for their own well-being. When questioned or challenged about their actions, vindictive narcissists will either strike back or retreat by withdrawing emotionally or physically. Their intent, in both cases, is to punish those who have dared to contest their sacrosanct views.

The self-serving focus on 'me, myself and I' can make these overly-confident narcissists into scheming exploiters who expect others to serve and attend to their wishes and take on their personal responsibilities. In return, they break promises with ease and are often unfaithful partners. They are capable of deceit, fraud and debt because loyalty, honesty and compassion are missing when the Feeling function does not register. Instead, repressed feelings cause them to take everything personally. These moody people hold grudges, seethe with vindictive resentment, and play a martyr-victim game that no one can win.

THE INTERNAL DYNAMICS OF OBSESSION

There are two crucial turning points in the breakdown syndrome that the workaholic addiction follows – the loss of feeling and the loss of integrity. To explain why this happens, we must first understand how the obsessional component of workaholism destabilizes one's personality and functioning abilities.

The Paradigm for obsession (Figure 3.1) is the author's conceptualization of what happens internally within the psyche when obsessional thoughts and compulsive acts reach the stage where they dominate the personality through first compelling, then dictating, and eventually controlling how a workaholic thinks and behaves. This paradigm is based on C.G. Jung's theory of psychological types that he developed in the early 1920s to explain personality differences. The diagram and a more comprehensive review of these dynamics can be found in Killinger (2004, p. 92).

The primary functions of Thinking, Feeling, Intuition and Sensation are adversely affected by the inner dynamics of obsession. Ironically, as the

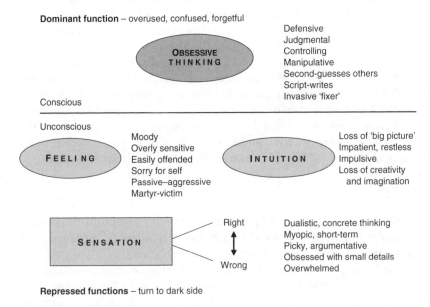

Figure 3.1   Paradigm for obsession

fixation on work begins to consume all of their energy and resources, workaholics lose the coveted control they so ardently seek. Inevitably, the dark side of each of these functions will begin to dominate and distort the workaholic's character.

Thinking

Healthy Thinking is rational, logical, analytical, pragmatic, fair and realistic. This goal-oriented, problem-solving function has a single-focused awareness that allows it to zero in on a particular subject and disregard all extraneous distractions. It examines the situation logically and objectively in order to arrive at a practical and reasoned conclusion.

Obsessional thinking, on the other hand, narrows its focus even further and becomes fixated on an object, person or some desired goal that becomes an end in itself. Obsessional dark thoughts become persistent and overtax rationality as the individual attempts to control all the details of a situation and to manipulate others to ensure a chosen end result. Second-guessing others and script-writing what will happen ahead of time becomes part of this externalizing process.

The negative side of thinking tends to be narrowly subjective, opinionated, judgmental, skeptical, and often irrational and illogical. Ruminations of this sort cloud meaning, purpose and clarity. Extraneous but frequently relevant information fails to register. Such tunnel vision typically diverts psychic energy away from personal concerns to safer impersonal and concrete issues.

Unfortunately, because the Thinking function is hierarchical, it loves to be one-up and problem-solve for others. Pre-occupied, self-serving workaholics are rarely good listeners. Because their ego boundaries tend to be ill-defined, they often become invasive 'fixers' who give unsolicited advice, while simultaneously serving their own agenda. Such manipulative one-sided communications are often confusing and convoluted, and rarely helpful or respectful. By taking on someone else's problem, the 'fixer' robs that individual of an opportunity to solve his or her own problem and thus build self-esteem.

Feeling

Feeling is the watchdog of ethical and moral values. The health of integrity in society and within the individual depends on its other-directed focus. The dark side of feeling is too self-absorbed to truly care.

The Feeling function has a capacity for diffuse awareness that allows it to do a number of things at once. This problem-solving function makes its decisions based on what it values and appreciates. Its outwardly-directed focus anticipates how others will be affected by some action or word.

Healthy feeling is the nurturing function. It is empathic, sensitive, thoughtful, gracious, appreciative and kind. It highly values harmony, honesty and generosity. Sharing is therefore important.

Positive Feeling in general loses out when obsessional Thinking dominates the personality. When the Feeling function is repressed, it turns to its dark passive–aggressive side. Blocked feelings produce sullen moods and seething resentments that simmer just below the surface of consciousness. Easily offended, it takes everything personally, feels sorry for itself, and plays the martyr-victim game with ease. Jaws set, and eyes glare or stare coldly. Some obsessive people withdraw into a hostile swirl of emotions, tune out, or leave the scene. Many use fatigue as an excuse to procrastinate or 'forget'.

Touchy oversensitivity is a misguided form of feeling that distorts the truth. Emotionally unavailable individuals are not good at sorting out 'who did what to whom'. No wonder Feeling's key values grow fuzzy, and obsessive workaholics don't know what they want or what is right. Such confusion makes it easy to slip into dark moods, and eventually into depression and despair.

Intensity quickly replaces Feeling's playful attitude. Taking the time to be sociable, to show sensitivity, concern and appreciation for others is considered a costly waste of effort and precious time. Self-nurturing activities also lose out when time is of the essence.

The repression of compassion and empathy affects the fair application of rules, regulations and judgments. Negative Feeling is no longer pliable when assessing a situation because it fails to take into consideration such realities as context, safety, and the health and welfare of all parties. Compassion is an integral component of integrity.

Chronic fatigue also contributes to carelessness and errors in judgment when the driven workaholic is compelled to recheck countless details, make long involved lists or plans, and overwork countless drafts in an effort to ease their dreaded fear of failure. Such excessive efforts drain the psyche of all its positive energy. No wonder distractions and interruptions are barely tolerated.

Intuition

Intuition loses its 'big picture' vision when the individual crosses the line into obsession. Ordinarily, Intuition uses an instinctive sixth sense to gather information in an unconscious way. Answers or solutions simply 'pop up' whole and complete, seemingly unannounced. Intuition is experienced as a 'gut reaction'.

Intuition sees meaning and relationship in concepts, and its insights stretch beyond the concrete information that the five senses provide. When presented with an array of possibilities, Intuition can often discern some probabilities that might remain 'invisible' otherwise. Its imaginative creativity is used in brainstorming techniques.

Positive Intuition is quick, curious, imaginative and often ingenious and clever. It is future-oriented and can be visionary.

Negative Intuition, on the other hand, works more slowly. It can get easily bored, impatient, impulsive and even reckless. Obsession turns brainstorming into tortuous 'script-writing', a rehearsing of endless possibilities. The 'big picture' disappears as workaholics find themselves flooding with wild or improbable ideas or thoughts, some of which are distorted by paranoia. 'It's like a tap that can't be turned off' is one man's description.

Such chaotic processes block creativity, dull artistic talents and spiritual inspiration, and jeopardize imaginative enterprises and innovative scientific discovery. It is very frightening when a clever workaholic can no longer innovate and generate sound ideas. Wisdom is replaced by self-doubt and confused anxiety.

The obsessive personality is clearly in trouble when the dark Shadow side of Thinking, as well as those of Feeling and Intuition, all begin to sabotage healthy functioning. Wise thoughts grow scarce, and a powerful negativity warps perception. Sadly, Sensation suffers a similar fate, but with even more dire consequences as the individual's neurosis deepens.

Sensation

Healthy Sensation perceives the physical reality of people and objects through its five senses – sight, sound, taste, smell and touch. Sense impressions are made up of observable data such as the shape, size and texture of an object. No judgment is involved when these details are registered into consciousness.

On another level, sense faculties respond physiologically, and these sense impressions are translated by the brain into thoughts and feelings about the concrete image. Sensation focuses on here-and-now experiences and concrete realities. It then devises practical and pragmatic reasons to explain what is occurring or what is being done.

Obsessional thinking changes all of this. Sensation's systematic slow but thorough step-by-step processing of data starts to go awry. These are the signs to watch for when negative Sensation is in charge.

A dualistic type of thinking develops which is concrete and often extreme. Things are black or white, right or wrong – there are no shades of grey. If someone challenges the superiority of their ideas, workaholics get defensive and can become picky, petty and argumentative in defense of some firmly-held position. Negative Sensation distrusts words and wants concrete evidence. Therefore, the anxious workaholic demands that the other person 'show me!' or 'prove it!'

The opinions of an 'opponent' are often disregarded or put down with disdain. 'Others should think like I do!' is the not so subtle message.

Listening is largely selective and usually focused on information and facts that support their own point of view. More often than not, rather than listening, workaholics will be rehearsing what they plan to say or do next.

More and more, short-term thinking dominates, and choices are made solely on the immediate practicality of any proposed action. Future long-term consequences are largely ignored when Intuition no longer informs decisions. Doing something in the immediate present temporarily eases growing self-doubt.

Negative Sensation *craves* enjoyment. Repressed feelings have left the workaholic experiencing a flat affect, a numb and scary emptiness. It is no longer enough to savor simple things like the beautiful sights and sounds of nature or just be satisfied with what *is*.

Impulsive neediness distorts Sensation's normal sense of well-being into a voracious appetite. It is not surprising, therefore, that seductive temptations that offer immediate gratification or a 'high' such as smoking and drug addictions, sexual acting-out or fraud become highly attractive.

Seemingly overnight, a workaholic can become fixated on food, or atypically start to smoke packs of cigarettes a day and frequent smoky bars. Some develop a heightened awareness of all things sexual and seek after younger attractive companions, who are often from a lower social economic level, to wine and dine and bed. Many extra-marital affairs last for years with promises to leave the marriage never met. A committed and genuine intimacy has become just too threatening.

A keen interest in wine can soon turn into alcoholism. Reports of this slippery slope of cross-addictions and excesses are written about in our newspapers every day. People are losing their hard-won integrity in dubious affairs, shady deals and neglected health. Corporate fraud and accounting scandals such as Enron and WorldCom are all too common.

Workaholism, unfortunately, is a contributing factor to this shocking large-scale loss of integrity. Our attention will now turn to the dangerous path that this insidious addiction follows.

THE BREAKDOWN SYNDROME OF WORKAHOLISM

Fears underlie every obsession, so it is important to identify and acknowledge the particular fears that destabilize the functioning abilities of the

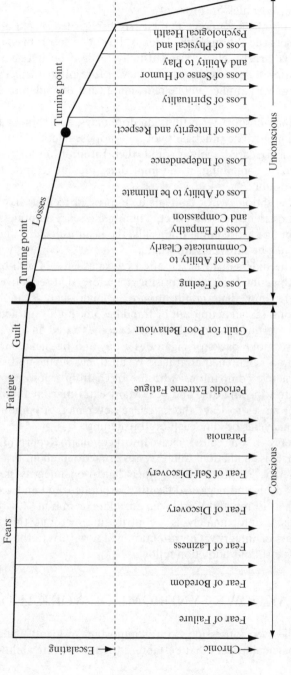

Figure 3.2   The breakdown syndrome

workaholic. Figure 3.2 first appeared in Killinger (1995, p. 59). Because the breakdown is internal, it is not readily observed. Self-reflection is rarely in evidence when the externalized doing–performing persona gradually eclipses the Self, the being–feeling side.

In retrospect, recovering workaholics recognize that seemingly overnight, or so it seems, at the height of their success when they are the most confident, cocky and arrogant, an insidious undercurrent of troubling self-doubt begins to seep into consciousness.

Gerald, a partner in his law firm, couldn't do enough for his clients. 'I was the perfect Mr Nice Guy who thought he had finally got the world by the tail. Publicly, I was the proverbial success story – great job, beautiful wife, and three model children. In my private life, I refused to acknowledge that everything was starting to fall apart.

'I woke up one red-letter day in a cold sweat. The thought jumped into my head that I was a complete and utter phony! My depressed, pill-popping wife was traumatized by my rages, and my middle daughter had recently developed anorexia. Our oldest son, who had been diagnosed as having Attention Deficit Disorder as a child, was failing miserably, while my youngest pride and joy was following in my footsteps, a perfectionist nail-biting achiever. Yet she could do no wrong in my eyes.

'And', he paused while experiencing a painful but necessary insight, 'I hadn't been there for any of them!'

Later, Gerald told me that he honestly believed that he had nothing to do with what he called 'the kids thing'. That was his wife's department and 'she was a wonderful mother!' Such an illogical statement typifies the twisted pseudo-logic of a floundering workaholic.

The Escalation of Fear

Fear is present in all situations where there is the potential for criticism, rejection or abandonment. The perfectionistic workaholic who grew up with conditional love and a performance-oriented value system cannot afford to not 'deliver the goods' lest he jeopardize the elusive acceptance that comes only when one fulfills the expectations of significant others. Performance becomes the primary yardstick by which to measure a person's worth.

Workaholism follows a highly predictable and personally tragic downward spiral. On the conscious level, a number of specific fears fluctuate, but ultimately escalate, accompanied by increasing levels of fatigue and troubling guilt. The values and behavior of the workaholic begin to change as the Feeling function shuts down and guilt turns to shame.

Fears recede in good times, only to erupt with a vengeance when plans go awry. Weakening defense mechanisms can no longer protect the workaholic from an increasingly troubled reality. There is a gradual transformation as Dr Jekyll becomes a Mr Hyde.

The major turning point in the breakdown is the acute loss of feeling that produces unconscious but profound personality changes, the ones that damage other family members and cause associates and the public much grief.

Recovery is only possible if workaholics can break through the powerful defense mechanisms that allow them to disown their own Shadow side, and recognize just how controlling and addicted to power they really are. It is important to note that the earlier the workaholic seeks help to stop this inevitable decline into chaos, the more chance there is for a restoration of both psychological and physical health.

Fear of Failure

The ultimate fear is to be fired or let go, but demotions or forced transfers can also be devastating.

The determined strivings of perfectionistic workaholics ensure that failure remains an unfamiliar experience, at least in the early years. To fail at anything is an unforgivable betrayal of an idealized image, of who the person wants to be; or, even more importantly, who he or she wants to be seen to be. Yet lurking deep within the realm of this repressed reality is a deep-seated fear of failure.

'It's huge! It's always been one of my worst nightmares' is how Sally, an economist, describes her fear of failure. The more Sally's sense of self folded into her carefully crafted persona, the more acute this nemesis became. When a significant failure at work did occur, her defenses crashed. She was immobilized for weeks and came close to suffering a nervous breakdown. She no longer knew who she was.

Whether the threat is real or perceived, it can set the workaholic morally and spiritually adrift. To avoid humiliation, stressed-out workaholics willingly take questionable risks to shore up an endangered reputation, or use others to bolster a sagging ego. When ethical or moral issues get in the way, some workaholics have no problem rationalizing that 'the end justifies the means'.

When the collapse of a relationship threatens, workaholics set themselves up for failure by denying the accusations of cruel insensitivity and angry outbursts, and justify their often outrageous behavior by blaming the partner. Too self-absorbed to acknowledge the pain that the loved one is experiencing, they hear only criticism.

Fear of Boredom

When only the dark side of intuition works and the 'big picture' is not clear, workaholics do get bored quickly, become restless and impulsive, and sometimes plain reckless. They are impatient with others and want things done now. Easily agitated and quick to judge, they make snap decisions that lead to serious errors in judgment. Faster is not necessarily smarter, and efficiency can suffer seriously over time.

Zeroing in on a goal-directed project or just 'doing something' to keep busy gives them a sense of purpose and accomplishment. This 'busy work' also serves as a distraction when the workaholic's life starts to unravel and plans go awry. Other people don't respond well to their need to rush and always move on. Children become anxious and feel pressure to conform, to fit into the parent's demanding and whirlwind schedule. Anxiety becomes pervasive, and a tense atmosphere builds. No one knows when it is safe to relax, to just be oneself.

Any enforced rest such as an illness, a long vacation or future retirement are all threatening. Without the drug of an adrenalin 'fix', the workaholic's fear of boredom looms large. Consequently, workaholics plan brief weekend jaunts or a week's holiday jammed full of activities. Many interrupt these junkets by plugging back into the office by phone or making an excuse to go back to the city for an 'important meeting'.

This leaves no time to contemplate nature, bask in the sun, and spend generous amounts of time playing quiet games or reading to the children, the kind of relaxed playtime that encourages the emotional security and predictability that youngsters need. Instead, workaholics boast to me about the short bursts of 'quality time' that they spend with their children.

To get workaholics to test out their awareness of the fear of boredom, I sometimes suggest that my clients go down to the waterfront, and sit on a bench and 'watch water' for at least a half-hour without moving or reading anything. One woman refused because she didn't want anyone thinking she was a 'bag lady', but she did admit to getting a knot in her stomach even thinking about it. In this situation, the fear of what others think prevented Cynthia from experiencing some of the positive sensations needed to ground herself, to help fill up the emptiness deep inside. Sadly, she just didn't get the point of the exercise, one that had helped so many other workaholics become more aware of this ever-present fear.

Fear of Laziness
The idea that driven workaholics fear laziness sounds paradoxical. However, the only time these achievers are fully present and feel alive is when they are pumping adrenalin and hell-bent on getting to the next desired goal. They pride themselves on being identified as hard workers.

A frenetic lifestyle of over-scheduling and unrealistic expectations belies the fear of laziness. Yet I'm told that, deep down inside, workaholics do suspect that if they let up, even for a short time, a natural laziness would take over. Their work spills into the weekend as briefcases and cell phones come home, or they make excuses to escape back into the office. Anxiety can be acute on Sundays when nothing is scheduled and others seem content to just relax. They set themselves up for the 'Thank God it's Monday' syndrome.

Psychologically, workaholics are lazy. There seems to be little curiosity about what makes them tick or where their life might be headed. If they do read books unrelated to work, it won't likely be self-help books, unless someone else insists.

The fear of laziness is kept at bay by running flat-out on the proverbial Gerbil Wheel, overworking the countless details that perfectionism demands. The obsession is starting to take control of the workaholic's life. For someone who prides themselves on independence, this is a galling irony.

Fear of Discovery

As faulty obsessional thinking results in serious errors in judgment, efficiency suffers greatly, and panicking workaholics worry about the 'visibility' of their mistakes. Issues concerning secrecy and privacy are suddenly of prime concern. No one must suspect that it is taking them twelve hours to do what they used to do in eight. Just making a decision, about almost anything, is apt to become a torturous exercise. Trapped in the confusion of this internal chaos, frightened workaholics make up excuse after excuse and weave a tangled web of circuitous face-saving lies to continue to 'look good' in the eyes of others.

Crippled by anxiety, many stressed-out workaholics sit immobilized at their desks, yet attempt to look busy because they must be seen to be productive. After one CEO was fired, the staff discovered piles of files stuffed underneath the skirts of the sofa in his office. He had not been functioning for a very long while.

It's not just the compulsion that drives them to *have* to work all the time that prevents some workaholics from taking vacations. Sometimes, the anxiety that other staff members will have access to their offices and files while they are away is enough reason to cancel a vacation, often one that a frustrated and unhappy spouse has organized. Mistakes and cover-ups might be caught and become public knowledge. This fear is exaggerated as heightened levels of paranoia are experienced.

Taking even overdue vacations might jeopardize their coveted reputation of being a hard worker. One CEO justified his bail-out this way: 'It's just not worth going away! It takes too much of my energy to get everything in order before I leave. And then, when I get back, it's weeks before I catch up. That's just too much pressure right now!'

The thought of taking more than one week of vacation at any time becomes problematic for most workaholics as the breakdown progresses.

I once suggested to a client who was close to a burn-out that he ought to seriously consider taking a three-week vacation. This would allow him to slow down the first week and be prepared to handle the adrenalin withdrawal symptoms we discussed earlier that were sure to kick in during the second week. Hopefully by the third week, his body and mind would actually be in a truly relaxed state.

Saul reluctantly agreed to try this, but after three days of 'doing nothing', as he called it, he got a bright idea! To amuse himself, this controller thought it might be fun to single-handedly build a new deck on the family cottage that he and his family were staying at.

'It would be good for me', Saul rationalized, 'to do something entirely different'. Needless to say, the 'vacation' was a disaster for everyone. The perfectionism so inherent in his makeup took over, and this exhausted and demoralized workaholic found out the hard way that construction was not his forte. An exhausted Saul returned to his office and one week later suffered a serious heart attack. Pumping excesses of adrenalin into his system had finally taken its toll.

Not only do workaholics want to fool others, they also become delusional about their uniquely singular view of themselves.

Fear of Self-Discovery

A major threat to the ego-inflated arrogance of the workaholic is the emergence of its polar opposite, a repressed self-loathing.

Workaholics desperately want to believe in their hard-won public persona. They have learned to externalize and typically form their definition of self by second-guessing how others view them. However, self-doubt does set in as the breakdown progresses when complaints by family members and others protesting their insensitive behavior become more frequent. From their point of view, however, such feedback is grossly exaggerated.

The truth is that, once the Feeling function is repressed, it can no longer offer accurate feedback information. Consequently, troubled workaholics lack the insight to know how they actually do affect others. Increasingly, they do not know who they really are or how they should behave. Crippled by the anxiety of self-doubt, they project unwanted and unacknowledged weaknesses onto a long-suffering spouse or colleague who can do nothing right.

As the marital relationship inevitably begins to break down, and spouses threaten to leave unless the workaholic will go for counseling, the inherent danger in 'opening up Pandora's box' looms large. On the defensive, some narcissistic Controller-type workaholics may go once or twice to appease a livid spouse, put on their best behavior and try to convince the therapist that it is their spouse that is the problem.

'She's bitching at me constantly,' Abdul complains. He lacks the insight to know that his own passive–aggressive avoidance of personal responsibility in the relationship is forcing his wife into a position where she must become aggressive, or else retreat into a stony silence. In either case, her depression worsens. She loses hope that their problems can be solved. No one can keep a marriage healthy, all by oneself.

'If I hadn't read your book,' his wife, Ava, tells me, 'I was going to commit suicide. Now I know what is really going on at our house!'

As the breakdown progresses, the powerful defense mechanisms of denial, rationalization, projection of blame, compartmentalization and dissociation no longer serve to protect the frightened workaholic. Cumulative fears that generate fierce anger surface as rage. These terrible outbursts threaten everyone's security. Set jaws, stony faces and blank expressionless eyes reveal the workaholic's lack of understanding, empathy or compassion.

As Carl Jung warned, unless we become fully aware of our Shadow side, we are not safe. Nor, indeed, are those who must deal with us. That is why so much attention is given in my practice to helping workaholics and their families become acquainted with the Shadow side of their personality. Only through awareness can one bring these troublesome attributes up to consciousness. It then becomes possible to transform a particular weakness into a strength by developing the positive side of that trait or function.

Paranoia

Paranoia, the fear of persecution, is described by Campbell (1981) as a personality disorder in which the person so affected is

> hypersensitive, rigid and unwarrantably suspicious, jealous, and envious. He often has an exaggerated sense of self-importance, must always be right and/or prove others to be in the wrong, and has a tendency to blame others and to ascribe evil to them.

The increasing self-doubts and extreme defensiveness that come with the fear of discovery and self-discovery can lead to similar persecution phobias in the later stages of workaholism.

The fear of being victimized can traumatize the hypersensitive workaholic, who takes everything personally. Paranoia, in fact, is almost a self-fulfilling prophecy in that what the person fears eventually does come to pass. As cracks appear in the persona, the workaholic begins to suffer periodic bouts of acute anxiety or an increasingly debilitating depression. Some 'act out' their anxiety by threatening or intimidating others, while others 'act in' by withdrawing into a protective shell. Both responses are apt to offend or alienate the very people they were formerly trying to impress.

Not only do paranoid workaholics not trust anyone else, but they themselves are not trustworthy. There is a strong vindictive streak that motivates them to punish others who dare to challenge or disagree with their agenda. As Terry, a cocky sales manager, boasted: 'I get a real kick out of settling scores! You should have seen the shocked look on that guy's face. He didn't know what hit him!' Then he added: 'I love to see people like him squirm. They've always deserved their fate.'

The irony in his situation was clear. Only the week before, Terry had proudly told me that he was really in touch with his feelings now, and thought he might do some sensitivity training with his fractious staff. He had no idea why there was so much tension in the office, but he meant to do something about it. Self-confrontation was not something that Terry was ready to initiate.

Controllers manage up well, but down poorly. They play favorites and weed out those whistle-blowers who protest at the wisdom of their decisions, and establish a small circle of like-minded 'yeah saying' insiders. Ultimately, they trust no one.

Chronic Fatigue

Chronic fatigue occurs when both the mind and the body are drained of all energy by the excessively long hours of work, emotional turmoil, self-doubt and growing relationship problems. More frequent and severe crashing bouts of fatigue serve as a circuit breaker to immobilize the frenetic workaholic. Adrenalin, after all, was intended for emergency situations, for fight or flight.

As stress begins to take its toll, workaholics must rely on an adrenalin 'fix' just to keep going. For a while, caffeine stimulants do help them stay alert. Like alcoholics, however, a greater intake is necessary as periodic bouts of fatigue become more frequent and acute. The adrenalin system, like a worn-out elastic that has lost its spring, eventually crashes, and workaholics slip into a serious state of prolonged chronic fatigue. The phenomenon called Chronic Fatigue Syndrome, so common today, may simply be misdiagnosed workaholism.

Health eventually does break down. As Dr Archibald Hart warns, stress causes an enlargement of the adrenal cortex, a shrinking of important lymph nodes, and irritation in the stomach and intestines. There is an increase in the production of blood cholesterol, but a decrease in the ability of the body to remove it. Capillaries and other blood vessels shut down the blood supply to the heart muscle, blood has an increased tendency to clot, and deposits of plaque build up on the walls of the arteries (Hart, 1991, p. 21).

The most common manifestation of this damage can be witnessed in what has become known as the 'couch potato', someone who can fall asleep anywhere, any time, even in mid-sentence! This individual can stare unseeing at the TV for hours on end, or may escape to dens or bedrooms where no 'performance' is expected.

However, such physical and emotional exhaustion can also be masked by hyperactivity or acute restlessness. Relaxation has become impossible. Hyper types jump from one activity to the next, and often have trouble winding down at night. There is little awareness of how tired, cramped and tense they actually are.

Guilt

If the Feeling function is still working well enough to allow insight into how one's behavior affects other people, then the discomfort that guilt causes can signal the need to make a healthy corrective response. It allows the workaholic to apologize and ask for forgiveness for some irresponsible behavior or wrong-doing. Sincere efforts can then be undertaken to permanently change that behavior, and by doing so, make amends.

That precious insight is lost, however, once the dynamics of obsession cause repressed feelings to become numb and flat. Increasingly immobilized by their fears and anxiety, workaholics cannot risk facing the truth that their behavior and decisions are harming others. The moral and ethical values that allowed them to make fair and equitable judgments no longer register sufficiently. Their conscience is consequently flawed.

During this period, many well-intentioned workaholics do make promises to work less, usually after some crisis in the family. However, spouses sooner or later discover that their partner has been seduced into taking on yet another more visible or prestigious task. The temptation was too great, and the excuses given are once again 'all about them'.

Caught in his lie, Matthew vehemently protests: 'You *must* understand. I can't afford to refuse this job.' Then he rationalizes, 'Besides, you must know by now that everything I do is for you and the kids!'

Guilt is actually unacknowledged self-anger. Its remorse too often is fueled by fears of rejection, punishment or retaliation, rather than by genuine sorrow. Disowned anger gets projected outwards, and others may be falsely accused. When his teenaged son Mark dared to call his enraged father a 'pathetic workaholic', Donald retaliated by slamming him into a wall and then chased his fleeing son back to his bedroom. Elaine, his distraught wife, screamed at him to stop and intervened by placing herself between them.

Not wanting to acknowledge Elaine's alarmed reaction, Donald yelled at her: 'You're just getting hysterical. Get a hold of yourself. Everything is fine here!' By doing so, Donald was absolving himself of guilt, and thereby rejecting his feelings of inadequacy at losing control.

When guilt is repressed, shame takes its place. This largely unconscious state manifests itself in ugly moods, cruel put-downs, caustic sarcasm, and a vindictive outrage that punishes others when things go wrong. Directed inwards, emotionally-crippled workaholics unwittingly punish themselves by overworking, and neglecting to eat properly or get enough sleep. Too busy to see a doctor, they ignore the warning signals that would ordinarily signal bodily distress. The ability to nurture oneself and others is lost when sensitivity and compassion are compromised.

The Losses that Lead to Personality Changes

Why do workaholics suffer largely unconscious but profound personality changes as the Feeling–Being side is slowly eclipsed by the powerful Doing–Performing side?

Loss of Feeling

The loss of feeling plays a major role in the breakdown syndrome that this addiction follows, and in the subsequent changes that occur within the individual.

Partly, this has to do with the dynamics of obsession described earlier. Remember, as the obsession with work starts to run the workaholic, all the functions begin to transform to their dark side. Obsessive thoughts overtax Thinking and it becomes fuzzy, confused and faulty. Repressed Feeling is overly-sensitive, takes everything personally, and turns moody and resentful. Negative Intuition is impatient, impulsive and reckless, and having lost touch with the 'big picture' it is attracted to pragmatic short-term gains. Negative Sensation's dualistic black–white thinking gets picky and argumentative, and an awful emptiness fuels a greedy neediness that must be assuaged.

The other contributing factor concerns the increase in narcissistic tendencies that occur as fearful workaholics fight for their survival. More and more self-centered and self-serving, emotionally-crippled workaholics are determined to be right and to get their own way. They fail to recognize the rights and individuality of others because ego boundaries are hopelessly blurred. As a consequence, they lack the insight necessary to discern how their invasive actions might impact and offend others. 'Others should think like I do, want what I want' is their unspoken expectation.

Repressed feelings work slowly, if at all. It may take hours to translate thoughts into feeling. If you ask workaholics how they feel, they will tell you what they think instead, or fake a standard reaction they guess might be appropriate. Or, as often happens in my office, workaholics will turn to their spouses looking for the 'right' answer. Because they lack feeling language and behavior, their jarring responses often leave the listener on the defensive, unsettled or simply puzzled.

Unlike the previously mentioned fears which are conscious, the changes in personality that repressed feeling creates are barely perceptible to the idealistic Dr Jekyll who does not wish to acknowledge Mr Hyde. The family cannot pinpoint what is happening either. Something is terribly wrong, but no one knows what to do about it. The instant success that *Workaholics: The Respectable Addicts* received attests to this fact. Finally, someone understood what was going on. 'As I turned each page, there we were! I couldn't believe it. You must have been living at our house' is a familiar, often repeated remark.

What must it be like not to feel? Patrick, a recovering workaholic who described himself as a 'distant observer' when we first met, admitted that he was functioning on one level, but understood little of what had happened to make him so critical, cynical and empty. Now that he was in touch with his feelings and reconnected to the significant people in his life, his plaintive cry was 'Please God, let me never have to live that way again!'

Loss of Communication Skills

Obsessive thinking can be confusing and even bizarre because it is often inconsistent, circular or convoluted. Communication appears logical, but goes nowhere. Thoughts get added or retracted as messages change or are too cryptic to be understood. There is no feeling input to moderate extreme thoughts or clarify meaning.

Such quasi-logical communication goes something like this. Peter, a respected physician, insisted in all seriousness: 'My wife and I are just fine. We're intelligent, well-adjusted and mature. The problem is the relationship!' If Mary had an opinion different from Peter's, this meant that Mary thought that he was wrong. In Peter's mind, two people could not possibly both be right. He was refusing to acknowledge his neglect and the trauma that his increasingly frequent eruptions of rage caused in the family.

When Mary tried to share some knowledge that she was acquiring to improve their relationship, Peter would make sneering remarks like 'You only read books you agree with!' These two were locked in a power struggle. Mary was trying to assert herself in an effort to be heard and affirmed, while Peter had to win and stay one-up in any conversation. If he did not like what was being said, he would exit mid-sentence.

No wonder communication breaks down. Outwardly, workaholics like Peter appear calm, controlled and poker-faced. Inside they are in a state of confused anxiety, yet remain indifferent to its source.

Loss of Empathy and Compassion

Empathy is the ability to place oneself in another's psychological space in an attempt to imagine what that person *might* be experiencing. It is important, however, to respect ego boundaries and not to make assumptions about the other person's behavior or motivation. Workaholics rarely take the important second step of actually asking that person what he or she does feel or think about what has happened. If requesting this information is not possible or it is inappropriate to ask, then care must be taken not to assume that one does know the real story.

The loss of empathy and the ability to show compassion affects family members greatly. To be understanding and loving, one must feel and be able to express genuine emotional support. Feeling language does this best. Maurice Boyd refers to William James's thought that by expressing an emotion we strengthen it. This minister then adds: 'When we express love we don't merely express how we already feel; we increase our capacity for loving' (Boyd, 1985, p. 90).

The opposite happens as the Shadow side of the workaholic's personality erupts. People become a nuisance. Their demands for some attention become annoyances which are best ignored. Any interruptions that waylay the workaholic's own agenda are barely tolerated. Negative Intuition's quick impatience and its impulsive and restless nature both work against taking the time to understand someone else's upset state.

Self-centeredness replaces empathy, and intolerance destroys compassion. Workaholics become self-absorbed people who refuse to acknowledge the rights and dignity of others. Trust and respect are undermined as a hurry-hurry, rush-rush attitude leaves no time or energy for working things out, solving unfinished problems, or gaining insight into another's needs and wishes.

Loss of the Ability to be Intimate

Maggie Scarf reminds us that 'Intimacy is a merging and fusion of the self and other – which involves the threat of losing one's own separate personality' (Scarf, 1987, p. 362). As the breakdown progresses, the authentic Self which has been sacrificed to the public persona, is not strong enough for workaholics to give up control and risk self-annihilation. They therefore assume an autonomous stance in the relationship. By default, the partner is left in charge of intimacy. Scarf describes the mutual frustration:

> In truth, the intimacy seeker has promised to chase but never to overtake the partner, just as the autonomy seeker has promised to run but never to get too distant from her breathless, dissatisfied pursuer. (ibid., p. 365)

Real intimacy requires a sharing of power. No wonder these partners remain locked in control struggles that destroy the trust, respect and friendship necessary for real love. Many of the couples I see have not been sexual for years. There is no real intimacy in affairs because everyone can go home to their own world afterwards, and distance creates its own barrier.

Loss of Independence

There is a certain irony involved in this loss because workaholics take great pride in being independent. However, when these people no longer know exactly how they feel or how they should react, and there is little insight into how their behavior affects other people, shame sets in. It is humiliating if one must depend on others just to cope.

A dependency develops where workaholics must guess how they should feel or are expected to act, especially in situations where relationship issues are involved. They can be observed closely watching others for clues as confidence wanes. Arthur, for instance, would go into great detail about an altercation at work that day. He would watch his wife's reaction, and next day Arthur would use her reaction and words to guide his behavior.

Such inner confusion often gets played out in controlling behavior as workaholics struggle to maintain some semblance of stability. This client's response is not atypical. When Sam was asked how he felt about an incident that was being discussed in our session, he hesitated and then turned to his wife, looking for the right answer. He needed Rachel to bail him out in order to 'look good' in front of an outsider. She, in turn, was trying to 'help' Sam by quickly filling in the blank, unconsciously playing out the role of the enabler.

Yet not five minutes later, Sam came out with a bitingly cruel remark that just devastated Rachel. Unwittingly, he was acting out his shame of dependency by punishing his loyal partner, the person he depended on for nurturance and support. Deep in denial, he had twisted the facts around so that his insensitive and inappropriate behavior did not count, and everything was Rachel's fault. According to Sam, her 'unjustly angry response' had completely ruined their vacation.

'The Terrible Twist', as I call such distortions, is a form of emotional cruelty. Falsely accusing someone by twisting the other's view of reality so that the workaholic can appear to be innocent of wrongdoing is far too common a dynamic in these families.

When depression sets in, Pleasers often tend to cling to the family. Self-absorbed, they refuse to go anywhere or do anything, so spouses become isolated. Friends disappear as plans get canceled or promises are 'forgotten'.

Paranoid workaholics worry excessively about public opinion, so they restrict their actions and may fail to follow through on their intentions rather than risk possible rejection or failure. The independent initiative and bravery necessary to confront denial and seek help are soon lost.

Loss of Integrity and Respect
The loss of integrity, one of the great tragedies of workaholism, usually takes place in incremental stages. It becomes easier each time one lies, cheats or steals, and the stakes inevitably rise accordingly. Because power eventually corrupts, morality and ethics are inevitably sacrificed for public success as chronic workaholics become unscrupulous, cruel and vindictive. Reaching some sought-after goal is all that matters. Infidelities are used to build up sagging egos as spouses, who have gone unappreciated and been taken for granted for years, are punished for finally standing up and threatening to leave if things don't change. 'What about me!' is their plaintive cry for help.

Saying what others want you to say rather than telling the truth is dishonest, yet workaholics are masters of such manipulation. It is hard for these people to accept the concept that the passive–aggressive behavior of neglecting to tell the truth is lying. Avoiding saying what you want to do and then sabotaging others' plans is irresponsible. Showing up alarmingly late, canceling at the last moment, or not being fully present by sleeping through the symphony or a church service is rude and insensitive. Worst of all, making promises to children and not keeping them is emotionally cruel behavior.

Beware! Respectability and trust earned through hard work and ambition can be lost seemingly overnight. The fall from grace can be cushioned for those wealthy enough to afford a prominent lawyer, or those who manage to avoid censure by insisting on telling the world that they are innocent. The media reports of yet another tale of indiscretion, of inappropriate, foolish and amoral behavior sicken us all. Headlines of unimaginable fraud and theft scream out from all the papers, and trials seem to go on forever.

Ironically, this unwanted publicity means that workaholics can no longer hide behind their Nice Guy or Gal persona. Harsh reality must be faced, but often not in time to save marriages or careers. One can only imagine the shame that is imposed on innocent family members, especially unsuspecting children who had idealized a powerful, yet neglectful parent.

Sometimes, the enormity of the workaholic's wrongdoing does hit home. A spouse leaves because of abuse and neglect, or a boss uncovers a fraudulent act. If shame and humiliation do break through to consciousness, workaholics must face the reality of what they have done to others. They must cope with deep self-loathing as the overwhelming pain and remorse for past actions finally surfaces. These awful but necessary insights allow workaholics to begin the difficult work of transformation. It is a journey that hopefully will help restore their integrity and allow them to feel again, so that they are capable of true intimacy.

Unfortunately, those whose defense mechanisms work all too well may never learn to face the reality of past misdeeds. Some eventually sink into deep states of depression, suffer from extreme anxiety attacks, or commit suicide. Other more hardy types manage to resurface seemingly unscathed, to reinvent or resurrect their public persona. Going on to another career with a new youthful trophy wife, these infamous celebrities leave behind a trail of broken dreams, bankrupt companies, and lost jobs.

Integrity is not possible without compassion. Unwittingly, these formerly idealistic, overly-ambitious people have lost this most precious and admired character trait.

Loss of Spirituality

When work becomes the 'sacred cow', personal values usually change. Faith often weakens because no energy is given over to the spiritual side of life. For those who have lost their spirituality, or never had it, this is a grim picture indeed. It is impossible for workaholics to give up control if they have no faith that letting go and allowing themselves to trust God will only thrust them further back into chaos. Opening up Pandora's Box to take ownership of their Shadow traits is just too scary.

One has to learn the love of self before spirituality is possible. Self-love is eroded by gnawing fears and self-doubt, haunting obsessions, and the many losses that occur when feelings are flattened and one's conscience barely works. Mr Hyde is not lovable. Self-loathing, the polar opposite of arrogance, is ordinarily repressed. When fragile workaholics are suddenly threatened by an unwelcome challenge or their plans are thwarted, however, these soulless people can suffer periodic psychotic bursts of rage which frighten others. Later, workaholics will deny their loss of control, as if nothing at all happened.

As the breakdown progresses, fatalistic workaholics expect the worst because it appears their decisions no longer make a difference. If things do work out well, it is a result of luck, accident or odds. Both positions reveal a splitting-off of self, a projection onto someone or something else. It is an abandonment of personal responsibility for one's own role in a given situation.

Religious affiliation may play a role in the workaholic's life, partly because it may be part of the Nice Guy or Gal's need to be seen as a respectable pillar of the community. Some do recognize the need for spiritual support and are physically present at their house of worship, but cannot concentrate because of fatigue, or are lost in work-related thoughts. Some still perform good deeds for others, but a 'do-gooder' philosophy can end up being a form of self-aggrandizement, or a way of controlling people by placing them in your debt.

Self-made Controller-types who still experience themselves as independently powerful and omnipotent often find the idea of letting go of control to anyone, even God, particularly offensive. However, when depression and anxiety hit, this means there is no spiritual guidance to ease the pain, to help the troubled individual find a more meaningful existence.

In their search for an authentic Self, many recovering workaholics rediscover their religious beliefs and faithfully attend their place of worship once again. For some, it is the first time they have fully participated in the life of a congregation. Searching for a new meaning in life inevitably sets one on a spiritual path. Answers must be found to questions such as 'Who am I separate from my work?', 'Where am I going?', 'Why am I killing myself?' Illnesses and lay-offs often trigger such existential searching. Forgiveness for harm done to others must also be sought if workaholics are to fully recover from their addiction to power and control. They must find the elusive inner peace that fosters a genuine love of self and of others.

Loss of a Sense of Humor and the Ability to Play

Driven workaholics are seriously intense and determined individuals who eventually experience little joy, laughter or optimism as psychological and physical health breaks down. They have lost the childlike wonder and spontaneous appreciation that bubbles forth and erupts when something strikes children as funny. Instead, they use black humor such as sarcasm, ridicule or caustic put-downs that serve to defend themselves from getting too close or involved. Sometimes they will respond with a diabolical laugh, or a chilling sneer that highlights their superiority. Young children, who have not as yet developed abstract thinking, hear only the concrete derogatory remark, not the double entendre. Consequently, sarcasm can seriously damage a child's self-esteem.

The ability to produce and to appreciate humor is an essential component of maturity. In my doctoral dissertation (Killinger, 1976) I concluded that one of the attributes of a mature individual is the ability to laugh at oneself and to see one's own situation in a humorous light. Humor moderates intense feelings and helps us to accept our weaknesses and shortcomings without playing the victim-martyr game. It gives us the objectivity and perspective necessary to not take everything personally, something workaholics tend to do when paranoia and the dark side of Feeling translate into ugly moods, depression and pessimism.

In the later stages of workaholism, genuine play is almost non-existent. Earlier, these competitive people worked at their play, analyzed each shot, and diligently compared their progress based on the scores of others. If dissatisfied, they would practice until their scores were higher than last time. If things went badly, they used foul language and threw bats and racquets in disgust. Some workaholics will not play golf, they say, because it takes too long. I suspect that it is more likely that they would not play unless they were good, and it would take too much of their precious time to hone their skills. I challenge those clients who do still play to try not keeping score some time. They look at me in disbelief. As one exasperated man said, 'What would be the point?'

Because they over-schedule, frazzled workaholics often come rushing onto the court to 'play' squash, which is of course a shorter game. Pleasure for its own sake is alien to their thinking because workaholics must compete, win or 'shoot to score'. Genuine play, in contrast, is fun, carefree and purposeless. It restores our energy, helps us relax, and provides a healthy balance to counteract the stress generated by the pace of our busy lives.

Loss of Physical and Psychological Health

An early sign that the psyche has become rigid occurs when workaholics develop a rigid, stiff way of carrying their body. Movements appear almost robot-like, and back problems are common.

Out of touch with their body because their Feeling function is repressed, workaholics remain unaware of the increases in adrenalin. Tightly crossed arms and legs, taut facial muscles and locked jaws reflect their defensive attitude. They walk fast, eat fast, and drink copious amounts of coffee just to keep going. Excessive pumping of adrenalin produces a fatigue that should act as a circuit breaker to warn of danger to all the body's functioning systems. Instead, workaholics just drive themselves even harder until chronic fatigue shuts them down.

Severe fatigue is also a symptom of the hopelessness that feeds depression. Some of the other signs of depression to watch for are changes in eating and sleeping patterns, poor concentration, loss of motivation, emotional and physical exhaustion, crying spells and a loss of libido. Neediness sometimes results in an increase in sexual drive. Depersonalization results in a distancing of oneself from a problem and not caring any more. Anger and cynicism are irrational, and there is a tendency to isolate from family and friends. Loss of memory and forgetfulness are severe problems for workaholics, who can appear to have a mind like a sieve.

Depression can be a downward spiral that moves very fast, or it can go on for years and become a habitual life-pattern. Some workaholics have remarkable stamina and persevere at their work throughout their lifetime.

Some never retire, and work into their eighties. Privately, they complain about aches and pains, but they stubbornly refuse to get medical attention.

Other workaholics are immobilized by stress and suffer debilitating anxiety. Panic attacks and claustrophobia are common as heart activity increases and breathing is disturbed. There are vasomotor changes and musculoskeletal disturbances such as trembling or paralysis, or increased sweating. Physiological responses may come from external stimuli and the demands of reality, or from internal pressures to push forward, to keep performing and seek gratification of blocked drives. Other signs of anxiety include excess stomach sensitivity, ulcers, abnormal blood pressure, heart trouble, nervousness, lack of vitality and a total inability to relax. Workaholics often report a feeling of pressure in their chest, constricted breathing, dizziness and light-headedness.

Unfortunately, all this stress can lead to strokes and heart attacks, what the Japanese call 'karoshi', death from overwork. Those who exaggerate and falsify reality often retreat into a psychotic state where reality and fantasy blur. A complete disintegration of the ego may occur, or suicide may be the tragic end.

DENIAL, CONTROL AND POWER – THE WORKAHOLIC TRAP

The seductive combination of denial, control and power, the BIG THREE as I call them, is the chief reason why workaholics cannot escape this addiction to save themselves from the grievous losses that have been presented.

Denial becomes a comfortable ally to maintain the illusion of perfection, to avoid dealing with what the workaholic is doing to others. Impression management is the workaholic's art. The public persona or professional mask must be protected at all costs. The real person gets lost in the self-sacrificing hero-turned-martyr who only feels alive and exhilarated in the impersonal workplace.

Control is the way to achieve the power and influence that wealth and prestige bring. Blatant controlling behavior is hard to miss. The passive–aggressive forms are less obvious, but equally destructive.

Power is the seductive mistress that lures the insecure workaholic away from the family. Power can be used for good or evil, but an excess of power, when it is combined with a growing arrogance, spells trouble in all areas of life.

The power of greed arises out of the aggressive instinct. It is fed by ambition, perfectionism, competition, anger and shame. Its language is strategies, tactics, manipulation, gamesmanship and exploitation.

Power coupled with love, on the other hand, has infinite possibilities for good. Love is the opposite of greed in all aspects. It is fed by the nurturing and sexual instincts. Love encourages empathy, compassion, generosity, goodwill and compromise. Its language is appreciation, support, enthusiasm and sharing.

Competition and compassion are like oil and water; they do not mix. Compassion does not deal in winners and losers. It does not isolate, separate or estrange. Competition can be constructive and creative, but it becomes destructive when one constantly needs to measure oneself against another to come out ahead, or when it is motivated by a desire to punish others in order to vindicate one's own self-worth. Only through gaining wisdom and insight and exercising his or her compassion will the workaholic be able to ensure that personal power is used for good, not evil.

I am often asked: 'How can I recover from workaholism?' My answer, in brief, is that you will be well on your way to recovery when the power of love becomes infinitely stronger than the power of greed.

REFERENCES

Boyd, R.M. (1985), *A Lover's Quarrel with the World*, Burlington, Canada: Welch Publishing Co.

Campbell, R. (1981), *Psychiatric Dictionary*, 5th edn, New York: Oxford University Press.

Hart, A. (1991), *The Hidden Link Between Adrenalin and Stress*, Dallas: Word Publishing.

Killinger, B. (1976), 'The place of humour in adult psychotherapy', Ph.D. dissertation (unpublished), York University.

Killinger, B. (1991), *Workaholics: The Respectable Addicts*, Toronto: Key Porter Books.

Killinger, B. (1995), *The Balancing Act: Rediscovering Your Feelings*, Toronto: Key Porter Books.

Killinger, B. (2004), *Workaholics: The Respectable Addicts*, Toronto: Key Porter Books.

Oates, W. (1971), *Confessions of a Workaholic*, Nashville: Abingdon.

Scarf, M. (1987), *The Intimate Partners: Patterns in Love and Marriage*, New York: Random House.

4. Exploring new frontiers to generate an integrated definition of workaholism

Lynley H.W. McMillan and Michael P. O'Driscoll

Workaholism is generally understood to involve an unwillingness to disengage from work. Workaholics' most notable characteristics are tendencies to:

(a) work with a passion that is obvious to the outside observer
(b) think about work four times more frequently, compared to non-workaholics, after most other people have mentally 'switched off'
(c) focus their conversation on work, even in social situations
(d) strive for tangible achievements in the workplace
(e) work slightly more hours than others.

(McMillan et al., 2004)

In general, contemporary data indicate that workaholism represents a value system about the importance of working and achieving that certainly does not meet the scientific criteria for addiction, as it is associated with a similar quality of health and relationships to that of the rest of the adult population, and generally does not worsen over time (McMillan and O'Driscoll, 2004). Interestingly, while the majority of workaholics appear to derive high enjoyment from their work *and* their leisure, it is their reluctance to utilize psychological 'off-buttons' that potentially makes them a challenging group for management professionals (Machlowitz, 1980).

In order to address some of these issues, this chapter comprises four major sections: (a) philosophical and epistemological frameworks underpinning current research, (b) a review of contemporary definitions, (c) illustrative data from an inductive/qualitatitive study, and (d) conclusions and a preliminary conceptual model based on an integration of the deductive and inductive data. Given that the extant body of knowledge is largely based in positivist research designs, the alternate framework for generating a definition of workaholism is based on triangulated data sources (from workers, their colleagues and their partners). The initial section therefore provides an overview of the philosophical and epistemological frameworks of current research, which generates a précis of the range of design parameters available to researchers. This will provide a succinct orientation for researchers who want to enter, review, or change their research approach in the workaholism domain.

PHILOSOPHICAL AND EPISTEMOLOGICAL FRAMEWORKS

Workaholism research is conducted predominantly from within a social science paradigm. Social scientists formally define a theory as a system of logical statements that explain the relationship between two or more phenomena (Berg, 1995). For example, workaholism researchers have investigated relationships between workaholism and constructs such as hours worked, health, relationships and work attitudes. Theory is used to (a) develop explanations about reality, (b) provide a means to classify and organize events, and (c) predict future occurrences of events (Berg, 1995). However, whether research designs *start* or *end* with theory is a point of ongoing debate among researchers in many of the social sciences. Thus, it is potentially possible to explore workaholism either by espousing a theory and then investigating its implications or by collecting some data and evolving a theory to explain its patterns. The present section therefore expands these two design options (deductive/inductive), in addition to reviewing alternate methodologies (quantitative/qualitative) and data sources (single source/multiple source).

Design Options (Deductive versus Inductive)

Deductive investigations (that is, theory before research) begin with ideas and then attempt to disprove them through tests of empirical research (refutation). *Inductive* investigations, in contrast, begin with data, then generate theoretical innovation afterward (that is, research before theory). Deductive research designs begin with theory then move on to gather data (see Figure 4.1), whereas inductive designs follow the inverse pattern, beginning with data and ending with generating a theory.

Whilst these two approaches represent differing underlying philosophies, some authors suggest that the approaches may actually coexist on a continuum (see, for instance, Berg, 1995). Thus, it is possible, at least theoretically, to investigate workaholism by (a) starting with a theory and

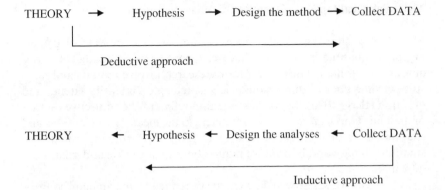

Figure 4.1   Comparison of deductive and inductive models of research

developing hypotheses, research designs and data analysis techniques, or (b) starting by gathering data, allowing them to suggest which analyses are required, then building a theory based on the findings, or (c) utilizing both approaches within the same sample (that is, a composite approach). The benefits of the approaches differ. For instance, theory-first allows researchers to contextualize designs and findings within other scientific disciplines (for example, relate workaholism to both psychological and business theories) and allows for prediction and control of variables. In contrast, a data-first approach could elucidate more diverse trends (such as exceptions to what theory may predict) and may be more sensitive to early changes in behaviour (such as responsiveness of workaholism to evolving mobile technologies). Alternately, a combined approach would allow for both sensitivity and breadth and thus provide a broad range of data on a phenomenon.

However, whilst many fields of psychological enquiry have adopted the composite paradigm (for instance, attitude research), workaholism designs are predominantly deductive. This suggests there is an extraordinary amount of information about workaholism about which we remain unaware. Importantly, if data from the composite approaches converged on the same conclusion, then the present body of knowledge about workaholism could be taken as considerably more reliable, more robust, and perhaps more representative of the phenomenon in question.

Currently, however, because workaholism research has used mostly a theory-down (deductive) approach, it is entirely feasible that how academics *view* workaholism and how the general public *experiences* it may be two completely different things. Clearly, if science is committed to thoroughly investigating constructs, we would be prudent to incorporate diverse research epistemologies in exploring the workaholism construct.

Methodological Options (Quantitative versus Qualitative)

Methodologically, the social sciences employ two generic ways of gathering data: quantitative and qualitative. Quantity refers to the objective amount of an item. Thus, *quantitative* research involves counts and measures of things across dimensions, such as frequency, intensity, latency and duration (Berg, 1995). In contrast, quality refers to the subjective essence of an item. Thus *qualitative* research refers to the meanings, definitions and characteristics of constructs. Clearly, in terms of furthering our understanding about workaholism, we require both quantitative and qualitative information.

In general terms, research data can be generated from two main sources; single-source (self-report) and multiple-source (multidimensional) data. Multidimensional data are typically generated through *triangulation*. Triangulation is commonly used in surveying, map-making and navigation, where three points are used to draw sighting lines toward an unknown object to estimate its size and characteristics. While two lines could be used, the third line permits a more accurate estimate of the unknown object (Berg, 1995).

Triangulation has been used in the social sciences since 1956 (see Campbell and Fiske, 1959). As outlined in the stress literature, triangulation is considered a desirable design element (Ivancevich and Matteson, 1988). In terms of workaholism research, this would involve informants such as spouses and colleagues (see for instance McMillan and O'Driscoll, 2004). However, the vast majority of data have been single-source, based on self-report, meaning we know little of how people living and working alongside workaholics define, understand and experience the behaviour.

REVIEW OF LAST FOUR DECADES OF PUBLISHED DEFINITIONS

Given that a wide variety of research designs is available to workaholism researchers, the present section discusses in more detail the definitions of workaholism developed over the last four decades of research.

In general, as outlined in Table 4.1, the majority of definitions of workaholism have been generated deductively and investigated using quantitative frameworks and unidimensional data sources. This trend has largely remained unchanged since the term 'workaholic' came into general usage in 1968. Although Oates's (1968) writing became the basis for much of the later work in the field, his work was rooted in personal conjecture rather than empirical data.

Table 4.1   Summary of major workaholism definitions, 1968–2004

Author	Year	Method	Criteria	Underlying framework
Oates	1968	Qualitative Anecdotal Introspective Generically inductive	1. Excessive need for work 2. Disrupted health, happiness, relationships, social functioning 3. Withdrawal – takes work home 4. Works outside work time and conceals it 5. Starts early and needs less sleep than others 6. Works weekends or 2 jobs	Pathological Addiction theory
Machlowitz	1980	Qualitative Inductive	1. Intrinsic desire to work long and hard 2. Work exceeds others' expectations 3. Intense, energetic, competitive, driven 4. Strong self-doubts, needs reassurance 5. Prefers labour to leisure 6. Works anywhere, any time 7. Maximizes time usage 8. Blurs business and pleasure	Strengths-based
Robinson	1989	Quantitative Deductive Anecdotal	1. Overdoing/ hurrying/binges 2. Low self-worth/ignore personal needs 3. Control/perfectionism 4. Intimacy difficulties/ impatience 5. Mental preoccupation	Pathological Addiction theory
Fassel	1992	Qualitative Anecdotal Clinical interviews	1. Multiple addictions 2. Denial 3. Self-esteem problems 4. External referencing	Psychological Addiction theory

Table 4.1   (continued)

Author	Year	Method	Criteria	Underlying framework
			5. Ability to relax 6. Obsessiveness	
Spence and Robbins	1992	Quantitative Deductive Cluster analyses	1. Work involvement 2. Drive 3. Enjoyment	Observable Behavioural
Clark et al.	1993	Quantitative Deductive Conceptual sorting	1. Personality factor = conscientiousness 2. Personality trait = obsessive-compulsive 3. Style = perfectionism, compulsion, energy	Personality theory Clinical psycho-pathology
Scott et al.	1997	Quantitative Deductive	1. Discretionary time spent working 2. Thinking about work when not at work 3. Working beyond requirements	Observable Behavioural
McMillan et al.	2002	Quantitative Deductive Confirmatory factor analyses	1. Reluctance to disengage from work 2. Enjoyment 3. Drive 4. Work or think about work 5. Work any time or anywhere	Observable Behavioural
Snir and Harpaz	2004	Deductive	1. Behavioural and cognitive elements 2. Steady/stable trait 3. Not externally imposed 4. Not solely attitudes/values/beliefs	Observable Behavioural

In 1980, Machlowitz published the first empirically based writing on workaholism. Workaholism was conceptualized as a trait that involved an intrinsic desire to work long and hard, led to working beyond job prescriptions, and earned the psychic incomes of responsibility, opportunity and recognition (Machlowitz, 1980). Machlowitz emphasized that workaholics' attitudes toward work, rather than the actual number of hours they worked, differentiated them from healthy workers. While the framework involved a partially qualitative design (participants were given open-ended questions and had their responses recorded, coded and analysed), this research prototype appears to have been largely ignored by subsequent workaholism researchers. This is possibly because the results (workaholics reported satisfaction and no more difficulties than other people) contradicted the popular stereotype of the day that workaholics were 'miserable slaves'. Machlowitz' work remains one of the few published qualitative studies in the field.

The next influential studies were produced by an American researcher, Bryan Robinson, commencing in 1989. Robinson followed Oates's conceptualization of workaholism and worked primarily from within a family therapy paradigm (Robinson, 1998). Robinson's definition was developed deductively using an addiction paradigm, where the symptoms of addiction were overlaid onto work-specific behaviour. The Robinson definition comprises five aspects: (a) overdoing (hurrying/binges), (b) self-worth (productivity at expense of personal needs), (c) control – perfectionism, (d) intimacy (relationship difficulties/impatience), and (e) mental preoccupation (brownouts/difficulty relaxing). A corresponding measure (the Work Addiction Risk Test: WART) and conceptual models have been developed (Robinson et al., 2001).

Fassel (1992) approached workaholism from an organizational consulting perspective. Based on anecdotal data from organizational clients and Workaholics Anonymous groups, Fassel defined workaholism as comprising six characteristics: (a) multiple addictions, (b) denial, (c) self-esteem problems, (d) external referencing, (e) inability to relax, and (f) obsessiveness. Fassel conceptualized workaholism as following the early–middle–late stage continuum of worsening disease, borrowed from the addiction paradigm. However, while Fassel's work represents an encouraging start at qualitatitive and inductive development of a definition, there was no formal research undertaken, nor systematic descriptions of participants or data analysis. While the ideological approach (qualitatitive/inductive) was of potential utility, the lack of scientific analysis means the definition remains speculative. Additionally, some of the components appear to represent outcomes of workaholism, rather than elements of the construct per se.

Spence and Robbins' (1992) deductively based framework was based on a review of theory and literature that was used to produce a model of workaholism, which was subsequently tested on homogenous samples of students and social workers. Workaholism was defined as a stable trait that involves (a) a high degree of commitment to work, (b) a good deal of time spent working, and (c) a compulsion to work even when it is not necessary (Spence and Robbins, 1992). Burke (1999) has subsequently produced a sequence of deductive studies based on the Spence and Robbins' definition.

Clark et al. (1993) used a deductive method based on personality theory and psychometric paradigms to devise and then test a model of Non-adaptive and Adaptive personality. Workaholism was classified as most closely related to the 'big five' personality trait of conscientiousness, fell into the subcategory of obsessive compulsiveness, and involved perfectionism, compulsion and high energy (Clark et al., 1996). However, their conceptualization does not appear to have been utilized specifically by workaholism researchers. Given the robust design methodology, this is somewhat surprising, although the constraints experienced by the present authors in accessing the measure, owing to copyright issues, may provide some explanation. Furthermore, the measure forms part of a larger battery, which may preclude its use in a research-specific context.

Scott et al. (1997) have published perhaps the most rigorous deductive methodology, commencing with an extensive review and critique of the literature, followed by a comprehensive conceptual model, and predicted relationships between variables and resultant research hypotheses. Their analysis suggested a definition that involves three components: (a) discretionary time spent working, (b) thinking about work when not at work, and (c) working beyond requirements. Unfortunately, however, there does not appear to have been any subsequent research that specifically tested their model, and it remains to this day speculative.

At the turn of the century, McMillan et al. (2002) concurrently tested the Spence and Robbins (1992) and the Clark et al. (1996) definitions of workaholism. On the basis of several deductive, data-based studies, McMillan et al. (2004) defined workaholism as comprising five elements: (a) reluctance to disengage from work, (b) enjoyment, (c) drive, (d) work or think about work (e) work any time or anywhere. The important contribution provided by this series of studies is that both the data *and* measurement sources have been triangulated (see McMillan and O'Driscoll, 2004). Around the same time, Mudrack and Naughton (2001) proposed a behaviourally-based definition of workaholism comprising two elements: (a) non-required work and (b) attempts to control others. This latter criterion (controlling others) is a new concept in workaholism research and still at the preliminary stages of testing. Whilst the Mudrack and Naughton measure has been used in later research (cf. Mudrack, 2004), there does not yet appear to have been any psychometric validation analysis conducted, which means data remain tentative at this stage.

More recently, Snir and Harpaz (2004) suggested that many existing definitions were implicitly value-laden, and argued for the importance of researchers to adopt neutral ('non-judgmental') definitions. They proposed that any definition of workaholism should reflect that it is (a) a steady state that involves (b) considerable allocation of time to (c) work-related activities and (d) work-related thoughts (e) that are not derived from external necessity. This definition shares considerable overlap with the McMillan et al. and Scott et al. definitions (see Table 4.1).

Altogether, therefore, the quantitative data on workaholism is predominantly generated from deductive techniques, and, with the exception of McMillan and O'Driscoll (2004), produced from single-source, self-reports. On the other hand, while some encouraging qualitative work has been commenced (for example, Oates, Machlowitz, Fassel) it is largely anecdotal in nature and not tested using scientific frameworks and peer review processes. The following section therefore reviews some preliminary inductively generated data that has been scientifically analysed, in order to compare two definitions, one inductively and one deductively derived.

DATA FROM AN ILLUSTRATIVE INDUCTIVE/ QUALITATIVE STUDY

The present section reports data from an *inductively* generated definition of workaholism where *participants* defined the construct. The epistemological perspective involved applied research in a naturalistic setting, using qualitatitive data from a contrasted group design and data gathered from multivariate sources (that is, triangulated data). The aim was (a) to generate an inductive definition by asking workers, their colleagues and their partners how they would describe someone who was workaholic, then (b) compare their descriptions with a published deductive definition to (c) establish whether the general public concur with the academic definitions of workaholism.

Sample

The study was conducted in New Zealand in 2001. The sample comprised four groups; workers (n = 55), work colleagues (n = 52), partners (n = 24) and content analysts (n = 9).

Workers
The workers (24 male, 31 female) had a mean age of 36.8 years (range = 20–63, *SD* = 11.6). Half of the sample held a tertiary qualification (apprenticeships through to masters degrees), the majority (80 per cent)

were New Zealand European, and most lived in married or de-facto relationships, working in technical, clerical, sales or financial services roles.
Workers were categorized into two contrasting groups (workaholic and
non-workaholic) using their responses to the Workaholism Battery-
Revised (WorkBAT-R: McMillan et al., 2002): a 14-item measure of
workaholism comprising two factors, Drive and Enjoyment, that has been
previously validated in New Zealand on two separate samples. A detailed
description of the classification into groups is provided in McMillan and
O'Driscoll (2004). The groups did not differ significantly in terms of
gender, age, income or highest qualification. Workaholics had a mean
Enjoyment-R score of 5.57 (range = 4.43 to 6.71) and a mean Drive-R of
5.81 (range = 4.86 to 6.71). Non-workaholics had a mean Enjoyment-R
score of 3.62 (range = 1.57 to 4.43) and a mean Drive-R score of 4.05
(range = 2.29 to 4.83).

Colleagues
Work colleagues of the workaholic group consisted of 12 males and 40
females. While Mann Whitney U tests indicated that none of the following differences were significant, workaholics' colleagues tended to be
female (n_w = 85 per cent, n_{nw} = 69 per cent), junior (n_w = 12 per cent,
n_{nw} = 27 per cent) and knew each other for less time (n_w = 12 per cent,
n_{nw} = 46 per cent) than non-workaholic colleagues. Most colleagues
worked in the same department as their corresponding worker (n_w = 85
per cent, n_{nw} = 81 per cent).

Partners
Of the partners, 16 lived with workaholics (12 male, 4 female) and 8 with
non-workaholics (5 male, 3 female). While Mann Whitney U tests indicated
that none of the following differences were significant, workaholics' partners tended to be older (M_w = 42.4, M_{nw} = 34.5) and in relationships longer
(M_w = 13.8, M_{nw} = 11.1) than non-workaholics' partners.

Content analysts
The three groups of content analysts (n = 3 members each) comprised nine
tertiary qualified people (2 male, 7 female), seven of whom were degree-
qualified psychologists, and two held tertiary qualifications in business
studies. Each group had a specific role; the first group simplified the raw
data into discrete concepts, the second group conducted a thematic analysis on the simplified raw data to produce clusters of statements, and the
third group cross-validated the two sets of data. None had particular
expertise in the area of workaholism.

Measures

Inductive
The qualitatitive, written question posed to workers, colleagues and partners was 'How would you describe someone who is workaholic?'

Deductive
The theoretically derived definition used as a comparison was deductively generated from prior literature reviews, theoretical critiques, and studies conducted on New Zealand working populations (cf. McMillan et al., 2001, 2002, 2003). This particular definition was selected as it had been previously validated on New Zealand samples. The definition was: (a) a personal reluctance to disengage from work, (b) a strong drive to work, (c) intense enjoyment of work, (d) a tendency to work or think about work, and (e) to do this any time and anywhere (McMillan et al., 2004).

Procedure

Step 1: generating raw data
Workers, colleagues and partners (n=132) returned their written responses directly to the researcher as part of a larger study (see McMillan and O'Driscoll, 2004).

Step 2: conceptual simplification
The first group of content analysts simplified the inductive data by subdividing the raw responses (which contained multiple themes) into discrete concepts. Instructions were: 'Here are some definitions of workaholism. Please break every response into single concepts.' Each definition of workaholism was reduced to phrases where only one idea was expressed. 'Agreement' was defined to have occurred where *all three* analysts concurred. The analysts reached 45 per cent initial agreements and 100 per cent agreements after discussion, and produced 298 final statements.

Step 3: thematic analysis
The second group of analysts clustered the 298 statements into seven themes. Instructions were: 'Here are some statements about workaholics. Please read all the statements and create 5–7 categories that capture the main themes expressed in the statements.' They reached 100 per cent final agreement and produced five final categories: (a) obsessive personal style, (b) driven by internal reasons, (c) time spent working and thinking about work, (d) work–leisure balance, and (e) work–relationships balance. The group emphasized that the 'driven' category represented a positive,

constructive aspect of workaholism, whereas the 'obsessive' category was intended to represent a less functional and ostensibly more negative aspect of workaholism.

Step 4: cross-validation

The third group of analysts matched the randomized list of statements generated by the first group ($n = 298$) with the categories generated by the second group ($n = 5$). Instructions were: 'Here are some statements about workaholics and some categories that they are likely to fit into. Please place each statement into the most suitable category.' After individually coding each statement, ($n = 162$ unanimous categorizations) they met as a group to discuss their differing decisions ($n = 136$ categorizations) with the researcher present as a data recorder, where 100 per cent final agreement was reached ($n = 298$ categorizations). The most frequently used category of classification by the third analyst group was time spent working or thinking about work (39 per cent), followed by obsessive personal style (22 per cent), which together accounted for the majority of definitions (61 per cent; see Figure 4.2). The remaining categories were used substantially less frequently: work–relationships balance was used 16 per cent of the time, driven to work by internal positive reasons was used 14 per cent, and, lastly, work–leisure balance was used only 9 per cent of the time.

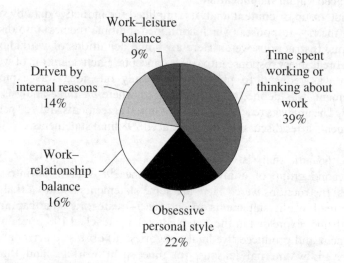

Figure 4.2   Pie chart depicting percentage of participants' statements categorized into each theme after cross-validation

Results

The final five categories proposed by the content analysts were: (a) obsessive personal style [that is, unable to stop, lack of control] (b) driven by internal (positive) reasons [such as passion, exceeding goals] (c) time spent working and thinking about work [that is, comparatively excessive], (d) work–leisure balance, and (e) work–relationships balance. In comparison, the theoretically derived (deductive) definition also comprised five aspects: (a) a personal reluctance to disengage from work, (b) a strong drive to work, (c) intense enjoyment of work, (d) a tendency to work or think about work, and (e) to do this any time and anywhere. These categories are presented in Table 4.2.

While much of contemporary workaholism research adopts the implicit assumption: *Enjoyment + Drive = Workaholism*, the (E+D) category in the

Table 4.2   Comparison of the deductive and inductive definitions of workaholism

Category number	Inductive (empirical) definition	Deductive (theoretical) definition
1	Obsessive personal style [i.e. unable to stop, lack of control, addicted, can't help it]	Personal reluctance to disengage from work
2	Driven by internal (positive) reasons [e.g. passion, satisfaction, focus, task orientations, developing competencies,	Driven to work
3	exceeding goals]	High enjoyment in work
4	Time spent working or thinking about work [i.e. comparatively excessive, in terms of quantity and quality]	Tendency to work or think about work
5	Work–leisure balance [i.e. chooses work over leisure time] Work–relationships balance [i.e. unclear boundaries between home life/ relationships and work life]	Tendency to work any time, anywhere

inductive data accounted for only one seventh (14 per cent) of the participants' definitions. In fact, the lay conceptualization suggests that workaholism comprises predominantly hours worked and thinking/talking about
work (these elements accounted for 39 per cent of their definition). Thus it
appears that a sizeable proportion of workaholism remained unexplained
by combining (E +D). Patently, we do not have clear evidence that a simplistic summing of enjoyment and drive fully accounts for workaholism.

Discussion of Data

The inductively generated definitions provided by participants hold some
interesting implications for workaholism research. Firstly, as outlined in
Table 4.2, the five inductively generated categories share considerable conceptual overlap with the five deductively generated (theoretically based)
categories. For instance, there are parallels between both statements in category one, which concern difficulty disengaging from work and an obsessive personal style that includes being unable to stop. There are also direct
overlaps between both statements in category four, which concern a tendency to work or think about work, and time spent working or thinking
about work. Both statements in category five (working any time, anywhere,
and an imbalance in leisure and relationships) also share a common theme,
although it is important to note that the content analysis differentiated
between leisure and relationships (see Table 4.2).

It is interesting, however, that two of the separate theoretical components of workaholism (Drive and Enjoyment) have been collapsed into one
category in the inductive definition (see Table 4.2). This is not a new
concept; Perez-Prada (1996) argued that the drive items of the (original)
WorkBAT were confounded with enjoyment themes. For instance, the item
'It is important to me to work hard, even when I do not enjoy what I am
doing' appeared to tap both constructs. This provides an interesting
hypothesis for future research.

Importantly, both the inductively generated (that is, qualitative) and
deductively generated (that is, quantitative) definitions are consistent with
the majority of existing theoretical literature. Firstly, neither data set
includes disturbances in health, happiness and relationships, as suggested
by Oates (1968). However, both definitions specify the structure and magnitude of workaholism. In particular, the present definitions encompass
the desire to work long and hard, as noted by Machlowitz (1980), and the
excessive involvement in work noted by Porter (1996). However, both
definitions are relatively operational as they specify *how* to generate the
dependent variable (workaholism). The data also gave qualified support to
the Scott et al. (1997) definition that included (a) discretionary time spent

working, (b) thinking about work when not at work, and (c) working beyond requirements, and Snir and Harpaz's (2004) definition involving time allocated to work activities and work thoughts. Overall, the present quantitative–qualitative definitions integrate and link several of the themes in the literature and, on this basis, provide an important foundation from which to conduct further research.

CONCLUSIONS: PRELIMINARY CONCEPTUAL MODEL

The apparent failings of contemporary research designs to substantiate the (E + D) proposition as the sole explanatory factor in workaholism prompt such questions as 'What is workaholism?' and challenge the notion that it is a unitary phenomenon. Perhaps, as Mudrack and Naughton (2001) suggested, the tendency to work or think about work is actually the essence of workaholism, while Enjoyment and Drive are merely antecedents that trigger the workaholic behaviour. Although Spence and Robbins' (1992) Work Involvement factor has repeatedly performed poorly in terms of psychometric qualities (it yields low internal consistency and is often saturated into the other two variables), it may capture some of this time-related aspect of workaholism. Clearly, our understanding of the antecedents and components of workaholism could benefit from further empirical enquiry. It is certainly feasible that Enjoyment and Drive are constructs that are related to workaholism, but whether they merely *describe* workaholic behaviour, as opposed to *explaining* its origins and causes, remains unknown. Therefore, it is feasible that Enjoyment and Drive are *antecedents* that trigger a repertoire of workaholic *behaviours* that consist of working, thinking and talking about work, striving for achievement and demonstrating a strong work ethic.

This raises the contention that perhaps researchers should abandon the unitary workaholism construct, much as they have done with Type A, and focus instead on studying enjoyment, drive and hours worked as separate constructs, albeit inter-related. In any event, it is apparent that the nature of workaholism remains unclear and further research is required to determine (a) whether the construct is unitary or multifaceted, (b) whether it has utility, and (c) whether it merely describes a set of behaviours that are triggered by the independent constructs of Enjoyment and Drive. Thus, workaholism may represent an abstract concept that acts as an umbrella for specific variables, rather than being a variable or construct in its own right. If this is the case, logic dictates that future research should explore Drive, Enjoyment, hours worked and hours thinking about work as specific manifestations of this umbrella concept, rather than subsuming them under one label.

It is conceivable that drive and an obsessive personal style are *antecedent traits* that interact with and are reinforced by enjoyment to produce *workaholic behaviour* that involves a tendency to work or think about work incessantly. This behaviour produces *consequences* that include working any time, anywhere. In turn, these consequences are likely to provide discriminative stimuli for further working. These propositions are modelled in Figure 4.3, which, it must be reiterated, is very tentative and intended to spur further research questions, rather than provide definitive answers about the nature of workaholism. Clearly, further testing is required to examine these propositions.

The working model yields several other potential hypotheses. For instance, the model implies that certain personality traits (such as Obsessiveness) precede workaholism. Furthermore, the reluctance to disengage from work is implied, but has not actually been measured – for instance, research taken 'at the point of disengaging from work' could elucidate the subtleties of this process. Does the person attempt to disengage

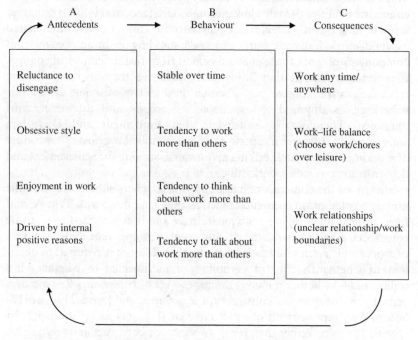

Figure 4.3   An integrated model of workaholism based on inductive–deductive data

several times before they succeed? Do they use certain cognitive tactics to help themselves disengage from work each day? Specifically, further theoretical development, hypothesis testing and structural equation modelling are required to ascertain the scientific and applied utility of this tentative model.

SUMMARY

Overall, the majority of workaholism data and definitions are quantitatively based and rooted in positivist, deductive paradigms. While some encouraging qualitative work has been published, it is largely anecdotal and remains untested by either scientific frameworks or peer review processes. The present comparison of an inductively and a deductively generated definition illustrates that both academics and the general public view workaholism in similar terms, involving (a) reluctance to disengage [obsessive style] (b) a strong drive to work [driven by positive reasons] (c) enjoyment in work, (d) a tendency to work or think about work [time spent working and thinking about work] that (d) occurs any time and anywhere [work–leisure and work–relationships balance]. This raises the interesting possibility that workaholism represents an *approach* to work, (that is, *intensity* of working), as opposed to a frequency, and may be observed as a *qualitative* characteristic that distinguishes workaholics from other workers.

As the present chapter has demonstrated, integrating both deductive/positivist and inductive/post-modernist epistemologies may provide substantial insight into the nature of, and mechanisms underlying, workaholism. Given that research on this construct has been conducted for four decades now, it is timely to leave behind the simplistic pen and paper studies and adopt more sophisticated research methodologies such as triangulated data sources, composite qualitatitive–quantitative designs, and epistemologies that elucidate the factors that perpetuate and maintain workaholism.

REFERENCES

Berg, B.L. (1995), *Qualitatitive Research Methods for the Social Sciences*, 2nd edn., Needham Heights, MA, USA: Allyn and Bacon.

Burke, R.J. (1999), 'Workaholism among women managers: work and life satisfactions and psychological well-being', *Equal Opportunities International*, **18** (7), 25–35.

Campbell, D.T. and Fiske, D.W. (1959), 'Convergent and discriminant validation by the multivariate–multimethod matrix', *Psychological Bulletin*, **56**, 81–105.

Clark, L.A., Livesley, W.J., Schroeder, M.L. and Irish, S.L. (1996), 'Convergence of two systems for assessing specific traits of personality disorder', *Psychological Assessment*, **8**, 294–303.

Clark, L.A., McEwen, J.L., Collard, L.M. and Hickok, L.G. (1993), 'Symptoms and traits of personality disorder: two new methods in their assessment', *Psychological Assessment*, **5**, 81–91.

Fassel, D. (1992), *Working Ourselves to Death*, London: HarperCollins.

Ivancevich, J.M. and Matteson, M.T. (1988), 'Application of the triangulation strategy to stress research', in J.J. Hurrell, L.R. Murphy, S.L. Sauter and C.L. Cooper (eds), *Issues and Developments in Research*, New York: Taylor and Francis, pp. 200–215.

Machlowitz, M.M. (1980), *Workaholics: Living with Them, Working with Them*, Reading, MA, US: Addison-Wesley.

McMillan, L.H.W. and O'Driscoll, M.P. (2004), 'Workaholism and health: implications for organisations', *Journal of Organizational Change Management*, **17** (5), 509–19.

McMillan, L.H.W., O'Driscoll, M.P. and Brady, E.C. (2004), 'The impact of workaholism on personal relationships', *British Journal of Guidance and Counselling*, **32** (2), 171–86.

McMillan, L.H.W., O'Driscoll, M.P. and Burke, R. (2003), 'Workaholism: a review of theory, research and future directions', in C.L. Cooper and I.T. Robertson (eds), *International Review of Industrial and Organizational Psychology*, **18**, 207–30, NY: John Wiley and Sons.

McMillan, L.H.W., O'Driscoll, M.P., Marsh, N.V. and Brady, E.C. (2001), 'Understanding workaholism: data synthesis, theoretical critique and future design strategies', *International Journal of Stress Management*, **8** (2), 69–91.

McMillan, L.H.W., Brady, E.C., O'Driscoll, M.P. and Marsh, N.V. (2002), 'A multifaceted validation study of Spence and Robbins' (1992) Workaholism Battery', *Journal of Occupational and Organizational Psychology*, **75**, 357–68.

Mudrack, P.E. (2004), 'Job involvement, obsessive-compulsive personality traits, and workaholic behavioural tendencies', *Journal of Organizational Change Management*, **17** (5), 490–508.

Mudrack, P.E. and Naughton, T.J. (2001), 'The assessment of workaholism as behavioral tendencies: scale development and preliminary empirical testing', *International Journal of Stress Management*, **8** (2), 93–111.

Oates, W.E. (1968), 'On being a "workaholic" (a serious jest)', *Pastoral Psychology*, **19**, 16–20.

Perez-Prada, E. (1996), 'Personality at work', unpublished doctoral dissertation, Saint Louis University. USA.

Porter, G. (1996), 'Organizational impact of workaholism: suggestions for researching the negative outcomes of excessive work', *Journal of Occupational Health Psychology*, **1**, 70–84.

Robinson, B.E. (1989), *Work Addiction: Hidden Legacies of Adult Children*, Florida, US: Health Communications.

Robinson, B.E. (1998), *Chained to the Desk: A Guidebook for Workaholics, their Partners and Children and the Clinicians who Treat them*, New York: New York University Press.

Robinson, B.E., Flowers, C. and Carroll, J. (2001), 'Work stress and marriage: a theoretical model examining the relationship between workaholism and marital cohesion', *International Journal of Stress Management*, **8** (2), 165–75.

Scott, K.S., Moore, K.S. and Miceli, M.P. (1997), 'An exploration of the meaning and consequences of workaholism', *Human Relations*, **50**, 287–314.

Snir, R. and Harpaz, I. (2004), 'Attitudinal and demographic antecedents of workaholism', *Journal of Organizational Change Management*, **17** (5), 520–36.

Spence, J.T. and Robbins, A.S. (1992), 'Workaholism: definition, measurement, and preliminary results', *Journal of Personality Assessment*, **58**, 160–78.

5. Understanding workaholism: the case for behavioral tendencies

Peter E. Mudrack

INTRODUCTION: UNTANGLING THE TANGLED WEB OF WORKAHOLISM

Workaholism is a concept that seems intuitively easy to understand, and the term is used regularly in everyday conversation. A workaholic obviously works 'too much' and is consumed with work to the exclusion of other activities. Implicit in workaholism is an element of free choice. Workaholics work more and invest more energy in work than is absolutely required. Workaholics, therefore, must do more than simply work 'a lot'. Their time spent at work must be, relatively speaking, optional rather than obligatory. If 80-hour work weeks are required on a job in order not to get fired, then someone who works 80 hours a week is not necessarily a workaholic. Any measure of workaholism, therefore, that is based largely on hours worked (for example, Snir and Harpaz, 2004) may be interesting and worthwhile, but also may not capture fully the notion of workaholism.

The preceding discussion suggests that workaholism is perhaps not as straightforward as it might seem at first glance. Whether someone who works 'a lot' can fairly be labeled a workaholic depends partly on the context in which work occurs (for example, the extent to which work is discretionary) and partly on the individual's attitude or approach to work. Persons who feel compelled to work in response to internal pressures (for example, to ward off feelings of guilt) (Spence and Robbins, 1992, p. 161) seem more likely candidates for the workaholism label than do persons for whom such feelings are absent.

Workaholism could seemingly include both attitudes and behaviors. As discussed above, if hours worked are insufficient by themselves as a behavioral indicator of workaholism, then what behaviors might qualify? Scott et al. (1997) identified three behavioral patterns in workaholism. Workaholics must spend discretionary time in work activities, must think about work when not at work, and must work beyond organizational or economic requirements. With regard to attitudes, Spence and Robbins (1992, p. 162) proposed that workaholics are highly involved in their work, feel driven to work, and tend not to enjoy work. Individual scores on these three workaholism components (the 'workaholic triad') can be used to construct profiles. A 'Workaholic' scores highly on work involvement and drive, but not on enjoyment. In contrast, 'Enthusiastic Workaholics' score highly on all three scales.[1]

Not all three of these attitudes may necessarily be relevant to workaholism, however. McMillan et al. (2002, p. 358), for example, seemingly utilized the behavioral perspective of Scott et al. (1997) to argue that workaholism is a pattern of behavior, and that work involvement, as an attitude, may not adequately represent workaholism. Indeed, these authors concluded that the work involvement scale should be eliminated altogether when assessing workaholism. Interestingly, McMillan et al. did not use the same logic when deciding to retain work enjoyment, also an attitude, as a component of workaholism. Using the rationale applied to work involvement, work enjoyment also seems of questionable relevance. Moreover, it is not entirely clear whether workaholism implies low enjoyment (Spence and Robbins, 1992) or high enjoyment (McMillan et al., 2002). Many workaholics may enjoy their work, while others may not (cf. Porter, 2001, p. 150).

Determining whether individuals enjoy work is undoubtedly meaningful on many levels. However, work enjoyment, whether high or low, is simply not a defining characteristic of workaholism. Spence and Robbins (1992, p. 161) defined this as a drive or compulsion to work emerging from internal pressures, and Scott et al. (1997) described three behavioral patterns. Work enjoyment is conspicuous by its absence in these definitions. Therefore, any study that assesses workaholism with a scale designed to measure work enjoyment has seemingly not assessed workaholism at all. Of the two scales retained by McMillan et al. (2002), only the Drive scale seems consistent with the conceptual definition of workaholism offered by Spence and Robbins.

Operationally, McMillan and colleagues classified employees as workaholics if they scored highly on both drive and enjoyment, and this implies (erroneously) that enjoying a job is a defining characteristic of workaholism. This approach seems to ignore evidence that many workaholics do *not* enjoy their jobs (Spence and Robbins, 1992), but more importantly has apparently led to research hypotheses that are of questionable value and make little sense (if work enjoyment is simply 'work enjoyment' and not 'workaholism'). Consider the second hypothesis advanced by McMillan et al. (2004, p. 173): 'People classified as workaholic will experience greater disturbances in close relationships than will non-workaholics.' Rephrasing this hypothesis to emphasize work enjoyment renders it of dubious relevance: 'People who enjoy their jobs will experience greater disturbances in close relationships than people who do not enjoy their jobs.' Consider also the second hypothesis put forth by McMillan and O'Driscoll (2004, p. 511): 'In comparison to non-workaholics, workaholics report poorer emotional health.' Slight rephrasing would alter this hypothesis to: 'In comparison to people who do not enjoy their jobs, people who enjoy their jobs report poorer emotional health.' Is it surprising to learn that neither of these hypotheses received empirical support? There seems to be no *a priori* reason to expect that people who enjoy their jobs would necessarily experience any negative outcomes, let alone relationship disturbances or poor health.

The purpose of this discussion is not to criticize the important work of McMillan and colleagues. Nonetheless, for workaholism research to move forward in a productive and fruitful manner, work enjoyment must not be used as a proxy for workaholism. The erroneous notion that work enjoyment partly defines workaholism is not unique to the research of McMillan and colleagues. Indeed, any study that uses the Workaholism Battery of Spence and Robbins (1992) automatically assesses workaholism with two scales that are conceptually independent of workaholism (that is, work involvement and work enjoyment). Some studies omit some of the original items (for example, Kanai and Wakabayashi, 2001), others use items emerging from only one of the subscales (for example, Joy in Work: Porter, 2001), and still others use all three scales but apparently none of the original items (for example, Buelens and Poelmans, 2004). Although it may be worth knowing that work enjoyment correlated positively and relatively strongly with job satisfaction, life satisfaction and purpose in life, and negatively and relatively strongly with job stress and emotional exhaustion (for example, Bonebright et al., 2000; Burke, 2001b; Burke and Koksal, 2002; Burke et al., 2004), such findings have no obvious connection to *workaholism*. Therefore, one characteristic of much workaholism research is that many ostensibly relevant results shed little light on the phenomenon in question.

Negative Aspects of Workaholism

Intuitively, workaholism seems, at least potentially, to have negative, harmful and deleterious aspects that have been noted in 'long-held clinical observations' (Robinson, 1999, p. 207). Naughton (1987) suggested that workaholics might be poor employees who focus on ritualized and time-consuming activities (for example, checking and rechecking completed work), rather than on potentially more urgent ones. Research using the Spence and Robbins (1992) measure (or similar measures), however, seems curiously unable to uncover much evidence that workaholism has *any* associated negative qualities. For example, 'workaholics' and 'non-workaholics' differed little on relationship disturbances (McMillan et al., 2004), emotional health (McMillan and O'Driscoll, 2004), or likelihood of being divorced (Burke, 2000a; Burke et al., 2003). In general, any negative results seem associated only with the Drive scale. For example, high drive was associated with high work–life conflict (Bonebright et al., 2000), psychosomatic symptoms (Burke, 2001a) and high job stress (Burke, 2001b).[2]

Robinson's (1999) Work Addiction Risk Test (WART) differs from the Spence and Robbins (1992) measure in its ability to generate more consistent negative results. Flowers and Robinson (2002) defined workaholism as the overindulgence in and preoccupation with work, often to the exclusion of health and relationships. Parenthetically, although Robinson (1999) was cited as the source for this definition, workaholism was not actually defined in this paper. Nonetheless, the 25 WART items emerged from symptoms of workaholism identified by clinicians and describe potentially undesirable aspects of workaholism. High scorers on the WART scale, for example, might tend to be impatient and irritable, to do several things at once, to feel guilty when not working, to have difficulty relaxing, and to invest more time and energy in work than in relationships. Some examples of potentially 'negative' results emerging from the WART scale are positive (and relatively strong) correlations with measures of anxiety, Type A Speed and Impatience (Robinson, 1999), job stress, work–nonwork conflict, exhaustion (Taris et al., 2005), symptoms of poor mental health, and reduced marital cohesion (Robinson et al., 2001).

One reasonable conclusion from this discussion is that Spence and Robbins' (1992) Workaholism Battery and Robinson's (1999) WART do not obviously assess the same underlying construct, are not necessarily alternative measures of workaholism, and thus cannot simply be substituted for each other in research applications. Investigators may need to think carefully about the conceptual implications of their choice of workaholism measure, because the measure used may profoundly affect the degree of hypothesis support. Although 'it is not surprising that joy in work was found to be positively related to levels of work and career satisfaction and higher levels of psychological health' (Burke, 1999a, p. 238), it would most definitely be surprising to learn that WART scores correlated positively with these variables.

Taris et al. (2005, pp. 39–40) concluded that only one WART subscale seems conceptually consistent with Scott et al.'s (1997) definition of workaholism. Even then, only two Compulsive Tendencies items specifically met this criterion (p. 47).[3] Other items seem only loosely connected (for example, staying busy, feeling guilty, hard to relax, hurried, multitasking). In fairness, of course, Flowers and Robinson (2002) defined workaholism as an overindulgence in and preoccupation with work. Post hoc attempts to make the WART scale items conform to the Scott et al. conceptualization seem somewhat unreasonable and inappropriate (although such attempts suggest how influential this conceptualization has been). None-theless, the WART measure (and even its Compulsive Tendencies subscale) seems to overlap little with this widely accepted view of workaholism.

To summarize, two measures are used regularly in workaholism research. The Spence and Robbins (1992) measure focuses on work attitudes, and includes two subscales that may be inconsistent with workaholism (work involvement, work enjoyment). The Robinson (1999) WART measure addresses a preoccupation with work and uncovers evidence that work-aholism may have negative side effects, but also may partly assess Type A behavior (for example, impatience, irritability, perfectionism, time pres-sure). A third measure, however, used the influential behaviorally-focused definition of Scott et al. (1997) as its starting point, and this is the subject of the following section.

WORKAHOLISM AS BEHAVIORAL TENDENCIES

Mudrack and Naughton (2001) developed workaholism survey items based on Scott et al.'s (1997) conceptual definition that identified three behavioral patterns: (1) spending discretionary time in work activities; (2) thinking about work when not at work; and (3) working beyond organizational or economic requirements. No other workaholism measure has clearly and unambiguously used this definition as its basis, in spite of the frequency with which the Scott et al. paper is cited. Perhaps one reason for this is the difficulties associated with developing appropriate items. These cannot refer to obligatory work activities, and must imply an element of free choice. As discussed earlier, hours worked, by itself, seems an imperfect indicator of workaholism at best (as does how hard one works, and how intently one focuses on work). Hard-working and focused employees are not necessarily workaholics if they forget about work when not at work, at least according to the Scott et al. conceptualization.

Survey items could simply ask directly whether respondents work more than absolutely necessary, or spend time on work activities away from work. However, workaholics may rationalize and claim that their work behavior is not really optional (cf. Scott et al., 1997; Schaef and Fassel, 1988). McMillan et al. (2004, p. 173) argued that the denial hypothesis 'has been given more weight than it perhaps deserves', but also admitted that 'data have not been forthcoming' (p. 173) on the extent to which work-aholics deny their workaholism. Given the mere possibility of denial, however, Mudrack and Naughton (2001) sought to minimize its potential impact on survey responses. They did this by asking about specific work activities (not obviously suggesting 'workaholism') instead of generally asking whether work behaviors were optional ('workaholics' in denial might simply say 'no').

Ideally, researchers who design survey items would have detailed knowledge about specific work contexts that would enable them to know which activities were technically necessary and which were discretionary (and thus a possible indicator of workaholism). In spite of its intuitive appeal, this approach contains numerous pitfalls. Detailed knowledge about a specific environment is not always easy to obtain. Survey items that refer to context-specific work activities would probably require substantial modification before they could be applied in other settings, and thus results from different settings might not be comparable. Researchers should not be required to 'reinvent the wheel' and develop their own items (otherwise, the original items have little practical value). Moreover, even in the same work setting, a necessary activity for Employee A might very well be discretionary for Employee B. If both employees engaged regularly in this activity and responded identically on their surveys, workaholism would be suggested only in Employee B.

If context-specific survey items are undesirable, then perhaps items should refer to activities that seem discretionary across multiple contexts. All employees are obligated to do their jobs and execute assigned work. Few employees, however, are required to initiate work and think of ways to do work 'better'. Moreover, few employees (even supervisors) are required to monitor the work activities of other employees actively and intrusively. These notions of thinking about how to do work 'better' and intrusive interference in the work of others seem broadly relevant and applicable, and consistent with the behaviorally-focused definition of workaholism (Scott et al., 1997). Such activities go beyond economic or organizational requirements, are largely discretionary, and are demanding enough to make employees liable to think about work in their spare time.

Although generally operationalized as an *intrapersonal* phenomenon, there may be a somewhat overlooked *interpersonal* component in workaholism. Workaholic tendencies certainly have the potential to affect others profoundly. Workaholics have an intense dedication to work that few of their peers can match, and this may lead to relations that are adversarial or even hostile (Oates, 1971; Scott et al., 1997). For instance, Machlowitz (1980) described the pressure cooker atmosphere that workaholics often create for the people around them, and their tendencies to meddle in the work of others and look over their shoulders (see also Scott et al., 1997; Seybold and Salomone, 1994). Porter (2001) specifically examined connections between workaholic tendencies and signs of stress in co-workers. In short, workaholic individuals may affect others negatively, and be unwilling to allow others to work without interference. This controlling element to workaholism is captured in the Control of Others scale described below. Thinking about how to do work better is reflected in the Non-Required Work scale.

Item Content

Mudrack and Naughton (2001) created eight survey items to assess workaholism as behavioral tendencies. Instructions to respondents asked them to 'please indicate how much time and energy you spend on each of the job related activities listed below. Use the following scale: 1 = None or not applicable; 2 = Little time and energy spent; 3 = Moderate time and energy spent; 4 = A considerable amount of time and energy spent; 5 = A very large amount of time and energy spent. For your job, how much time and energy do you now spend on the following activities?'

The four *Non-Required Work* items asked about time and energy spent on: (1) 'Thinking of ways to improve the *quality* of work provided to customers and/or co-workers'; (2) 'Thinking of ways to improve the *quantity* of work provided to customers and/or co-workers'; (3) 'Thinking of ways to be more productive'; (4) 'Taking responsibility for initiating assignments and projects'. The *Control of Others* scale reflects the interpersonal and intrusive nature of workaholism, and also contained four items: (1) 'Fixing problems created by other people'; (2) 'Checking on the accuracy of other people's work'; (3) 'Taking responsibility for the work of other people'; (4) 'Dealing with crisis situations'. As discussed above, few (if any) employees would be required to spend considerable time and energy on such activities, which makes these plausible behavioral indicators of workaholism. With regard to crises, workaholics may create these in order to spend more time at work and to make it more 'interesting'. Similarly, those who enjoy fighting fires might start fires or fan the flames of existing fires (Machlowitz, 1980, pp. 56–7).

In the section immediately below, relationships proposed by Mudrack and Naughton (2001) between the two workaholism scales and various work attitudes are discussed. Following that is a section pertaining to connections between workaholism and personality traits.

WORKAHOLIC BEHAVIORS AND WORK ATTITUDES

Job Involvement

Despite the existence of well-established measures of job involvement, Spence and Robbins (1992) developed their own eight-item scale. Scores on this measure tended to associate positively with the 'workaholism triad' scales (for example, Burke, 1999a, 1999b; Burke et al., 2004). How might job involvement relate to the two behaviorally-focused workaholism scales? Job involvement refers to the degree to which individuals psychologically identify with their present job (Kanungo, 1982), and highly involved persons seem both disinterested in non-work activities (for example, Cohen, 1995; Ettington, 1998; Porter, 1996; Rosin and Korabik, 1995) and inclined to engage in organizational citizenship behaviors such as helping others (Cohen, 1999; Hoffi-Hofstetter and Mannheim, 1999). Such results suggest that highly involved individuals might be inclined both to think about their jobs when away from work (given their relative disinterest in nonwork activities) and to 'assist' others on the job (that is, attempt to exert control over others). Mudrack and Naughton (2001) thus anticipated positive relationships between job involvement and both Non-Required Work and Control of Others. Mudrack (2004) also suggested that the relationship between job involvement and Non-Required Work might be moderated by various obsessive-compulsive personality traits. The rationale behind this proposal will be addressed later.

Job Satisfaction

As discussed earlier, the extent to which workaholic individuals enjoy their work seems an open question. Some workaholics, even if they are in denial or only rationalizing, may very well love their work. Others, however, may persist in their work grimly in spite of an absence of satisfaction or fun. Research with the 'workaholic triad' has typically reported weak relationships at best between work enjoyment and the other workaholism components (Burke, 1999a, 1999b; Spence and Robbins, 1992). Mudrack and Naughton (2001) did not expect clear relationships between their workaholism measures and either job satisfaction or self-reports of fun at work.

Job Stress

The potentially negative and harmful aspects of workaholism suggest possible connections with job stress. Indeed, drive scores generally correlate positively and relatively strongly with measures of stress (Burke, 2000b, 2001b; Spence and Robbins, 1992). High scorers on the WART measure (and its Compulsive Tendencies subscale) also seem stressed. They tend to perceive high job demands and also to be exhausted at work (Taris et al., 2005). Nonetheless, there seems no logical reason to expect that thinking about ways to perform one's job better would necessarily be stressful. On the other hand, high scorers on the Control of Others scale are involved in problems and crises at work. Although perhaps self-created (for example, Machlowitz, 1980), these certainly seem stressful, as do tendencies to intrude on the work of others (which may provoke hostile reactions). Mudrack and Naughton (2001) proposed a positive relationship between job stress and Control of Others.

Work–nonwork Conflict

Conflict between the work and nonwork spheres of life might be another potentially negative consequence of workaholism. Scores on both the Drive scale and the WART measure tend to correlate positively and relatively strongly with work–nonwork conflict (Bonebright et al., 2000; Taris et al., 2005). Employees who attempt to control others at work and who deal regularly with crises seem likely candidates to be irritable at home and too tired for other activities. Mudrack and Naughton (2001) thus expected a positive relationship between work–nonwork conflict and Control of Others, but no clear relationship with Non-Required Work. Simply thinking about how to do one's job better seems unlikely to provoke irritability and fatigue.

Role Conflict

Role conflict involves a sense that work activities should be done differently, and that doing work 'properly' may involve defying existing policies and rules. One manifestation of role conflict may be active intrusion in the work of others and a belief that the ideal person to be in charge is oneself. Employees who attempt to control others at work seem to be overstepping their authority (that is, they are playing a role that conflicts with their assigned role). Mudrack and Naughton (2001) thus predicted that role conflict would correlate positively with Control of Others. On the other hand, role conflict seems unlikely to be associated with simply thinking about one's job.

WORKAHOLIC BEHAVIORS AND PERSONALITY TRAITS

Need for Dominance and Self-monitoring

The Control of Others scale has clear interpersonal implications, and thus may be associated with personality traits relevant to relationships with others. Mudrack and Naughton (2001) examined two such traits, dominance and self-monitoring, and expected both to relate positively to Control of Others. Dominant individuals assume leadership and influence roles, and are controlling (Jackson, 1984; Steers and Braunstein, 1976). High self-monitors are keenly aware of moods and reactions, and will alter their own behavior to elicit others' approval. As attempts to control the work of others might be interpreted negatively, high self-monitoring might increase the success of such attempts and thus be valuable.

Need for Achievement, Affiliation, Autonomy

Mudrack and Naughton (2001) expected scores on three traits to be associated positively with scores on the Non-Required Work scale. High need achievers, for example, seem generally inclined to go above and beyond the call of duty at work. Doing 'unnecessary' work and thinking of ways to do work 'better' seems a solitary and independent activity that might have great appeal for someone with high autonomy needs. Taking the initiative on 'unnecessary' but perhaps important work might garner the appreciation of others, and thus help to satisfy someone with high affiliation needs. Workaholics may need to be needed (Baechler, 1996).

INVESTIGATING THE ORIGINS OF WORKAHOLIC BEHAVIORS

Naughton (1987) addressed the origins of workaholism and proposed that high job involvement combined with an obsessive-compulsive personality might help to trigger workaholic tendencies. Highly involved employees seem generally inclined to *want* to perform non-required work, but obsessive-compulsive traits may be the deciding factor that tips the balance toward *actually doing* more work than necessary. Mudrack (2004) proposed that high job involvement coupled with high scores on the specific traits of obstinacy, orderliness, rigidity and superego (Lazare et al., 1966, 1970; Pollak, 1979) might produce high scores on the Non-Required Work scale. As obsessive-compulsive traits have few obvious interpersonal implications, these may not be relevant to the Control of Others scale.

Obstinacy

Obstinacy is associated with a stubborn, opinionated and defiant nature that is (perhaps unreasonably) convinced of the correctness of one's views and actions. Highly job involved persons who are also highly obstinate may spend time thinking of ways to perform work 'better' because they feel unusually qualified for this task. Involved employees who are less obstinate seem less intensely committed to the notion that they personally are obliged to improve their jobs.

Orderliness

Before employees are free to engage in non-required work, they may need to complete assigned duties. Orderliness suggests tendencies to be precise, methodical and well-organized, and highly orderly persons are likely to be 'on top of' work assignments. This trait, combined with high job involvement, may allow employees the time and energy needed to think of ways to do jobs 'better'. Less orderly, but highly involved, employees might lack the time or energy to perform non-required tasks.

Rigidity

Individuals who follow routines, dislike change, and are inflexibly 'set in their ways' are rigid. When coupled with high job involvement, high rigidity may produce employees who continue to perform non-required duties even when changing circumstances such as pressing deadlines might argue for postponing these. Highly involved employees who are less rigid seem more inclined to abandon their discretionary duties in the light of changing conditions that make required tasks more salient.

Superego

High superego scorers are suspicious of pleasure, believe themselves to be highly ethical, and are guided by conscience. Highly involved employees who have completed assigned tasks are now faced with the 'problem' of unstructured free time that could easily be circumvented by performing more work. Thus high job involvement coupled with high superego might produce tendencies to engage in non-required tasks. Highly involved employees without this acute sense of morality, on the other hand, seem less likely to feel compelled to fill unstructured free time with more work.

In summary, Mudrack (2004) predicted that the interaction between job involvement and four obsessive-compulsive traits (obstinacy, orderliness, rigidity, superego) would be significantly associated with employee tendencies to engage in non-required work. Specifically, such tendencies were predicted to be highest in the presence of high scores on both job involvement and obsessive-compulsive traits. Stated differently, the positive relationship between job involvement and Non-Required Work should be stronger when obsession-compulsion is high rather than low.

METHOD

Mudrack and Naughton (2001) administered self-report surveys to 278 adults who attended classes in an evening MBA program at Wayne State University in Detroit (Michigan, USA). All respondents worked full-time at paying jobs in a variety of companies (5.2 years with their current employer on average). Mean age in this sample of 163 men and 115 women was 29.9 years. Most respondents were currently married (162 married or equivalent, 116 not married) and many supervised other employees (127 managers, 151 non-managers).

All respondents completed the two workaholism scales, the measures of work attitudes, and the obsessive-compulsive personality traits. A subset of these respondents ($n = 183$) from four separate class sections completed the other personality measures (for example, self-monitoring). Details about the measures and sample survey items are available in Table 5.1. Self-monitoring and the needs for achievement, autonomy and affiliation featured a *true–false* response format (a 'false' response received zero points, and a 'true' response received one point). All other measures (except workaholism) appeared in a seven-point response format ranging from *strongly disagree* (one point) to *strongly agree* (seven points), with higher scores suggesting higher levels of the variable in question.

Results

The two workaholism scales developed by Mudrack and Naughton (2001) had acceptable levels of internal consistency ($\alpha = .74$ for Non-Required Work and $\alpha = .82$ for Control of Others), and were moderately correlated ($r = .25$, $p < .001$). Briggs and Cheek (1986) suggested that an optimal inter-item correlation within survey items lies between .20 and .40. Below this range, a single total score is unable to represent the complexity of the items adequately. Above this range, the items seem overly redundant. The mean item correlations of .41 for Non-Required Work and .37 for Control of Others are somewhat high, but nonetheless seem adequate. Both scales correlated positively, but relatively weakly, with respondent estimates of hours worked (defined broadly as hours spent per week engaged in job/career related activities, including time spent at the office, time spent traveling to/from work, time spent working at home on job activities, and time spent in graduate school activities).

Table 5.2 provides correlations between the two workaholism scales and the other variables assessed. Control of Others scores correlated positively, significantly, and relatively strongly with four work attitudes: job involvement, job stress, work–nonwork conflict and role conflict. Correlations

Table 5.1   Sample survey items

Job Involvement, Nine Items (Paterson and O'Driscoll, 1990; α = .83)
I am very much involved personally in my job.
I live, eat, and breathe my job.

Job Satisfaction, Three Items (Hackman and Lawler, 1971; α = .79)
Generally speaking, I am satisfied with my job.
I frequently think of quitting my job. (scoring reversed)

Fun At Work, Four Items (Mudrack and Naughton, 2001; α = .76)
I have fun at work.
I find very little to laugh about at work. (scoring reversed)

Job Stress, Four Items (Motowidlo et al. 1986; α = .86)
I feel a great deal of stress because of my job.
Very few stressful things happen to me at work. (scoring reversed)

Work–Nonwork Conflict, Eight Items (Kopelman et al., 1983; α = .88)
Because my work is demanding, at times I am irritable at home.
After work, I come home too tired to do some of the things I'd like to do.

Role Conflict, Eight Items (Rizzo et al., 1970; α = .80)
I have to do things at work that should be done differently.
I often have to buck a rule or policy in order to carry out an assignment at work.

Achievement, Sixteen Items, Personality Research Form E (Jackson, 1984; α = .74)
I enjoy difficult work.
I try to work just hard enough to get by. (scoring reversed)

Affiliation, Sixteen Items, Personality Research Form E (Jackson, 1984; α = .72)
People consider me to be quite friendly.
Sometimes I have to make a real effort to be sociable. (scoring reversed)

Autonomy, Sixteen Items, Personality Research Form E (Jackson, 1984; α = .69)
I would like to have a job in which I didn't have to answer to anyone.
My greatest desire is to be independent and free.

Dominance, Five Items (Steers and Braunstein, 1976; α = .80)
I strive to be 'in command' when I am working in a group.
I avoid trying to influence those around me to see things my way. (scoring reversed)

Self-monitoring, Eighteen Items (Snyder and Gangestad, 1986; α = .70)
I can only argue for ideas which I already believe. (scoring reversed)
I'm not always the person I appear to be.

Obstinacy, Seven Items (Lazare et al., 1966, 1970; α = .52)
I have strong opinions on many subjects.
I tend to be stubborn about things I consider important.

Orderliness, Seven Items (Lazare et al., 1966, 1970; α = .74)
I am systematic and methodical in my daily life.
Everything I do must be precise and accurate.

Table 5.1   (continued)

Rigidity, Seven Items (Lazare et al., 1966, 1970; α = .63)
I am usually consistent in my behavior, go about my work in the same way and frequent the same routes.
I am a creature of habit. I can even endure monotony without fretting.

Superego, Seven Items (Lazare et al., 1966, 1970; α = .76)
I think that I have a more rigorous standard of right and wrong than most people.
I carry a strict conscience with me wherever I go.

Table 5.2   Correlations involving non-required Work and Control of Others

Variables	1	2
Non-required Work (1)	–	–
Control of Others (2)	.25***	–
Job Involvement	.18**	.31***
Job Satisfaction	.13*	−.10*
Fun at Work	.02	−.13*
Job Stress	.15**	.49***
Work–nonwork Conflict	.19***	.38***
Role Conflict	.10*	.41***
Hours Worked	.20***	.14*
Achievement Needs	.29***	.17*
Autonomy Needs	.23**	−.03
Affiliation Needs	.26***	.10
Dominance Needs	.20**	.35***
Self-monitoring	.06	.32***
Obstinacy	.05	.16**
Orderliness	.22**	.04
Rigidity	−.16**	.08
Superego	.12*	.10*

Note: * $p < .05$; ** $p < .01$; *** $p < .001$.

involving Non-Required Work, although positive and significant, were considerably weaker. Neither workaholism scale correlated strongly with job satisfaction or fun at work. As expected, Control of Others correlated positively with dominance needs and self-monitoring. Non-Required Work correlated positively with dominance, achievement, affiliation and autonomy needs (as well as orderliness). These findings were consistent with theoretical expectations and provide evidence of 'importance' (Briggs and Cheek, 1986) in the workaholic behaviors scales (that is, different patterns of relationships with other variables of interest). Moreover, 'negative' results tend to cluster in the Control of Others scale (for example, high positive correlations with stress and work–nonwork conflict).

In the full sample, job involvement and Non-Required Work correlated modestly ($r = .18$). Among high obsessive-compulsive trait scorers alone, however, this relationship was clearly stronger: high obstinacy ($r = .29, p < .001, n = 138$); high orderliness ($r = .36, p < .001, n = 149$); high rigidity ($r = .28, p < .01, n = 147$); high superego ($r = .24, p < .01, n = 146$). In contrast, correlations between job involvement and Non-Required Work were notably weaker among low scorers: obstinacy ($r = .03, n = 140, ns$); orderliness ($r = -.03, n = 129, ns$); rigidity ($r = .11, n = 131, ns$); superego ($r = .07, n = 132, ns$). These results suggest that at least one aspect of workaholism may be attributable to a combination of high job involvement with an obsessive-compulsive personality (Naughton, 1987).

DISCUSSION

Although its meaning seems almost obvious, the concept of workaholism is surprisingly difficult to pin down precisely. Does workaholism refer to attitudes or behaviors? Which specific attitudes or behaviors are most relevant? Do existing measures adequately capture the meaning of workaholism?

The measure that most closely corresponds to the idea of workaholism as attitudes is the Workaholism Battery of Spence and Robbins (1992). This paper recommends an immediate moratorium on the use of this measure (at least in its present form), which has done little to advance our understanding of workaholism. Two of its three scales (work involvement and work enjoyment) are simply not relevant (at least not directly). The dubious relevance of work involvement has been recognized elsewhere. As no definition of workaholism refers even obliquely to work enjoyment (or to high enjoyment specifically), it seems surprising that much research explicitly regards this as a critical component of workaholism.

Many researchers construct profiles based on high and low scores on the 'workaholism triad'. If two of three scales are not relevant to workaholism, then this activity seems rather pointless. Beyond this, these profiles also seem unnecessarily complicated (that is, not parsimonious), difficult to interpret easily, of questionable practical value, and to shed little light on the phenomenon of workaholism.[4] However, the notion of profiles should not be discarded altogether. These may be simpler than typically represented, with one profile (pattern of relationships) occurring when work enjoyment is high and another when it is low. Stated differently, work enjoyment may be relevant to workaholism as a moderator variable. As a specific illustration, consider the positive relationship between drive scores and job stress (Burke, 2000b, 2001b; Spence and Robbins, 1992). Work enjoyment may act as a buffer that helps to insulate a highly driven person from experiencing the full negative effects of stress. Therefore, the afore-mentioned positive relationship seems likely to be stronger when enjoyment is low rather than high. As a general principle, parsimony is prized in scientific pursuits. Eight distinct profiles emerge from high and low 'worka-holism triad' scores. The approach to profiling advocated here is clearly more parsimonious, as only two distinct profiles are produced (some highly driven persons enjoy their work, and others do not).[5] Researchers who have used the Workaholism Battery should consider re-analyzing these data using work enjoyment as a moderator variable.

Additional study of the Work Addiction Risk Test (WART) of Robinson (1999) seems warranted in order to determine its proper role in the context of workaholism research. Conceptually, this measure seems partly to reflect Type A behavior, and thus may not completely capture the notion of workaholism. Nonetheless, the WART measure seems generally relevant, and is capable of producing results suggesting that workaholism may have some associated negative qualities.

This paper made a case for the assessment of workaholism as behavioral tendencies. The measures developed by Mudrack and Naughton (2001) emerged directly from the influential definition of Scott et al. (1997). In this view, workaholics must work during discretionary time, must think about work when away from work, and must work beyond any financial or job-related requirements. Two sets of behaviors consistent with this conceptual framework were engaging in non-required work (primarily thinking of ways to do work 'better') and intruding on and attempting to control the work of others. One interesting feature of these survey items is that work-aholism is not obviously being investigated at all. Therefore, any response biases associated with denial of workaholic tendencies might be circum-vented. Moreover, these workaholic behaviors seem broadly applicable and are not relevant only to specific contexts (otherwise the survey items would have limited value).

Mudrack and Naughton (2001) argued that few employees would be obligated to spend much time and energy thinking of ways to perform work 'better' or in initiating projects. Therefore, persons who *do* behave in such ways may be manifesting workaholic tendencies, and this was assessed with the Non-Required Work scale. High scorers take responsibility for initiat-ing work and spend time thinking of ways to be more productive and to improve the quality and quantity of work. Such activities seem to have few negative implications – they can be performed anywhere, are solitary and independent, and seem neither demanding nor stressful. In fact, employees who are performing such work may appear to be doing nothing more than daydreaming. High scorers on this scale tended to have high achievement needs (consistent with the driven nature of workaholics), high autonomy needs (consistent with the solitary nature of this work) and high affiliation needs (consistent with the need for workaholics to feel needed).

What 'causes' workaholism? Although multiple explanations seem possible (cf. McMillan et al., 2001), the results reported here suggest that one facet of workaholism may occur when high job involvement combines with an obsessive-compulsive personality (Naughton, 1987). Examples of relevant obsessive-compulsive traits are obstinacy, orderliness, rigidity and superego (high morality). Non-Required Work scores by themselves correlated positively with job involvement. However, among employees who (relatively speaking) were highly stubborn, orderly and well-organized, rigid and set in their ways, and convinced of their inherent morality, the aforementioned positive correlation was much stronger. Although additional research is needed on the origins of workaholism, such results represent some first steps on this path of discovery.

Mudrack and Naughton (2001) also claimed that few employees (even supervisors) would technically be required to spend considerable time and energy monitoring other employees to make sure that work was performed 'correctly'. Thus, persons who do such things may also be manifesting workaholic tendencies, and this was assessed with the Control of Others scale. High scorers interfere in the work of others; for example, they fix others' problems and take responsibility for others' work. Such behaviors emphasize the interpersonal and potentially negative aspects of workaholism. Indeed, Control of Others scores correlated positively with stress, work–nonwork conflict and role conflict, and also with dominance needs (consistent with desires to control others), self-monitoring and job involvement. Although research has uncovered few negative implications of high job involvement, highly involved employees do seem inclined to intrude on the work of others.

Briggs and Cheek (1986) addressed the notion of 'importance' within subscales of a potentially unitary construct. Evidence of importance includes different patterns of relationships involving the two workaholism subscales. Although Control of Others scores correlated relatively strongly with job stress ($r = .49$), work–nonwork conflict ($r = .38$) and role conflict ($r = .41$), no correlations involving Non-Required Work exceeded absolute .20. Non-Required Work scores correlated much more strongly with needs for achievement ($r = .29$), affiliation ($r = .26$) and autonomy

($r = .23$) than did Control of Others. Preliminary evidence therefore suggests that these workaholism scales may be 'important'. Obviously, however, more research is needed. Do these scales adequately capture the notion of workaholism? Are there other relevant workaholic behaviors that should be considered? How do these scales relate to existing workaholism measures, and do they 'perform better' (for example, provide stronger support for hypothesized relationships)? These seem open questions that await more definitive answers. In the meantime, however, these scales suggest a possible path through the 'tangled web' of workaholism (described at the outset) and offer hope of achieving greater understanding of this significant phenomenon.

NOTES

1. The attempt to classify workaholic individuals into types has a long history. Oates (1971), for example, identified five types of workaholics, while Machlowitz (1980) recognized four types.
2. This and other findings seem unnecessarily difficult to interpret, as high scores on the Drive scale suggested low drive (Burke, 2001b, p. 2344). Thus job stress correlated positively with drive scores (Burke, 2001b), with high scores on both suggesting low stress and low drive. Psychosomatic symptoms correlated negatively with the Drive scale (Burke, 2001a). Seemingly, high scores on symptoms suggested more symptoms or higher intensity symptoms, whereas high drive scores suggested low drive. In general, for ease of interpretation, higher scores on a variable should reflect 'more' rather than 'less'. Adding to the confusion is that scoring of variables varied across studies. For example, in findings from the same data set, Joy in Work correlated both positively ($r = .20$; Burke, 2001a) and negatively ($r = -.20$; Burke, 2001b) with a measure of Beliefs and Fears.
3. These were 'I find myself continuing to work after my co-workers have called it quits' and 'I spend more time working than on socializing with friends, on hobbies, or on leisure activities'.
4. The literature is filled with findings such as the following: Enthusiastic Workaholics (high scorers on all three variables) did not differ from non-workaholics (a label that combined three separate profiles) on life satisfaction, but scored higher than Non-Enthusiastic Workaholics; that is, high involvement and drive, but low enjoyment (Bonebright et al., 2000). Such findings lack parsimony and seem difficult to interpret easily and succinctly.
5. This recommended approach to profile construction seems consistent with early thinking by Machlowitz (1980) and Oates (1971), who attempted to identify different types of *workaholics*. In contrast, profiles derived from the Workaholism Battery seek to classify *everyone*; that is, workaholics and non-workaholics alike. Four out of eight possible 'types' emerging from this approach have low scores on at least two dimensions.

REFERENCES

Baechler, M. (1996), 'I'm Mary, and I'm a workaholic', *Inc.*, **18** (5), 29–30.
Bonebright, C.A., Clay, D.L. and Ankenmann, R.D. (2000), 'The relationship of workaholism with work–life conflict, life satisfaction, and purpose in life', *Journal of Counseling Psychology*, **47**, 469–77.

Briggs, S.R. and Cheek, J.M. (1986), 'The role of factor analysis in the development and evaluation of personality scales', *Journal of Personality*, **54**, 106–48.

Buelens, M. and Poelmans, S.A.Y. (2004), 'Enriching the Spence and Robbins' typology of workaholism: demographic, motivational and organizational correlates', *Journal of Organizational Change Management*, **17**, 440–58.

Burke, R.J. (1999a), 'It's not how hard you work but how you work hard: evaluating workaholism components', *International Journal of Stress Management*, **6**, 225–39.

Burke, R.J. (1999b), 'Workaholism in organizations: measurement validation and replication', *International Journal of Stress Management*, **6**, 45–55.

Burke, R.J. (2000a), 'Workaholism and divorce', *Psychological Reports*, **86**, 219–20.

Burke, R.J. (2000b), 'Workaholism in organizations: psychological and physical well-being consequences', *Stress Medicine*, **16**, 11–16.

Burke, R.J. (2001a), 'Predictors of workaholism components and behaviors', *International Journal of Stress Management*, **8**, 113–27.

Burke, R.J. (2001b), 'Workaholism components, job satisfaction, and career progress', *Journal of Applied Social Psychology*, **31**, 2339–56.

Burke, R.J. and Koksal, H. (2002), 'Workaholism among a sample of Turkish managers and professionals: an exploratory study', *Psychological Reports*, **91**, 60–68.

Burke, R.J., Burgess, Z. and Oberklaid, F. (2003), 'Workaholism and divorce among Australian psychologists', *Psychological Reports*, **93**, 91–2.

Burke, R.J., Richardsen, A.M. and Mortinussen, M. (2004), 'Workaholism among Norwegian managers', *Journal of Organizational Change Management*, **17**, 459–70.

Cohen, A. (1995), 'An examination of the relationships between work commitment and nonwork domains', *Human Relations*, **48**, 239–63.

Cohen, A. (1999), 'The relation between commitment forms and work outcomes in Jewish and Arab culture', *Human Relations*, **54**, 371–91.

Ettington, D.R. (1998), 'Successful career plateauing', *Journal of Vocational Behavior*, **52**, 72–88.

Flowers, C.P. and Robinson, B. (2002), 'A structural and discriminant analysis of the Work Addiction Risk Test', *Educational and Psychological Measurement*, **62**, 517–26.

Hackman, J.R. and Lawler, E.E., III (1971), 'Employee reactions to job characteristics', *Journal of Applied Psychology*, **55**, 259–86.

Hoffi-Hofstetter, H. and Mannheim, B. (1999), 'Managers' coping resources, perceived organizational patterns, and responses during organizational recovery from decline', *Journal of Organizational Behavior*, **20**, 665–85.

Jackson, D.N. (1984), *Personality Research Form Manual*, 3rd edn, Port Huron, MI: Research Psychologists Press.

Kanai, A. and Wakabayashi, M. (2001), 'Workaholism among Japanese blue-collar employees', *International Journal of Stress Management*, **8**, 129–45.

Kanungo, R.N. (1982), 'Measurement of job and work involvement', *Journal of Applied Psychology*, **67**, 341–9.

Kopelman, R.E., Greenhaus, J.H. and Connolly, T.F. (1983), 'A model of work, family and interrole conflict: a construct validation study', *Organizational Behavior and Human Performance*, **32**, 198–215.

Lazare, A., Klerman, G.L. and Armor, D.J. (1966), 'Oral, obsessive and hysterical personality patterns', *Archives of General Psychiatry*, **14**, 624–30.

Lazare, A., Klerman, G.L. and Armor, D.J. (1970), 'Oral, obsessive and hysterical personality patterns: replication of factor analysis in an independent sample', *Journal of Psychiatric Research*, **7**, 275–90.

Machlowitz, M. (1980), *Workaholics: Living with Them, Working with Them*, Reading, MA: Addison-Wesley.

McMillan, L.H.W. and O'Driscoll, M.P. (2004), 'Workaholism and health: implications for organizations', *Journal of Organizational Change Management*, **17**, 509–19.

McMillan, L.H.W., O'Driscoll, M.P. and Brady, E.C. (2004), 'The impact of workaholism on personal relationships', *British Journal of Guidance and Counselling*, **32**, 171–86.

McMillan, L.H.W., O'Driscoll, M.P., Marsh, N.V. and Brady, E.C. (2001), 'Understanding workaholism: data synthesis, theoretical critique, and future design strategies', *International Journal of Stress Management*, **8**, 69–91.

McMillan, L.H.W., Brady, E.C., O'Driscoll, M.P. and Marsh, N.V. (2002), 'A multi-faceted validation study of Spence and Robbins' (1992) Workaholism Battery', *Journal of Occupational and Organizational Psychology*, **75**, 357–68.

Motowidlo, S.J., Packard, J.S. and Manning, M.R. (1986), 'Occupational stress: its causes and consequences', *Journal of Applied Psychology*, **71**, 618–29.

Mudrack, P.E. (2004), 'Job involvement, obsessive-compulsive personality traits, and workaholic behavioral tendencies', *Journal of Organizational Change Management*, **17**, 490–508.

Mudrack, P.E. and Naughton, T.J. (2001), 'The assessment of workaholism as behavioral tendencies: scale development and preliminary empirical testing', *International Journal of Stress Management*, **8**, 93–111.

Naughton, T.J. (1987), 'A conceptual view of workaholism and implications for career counseling and research', *Career Development Quarterly*, **35**, 180–87.

Oates, W. (1971), *Confessions of a Workaholic: The Facts about Work Addiction*, New York: World.

Paterson, J.M. and O'Driscoll, M.P. (1990), 'An empirical assessment of Kanungo's (1982) concept and measure of job involvement', *Applied Psychology: An International Review*, **39**, 293–306.

Pollak, J.M. (1979), 'Obsessive-compulsive personality: a review', *Psychological Bulletin*, **86**, 225–41.

Porter, G. (1996), 'Organizational impact of workaholism: suggestions for researching the negative outcomes of excessive work', *Journal of Occupational Health Psychology*, **1**, 70–84.

Porter, G. (2001), 'Workaholic tendencies and the high potential for stress among co-workers', *International Journal of Stress Management*, **8**, 147–64.

Rizzo, J.R., House, R.J. and Lirtzman, S.I. (1970), 'Role conflict and ambiguity in complex organizations', *Administrative Science Quarterly*, **15**, 150–63.

Robinson, B.E. (1999), 'The Work Addiction Risk Test: development of a tentative measure of workaholism', *Perceptual and Motor Skills*, **88**, 199–210.

Robinson, B.E., Flowers, C. and Carroll, J. (2001), 'Work stress and marriage: a theoretical model examining the relationship between workaholism and marital cohesion', *International Journal of Stress Management*, **8**, 163–75.

Rosin, H. and Korabik, K. (1995), 'Organizational experiences and propensity to leave: a multivariate investigation of men and women managers', *Journal of Vocational Behavior*, **46**, 1–16.

Schaef, A.W. and Fassel, D. (1988), 'The addictive organization', San Francisco: Harper and Row.

Scott, K.S., Moore, K.S. and Miceli, M.P. (1997), 'An exploration of the meaning and consequences of workaholism', *Human Relations*, **50**, 287–314.

Seybold, K.C. and Salomone, P.R. (1994), 'Understanding workaholism: a review of causes and counseling approaches', *Journal of Counseling and Development*, **73** (1), 4–9.

Snir, R. and Harpaz, I. (2004), 'Attitudinal and demographic antecedents of workaholism', *Journal of Organizational Change Management*, **17**, 520–36.

Snyder, M. and Gangestad, S. (1986), 'On the nature of self-monitoring: matters of assessment, matters of validity', *Journal of Personality and Social Psychology*, **51**, 125–39.

Spence, J.T. and Robbins, A.S. (1992), 'Workaholism: definition, measurement, and preliminary results', *Journal of Personality Assessment*, **58**, 160–78.

Steers, R.M. and Braunstein, D.N. (1976), 'A behaviorally-based measure of manifest needs in work settings', *Journal of Vocational Behavior*, **9**, 251–66.

Taris, T.W., Schaufeli, W.B. and Verhoeven, L.C. (2005), 'Workaholism in the Netherlands: measurement and implications for job strain and work–nonwork conflict', *Applied Psychology: An International Review*, **54**, 37–60.

PART III

Antecedents and types of workaholics

6. Making sense of temporal organizational boundary control

Graeme MacDermid

INTRODUCTION

The increase in working time among knowledge workers over the last two decades is related to a number of phenomena. First, the competitive environment of business has grown more intense, owing to changes in technology, globalized competition and reduced regulation (Barkema et al., 2002). Second, organizational boundaries have become less well-defined, owing to the greater autonomy granted workers in higher status occupations and changing social norms which have allowed work and non-work spheres to become more intermingled. Third, organizational control has shifted from being instrumental, based on rewards and monitoring, to normative, based on conforming to and adopting accepted values and behavior and thus exerting self-control.

I propose that more research is needed to understand how knowledge workers make sense of organizational control, and temporal boundary control in particular. The problem of managing knowledge workers has been noted by Perlow (1998) and she has highlighted that, owing to the open-ended nature of the work, it is difficult for a manager to carefully specify a subordinate's task beforehand and to evaluate the results after the fact (see also Drucker, 1993). Thus organizations have tended to focus more on normative control of knowledge workers, where the worker adopts the organization's goals, values and behaviors as their own (Alvesson and Deetz, 1996; Hardy and Clegg, 1996).

In this chapter I put forward my research questions along with observations from preliminary field research at a small software firm, referred to as Webware, developing web applications for large institutional and commercial clients. The research generated data through in-depth semi-structured interviews with software developers and office managers, examination of company documents such as strategic plans and presentation, and on-site observation of work practices.

RESEARCH QUESTIONS AND INITIAL OBSERVATIONS

Research in this area needs to examine how people consciously reflect on their temporal organizational boundaries and thus how they perceive organizational control.

Organizational control can be exerted in various ways. Bureaucratic organizations have traditionally relied on instrumental control methods, including the use of rewards and punishments, for meeting organizational objectives and systems of monitoring and evaluating performance against standards (Etzioni, 1961). Increasingly in modern organizations, normative controls are used. These normative controls can become instrumental again as groups which have bought into the organizational values and goals exert concertive control on each other (Barker, 1993).

Thus the primary research question was:

How do individuals make sense of temporal organizational boundary control?

This question is important since much compliance with organizational control is believed to occur unconsciously (Lukes, 1974; Ranson et al., 1980). Critical theorists see individuals as unwittingly accepting organizational values and reaching a false consensus with their organizations regarding which values and goals are important, even if these values and goals do not reflect their own best interests. This perspective suggests that individuals are largely unaware of normative controls, although possibly still aware of instrumental controls. However, Alvesson and Willmott (1992) note the paradox of emancipation from normative control in that emancipation can be costly. Individuals may be unwilling to give up rewards that they value in order to be free of organizational domination. At Webware, developers experienced their work hours as being an inevitable consequence of working in the industry. That is, they saw work demands as being externally determined and there was nothing that they or the organization could do about them. Working when requested 'comes with the territory' said one developer.

Previous research in this area has been lacking in the following ways. First, much of the writing is at a theoretical level, noting the rise in use and effectiveness of normative controls in organizations (for example, Alvesson and Deetz, 1996; Hardy and Clegg, 1996). Second, where the research has studied the effect of organizational control (particularly normative) on individuals, it has generally not been self-reflective in that, while individuals have been interviewed and observed to see how they react to organizational control, the interpretation of these responses has largely been left to the researchers (for example, Casey, 1999; Gabriel, 1999; Kunda, 1992; Perlow, 1998). Third, the possibility that individuals understand the way in which they are being indoctrinated into a false consensus by the organizational culture and norms, but that they willingly accept this false consensus having given thought to the costs of not accepting it, has not been explored. Often individuals give little thought to temporal organizational boundaries. For instance, Robinson and Godbey (1997) found that people generally overestimated their hours of work, where initial estimates of working hours were compared with more precise time-diary results. In some cases work can be so all-encompassing that there is little else to represent a sphere other than the work sphere (Gorz, 1989). In other cases non-work pressures may impose themselves on the individual and force them to become aware of the boundary by examining the conflict between work and non-work needs. Thus my second question is:

> To what extent and in what ways are individuals aware of temporal organizational boundaries?

A structuralist view of organizational control proposes that people work long hours because the economic system demands it (Braverman, 1974). In a competitive environment, if the individual does not comply with organizational demands, they can be replaced by someone else who will. The 1990s saw more awareness of the lack of job security for individuals even in high status positions (for example, professionals, managers, knowledge workers), thus reducing the individual's feelings of power to resist organizational demands. On the other hand, these high status workers are relatively privileged compared with blue-collar and unskilled labor. They have more freedom to define how, when and where, they will carry out their task (Drucker, 1993). Thus individuals will probably express a range of feelings. Thus:

> How and to what extent do individuals feel relative autonomy or dependence in their work domain?
> How do individuals make sense of their relative control or independence?

Regardless of individuals' perceptions of organizational control, they will somehow react to organizational controls. Even those employees who feel relatively dependent on the organization will find areas or opportunities to resist organizational demands. Thus:

> How do individuals react to organizational control?
> How do they exhibit compliance and resistance?

The key gap in the literature that needs to be examined is how the individual makes sense of the temporal organizational boundary control that he or she is experiencing. Critical theory suggests that the individual is unaware of being controlled, having been indoctrinated in the organization's culture. Positivist theory suggests that the individual has made a rational decision about the rewards to be gained from complying with organizational demands. Labor process theory suggests that the individual, while making a rational decision, has little choice but to comply, given the structure of the economic system.

Previous research has shown that normative control systems are effective in controlling the behavior of high status workers (Peters and Waterman, 1984; Casey, 1999), but that instrumental control is still important as well (Perlow, 1998). While previous research shows how people respond to organizational control, none of it allows the subjects to speak for themselves, in order to provide an understanding of how they perceive and interpret the control systems that they are subject to.

Taking Perlow's (1998) case as an example, organizational control is seen to be carried out by modeling behavior, directing and monitoring. Subordinates are seen as either compliant or resistant, with resistant employees acknowledging the cost of resistance in terms of career progress and rewards. What is not examined here (or elsewhere) is how individuals perceive these methods of control, or whether they are even acknowledged. Take, for example, the managerial behavior of staying late. This could be seen as modeling behavior (manager is setting an example), as directing behavior (manager calls a late meeting, forcing people to stay), or as monitoring behavior (manager is seeing who else is staying late). The subordinate could interpret this action in a variety of ways:

- the subordinate may or may not be aware that the boss is staying late;
- if aware, the subordinate may not even recognize that this means anything;
- the subordinate could interpret the behavior positively as being supportive;
- the subordinate could interpret the behavior negatively as controlling or manipulative;
- if aware of controlling behavior, the subordinate could see it as modeling, directive or monitoring behavior.

Thus, prior research acknowledges the existence of control, both normative and instrumental, and that individuals react to it with degrees of compliance or resistance, but we know little about how individuals interpret this control.

I have chosen temporal organizational boundaries as the terrain in which to examine organizational control since the boundaries in contemporary organizations, and especially for knowledge workers, are relatively flexible and permeable, and thus represent a highly contestable terrain in which to examine various understandings of and reactions to organizational control. Given the relative economic advantage and organizational autonomy of these individuals, it is interesting that in general they have been choosing to commit more time to work, rather than less.

LITERATURE REVIEW

The literature review for this research touches on the following areas. First, there is a brief look at the trends in working time, since working time, or the temporal organizational boundary, is the contested terrain that I am examining in this study. Since working time constitutes a major part of our existence it should be an important phenomenon to study. I follow this with a section on preferences for working hours, since it is not clear whether people in general are satisfied with working as much as (or as little as) they do. Labor is not generally a commodity that can be sold in variable amounts as preferred; rather, organizations (buyers of labor) prefer a predictable supply in standard units (for example, 8 hours per day, 40 hours per week, 50 weeks per year) or may make further demands for flexibility or extension to suit the organization's needs.

Next I review the literature on organizational control. This review is dominated by a critical theory perspective on power which extends the traditional literature on organizational control, based on instrumental controls such as reward and punishment, monitoring, and rules and procedures to a growing body of literature on normative control methods such as the use of organizational culture to a largely critical body of literature on normative control, such as the use of organizational culture and the embeddedness of organizational values in everyday life. This form of control is important to look at, since its use in organizations is expanding and yet the methods of control are generally less apparent to those being controlled.

Then I look at the literature on boundary creation and organizational boundary control. It is important to look at boundary creation, since this is the frontier at which control over working time, in the case of temporal boundaries, is contested. The literature on organizational boundary control is limited, but provides some categories of boundary control in the workplace.

The final section describes the unique organizational issues facing knowledge workers. I have chosen to study knowledge workers since they typically have a great deal of organizational autonomy and economic power. This means that, first of all, they typically have poorly defined organizational boundaries, thus understanding of the temporal boundary is an interesting problem. Secondly, the nature of their work means that they are subject more to the less obtrusive normative controls than to more obvious instrumental controls. Again, understanding how and to what degree the individuals are aware of control is an interesting problem. Thirdly, knowledge workers have a relatively high degree of economic power. This means that, where the temporal boundaries are contested, there is at least some opportunity for the individual to contest the organizational demands.

History of Work Time

Working time is a representation of the extent of the temporal organizational boundary. The long working hours of high status workers is significant, given that they are high both in the historical context and in relation to other occupational groups. Normal working hours have varied historically. In pre-industrial times, estimates of working hours vary from 1440 to 2300 hours per year, with lower estimates very common. Sahlins (1972) found similarly low working hours for hunting and gathering tribes. With the industrial revolution, working hours rose to 3100 to 3600 hours per year (Schor, 1993). There are various explanations for the rise in working hours during the industrial revolution. Agricultural work was paced and limited by the needs of the land and the animals, whereas industrial work was detached from any natural pacing. Labor time became commoditized and thus industrialists sought to maximize the amount of time individuals spent in production. In the twentieth century, the workweek fell from 60 hours in 1900 to only 40 hours by 1960. A key initiative was the establishment of the 40-hour workweek in the United States in 1938 (Hunnicut, 1988).

Since 1960 average working hours have been constant. However, since 1980 there has been growing polarization in the distribution of work hours, with more people working long hours along with more people working part-time (or less than 35 hours per week) (Drolet and Morissette, 1997; Sunter and Morissette, 1994). In particular, working hours have increased for professionals and managers (Rones et al., 1997). For those with college education, 40 per cent of men and 25 per cent of women work more than 50 hours per week (Jacobs and Gerson, 1998).

While this research tends to examine organizational control in affecting individuals' temporal organizational boundaries, there are other factors put forward by economics scholars (especially Schor, 1993). They have attempted to explain the rise in working hours as being due to increased organizational demands imposed on the individual, as well as individuals' own increased demands for income arising from increased consumption.

Organizational scholars have explained the long work hours both in terms of organizational demands and in terms of individual preferences (for example, Perlow, 1998; Hochschild, 1997).

Schor (1993) contends that the rising work hours are partly due to individual choice and partly due to organizational pressure. The individual's choice is seen by these theorists to be largely influenced by social pressure to consume increasing quantities of products and services, which in turn makes them more dependent on organizational compensation. The organizational pressure is influenced by the large fixed costs associated with each worker (for example, benefits, pensions, training, recruiting, communication) which mean it is more productive to get more output from each existing worker rather than increase the number of workers. Rising working hours are also considered to be caused by the downsizing that has occurred and the resulting job insecurity that has been felt by those who are left behind (Harrison and Bluestone, 1988). Alternately, Hochschild (1997) found that employees spent more time at work since it was more rewarding than spending time at home. Jacobs and Gerson (1998) found that long working hours were due to the high human capital value of high status workers; as with any piece of capital with a high investment, maximizing usage is preferred. Maume and Bellas (2001) found support for Schor's (1993) and Jacobs and Gerson's (1998) contentions.

At Webware, for the most part the developers put in a normal week of about forty hours. Around software update releases, there was usually a rush to get the work finished and thus some extra hours during the week and possibly working Saturday. Also, as Robinson (Robinson and Godbey, 1997) notes, work time would not be so regulated that there would be no non-work activity going on. The office manager noted that a certain amount of non-work related Internet activity was unavoidable.

Work Hours Preferences

Notwithstanding these findings, the increased work hours may only mean that that is what people are rationally choosing to do. The evidence regarding individuals' preferences for working or other activities is not clear.

Knowledge work often has a lot of intrinsic appeal and the higher wages mean that the opportunity cost of not working is higher. Most of the work hours preference data comes out of surveys rather than from academic studies. This would suggest that increased working hours are beneficial to both parties (employer and employee).

Surveys of individuals' work hours preferences show mixed results. Statistics Canada found that most people are satisfied with the amount of time they spend at work (66 per cent), while 27 per cent would choose to work longer hours, and only 6 per cent would choose to work shorter hours (Drolet and Morissette, 1997). Golden (1996) found a more even split between overworked and underworked individuals, while others found a greater preference for reduced working hours (Jacobs and Gerson 1998). Some workers are thought to prefer longer hours at work since the work environment is more rewarding than the home environment (Hochschild, 1997).

A *Fast Company*–Roper survey (1999) found contradictions within the same group of respondents. While 88 per cent said it was possible to find a balance between work and non-work if one wanted to, 50 per cent said that they did not in fact have any control over working hours and 89 per cent said they had to work as hard as possible in order to compete (Schwartz, 2000). Thus, individual preferences appear confusing. The report explained part of this contradiction in the finding that career and money were very important for this group. Thus, while the group feel that they have little choice but to work, the unspoken or more complete explanation may be that they feel 'no choice to work, *if* they want to have career success'. George (1997) concurs, suggesting that, while on the surface most individuals are satisfied with their current work boundaries, with reflection they would prefer to want less, and thus be able to work less, seeing other areas of life which would be more satisfying if only more time were spent on them.

However, mixed results may reflect individuals' limited awareness of the possibility of choosing different work routines. In cases where workers have been forced to give up steady overtime, it has been shown that the first reaction is unease, partly due to the financial loss (workers had adjusted their lifestyles to the higher income) and partly due to not having other activities to fill their time. After some time at a normal workload, these workers re-establish relationships, join clubs, attend courses and take up hobbies. When asked to work overtime again, the response this time is reluctance to go back to what they were previously reluctant to give up (Gorz, 1989; Wilson, 1998). One of the steps towards voluntary work reduction, an aim of the voluntary simplicity movement, is to raise individual awareness of the net costs and benefits of work (Dominguez and Robin, 1992; Rothenberg, 1995).

These mixed results suggest that it is necessary to take a more in-depth look at how individuals see their personal involvement in the construction of organizational boundaries and to see how they take into account organizational control. The respondents seem to want to hold opposite positions: that they have freedom to choose how much they work, but that they have to work long hours in order to have a good career. If a 'good career' is the only alternative they can imagine, it appears they do not really feel they have the freedom. Alternately, they may have considered the choice between having a good career or not and freely chosen the long work hours as the sacrifice necessary to attain that goal. The shortcoming, however, is that the surveys ask people to make choices where, first, they may have little understanding of the alternatives; second, they may feel they have no choice (and may not take the question seriously); and third, they may be economically dependent in the short run on their current level of wages, but in the long run prefer something else. (I have found similar ambiguous responses when discussing working hours preferences with students.)

Normative control and instrumental control are not mutually exclusive and in fact tend to support each other. While normative control is increasing in handling complex tasks, instrumental control plays a bigger role in managing peripheral activities (Leifer and Mills, 1996).

It is here that this research, through a deeper questioning of individual choices and actions, will examine how individuals perceive the various organizational controls (or normative forces) affecting their perceptions of temporal boundary control and the degree to which they are aware of these normative influences.

Organizational Control

The modern organization is situated in a competitive context where the primary objective is to maximize efficiency in order to stay in the market. Given that markets are imperfect, there is generally some room for slack or temporary economic rents, but it appears that this slack is being diminished with more global trade and ease of access to knowledge. Organizational control is the means by which organizations encourage or compel their constituent members to work towards the organizations' objectives even when they are in conflict with their own individual objectives.

Traditionally organizations have relied on instrumental controls, but in the modern organization normative control is increasingly being used. Instrumental organizational control relies on exchange, coercion, monitoring, and rules and procedures to ensure compliance with organizational goals. Individuals may not see their interests being coincident with the organization's, but they see their interests being served as well as possible through the exchange (Hodson, 1995).

However, as organizational tasks become more complex, as is typical in knowledge work, it becomes difficult to create procedures in advance of carrying out the task and to properly evaluate the results after the fact. The individual, by necessity, has more autonomy in determining how the task is to be carried out and to what standard it is completed. Therefore normative control has grown in use, although it has not replaced instrumental control. Normative control relies on tools such as organizational culture, organizational socialization and embedded social values to instill the values and objectives of the organization in the individual. Thus the individual, in adopting the organization's values and goals, can be relied on to serve the organization's interest with less emphasis on performance being directed, monitored and evaluated.

Organizational Power

Compliance with organizational control depends on the power relationship between the organization and the individual. Where the organization is in a relatively powerful position, there will be correspondingly more compliance with organizational interests wherever there may be potential conflict. In this section I look at the literature on organizational power in three forms: resource power, process power and normative power (Lukes, 1974). I am placing more emphasis on normative power, since it parallels the normative control that this research proposal is designed to investigate.

Resource power

In this aspect of power, the relationship is governed by resources that one party possesses and that the other party desires. In addition to desirability, each party's resources may be substitutable by others who can provide the resource. This leads to the following strategies of increasing dominance or reducing subordination (Emerson, 1962):

- increase the desirability, the value of one's resource to others (for example, increase expertise, increase one's stock of rewards)
- decrease the substitutability of one's resource to others (for example, prevent other experts from being available, prevent others from rewarding those you have relations with)
- decrease the desirability of the other's resource (for example, reduce expense to reduce the need for additional income)
- increase the substitutability of the other's resource (for example, make contact with more experts, find other methods of attaining your goals that make use of others' resources).

In the workplace resource power is evident in the discretion of managers to award or deny bonuses or promotions and to provide ongoing work. Individuals can take measures, as well, to increase their power over (or lessen their dependence on) the organization. Market conditions for labor can be an external factor that also affects the power relationship, increasing the substitutability of either labor or employers. Resource power was felt in that employees noted there was a weak market for software developers. Two developers had experienced six months or more of unemployment before joining Webware.

Process power
Process power is the use of regulations and procedures to forestall the ability to negotiate over conflicting goals (Bachrach and Baratz, 1962, 1963). In this case conflicting goals may exist and be acknowledged, but without a mechanism for negotiating a compromise the individual is forced to accept the organizational demands or withdraw. For instance, an organization may have a non-negotiable policy on work hours or vacations. This may be established for the convenience and efficiency of managing a large workforce. Regulations and procedures may be framed as neutral or efficient, but their nature reflects the interests of those who created them. After the fact, they may prove to be impersonal and difficult to challenge. Certainly organizational regulations and procedures remove discretion from managers as well as subordinates, but this removal of discretion can benefit the manager by allowing responsibility for difficult decisions to be passed on to the impersonal regulations.

At Webware, one developer noted that he would like to have more than two weeks vacation, but accepted that this was what was normal for North American workers and that it was 'in the company policy'. Thus the possibility of having a longer vacation is pre-empted since it is undiscussable. However, the interview process itself provoked him to consider asking about the policy.

Normative power
This form of power, what Lukes (1974) termed the 'third dimension of power' or Hardy (1985) termed unobtrusive power, works by providing models of appropriate behavior that the individual accepts as their own. The individual comes to accept these models due to their embeddedness and persistence in organizational culture and socialization processes and in wider social norms. Since these practices and norms are persistent and held by the dominant party, they are considered legitimate and examination of alternative arrangements is not even considered. The individual then becomes essentially self controlling. Critical theory contends that the individual's adoption of organizational goals as their own is due to a false consensus, since the organizational goals may conflict with their own interests, however in adopting the organizational goals, the individual suppresses their recognition of their own interests (Alvesson and Deetz, 1996; Hardy and Clegg, 1996).

From this perspective some of the intrinsic value individuals attribute to their work and organizational sphere can be seen as falsely created. For instance, organizations may seek to provide a culture which emphasizes values such as 'working as a team' or 'being family' (Casey, 1999; Peters and Waterman, 1984), they may seek to make work more fulfilling through empowerment or job enrichment, or they may encourage the view that work is a calling or is sacred (Weber, 1930). Popular business writing also provides a romantic, even heroic, view of work, raising the significance of organizational activities relative to others. All of these initiatives can make the experience of work more satisfying for the individual in carrying out their necessary tasks. However, the creation of meaning in work also serves to place more emphasis on the organizational domain as the primary one in which to find satisfaction in one's life.

Power and Compliance

Given that there is potential conflict between organizational and individual interests and that the weight of tradition, legitimacy and coordinated action will generally favor the interests of the organization, there will still be variety in how individuals comply with or resist organizational demands. In Perlow's (1998) study of an engineering team designing a printer, there were varying degrees of resistance and compliance. More compliant workers would return to the office during a vacation if asked. Resistors would refuse to come in at weekends or find ways to avoid staying late. Some found strategies to legitimize their resistance (for example, family needs) or to put a favorable light on their resistance (for example, 'a temporary situation'). Nevertheless, resistors were generally aware that they were less likely to get good evaluations, which would lead to higher salaries, bonuses or promotions. Even within individuals, compliance could vary over time. A manager would one day rationalize his decision to leave early and the next day feel regret (even shame) about doing so. At Webware, managers felt that they could evaluate their developers according to the quality of their coding. One manager noted how one of the developers could always be counted on for top quality work. Yet in the same conversation, there were comments such as 'some of them are just nine-to-five-ers' or concern over non-work internet use that hinted that putting in time showed commitment and was valued. This need to put in time was felt by the developers. As one stated when asked how the boss knew whether he was doing good work: 'First of all, I'm putting in long hours – it doesn't mean I'm doing a good job, because you can spend 12 hours and do nothing.'

Bradshaw and Wicks (1997) showed that individuals could go through periods of compliance and resistance marked by changing levels of consciousness of their organizational situation. In this case, feminist consciousness provided the stimulus to at least consider challenging the status quo. One Webware employee, who had some issues with the limited vacation time (two weeks after one year), did so conscious of the much more generous vacation allowance of his German counterparts (five to eight weeks). The discussion of vacation time during the interview, in fact, led him to consider asking for more time off.

Much of the resistance literature is based on studies of unionized or factory workplaces. Collinson (1994) noted that resistance increases with managerial control. However Hodson (1995) found that there was no relationship between the type of organizational control and employee resistance. This would suggest that in higher level positions, where control is both less obtrusive and also less enacted, workers would see less reason to resist (it is less likely you will resist if satisfied) and resist in less obvious ways. Bradshaw and Wicks (1997) is the only study to examine the individual's awareness of organizational control. However, the sample group, university professors, are a group who are likely to be more prone to reflecting on issues of organizational power, especially at the level discussed in this proposal. In this research I hope to discover that other forms of consciousness (beyond feminist consciousness) inform individuals' understandings of organizational control.

At Webware only one respondent seemed to have experiences that gave him an awareness of alternative ways of arranging working time. He noted both the longer vacation time granted to European partners he had worked with and the more flexible working hours and self-management he experienced in a research environment.

Temporal Organizational Boundary Control

This research focuses on the temporal organizational boundary as the domain of interest. As noted above, work consumes a major portion of our waking lives. Organizations generally seek more of an individual's time, since to a large degree working time is the factor upon which performance is evaluated (Perlow, 1998).

Perlow (1998) examined the concept of boundary control in knowledge work. She defined temporal boundary control as 'managers' ability to affect how employees divide their time between their work and nonwork spheres of life'. The reason temporal boundary control is important is that it is difficult for managers to direct and evaluate the complex tasks to be performed. The tasks cannot be easily standardized or specified in advance, they often involve teamwork, and their effectiveness cannot often be determined immediately. Rather the knowledge worker is given more autonomy in determining how to do the task and in evaluating whether the task has been done well. Given that managers have difficulty evaluating the value of the work itself, they will tend to at least encourage more work rather than less. Thus managers will find ways to 'cajole, encourage, coerce, or otherwise influence the amount of time employees physically spend in the workplace' (p. 329).

Given unlimited organizational demands for more output (Kanter, 1977) managers will try to expand the organizational boundaries, rather than focus on other ways of increasing output. Since output control is less viable for this type of work, organizations will tend to control through more subtle means such as requiring shows of commitment and intrinsic satisfaction with work (Kunda, 1992).

Perlow (1998) found that managers controlled their subordinates' time by imposing demands (for example, scheduling meetings and setting deadlines), by monitoring (for example, checking up on them), and by modeling expected behavior (for example, working long hours themselves). Subordinates' time can also be controlled through entrenching organizational cultural values and through enacting professional or sector norms. In fact the setting of and meeting deadlines was mentioned consistently by all the participants as an important factor in controlling their work. Monitoring was prevalent through frequent meetings, daily at the beginning of a project, weekly as it matured, and owing to the open design of the office. The office partitions offered little privacy.

Boundary control need not be imposed by managers and organizational standards. Control may be imposed by the group. In the case of a work group given autonomy to decide on work design and intensity, they established rules and norms that were just as controlling as those that the company had imposed on them under the old system (Barker, 1993). When team monitoring is combined with traditional accounting control or monitoring, the organizational control autonomy may be reduced even further (Sewell, 1998; Ezzamel and Willmott, 1998). Only where management surveillance is reduced or poorly implemented is resistance to organizational control likely (McKinlay and Taylor, 1996).

Control may be imposed on oneself. In a case where workers began to work from home after a reorganization, they replicated the organizational boundaries from the office (Brocklehurst, 2001); for instance, separating the work area from the rest of the house, getting dressed in 'work' clothes, setting start and finish times. To some degree the control was not imposed by the company, which only occasionally checked up on people by phone to see that they were at their stations.

My work builds on Perlow's (1998) concept of boundary control, but, rather than looking at how managers impose control on subordinates, I will be looking at how the subordinates, in this case knowledge workers, come to make sense of these various controls and thus negotiate and socially construct their own organizational boundaries.

Making Sense of Boundary Control

While the literature has discussed how organizations attempt to impose their goals through boundary control and while the power literature shows that there are different ways that individuals are subjected to organizational power, the individual still has a degree of freedom in selecting their hours of work. For knowledge workers, there are not likely to be time clocks or even a regular start/end time. Supervision is likely to be incomplete. Even the geographic location is unlikely to signify a sharp boundary.

The question is, then, how do knowledge workers make sense of the various attempts to control and expand organizational boundaries and how do they construct their own boundaries?

Organizations may attempt to impose greater boundary control, but these efforts will not be uniformly experienced and accepted by the individuals. Individuals will construct their own boundaries, albeit built from the 'material' (controlling influences) taken from managerial behavior, organizational culture, and professional and societal norms.

Perlow (1998) noted that managers used modeling, monitoring and setting tasks as methods of control. However, how does the subordinate perceive managerial control?

Workers may react to boundary controls with ambivalence (Gabriel, 1999). The imposition of a Total Quality Management (TQM) culture espousing values of 'family' and 'team' left people feeling anxious and confused (Casey, 1999). Employees were happy to see the company stress family and team work; they felt it made them better employees and better people. Yet at the same time many of these same individuals expressed negative attitudes toward the long hours and domination of the organization. Similarly accountants in transitioning from a professional to a managerial form of practice felt pride in fulfilling newly set objectives, yet at the same time felt highly stressed by the new demands (Covaleski et al., 1998). In a government department, the change in culture to a more business-oriented practice focused on the acceptance of and resistance to the new language (Oakes et al., 1998).

Nippert-Eng (1996) found that organizational and private lives overlapped to some degree and thus boundaries were ambiguous. Work is brought home (the computer, the briefcase) and the home is brought into the workplace (personal calls in company time, family photos on the desk). In some cases individuals carefully negotiate these boundaries, keeping the two domains separate. For others, there is more integration and at times confusion over which domain they are occupying at the moment. In one example, a supervisor reprimands an employee for speaking out against the company during a work break, but waits until breaktime is over to speak, thus acknowledging a type of boundary between work and non-work. To the worker it is not important whether or not he was on a break when he criticized the company, believing that his opinions are not something the company has dominion over during his time or company time.

At Webware the dominant means of temporal boundary control was the deadline. All respondents noted that deadlines affected their management of working time. Overtime was more likely as deadlines approached. Most respondents stated that most estimates of the time required to complete a task or a project were fair, reflecting the experience of the project managers with input from the developers. However, if the deadline turned out to be unmanageable, deadlines would be revised. One developer speaking about tight deadlines noted: 'Yeah, probably sometimes the deadline is not reasonable, I cannot finish, I will tell them.' Another said, 'I mean usually . . . sometime in advance of the deadline we will raise a flag saying "This is impossible" or something like that. So whoever's managing the project . . . will have to work something out.'

External boundaries were also used. One respondent had limits as to how early or how late he could work, determined by transit schedules: 'Because I take the train, and I am on the first train, I cannot be here any earlier.' Family obligations also imposed boundaries: 'Typically I try to keep it at 40 hours a week, because I do have a family and a life and stuff like that.' In a couple of cases vacations were only taken where they could be seen as significant uses of time. 'I want to get away and travel somewhere. I don't want time off just to hang around,' said one respondent.

Environmental Changes Affecting Organizational Boundaries

Organizational boundaries were once better defined. Temporally, work would begin and end at defined hours (for example, a nine-to-five job). In some cases workers had to record the time they started and ended a shift (for example, clocking in). In a highly regulated environment, even break-times would be defined by contract. The geographic boundaries were marked by the office door. Other markers of the work domain include special work clothing and the use of specialized equipment. In modern organizations these boundaries are less well defined. Today, greater autonomy and less supervision mean that workers have more freedom in setting when and how they work. Employee-friendly work practices such as work-sharing and flexitime mean that start and end times are fluid.

Aiding the softening of work boundaries are technological changes which allow more work to be conducted outside the office. Cordless phones and pagers allow, and sometimes require, employees to be in continuous contact with their organization or clients. Cheaper and faster telecommunications and increased use of portable computers and other devices allow work to be done from home or other remote locations more readily. All of this is accompanied by greater social acceptance of the use of such technologies (doing business on the phone while driving; being available around the clock with a pager). Moreover, the equipment (computers, wireless devices) is no longer seen as just tools of the workplace, but is used for leisure as well.

At Webware, the technology allowed non-work to permeate the work domain through Internet technologies such as email, instant messaging and web browsers. For the most part this was fairly discreet. I rarely saw an employee browsing a non-work-related site, but the office manager noted that if the Internet connection went down he knew sooner than he would expect if developers were only using the Internet for work-related communication. Webware does not provide desk phones, owing to their just-getting-by start-up nature, but mobile phones fill the gap for some employees. The tendency is for developers to keep calls short, or, given the openness of the office, to leave the office and talk in the reception area or the corridor outside.

What this means is that contemporary knowledge workers have much less definite organizational boundaries than do workers in other occupational sectors, but also less than their counterparts did a generation before.

Boundaries

The contested domain of interest is the temporal organizational boundary. Boundaries are constructed to limit the domain of an individual or a group. Kreiner (2002) proposes that there are external boundaries defining the limits of an individual or a group and internal boundaries defining domains within the individual or group. In referring to the temporal organizational boundary, I am referring to the domain within the individual that is identified with the organization and its tasks.

Boundaries can be physical, temporal or cognitive. Physical organizational boundaries could be limited to the office where one works; however, for many it is common to take work outside the office, in a car, in a hotel, or to home. Thus physical boundaries can be variously well-defined or poorly defined. Temporal boundaries could be well-defined if there is a regular beginning and ending time (for example, nine-to-five, a 40-hour week), but flexitime arrangements, extensive overtime or just a lack of regular working hours indicate poorly defined working hours. Home workers often replicate the workplace boundaries at home by establishing regular working hours and setting aside a part of the house for work only (Brocklehurst, 2001).

Organizational boundaries have properties of flexibility and permeability (Campbell Clark, 2002). Flexibility refers to whether the individual can set their own hours for arriving and leaving. Flexitime arrangements, where individuals must be present for core hours but have discretion within a few hours, would represent a middle level of flexibility. Permeability refers to how easily non-work activities can be carried out in the workplace or how easily workplace activities can be carried out outside of the workplace and working hours. For example, can one take calls from friends or book personal appointments while at work? On the other hand, permeability can also mean that one's non-work life is easily interrupted by work requests.

At Webware, the office design lent itself to creating firm boundaries to keep the nonwork world out. The windows offered no views except a brick wall of a facing building, or blinds were pulled to keep out the sun. There were no desk phones, only two cordless handsets generally answered by one of the managers, although most employees carried mobile phones. The office was located in the back corner of a renovated industrial building, and offered little in the way of convenient refreshment services; the nearest convenience store and snack bar were a ten-minute walk away. The open design allowed easy self-monitoring of who was working. There were many times when the place was silent – everyone working at their workstations. As noted previously, boundaries between work and other domains can be highly integrated or highly segregated. Nippert-Eng (1996) also found that individuals struggled with the issue of segregating domains, but sometimes failed.

Knowledge Workers

Knowledge work is an important domain for study for the following reasons. First, knowledge work is generally complex, non-routine and difficult to codify into standard procedures. This means that the task is difficult to prescribe in advance and to evaluate afterward. Thus normative control becomes an important means of controlling the work (Thompson, 1967; Dornbusch and Scott, 1975; Zald, 1970). Second, knowledge workers have relatively high economic security and therefore are less dependent economically on their organizations. Thus the contest over establishing the temporal organizational boundary is a meaningful contest (as opposed to a completely one-sided contest where the individual is completely dependent on the organization). Thirdly, knowledge workers generally work in an environment where organizational boundaries are poorly specified. Thus the boundaries have two properties of interest in examining this contest over boundary control: the boundaries are not necessarily apparent (high permeability) and they are fairly flexible.

However there is some suggestion that software development is becoming routine and that managers are more able to codify it (Adler, 2005). Certainly the developers at Webware felt that the project managers did a good job of estimating how much time to assign to any given development task.

On the other hand, developers would take all the time granted to them to complete a task. If a developer were to get his task done by Thursday noon and he had promised it for Friday afternoon, he probably would not inform his project manager. Rather he would use the time either to work on another task to make sure it stayed on track or to do some online research and skills development (for example, checking developers' bulletin boards for shared code, checking software standards changes and new releases). The managers expressed some frustration at not knowing exactly when work was done, which reflects the limits of their ability to monitor the progress of their subordinates. It also suggests that software development here does have some aspects of being done on a 'piecework' basis, suggesting that there is less need for controlling time given to the workplace.

The interest in this study arises out of the rising working hours among knowledge workers. Knowledge workers constitute a growing and significant part of the labor force. Some characteristics of knowledge work are that it involves the transformation of knowledge, it is non-routine, and it requires higher education. It includes professionals, consultants, technologists, scientists and managers (Schultze, 2000). Workers in knowledge industries, defined as 'industries that conduct a higher than average level of research and development, and in which the professionals and engineers are a large part of the work force' (Drolet and Morissette, 2002) constitute 7 per cent of the overall workforce.

CRITICAL THEORY PERSPECTIVE

It is necessary to look at the critical theory perspective, since my approach is to take the perspective of the individual in his or her engagement with organizational control. A positivistic approach to organizational control would celebrate control as a tool for achieving greater productivity. This study is based on the critical theory assumption that individual consciousness is dominated by organizational ideologies which create a false consciousness, preventing individuals from finding true human fulfillment (Burrell and Morgan, 1979). The objective in critical theory is to reveal the domination of certain groups over other groups or individuals as unnatural in the hope that the subordinated parties will find emancipation from this unobtrusive domination.

Critical theory assumes that organizations are able to suppress conflict and even the awareness of conflict between individual and organizational goals. This contrasts with the traditional view of power as being based on relative resource dependence.

The discussion of work hours preferences in an earlier section is relevant to this discussion, since the ambiguity in people's expressions of preferences suggests that individuals do not fully explore the possibility of alternatives to long working hours, owing to the social and organizational norms which they have accepted.

Critical Theory Critique of Organizational Power

There are four main themes in the critique of organizational power from the critical theory perspective: the naturalization of the social order, managerial privilege, instrumental reasoning, and hegemony (Alvesson and Deetz, 1996).

Naturalization of the social order refers to the ways in which societal norms are often taken for granted and given status as belonging to the natural order of human relations. Critical theory notes that societal norms often reflect the interests of the dominant powers and thus are not neutral or natural at all. For employees of modern organizations the acceptance of organizational values and objectives, which may be in conflict with their own, can be justified by this appeal to the natural order.

Managerial privilege refers to the way modern organizations tend to follow a hierarchical process of decision making. Those at the top of the organization are given the power to determine the goals (and the process for setting those goals) for the organization. Nominally this is on behalf of the owners of the organization, but with multiple ways to serve owner interests there is much room for discretion. Often these goals are legitimated by the more widely accepted criterion of maximizing firm profit (Lukács, 1971; Giddens, 1979). The lack of workplace democracy, participation programs aside, is rarely questioned.

Instrumental reasoning refers to the dominance of economic values such as maximizing profit or efficiency in the firm, which means that all other values are subordinated. From this perspective, any technique which values bettering the condition of the individual within the organization is seen only as an ends to meeting the primary goal. This body of research includes a critique of human resource management, where new methods that improve the condition of individuals are implemented on the basis of what they will do for the organization's profit and efficiency as the prime consideration, even if positioned as methods for the betterment of employee conditions (Stablein and Nord, 1985; Alvesson and Willmott, 1992; Jermier, 1998). For instance, Dickson's (1981) study of implementing worker participation found that participation was limited and in fact increased managerial control. The current trend of bringing business models (along with the culture and language) to government and non-profit agencies is an example of trying to extend the efficiency imperative. A study of a government agency introducing business models, culture and language to its operations showed that this led to the employees having reduced autonomy, being now under the control of annual plans and objectives that had been legitimated by the new business model (Oakes et al., 1998).

Hegemony refers to the way the values of the dominant group become embedded in everyday life to such an extent that they are not questioned and are thus taken as natural. Social arrangements and laws tend to reinforce these assumptions. The dominant values are not necessarily wrong but they are seen as unchallengeable and as representing the best interests of all in society. Through constant reinforcement of the dominant value, individuals adopt the value as their own, even though it may not reflect their own best interests (Burawoy, 1979; Kunda, 1992; Clegg, 1989).

The use of corporate culture as a normative control mechanism represents a more local (organizational and group level) form of this embedding of dominant values. Individuals are seen as complicit in their own domination (Jermier, 1985; Knights and Wilmott, 1987; Rosen, 1985). While organizational culture has been recognized as an effective control mechanism by mainstream writers (Peters and Waterman, 1984), the critical theory perspective is concerned with the co-optation of the individuals' interests. As Willmott (1993) notes,

> under the guise of giving more autonomy to the individual than in organizations governed by bureaucratic rules, corporate culture threatens to promote a new, hyper-modern neo-authoritarianism which is more insidious and sinister than its bureaucratic predecessor.

To take a critical theory view is to question the apparently objective basis for individuals' attitudes towards and choices regarding organizational life compared with other life spheres. However questioning the apparent false consensus is challenging. At what point can one determine that an individual's true interests are contrary to their stated interests?

Making assumptions about the role of organizations in dominating individuals and preventing their fulfillment does not mean that organizations entirely prevent fulfillment. In fact one can argue that organizational values often contribute to one's sense of worth and develop one's skills. Work can contribute to self-esteem, self-worth and self-actualization, and certainly many of the participants in Casey's (1999) study felt their lives were improved by the new work culture. The point is that socially constructed work values, work ethics and organizational cultures create a false consensus whereby the individual finds meaning predominately in their work and in service to the organizational goals when finding meaning and serving goals in other domains would probably be more in their interests.

Limits to Emancipation

An aim of critical theory is to raise awareness of normative control so that the individual becomes aware of what are generally unobtrusive controls and reflects on his or her own complicity in accepting organizational control. However, Alvesson and Willmott (1992) suggest that there may be limits to the degree to which individuals indeed desire emancipation from the constraints of organizational life. First, the normative control systems are so deeply embedded in everyday life that it is difficult to become aware of them and to view them as being anything but natural. Secondly, there is the risk that, upon challenging certain taken for granted assumptions, the individual will not be able to deal with the contradictions embedded in the way they have practiced life, or they may not be able to give up the rewards that the system provides. They may willingly prefer the constraints of organizations and wish to suppress thoughts that contradict their existing self-image. Jermier (1998) notes how we 'celebrate efficiency' because of the good life it provides, yet 'struggles for control, which more fundamentally enable these lifestyles (at least for some percentage of the citizenry), are ignored or viewed with embarrassment.'

I hope that a better understanding of how individuals do perceive organizational control will help to address this issue. It is possible that the critical theoretical perspective is correct and individuals are co-opted, unaware, into reducing the priority of their own interests. However it is also possible that individuals, upon examination of the alternatives, gladly accept unobtrusive organizational control.

CONCLUSIONS

The context of this study was the changing work conditions, due to social and technological change, that are giving rise to more flexible and less defined organizational boundaries. Within this environmental change, knowledge workers had relatively high organizational autonomy and economic freedom, yet found their temporal organizational boundaries generally being expanded or at least being maintained at a high level.

Previous research has shown how organizations exert control through managerial action (Perlow, 1998) or through imposition of organizational cultural values (Peters and Waterman, 1984), how individuals become aware of and resist organizational controls (Bradshaw and Wicks, 1997), and how individuals can impose organizational controls on themselves (Barker, 1993). We also know that putting in time is an important part of how people are evaluated, given the complexity of knowledge work and post-modern organizations (Perlow, 1998).

The main finding of this preliminary study is seeing how management imposes boundary control through the use of organizational constructs such as vacation policies and deadlines, thus extending the work of Perlow (1998). These controls effectively left the employees feeling conflict with organizational demands, but feeling unable to challenge them, as in Lukes's (1974) model of power. Boundary control was also exerted through physical control, the design and location of the office, as well as temporal control.

Secondly, employees use externally imposed constraints (family, transit schedules) to help define or justify their boundaries.

The primary contribution of this research is towards understanding how individuals make sense of temporal organizational boundary control. Critical theory on power (Hardy and Clegg, 1996; Lukes, 1974) suggests that individuals are unwittingly co-opted into adopting organizational values and objectives as their own, suppressing their own, possibly competing, interests. However Alvesson and Willmott (1992) suggest two problems with the idea of false consensus. First, the social and organizational controls are so deeply embedded that there can only be limited awareness of them by individuals. Second, when faced with an awareness and understanding of organizational control, the individual may prefer not to be freed from it, since this can mean abandoning so much of what is held to be important to the individual. Thus some may willingly accept false consciousness over emancipation, since emancipation can be costly.

Second, while previous research (Perlow, 1998) examined how organizational boundary control is exerted, this research takes a more subject oriented approach. It examines how individuals interpret the previously acknowledged forms of organizational control. As I argued earlier, individuals could have a variety of interpretations of management behavior that is intended to control. The degree to which individuals acknowledge and interpret organizational control has been little studied. The managers in this study attempted to show that they do not use temporal boundary control, seeing other ways of managing or evaluating employees as being more effective, yet they found themselves resorting to boundary control unconsciously.

Third, it extends the literature on work practices in knowledge work and high technology work. This is considered to be an understudied area, given the changing dynamics and growth of the sector (Barley and Kunda, 2001). The knowledge workers in this study are not as overworked as the stereotypes would indicate, experiencing only occasional overtime when release dates are near.

The key contribution to practitioners, that is the workers experiencing similar workplace conditions (such as high autonomy, blurred organizational boundaries, long working hours), can be a raised awareness of how organizational control, especially normative control, is interpreted. So far the best we can say is that some workers feel ambiguity (Casey, 1999) or stress (Covaleski et al., 1998). An understanding of resource power allows individuals to develop strategies for managing the resources they control and the resources they require. An understanding of process power allows individuals the opportunity to press for regulatory change, given the energy, time and support of a critical mass of other organizational members, or allows the individual to withdraw from the organization, if he or she finds that change is impossible. However, understanding how to recognize and cope with normative control is rarely taught in business programs or written about in the popular business press. Thus, in addition to raising awareness, a long-term goal would be to develop strategies of negotiating with (or resisting) organizational control.

REFERENCES

Adler, P. (2005), 'The evolving object of software development', *Organization*, **12** (3): 401–35.

Alvesson, M. and Deetz, S. (1996), 'Critical theory and postmodernism approaches to organizational studies', in S.R. Clegg, C. Hardy and W.R. Nord (eds), *Handbook of Organization Studies*, Thousand Oaks, CA: Sage Publications, pp. 191–217.

Alvesson, M. and Willmott, H. (1992), 'On the idea of emancipation in management and organization studies', *Academy of Management Review*, **17** (3), 432–64.

Bacharach, S.B. (1989), 'Organizational theories: some criteria for evaluation', *Academy of Management Review*, **14** (4), 496–515.

Bachrach, P. and Baratz, M.S. (1962), 'Two faces of power', *American Political Science Review*, **56** (4), 947–52.

Bachrach, P. and Baratz, M.S. (1963), 'Decisions and nondecisions: an analytical framework', *American Political Science Review*, **57** (3), 633–42.

Barkema, H.G., Baum, J.A.C. and Mannix, E.A. (2002), 'Management challenges in a new time', *Academy of Management Journal*, **45** (5), 916–30.

Barker, J.R. (1993), 'Tightening the iron cage: concertive control in self-managing teams', *Administrative Science Quarterly*, **38**, 408–37.

Barley, S.R. and Kunda, G. (2001), 'Bringing work back in', *Organization Science*, **12** (1), 76–95.

Bradshaw, P. and Wicks, D. (1997), 'Women in the academy: cycles of resistance and compliance', in P. Prashad, A. Mills, M. Elmes and A. Prasad (eds), *Managing the Organizational Melting Pot: Dilemma of Workplace Diversity*: Thousand Oaks, CA: Sage Publications, pp. 199–225.

Braverman, H. (1974), *Labor and Monopoly Capital: The Degradation of Work in the Twentieth Century*, New York: Monthly Review Press.

Brocklehurst, M. (2001), 'Power, identity and new technology homework: implications for "new forms" of organization', *Organization Studies*, **22** (3), 445–66.

Burawoy, M. (1979), *Manufacturing Consent: Changes in the Labor Process under Monopoly Capitalism*, Chicago: University of Chicago Press.

Burrell, G. and Morgan, G. (1979), *Sociological Paradigms and Organizational Analysis*, London: Heinemann.

Campbell Clark, S. (2002), 'Borders between work and home, and work/family conflict', Academy of Management Annual Meetings, Denver, Colorado.

Casey, C. (1999), ' "Come, join our family": discipline and integration in corporate organizational culture', *Human Relations*, **52** (2), 155–78.

Clegg, S. (1989), *Frameworks of Power*, London: Sage Publications.

Collinson, D. (1994), 'Strategies of resistance: power, knowledge and subjectivity in the workplace', in J.M. Jermier, D. Knights and W.R. Nord (eds), *Resistance and Power in Organizations*, London: Routledge, pp. 25–68.

Covaleski, M.A., Dirsmith, M.W., Heian, J.B. and Samuel, S. (1998), 'The calculated and the avowed: techniques of discipline and struggles over identity in Big Six public accounting firms', *Administrative Science Quarterly*, **43** (2), 293–327.

Dickson, J.W. (1981), 'Participation as a means of organizational control', *Journal of Management Studies*, **18** (2), 159–76.

Dominguez, J. and Robin, V. (1992), *Your Money or your Life: Transforming your Relationship with Money and Achieving Financial Independence*, New York: Penguin Books.

Dornbusch, S.M. and Scott, W.R. (1975), *Evaluation and the Exercise of Authority*, 1st edn, San Francisco: Jossey–Bass Publishers.

Drolet, M. and Morissette, R. (1997), 'Working more? Less? What do workers prefer?', *Perspectives on Labour and Income* (Statistics Canada, Catalogue no. 75-001-XPE), Vol. 9, 32–8.

Drolet, M. and Morissette, R. (2002), 'Better jobs in the new economy?', *Perspectives on Labour and Income* (Statistics Canada, Catalogue no. 75-001-XIE), Vol. 3, 4, Ottawa: Minister of Supply and Services Canada.

Drucker, P. (1993), *Post-Capitalist Society*, New York: HarperBusiness.

Emerson, R.M. (1962), 'Power-dependence relations', *American Sociological Review*, **27** (1), 31–41.

Etzioni, A. (1961), *A Comparative Analysis Of Complex Organizations*, New York: Free Press.

Ezzamel, M. and Willmott, H. (1998), 'Accounting for teamwork: a critical study of group-based systems of organizational control', *Administrative Science Quarterly*, **43**, 358–96.

Fast Company (1999), 'Great expectations', **29**, 212.

Gabriel, Y. (1999), 'Beyond happy families: a critical re-evaluation of the control-resistance-identity triangle', *Human Relations*, **52** (2), 179–203.

George, D. (1997), 'Working longer hours: pressure from the boss or pressure from the marketers?', *Review of Social Economy*, **LV**(1), 33–65.

Giddens, A. (1979), *Central Problems in Social Theory: Action, Structure and Contradiction in Social Analysis*, Berkeley, CA: University of California Press.

Golden, L. (1996), 'The economics of worktime length, adjustment, and flexibility: a synthesis of contributions from competing models of the labor market', *Review of Social Economy*, **LIV**(1), 1–45.

Gorz, A. (1989), *Critique of Economic Reason (Métamorphoses du Travail)*, trans. by G. Handyside and C. Turner, London: Verso.

Hardy, C. (1985), 'The nature of unobtrusive power', *Journal of Management Studies*, **22** (4), 384–99.

Hardy, C. and Clegg, S.C. (1996), 'Some dare call it power', in S.C. Clegg, C. Hardy and W.R. Nord (eds), *Handbook of Organization Studies*, Thousand Oaks, CA: Sage Publications, pp. 622–41.

Harrison, B. and Bluestone, B. (1988), *The Great U-turn: Corporate Restructuring and the Polarizing of America*, New York: Basic Books.

Hochschild, A.R. (1997), *The Time Bind: When Work Becomes Home and Home Becomes Work*, New York: Metropolitan Books.

Hodson, R. (1995), 'Worker resistance: an underdeveloped developed concept in the sociology of work', *Economic and Industrial Democracy*, **16**, 79–110.

Hunnicut, B.K. (1988), *Work Without End*, Philadelphia: Temple University Press.

Jacobs, J.A. and Gerson, K. (1998), 'Who are the overworked Americans?', *Review of Social Economy*, **LVI** (4), 442–59.

Jermier, J.M. (1985), ' "When the sleeper awakes": a short story extending themes in radical organization theory', *Journal of Management*, **11** (2), 67–80.

Jermier, J.M. (1998), 'Introduction: critical perspectives on organizational control', *Administrative Science Quarterly*, **43**, 235–56.

Kanter, R.M. (1977), *Work and Family in the United States: a Critical Review and Agenda for Research and Policy*, New York: Russel Sage Foundation.

Knights, D. and Willmott, H. (1987), 'Organisational culture as management strategy', *International Studies of Management and Organization*, **17** (3), 40–63.

Kreiner, G.E. (2002), 'On the edge of identity: boundary theory and work-self conflict', Academy of Management Annual Meetings, Denver, Colorado.

Kunda, G. (1992), *Engineering Culture: Control and Commitment in a High-tech Corporation*, Philadelphia: Temple University Press.

Leifer, R. and Mills, P.K. (1996), 'An information processing approach for deciding upon control strategies and reducing control loss in emerging organizations', *Journal of Management*, **22** (1), 113–37.

Lukács, G. (1971), *History and Class Consciousness*, trans. by R. Livingstone, London: Merlin Press.

Lukes, S. (1974), *Power: A Radical View*, London: Macmillan.

Maume Jr., D.J. and Bellas, M.L. (2001), 'The overworked American or the time bind?', *American Behavioral Scientist*, **44** (7), 1137–56.

McKinlay, A. and Taylor, P. (1996), 'Power, surveillance and resistance', in P. Achers, C. Smith and P. Smith (eds), *The New Workplace*, London: Routledge, pp. 279–300.

Nippert-Eng, C.E. (1996), *Home and Work: Negotiating Boundaries through Everyday Life*, Chicago: University of Chicago Press.

Oakes, L.S., Townley, B. and Cooper, D.J. (1998), 'Business planning as pedagogy: language and control in a changing world', *Administrative Science Quarterly*, **43** (2), 257–92.

Perlow, L.A. (1998), 'Boundary control: the social ordering of work and family time in a high-tech corporation', *Administrative Science Quarterly*, **43** (2), 328–57.

Peters, T.J. and Waterman, R.H. (1984), *In Search of Excellence*, New York: Warner Books.

Ranson, S., Hinings, R. and Greenwood, R. (1980), 'The structuring of organizational structure', *Administrative Science Quarterly*, **25** (1), 1–14.

Robinson, J.P. and Godbey, G. (1997), *Time for Life: The Surprising Ways Americans Use their Time*, University Park, PA: Pennsylvania State University Press.

Rones, P.L., Ilg, R.E. and Gardner, J.M. (1997), 'Trends in hours of work since the mid-1970s', *Monthly Labor Review*, **120**, 3–14.

Rosen, M. (1985), 'Breakfast at Spiro's: dramaturgy and dominance', *Journal of Management*, **11** (2), 31–48.

Rothenberg, R. (1995), 'What makes Sammy walk?', *Esquire*, pp. 72–9.

Sahlins, M. (1972), *Stone Age Economics*, Chicago: Aldine Atherton, Inc.

Schor, J.B. (1993), *The Overworked American: The Unexpected Decline of Leisure*, New York: Basic Books.

Schultze, U. (2000), 'A confessional acount of an ethnography about knowledge work', *MIS Quarterly*, **24** (1), 3–41.

Schwartz, T. (2000), 'How do you feel?', *Fast Company*, May, p. 296.

Sewell, G. (1998), 'The discipline of teams: the control of team-based work through electronic and peer surveillance', *Administrative Science Quarterly*, **43** (2), 397–482.

Stablein, R.E. and Nord, W.R. (1985), 'Practical and emancipatory interests in organizational symbolism', *Journal of Management*, **11** (2), 13–28.

Sunter, D. and Morissette, R. (1994), 'The hours people work', *Perspectives on Labour and Income*, (Statistics Canada, Catalogue no. 75-001E) **6** (3 (Autumn)), 8–13.

Thompson, E. (1967), 'Time, work-discipline and industrial capitalism', *Past and Present*, **238**, 56–97.

Weber, M. (1930), *The Protestant Ethic and the Spirit of Capitalism*, trans. by T. Parsons, London: George Allen and Unwin Ltd.

Willmott, H. (1993), 'Strength is ignorance, slavery is freedom: managing culture in modern organizations', *Journal of Management Studies*, **30**, 515–52.

Wilson, K. (1998), 'Hooked on killer overtime', *Now*, Toronto.

Zald, M.N. (1970), *Organizational Change: The Political Economy of the YMCA*, Chicago: University of Chicago Press.

7. Economic and employment conditions, karoshi (work to death) and the trend of studies on workaholism in Japan

Atsuko Kanai

INTRODUCTION

The purpose of this chapter is to provide an overview of economic and employment conditions in Japan, which are believed to be responsible for the current situation of karoshi (work to death), as well as to consider potential tasks for future studies in the area of workaholism. More specifically, we first review the Japanese economy and employment conditions, showing a pattern of the labor force being divided into two bipolar groups: workers who work very long hours and workers who work shorter hours than before owing to the influence of industry structure reform under the continued sluggish conditions of the economy and employment. Second, we discuss the problem of karoshi, which is unique to Japan. Karoshi has become an increasingly serious problem. We discuss this problem by focusing on the number of workers' accidents approved as work-related. On the basis of these facts, we review workaholism studies in Japan and demonstrate that workaholism is a result of excessive adaptation to work and that it greatly influences workers both mentally and physically. Finally, we discuss the future tasks for workaholism studies in Japan and the need for seeking the new working style of the twenty-first century. It became clear that the working style of the twentieth century does not work.

BACKGROUND TO WORKAHOLISM STUDIES

Economic and Employment Situation in Japan

When we examine workaholism studies in Japan, it is important to understand the trend in economic conditions. The Japanese economic situation is still sluggish after enjoying high economic growth in the 1980s followed by the collapse of the bubble economy in 1991. It has been slow for a long period, although there are some indications of improvement in recent years. This directly influences the employment situation.

Firstly, a wide-scale restructuring, including lay-off, has been taking place and the unemployment rate has increased. Figure 7.1 shows the changes in the total unemployment rate for males and females in Japan (Ministry of Health, Labor and Welfare, 2004; *Chunichi Shinbun*, 2005b).

The total unemployment rate is the ratio of the total unemployed against labor population. The labor population is the sum of the employed and unemployed who are 15 years or older and have the willingness and ability to work. The totally unemployed are those who satisfy the following three conditions: (1) they are not working only because a job is not found; (2) they are ready to work as soon as a job is found; (3) they have completed the preparation for job-seeking activity or starting their own business (including waiting for the result of the past job-seeking activity). The total unemployment ratio had been relatively low until the 1980s, but began to increase in the first half of the 1990s. The monthly total unemployment ratio for males reached 5.9 per cent in October 2002, which was the peak (*Chunichi Shinbun*, 2002). The rate improved in 2003 and 2004; however, it still remains in the high range.

As part of restructuring, various types of employment have been introduced. Particularly, non-regular employment, including part-time employment, employment on lease and temporary employment, has been

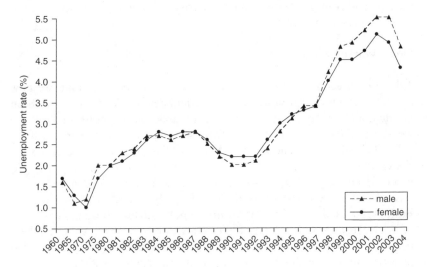

Figure 7.1   Unemployment rate in Japan

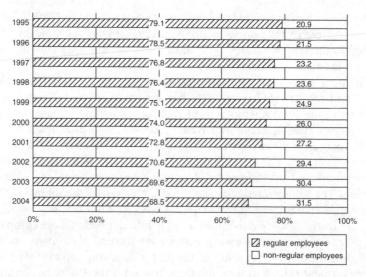

Figure 7.2   Increase in part-time employees

increasing. Figure 7.2 demonstrates the changes in the ratios between regular employees and non-regular employees (Ministry of Health, Labor and Welfare, 2004). Non-regular employment has increased from approximately 20 per cent in 1995 to over 30 per cent in 2004. Partly because welfare for these temporarily employed workers such as minimum wage security and continued employment security is not enough, the anxieties of such workers are increasing.

Hours Worked in Japan

Taking such economic and employment situations into account, we now examine the number of hours worked by Japanese workers, which has been pointed out to be too long. Figure 7.3 compares working hours of Japanese workers to those of other countries (Ministry of Health, Labor and Welfare, 2004). In 1988, the Amended Labor Standard Law was put into force despite the criticisms by other countries that Japanese people were working too much. Hours worked by Japanese workers were almost the same level of those of the USA and the UK. The Law on Temporary Measures to Promote Reduction of Working Hours – a policy to limit the annual number of hours worked by a worker to 1800 – was enforced in 1992. Although these movements were favored, in practice workers were gradually being divided into two bipolar groups by age and employment type, as discussed below. Hours worked by one of the two groups have become even longer.

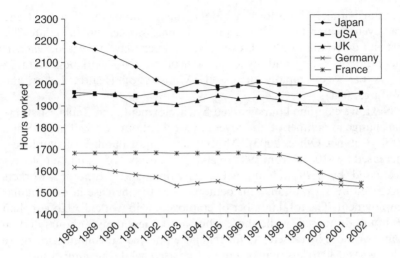

Figure 7.3   Comparison of total annual hours worked by country

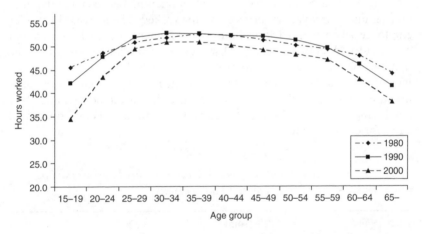

Figure 7.4   Average weekly hours worked by each age group: male workers

First, we examine hours worked by age group. Figure 7.4 shows changes in hours worked by males for each age group (Cabinet Office, 2002). Kanai and Wakabayashi (2004) pointed out that, although the average total labor hours in 2000 were shorter than those in 1980 and hours worked by young and senior male workers were shorter, the hours worked by male workers in their late 20s, 30s and early 40s remained long. This shows a bipolarized phenomenon. Such a trend was even clearer in 2003: the ratio of male workers in their late 20s, 30s and early 40s who work over 60 hours per week increased, whereas the ratio of young and senior male workers who work less than 35 hours per week rapidly increased (Ministry of Health, Labor and Welfare, 2004).

Next, we examine hours worked by employment type. Table 7.1 shows the change in number of employees by weekly hours worked in 1995 and 2001 (Cabinet Office, 2003). Although the total number of employees increased by 410 000 from 1995 to 2001, the number of regular employees decreased by 1.29 million, while part-time and temporary workers increased by 1.7 million. This demonstrates the increase in non-regular employment. The total number of employees who worked 30 to less than 60 hours decreased, while those who worked less than 30 hours and 60 hours or more increased. As for regular employees, the number of those who worked 30 to less than 60 hours decreased, while the number of those who worked 60 hours or more increased by 490 000. On the other hand, non-regular workers who worked less than 30 hours increased by 800 000. This demonstrates the bipolarized phenomenon between regular and non-regular employees in terms of hours worked. The increase in regular employees who worked long hours is prominent, which indicates that workload had shifted to them. However, it must also be noted that the number of non-regular employees who worked 60 hours or more increased by 70 000. This indicates that some non-regular employees have no choice but to work long hours because they are paid less and their employment status is so unstable as to be positioned as an adjustment valve for employment.

Table 7.1   Change in number of employees by weekly hours worked in 1995 and 2001 (unit: 10 000 persons)

	Total employees	Regular employees	Non-regular employees
Less than 30 hrs	△78	▼1	△80
30 to less than 40 hrs	▼12	▼40	△28
40 to less than 50 hrs	▼82	▼127	△45
50 to less than 60 hrs	▼0	▼9	△9
60 hrs and over	△56	△49	△7
Total	△41	▼129	△170

Note: △: increased from 1995 to 2001; ▼: decreased from 1995 to 2001.

Result of Working Long Hours – Karoshi

Karoshi can be considered as one of the consequences of working long hours that deteriorates an employee's health. Karoshi was named in the early 1980s, just before Japan entered the so-called bubble economy. It was defined as a

> condition of being permanently unable to work or dead due to acutely attacking ischemic heart disease such as myocardial infraction, or acute heart failure caused by cerebral vascular diseases such as cerebral hemorrhage, subarachnoid hemorrhage and cerebral infraction, because inherent health problems such as hypertension and arteriosclerosis are deteriorated by excessive work overload. (Hosokawa et al., 1982)

The National Defense Council for KAROSHI Victims (1989) describes karoshi as a 'fatal condition, in which the living rhythm of a human being is collapsed due to excessive fatigue and the life maintenance function is ruined'. Figure 7.5 shows the changes in the number of cases of worker's accident compensation approved as caused by cerebral/cardio diseases and mental disorders (Ministry of Health, Labor and Welfare, 2004; *Chunichi Shinbun*, 2005c). The number of death cases is not indicated for cerebral/cardio diseases in 1996 and before. Death caused by cerebral/cardio diseases corresponds to karoshi, and suicide or attempted suicide due to mental disorders corresponds to karo-jisatu (suicide by overwork).

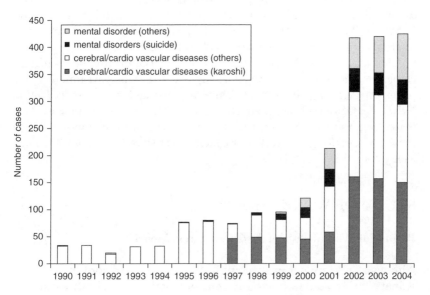

Figure 7.5   Worker's accident compensation approved as caused by karoshi or mental disorders

Even though the karoshi problem has been pointed out since the early 1980s (for example, National Family Group of Karoshi Victims, 1997), the Ministry of Health, Labor and Welfare was initially reluctant to approve karoshi. However, as harmful influences caused by excessive fatigue or weariness became evident, the Ministry modified standards for karoshi approval in 1995 and furthermore, relaxed such standards in 2002. Similarly, so-called karo-jisatsu – suicide committed by workers who were depressed owing to work overload – was not approved because it was considered international behavior on the part of the worker. However, in response to increases in karo-jisatsu, the Ministry relaxed approval standards for mental disorders in 1998. In Figure 7.5, the result of such relaxation can be confirmed with the increased approval of cases of cerebral/cardio diseases as from 1995 and mental disorders as from 1999, as well as the rapid increase in cases of approved cerebral/cardio diseases in 2002.

The approved number of cases of cerebral/cardio diseases as worker's accident was 294 (including 150 death cases) and that of mental disorders was 130 (including 45 death cases) in 2004, while the number of applications for worker's accident compensation was 816 for cerebral/cardio diseases and 524 for mental disorders. Only about one-third and one-fourth were approved respectively. This low approval ratio seems to discourage many from applying for worker's accident compensation, so that the actual number of karoshi and karo-jisatsu is hard to capture. Kawahito (1998) estimated, on the basis of statistics produced by the Ministry of Health, Labor and Welfare, that more than 10000 workers died annually owing to cerebral/cardio diseases caused by work overload.

Also, application for worker's accident compensation not only by regular employees but also by non-regular employees such as part-time workers (*Chunichi Shinbun*, 2004) and temporary workers on lease (*Chunichi Shinbun*, 2005a) has become approved. As mentioned above, some workers work long hours even though their employment status is non-regular. In these cases, non-regular workers are facing the risk of karoshi just the same as regular workers.

STUDY OF WORKAHOLISM IN JAPAN

Position of Workaholism in the Career Stress Model

Although there are not many empirical studies on workaholism in Japan, Kanai (2000) placed workaholism as an outcome variable in stress process, and proposed a career stress model (Figure 7.6). This model is based on Lazarus and Folksman's (1984) stress process model and placed a focus on

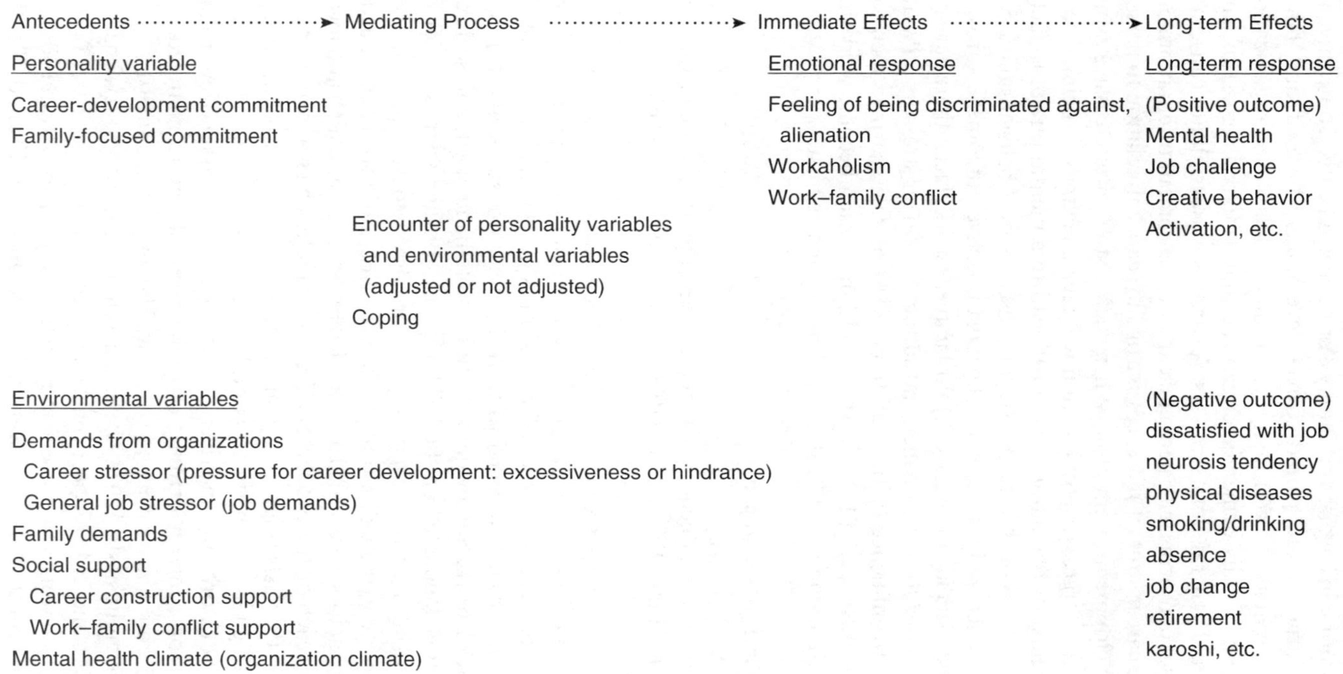

Antecedents ·········➤ Mediating Process ·········➤ Immediate Effects ·········➤ Long-term Effects

Personality variable

Career-development commitment
Family-focused commitment

Encounter of personality variables
and environmental variables
(adjusted or not adjusted)

Coping

Environmental variables

Demands from organizations
Career stressor (pressure for career development: excessiveness or hindrance)
General job stressor (job demands)
Family demands
Social support
Career construction support
Work–family conflict support
Mental health climate (organization climate)

Emotional response

Feeling of being discriminated against,
alienation
Workaholism
Work–family conflict

Long-term response

(Positive outcome)
Mental health
Job challenge
Creative behavior
Activation, etc.

(Negative outcome)
dissatisfied with job
neurosis tendency
physical diseases
smoking/drinking
absence
job change
retirement
karoshi, etc.

Figure 7.6 Career stress model in organizations

two main domains, work and family. As antecedents, two contrastive personality variables are paired, career-development-focused and family-focused, as well as two contrastive environmental variables, organizational demands and family demands. Organizational demands consist of career stressors and general work stressors. A career stressor will not cause stress as long as it conforms with personal career development orientation, but it will cause career stress if it is excessive or suffocative in relation to personal career development orientation. When such a stressor is excessive, workaholism will emerge, while suffocation will create feelings of being discriminated against or alienation. These will lead to a mental outcome such as depression, a physical outcome such as diseases or a behavioral outcome such as absence and job change. The most negative outcome is karoshi or karo-jisatsu (suicide by overwork). In Japanese workplaces, there have been excessive career stressors on men and suffocative career stressors on women owing to the influence of the traditional view of role sharing: 'men work outside, women stay at home'. As a result, men often become workaholic and women often feel suffocated or discriminated against.

Workaholic Types in Japan

Kanai et al. have conducted a few studies using the framework of this career stress model. First, Kanai et al. (1996a) translated the work addiction scale mentioned in Spence and Robbins (1992) and conducted a survey on Japanese workers. Spence and Robbins defined workaholism as consisting of three dimensions: work involvement, driven to work and enjoyment of work. They described characteristics of workaholics as: (1) high in work involvement, (2) driven or compelled to work by inner pressures, and (3) low in enjoyment of work. Survey questionnaires were handed out and scale construction was conducted on the 1072 responses (valid response rate of 87.5 per cent), using a factor analysis. Two factors, driven to work and enjoyment of work, were extracted, although the factor of job involvement was not. These two factors were scaled and divided into two groups, high and low. By combining each of the two factors, four workaholic types were constructed: (1) work enthusiasts (high in enjoyment of work, high in driven), (2) enjoying work (high in enjoyment of work, low in driven), (3) workaholic (low in enjoyment of work, high in driven) and (4) unengaged workers (low in enjoyment of work, low in driven). Only male samples were analyzed, since responses from female workers were few. The analysis found 301 (31.8 per cent) work enthusiasts, 180 (19.0 per cent) enjoying work, 201(21.2 per cent) workaholics and 264 (27.9 per cent) unengaged workers.

Unengaged workers were seen most in the age group of 20s and 30s, while more work enthusiasts were seen in the age group of 40s and 50s. With respect to position in the organization, there were more unengaged workers in the group of workers and assistant managers, and more enthusiasts were seen in the group of supervisors or above. It became evident that workaholics were most prevalent in the group of assistant managers.

Now we look at characteristics by type. Workaholics felt job stress most, and complained about nondelegation and health as much as work enthusiasts. Work enthusiasts had the highest scores for time involvement, job involvement and perfectionism. Work enthusiasts were characterized by being the lowest in job stress and health complaints.

Characteristics of the Japanese Version of the Workaholism Scale

Table 7.2 demonstrates the correlation between the two scales, enjoyment of work and driven to work, and the related characteristics. There was .32 correlation between enjoyment of work and driven to work. It was found that driven to work had significant positive correlation with time involvement, job involvement, job stress, perfectionism, nondelegation and health complaints, while enjoyment of work had significant positive correlation with time involvement, job involvement and perfectionism. An examination of scores for these related measures by workaholic type with a one-way analysis of variance found that job stress and health complaints were highest with workaholics and lowest with enjoying work. Also, persuasiveness of workaholic type, after control for demographic factors, was examined with a multiple regression analysis using health complaints as a dependent variable, and significant persuasiveness was found.

These examinations revealed that (1) workaholics had most job stress and health complaints; (2) driven to work was particularly related to job stress and health complaints; and (3) driven to work tended to overwork

Table 7.2   Characteristics of workaholic scale

	Driven to work	Enjoyment of work
Enjoyment of work	.32**	
Time involvement	.67**	.36**
Work involvement	.40**	.70**
Job stress	.57**	−.01
Perfectionism	.58**	.30**
Nondelegation	.38**	.07*
Health complaints	.31**	−.06

Note: $*p < .05$; $**p < .01$.

because of its strong connection with time involvement. This confirms the validity and reliability of the workaholic scale and types developed by Spence and Robbins (1992) in Japan. Another point revealed was that (4) enjoyment of work had the effect of loosening the relationship between driven to work and job stress. The reason for this was that enthusiasts had low scores for job stress, although their scores for time involvement, perfectionism and nondelegation were the same as or higher than those of workaholics. Another indicated point was that (5) workaholism could be a mode of adaptation to work overload, since it was most seen with assistant managers, who are in practice most burdened with job tasks.

Examination by Work Type and Age Group

Kanai and Wakabayashi (2001) conducted a study by work type, namely blue-collar employees, engineers, clerical workers and workers in sales, and found that (1) as for scores of enjoyment of work, there were no differences among work types, while driven to work was seen most with workers in sales divisions and (2) blue-collar workers had significantly low work overload compared with the others, while engineers had the highest work overload.

Examination of blue-collar workers (2247 respondents) by age group found that (1) scores of the young group for driven to work, enjoyment of work and work overload were lowest. (2) An examination of interaction between work overload and age using driven to work and enjoyment of work as dependent variables revealed that with higher work overload, the age group of 18–34 years old as well as the group over 35 years old showed high scores for driven to work, while enjoyment of work was low for the group of over 35 years old and high for 18–34 years old.

From these findings, it was evident that, although the young age group originally had low scores for both driven to work and enjoyment of work, if workload increased to a certain level, their scores for not only driven to work but also enjoyment of work went up at the same time. A higher score for enjoyment of work is supposed to be preferable for career construction, and it was indicated that a certain amount of workload plays an important role for career construction in the initial stage. On the other hand, the age group of over 35 years old had higher driven to work and lower enjoyment of work. Work overload strengthened workaholic tendency. This difference of response to workload between the group of young age and those over 35 years old seemed to be coming from the fact that workload was controlled low for the young group. Thus, an appropriate amount of workload is preferable for the young group as well.

Relation of Workaholism to Work Overload

The effects of work overload on driven to work and enjoyment of work for blue-collar workers were examined with a correlation analysis and multiple regression analysis. (1) Although significant correlation was not found between enjoyment of work and work overload, the coefficient between driven to work and work overload was .40 (p < .05). Multiple regression analysis, where other factors were controlled, revealed that (2) effects of work overload were significantly positive on driven to work (β = .19, p < .05) and significantly negative on enjoyment of work (β = −.11, p < .05). Thus, it was indicated that work overload accelerated the workaholic tendency, since work overload increased driven to work and decreased enjoyment of work.

The standardized partial regression coefficient of work overload was significant but at a low level. This was because the respondents were blue-collar workers, who worked on a manufacturing line. Their workload, work task, working hours and so forth were structured and controlled so that differences among individuals were small. An examination by work type, as already mentioned, revealed that blue-collar workers had least work overload in comparison with other work types. This fact indicates a possibility that effects of work overload may be larger in the case of other work types, where workload, work task or working hours are not structured. Further empirical examinations are needed.

Relation of Workaholism to the Economic Situation

Kanai and Wakabayashi (2004) examined the available data empirically to see whether the economic situation indeed influenced the workaholic tendency. As a result of examining seven data sets for men and three sets for women, it was revealed that (1) there were no changes as time went by in driven to work but enjoyment of work significantly decreased in the late 1990s to the early 2000s compared with the early 1990s, virtually showing a stronger workaholic tendency, and (2) in the late 1990s, although the overall workload became lower, the workload on workers in their 30s as age group and engineers as work type was just as much as or even more than that of the time of thriving economy in the early 1990s, which caused higher driven to work, thus a stronger workaholic tendency.

Kanai et al. considered that the decrease of enjoyment of work reflected the feeling of helplessness against the prolonged depression. The sluggish economy in the 1990s generated rapid changes in industry structure. Such sluggishness and the following changes were changes in the social structure, for which one's enthusiasm or efforts cannot do anything. They argued that it may be hard to enjoy work in the situation where only a feeling of exhaustion is strengthened against the prolonged sluggish economy. As for the heavier burden on engineers and workers in their 30s at the time of depression, they considered that this was because there were high expectations of engineers, who create new technologies, and workers in their 30s, who were going to shoulder responsibilities in the coming generation for conversion of industry structures. They concluded that all of them were influenced by the sluggish economic situation of Japan.

TASKS FOR THE FUTURE

To understand workaholism in Japan better, more studies are needed to demonstrate the relation between karoshi and workaholism. Such studies may be difficult to conduct. However, collaboration among psychologists as well as with the medical field has the potential to be fruitful.

Another point is that not enough data on women's workaholism are currently available (for example, Kanai et al., 1996b). When we look at the number of approved workers' accidents as caused by mental disorders, the ratio of women's cases is increasing year by year, reaching a record high of 46 (35.4 per cent) out of 130 cases in the fiscal year of 2004. Thus, it is essential to conduct studies for women employees.

The cultural background should be considered. Although the study by Spence and Robbins on university faculties (1992) found no correlation among the measures of the work addiction scale, a study on regular employees of Japanese private companies revealed a correlation ($r = .32$, $p < .01$) between driven to work and enjoyment of work (Kanai et al., 1996a) and the study by Burke (2004) on Canadian university students found that driven to work and enjoyment of work were correlated ($r = .26$, $p < .001$). Kanai et al. were unable to extract factors of work involvement with a factor analysis. These problems in scale construction may come from the difference in respondents or methodology; however, cultural factors should also be examined as a cause. Considering the fact that in Japan the relation between cerebral/cardiovascular diseases and long working hours or work overload was pointed out and karoshi (work to death) was named in the early stage, it is important to empirically examine whether a particular psychological process towards karoshi – unique to the Japanese – can be identified. These studies are in urgent need to be conducted in order to prevent workaholism from occurring, as well as to prevent karoshi.

Kanai (2002a) examined work–family conflict of three categories within the career stress model: working women whose husbands were working, working men whose wives were working and working men whose wives stayed at home. The following was revealed about working men whose wives stayed at home. (1) They were highest in family involvement among the three categories. However, (2) when they became busy with work, they thought less about family. (3) When they had a conflict between work and family, they tended to have a hostile feeling towards family. Kanai considered that this was because family involvement by those men decreased more and more. Their involvement was limited from the beginning, as the roles in family life were divided between them and their wives. When these men became busy with work, this tendency was accelerated. When a conflict occurred between work and family, these working men perceived family as a disturbance to their work and their inclination to avoid family went up, despite the fact that it was their family that inspired them to work. However, they were not working for their family any more if they had such feelings. Therefore, there was no doubt that an excessive shift towards work harmed their family life.

As for working men whose wives were working, (1) those who were high both in work commitment and family commitment had lowest work–family conflict and (2) those who were high in work commitment and low in family commitment had highest work–family conflict. On the basis of the above, it was considered that an appropriate involvement in both domains of work and family was proper for their mental health, since too much involvement in one of them would make requirement from the other stressful, since those men whose wives were working had to be involved in both work and family anyhow (Kanai, 2002b).

This chapter has reviewed workaholism studies conducted in Japan. These studies revealed that an excessive shift to work negatively influences mental and physical health. In addition, the studies on work–family conflict showed that an appropriate balance between work and family is required. After experiencing high economic growth in the latter half of the twentieth century, Japan faces various problems in the twenty-first century. What is indicated by these problems is that the working style of the twentieth century does not work any more. By examining workaholism problems, we need to think about how we want to work and explore a new working style for the twenty-first century.

REFERENCES

Burke, R.J. (2004), 'Workaholism, self-esteem and motives for money', *Psychological Reports*, **94**, 457–63.
Cabinet Office (2002), *White Paper on National Life Style* (in Japanese), Tokyo: Gyosei.
Cabinet Office (2003), *White Paper on National Life Style* (in Japanese), Tokyo: Gyosei.

Chunichi Shinbun (2002), '5.9 per cent: worst male unemployment rate', 29 November (in Japanese).

Chunichi Shinbun (2004), 'Temporary worker's death after 50 days of work: approved as karoshi', 31 August (in Japanese).

Chunichi Shinbun (2005a), 'Approving suicide by temporary workers as karo-jisatsu (suicide by overwork)', 1 April (in Japanese).

Chunichi Shinbun (2005b), 'Unemployment rate: improved to 4.6 per cent', 26 April (in Japanese).

Chunichi Shinbun (2005c), 'A record high approval of occupational disease as caused by mental disorders', 18 June (in Japanese).

Hosokawa, M., Tajiri, S. and Uehata, T. (1982), *Karoshi: Approval of Cerebral and Cardiovascular Diseases as Occupational Disease and How to Prevent them* (in Japanese), Tokyo: Rodo Keizaisha.

Kanai, A. (2000), *A Study on Career Stress: Approach to Mental Health from the Viewpoint of Career Development in Organizations*, (in Japanese): Kazama Shobo.

Kanai, A. (2002a), 'Examining determinants of work–family conflict and their effects on the mental health of male and female workers', *Japanese Association of Industrial/Organizational Psychology Journal*, **15** (2), 107–22 (in Japanese).

Kanai, A. (2002b), 'Career stress and work–life balance', *Japanese Journal of Labor Studies*, **503**, 54–62 (in Japanese).

Kanai, A. and Wakabayashi, M. (2001), 'Workaholism among Japanese blue-collar employees', *International Journal of Stress Management*, **8** (2), 129–45.

Kanai, A. and Wakabayashi, M. (2004), 'Effects of economic environmental changes on job demands and workaholism in Japan', *Journal of Organizational Change Management*, **17** (5), 537–48.

Kanai, A., Wakabayashi, M. and Fling, S. (1996a), 'Workaholism among employees in Japanese corporation: an examination based on the Japanese-version workaholism scale', *Japanese Psychological Research*, **38** (4), 192–203.

Kanai, A., Wakabayashi, M. and Fling, S. (1996b), 'Workaholism among Japanese employees: male and female differences', The Association of Japanese Business Studies, 9th annual meeting, Best Paper Proceedings, 223–36.

Kawahito, H. (1998), *Suicide by Overwork* (in Japanese), Iwanami Shinsho Series, Tokyo: Iwanami Shoten.

Lazarus, R.S. and Folksman, S. (1984), *Stress, Appraisal and Coping*, New York: Springer Publishing Company.

Ministry of Health, Labor and Welfare (2004), *White Paper on the Labor Economy* (in Japanese), Tokyo: Gyosei.

National Defense Council for KAROSHI Victims (1989), *KAROSHI* (in Japanese), Tokyo: Futabasha.

National Family Group of Karoshi Victims (1997), *Why do you work to death?* (in Japanese), Tokyo: Kyoikushiryo Shuppankai, Inc.

Spence, J.T. and Robbins, A.S. (1992), 'Workaholism: definition, measurement and preliminary results', *Journal of Personality Assessment*, **58** (1), 160–78.

ACKNOWLEDGMENT

I thank Professor Mitsuru Wakabayashi and Professor Yukari Okamoto for their helpful comments on the draft of this chapter.

8. Workaholic types: it's not how hard you work but why and how you work hard[1]

Ronald J. Burke

Although the popular press has paid considerable attention to 'workaholism' (Fassel, 1990; Garfield, 1987; Kiechel, 1989a, b; Killinger, 1991; Klaft and Kleiner, 1988; Machlowitz, 1980; Waddell, 1993), very little research has been undertaken to further our understanding of it (McMillan et al., 2003). Most writing has been anecdotal and clinical (Fassel, 1990; Killinger, 1991; Oates, 1971; Schaef and Fassel, 1988). Basic questions of definition have not been addressed and measurement concerns have been avoided (Scott et al., 1997).

It should come as no surprise then that opinions, observations and conclusions about workaholism are both varied and conflicting (McMillan et al., 2001). Some writers view workaholism positively from an organizational perspective (Korn, Pratt and Lambrou, 1987; Machlowitz, 1980; Sprankle and Ebel, 1987). Machlowitz (1980) conducted a qualitative interview study of 100 workaholics and found them to be very satisfied and productive. Others view workaholism negatively (Killinger, 1991; Schaef and Fassel, 1988; Oates, 1971). These writers equate workaholism with other addictions and depict workaholics as unhappy, obsessive, tragic figures who are not performing their jobs well and are creating difficulties for their co-workers (Naughton, 1987; Oates, 1971; Porter, 1996). The former would advocate the encouragement of workaholism; the latter would discourage it.

DEFINITIONS OF WORKAHOLISM

Research on workaholism has been hindered by the absence of acceptable definitions and measures (Scott et al., 1997). It is difficult to understand and research a phenomenon until one can define what it is. Mosier (1983) defined workaholism in terms of hours worked; workaholics were those

173

who worked at least 50 hours per week. Cherrington (1980, p. 257) sees workaholism as 'an irrational commitment to excessive work. Workaholics are unable to take time off or to comfortably divert their interests'. Machlowitz (1980, p. 11) defines workaholics as people 'who always devote more time and thoughts to their work than the situation demands . . . what sets workaholics apart from other workers is their attitude toward work, not the number of hours they work'. Killinger (1991, p. 6) defines a workaholic as 'a person who gradually becomes emotionally crippled and addicted to control and power in a compulsive drive to gain approval and success'. Robinson (1998, p. 81) defines workaholism 'as a progressive, potentially fatal disorder, characterized by self imposed demands, compulsive overworking, inability to regulate work habits and an over-indulgence in work to the exclusion of most other life activities'.

Oates (1971, p. 4), generally acknowledged as the first person to use the word 'workaholic', defined it as 'a person whose need for work has become so excessive that it creates noticeable disturbance or interference with his bodily health, personal happiness, and interpersonal relationships, and with his smooth social functioning'. Porter (1996, p. 71) defines workaholism as 'an excessive involvement with work evidenced by neglect in other areas of life and based on internal motives of behavior maintenance rather than requirements of the job or organization'. Most of these definitions have a negative connotation.

Scott et al. (1997) used a three-step process to develop what they term 'a reasonable definition' of the construct. They first collected characteristics attributed to workaholics in the practical and clinical literature. They then looked for conceptual similarities among these characteristics. They also differentiated the workaholic concept from similar constructs (such as job involvement) to reduce redundancy. They identified three elements in the workaholic behavior patterns using this process: discretionary time spent in work activities, thinking about work when not working, and working beyond organizational requirements.

Spence and Robbins (1992, p. 62) define the workaholic as a person who 'is highly work involved, feels compelled or driven to work because of inner pressures, and is low in enjoyment at work'. Most writers view workaholism as a stable individual characteristic (Scott et al., 1997; Spence and Robbins, 1992) and use the terms excessive work, workaholism and work addiction interchangeably.

Despite these broad and varying definitions, a compelling case could be made for devoting more research attention to workaholism. The concept has received considerable attention in the popular press. There also have been suggestions that workaholism may be increasing in North America (Fassel, 1990; Schor, 1991) and elsewhere (Kanai and

Wakabayashi, 2004). In addition it is not clear whether workaholism has positive or negative organizational consequences (Killinger, 1991; Machlowitz, 1980). There is also debate on the association of workaholic behaviors with a variety of personal well-being indicators, such as psychological and physical health and self-esteem. Finally, different types of workaholic behavior patterns probably exist, each having unique antecedents and outcomes. The question of whether workaholism can, or should be, reduced has also been raised (Killinger, 1991; Porter, 1996; Seybold and Salomone, 1994).

MEASURES OF WORKAHOLISM

Some writers have developed measures of workaholism (Engstrom and Juroe, 1979; Fassel, 1990; Killinger, 1991; Machlowitz, 1980; Spence and Robbins, 1992; Spruel, 1987; Robinson, 1998; Doerfler and Kammer, 1986), but with the exception of Robinson (1998) and Spence and Robbins (1992), they were not based on a clear definition of workaholism and did not provide psychometric information on the measure and its validity.

A number of measures of workaholism have been reported in both the popular and academic literatures. Many of these are listings of behaviors in checklist form, are used once and are never validated. Machlowitz (1980) lists 10 characteristics (for example, 'Do you get up early, no matter how late you go to bed?') in a yes/no format. She states that if you answer yes to eight or more questions you may be a workaholic. Doerfler and Kammer (1986) used this measure in a study of male and female attorneys, physicians and psychologists. Killinger (1991) lists 30 questions in her workaholic quiz (for example, 'Do you think you are special or different from other people?'), also answered in a yes/no format. She suggests that if you answer 20 or more yes, most probably you are a workaholic. There is no information about where these items came from nor any psychometric information about the properties of these two scales.

Two other measures of workaholism now used in several studies have been developed and reported along with information on some of each measure's properties (Robinson, 1998; Spence and Robbins, 1992). Robinson and his colleagues developed the Work Addiction Risk Test (WART). The WART contains 25 items drawn from symptoms (characteristics) reported by writers on workaholism (Robinson, 1998). Respondents rate items on a four-point Likert scale (1 = Never true, 4 = Always true) according to how well each item describes their work habits (for example, 'It's important that I see the concrete results of what I do'). Scores can range from 25 to 100. Robinson (ibid.) states that scores of 25 to 56 indicate that you are not work addicted, scores from 57 to 66, mildly work addicted, and scores from 67 to 100, highly work addicted. Scores above 65 fall more than one standard deviation above the mean. The items in the WART, based on a review of available literature, were grouped into five categories: over-doing, self-worth, control-perfectionism, intimacy and preoccupation–future reference.

Robinson and his colleagues report a number of brief studies providing psychometric information for the WART (for example, Robinson, 1996a). They indicate a test–retest reliability over a two-week period in a sample of 151 university students of .83, with a coefficient alpha of .85 (Robinson et al., 1992). Robinson and Post (1995a) reported split-half reliabilities in three data sets: 169 college students, 106 graduate students and 194 members of Workaholics Anonymous. On the basis of the 442 respondents, a Spearman–Brown split-half coefficient of .85 was obtained.

Robinson (1999) tested the criterion-related validity of the WART, again in a sample of students, by correlating WART scores with measures of Type A behavior and anxiety. Comparing high, medium and low WART scorers showed that students scoring higher on the WART also scored higher on anxiety and some Type A components. These findings are not surprising, given the conceptual and content overlap between the WART and the two criterion measures.

Spence and Robbins (1992) report the development of their workaholism measure, providing both reliability and concurrent validity information. On the basis of their definition of workaholism, developed from a review of the literature, they propose three workaholism components: work involvement, feeling driven to work and work enjoyment. They developed multi-item measures of these components, each having internal consistency reliabilities greater than .67 in a study of 368 social workers holding academic appointments.

TYPES OF WORKAHOLICS

Some researchers have proposed the existence of different types of workaholic behavior patterns, each having potentially different antecedents and associations with job performance, work and life outcomes. Naughton (1987) presents a typology of workaholism based on the dimensions of career commitment and obsession-compulsion. Job-involved workaholics (high work commitment, low obsession-compulsion) are hypothesized to perform well in demanding jobs and to be highly job satisfied, with low interest in non-work activities. Compulsive workaholics (high work commitment, high obsession-compulsion) are hypothesized to be potentially poor performers (staff problems resulting from impatience and ritualized work habits). Non-workaholics (low work commitment and obsession-compulsion) spend more time in other than work commitments. Compulsive non-workaholics (low work commitment, high obsession-compulsion) compulsively spend time in non-work activities.

Scott et al. (1997) suggest three types of workaholic behavior patterns: compulsive-dependent, perfectionist and achievement-oriented. They hypothesize that compulsive-dependent workaholism will be positively related to levels of anxiety, stress, and physical and psychological problems and negatively related to job performance and job and life satisfaction. Perfectionist workaholism will be positively related to levels of stress, physical and psychological problems, hostile interpersonal relationships, low job satisfaction and performance, and voluntary turnover and absenteeism. Finally, achievement-oriented workaholism will be positively related to physical and psychological health, job and life satisfaction, job performance, low voluntary turnover and pro-social behaviors.

Oates (1971) identified five types of workaholics: dyed-in-the-wool workaholics, converted workaholics, situational workaholics, pseudo-workaholics and escapists posing as workaholics. Fassel (1990) described four types of workaholics: compulsive workers, binge workers, closet workers and work anorexics. Robinson (1998) distinguished four types of workaholics; relentless workaholics, bulimic workaholics, attention deficit workaholics and savoring workaholics.

Spence and Robbins (1992) propose three workaholic types based on their workaholic triad notion. The workaholic triad consists of three concepts: work involvement, feeling driven to work, and work enjoyment. Profile analyses were undertaken, resulting in the emergence of three workaholism types. Several other studies (for example, Buelens and Poelmans, 2004; Elder and Spence, unpublished manuscript; Kanai et al., 1996; Robbins, 1993), using the same three scales, have produced essentially these same types: Work Addicts, Enthusiastic Addicts and Work Enthusiasts. Work Addicts (WAs) score high on work involvement and feeling driven to work and low on work enjoyment. Work Enthusiasts (WEs) score high on work involvement and work enjoyment and low on drivenness. Enthusiastic Addicts (EAs) score high on all three components. These researchers then offer a number of hypotheses as to how these three workaholic types might differ from each other. Thus, WAs would be more perfectionistic, would experience greater stress and would report more physical health symptoms. The existence of different types of workaholics might help reconcile conflicting observations and conclusions cited above.

RESEARCH FINDINGS

The following sections of the chapter will review selected research findings that compare the three types of workaholics proposed by Spence and Robbins (1992) on personal demographic and work situation characteristics, job behaviors, work outcomes, personal life and family functioning and indicators of psychological health. Fortunately the three workaholism types identified by Spence and Robbins have received much research attention.

Personal Demographic and Work Situation Characteristics

A critical question involves potential differences between the three workaholism types on both personal demographic and work situation characteristics, including hours worked per week. If the workaholism types were found to differ on these (for example, organizational level, marital status, hours worked per week), these differences would account for any differences found on work and health outcomes.

A number of studies (Spence and Robbins, 1992; Burke, 1999a; Burke et al., 2002; Bonebright et al., 2000) have reported essentially no differences between the workaholism types on a variety of personal and work situation characteristics. The workaholism types work the same number of hours and extra-hours per week; the workaholism types working significantly more hours per week and more extra-hours per week than the non-workaholism types. In addition these three workaholism types were similar on age, gender, marital and parental status, level of education, job and organizational tenure, income and organizational size.

Validating Job Behaviors

There has been considerable speculation regarding the job behaviors likely to be exhibited by workaholics. This list includes job involvement, job stress, non-delegation of job responsibilities to others, levels of job performance, levels of interpersonal conflict and trust. There is empirical research which examines some of these hypothesized relationships (Porter, 2001).

Both Spence and Robbins (1992) and Burke (1999a) provide evidence of the concurrent validity of the Spence and Robbins workaholism types. Both studies included the same measures of job behaviors (job involvement, job stress, psychological sense of, time committed to the job, perfectionism, non-delegation). These studies consistently showed that WAs exhibited higher levels of these validating job behaviors than did the two other workaholic profiles (WEs and EWs).

Comparisons of the workaholism types on a number of behavioral manifestations provided considerable support for the hypothesized relationships. EAs devoted more psychological sense of time to job than did both WEs and WAs. WAs reported greater job stress than did EAs, both reporting greater job stress than did WEs. Third, both EAs and WEs reported greater job involvement than did WAs. Fourth, WAs had greater unwillingness to delegate than both WEs and EAs. Fifth, EAs were more perfectionistic than were WEs.

Spence and Robbins (1992) found that WAs reported higher levels of job stress, perfectionism and unwillingness to delegate job duties to others than did WEs. Kanai et al. (1996), using the Spence and Robbins measures, reported that EAs and WAs scored higher than WEs on measures of job stress, perfectionism, non-delegation and sense of time committed to job.

Elder and Spence (unpublished manuscript) report that, in a sample of women and men MBA graduates, WAs and EAs scored higher than WEs on measures of perfectionism, job stress and non-delegation. In summary, Spence and Robbins WAs exhibit different job behaviors from those of individuals in their other two workaholism types.

Antecedents of Workaholism

Three potential antecedents of workaholism have received some conceptual and research attention. Two of these, family of origin and personal beliefs and fears, are the result of socialization practices within families and society at large. The third, organizational support for work–personal life balance, represents organizational values and priorities.

Family of origin
Robinson (1996b, 1998) has written about work addiction as a symptom of a diseased family system. Work addiction, similar to other addictive behaviors, is intergenerational and is passed on to future generations through family processes and dynamics. In this view, work addiction is seen as a learned addictive response to a dysfunctional family of origin system. Pietropinto (1986) suggests that children of workaholics learn that parental love is contingent on their (the children's) high performance.

Although this was not tested directly (that is, workaholism scores of parents were not examined in relation to workaholism scores of their children), Robinson and his colleagues equated elevated health symptoms of workaholic fathers with elevated health symptoms of their children (for example, anxiety and depression) as support for such a relationship (Robinson and Post, 1995b; Robinson and Kelley, 1998; Robinson and Post, 1997; Robinson, 1998).

Personal beliefs and fears
Burke (1999b) examined the relationship of personal beliefs and fears to workaholism. Beliefs and fears, a reflection of values, thoughts and interpersonal styles, have been shown to be precursors of Type A behavior (Price, 1982). Three measures of beliefs and fears developed by Lee et al. (1996) were used. One, Striving against others, had six items (for example, There can only be one winner in any situation). A second, No moral principles, had six items (for example, I think that nice guys finish last). The third, Prove yourself, had nine items (for example, I worry a great deal about what others think of me). A total score was also obtained by combining these three scales.

Burke compared the three Spence and Robbins workaholic types on these measures of beliefs and fears. Was there a relationship between cognitions that managers and professionals held about their broader environment and levels of workaholism? Analyses provided evidence of such a relationship. First, all three beliefs and fears were significantly correlated with measures of feeling driven to work (positively) and work enjoyment (negatively). Second, comparisons of workaholism types showed significant type effects on all three measures of beliefs and fears as well as on their composite.

More specifically, WAs scored significantly higher than WEs and EAs on measures of Striving against others and No moral principles, as well as on the composite measure. In addition, WAs scored higher on the need to prove oneself than did WEs. WAs scored higher on the composite measure than both WEs and EAs. Workaholism thus emerges as work behaviors in response to feelings of low self-worth and insecurity. This is best reflected in managers' feelings of being driven to work because of inner needs. Paradoxically these beliefs and fears were also found to be associated with lower levels of work enjoyment.

Type A behavior   Burke et al. (2004) found, in a study of 171 Norwegian owners and senior managers of construction companies, that WAs scored higher than WEs on Impatience–Irritation; EAs scored higher than WEs on Achievement–Striving, both being dimensions of Type A behavior. Impatience–Irritation has been shown to be predictive of psychological distress.

Organizational values
Burke (1999c) compared perceptions of organization culture values supporting work–personal life imbalance across the Spence and Robbins workaholism types. Organizational values encouraging work–family imbalance were measured by scales proposed by Kofodimos (1993). Organizational

values encouraging balance were measured by nine items (for example, 'Setting limits on hours spent at work'). Organizational values supporting imbalance were measured by eight items (for example, 'Traveling to and from work destinations on weekends'). A total imbalance score was obtained by combining both scales, reversing the balance scores.

There was considerable support for the hypothesized relationships. WEs reported greater organizational balance values then did both WAs and EAs. WAs reported greater imbalance values than both WEs and EAs. In summary, WAs see their workplaces as more supportive of work–personal life imbalance than the two other workaholism types.

Work Outcomes

The relationship between workaholism and indicators of job and career satisfaction and success is difficult to specify. It is likely that different types of workaholics will report varying work and career satisfactions (Scott et al., 1997).

Burke (1999d) compared levels of work and career satisfaction and success among the workaholism profiles observed by Spence and Robbins (1992). Four work outcomes, all significantly intercorrelated, were used. Intent to Quit was measured by two items (for example, 'Are you currently looking for a different job in a different organization?') This scale had been used previously by Burke (1991). Work Satisfaction was measured by a seven-item scale developed by Kofodimos (1993). An item was 'I feel challenged by my work'. Career Satisfaction was measured by a five-item scale developed by Greenhaus et al. (1990). One item was 'I am satisfied with the success I have achieved in my career'. Future Career Prospects was measured by a three-item scale developed by Greenhaus et al. (ibid.). An item was 'I expect to advance in my career to senior levels of management'.

WAs scored lower than WEs and EAs on job satisfaction, career satisfaction and future career prospects and higher than WEs on intent to quit. Interestingly, all three workaholic profiles (WAs, EAs, WEs) worked the same number of hours per week and had the same job and organizational tenure.

Psychological Well-being

There is considerable consensus in the workaholism literature on the association of workaholism with poorer psychological and physical well-being (McMillan et al., 2003). In fact, some definitions of workaholism incorporate aspects of diminished health as central elements. It is not surprising that this relationship has received research attention.

Burke (1999e) compared the three workaholism types on three indicators of psychological and physical well-being. Data were obtained from 530 employed women and men MBAs using questionnaires. Psychosomatic symptoms were measured by 19 items developed by Quinn and Shepard (1974). Respondents indicated how often they experienced each physical condition (such as 'headaches') in the past year. Lifestyle behaviors were measured by five items developed by Kofodimos (1993). One item was 'I participate in a regular exercise program'. Emotional well-being was measured by six items developed by Kofodimos (ibid.). An item was 'I actively seek to understand and improve my emotional well-being'.

The comparisons of the workaholism types on the three measures of psychological and physical well-being provided considerable support for the hypothesized relationships. Thus, WEs and EAs had fewer psychosomatic symptoms than did WAs; WEs had more positive lifestyle behaviors than did WAs; WAs had more psychosomatic symptoms than both WEs and EAs and poorer physical and emotional well-being than WEs.

Other researchers have shown similar results. Kanai et al. (1996), using the workaholism triad components developed by Spence and Robbins in a sample of 1072 Japanese workers from ten companies, found that both WAs and EAs reported more health complaints than did WEs. There was no difference between these three groups on measures of smoking, alcohol consumption and serious illness, however. Spence and Robbins (1992) noted that, in a sample of men and women social work professors, WAs indicated more health complaints than did individuals in their other profiles. Elder and Spence (unpublished manuscript), in their study of women and men MBA graduates, observed that WAs and EAs indicated more health complaints than did WEs. They also reported that WAs were less satisfied with their jobs and lives than were EAs and WEs.

Extra-work Satisfactions and Family Functioning

A number of writers have hypothesized that workaholism is likely to impact negatively on family functioning (Killinger, 1991; Porter, 1996; Robinson, 1998). Empirical examinations of this hypothesis are unfortunately few. Robinson and Post (1997) report data from a sample of 107 self-identified workaholics (members of Workaholics Anonymous chapters in North America) who completed the WART and a family assessment instrument. Three levels of WART scores, representing increasing levels of workaholism, were compared. High scores differed from low and medium scores on six of the seven family assessment scales, indicating lower (poorer) family functioning in all cases.

Robinson (1990) also reviews the literature on children of workaholics. Robinson and Kelley (1998) asked 211 young adults (college students) to think back to their childhoods and rate the workaholism of their parents on the WART. Participants also completed measures of depression, anxiety, self-concept and locus of control. College students who perceived their parents as workaholics scored higher on depression and external locus of control. Children of workaholic fathers scored higher on anxiety than did children of non-workaholic fathers. Interestingly mothers' workaholism had no effect on these outcomes. Robinson (2000, 2001) and Robinson and Rhoden (1998) attribute the distress of children of workaholic fathers to the presence of a diseased family system, more evidence that work addiction contributes to family dysfunction (Pietropinto, 1986).

Burke (1999f) considered the relationship between workaholism types identified by Spence and Robbins (1992) and extra-work satisfactions. Three aspects of life or extra-work satisfaction were included. Family satisfaction was measured by a seven-item scale developed by Kofodimos (1993). One item was 'I have a good relationship with my family members'. Friend Satisfaction was measured by three items developed by Kofodimos (ibid.). An item was 'My friends and I do enjoyable things together'. Community Satisfaction was measured by four items also developed by Kofodimos (ibid.). A sample item was 'I contribute and give back to my community'.

The comparisons of the workaholism types on the three measures of life or extra-work satisfactions provided moderate support for the hypothesized relationships. First, WAs reported less family satisfaction than did the two other types. Second, WAs reported less friend satisfaction than WEs. Third, WAs and EAs reported less community satisfaction than did WEs. Thus, WAs reported less satisfaction on all three measures than did WEs and less satisfaction on one (family) than did EAs.

Evaluating Workaholism Components

The two workaholism measures used in two or more research studies (that is, Robinson, 1998; Spence and Robbins, 1992) both contain components or factors. Do each of these factors have similar and independent relationships with particular outcomes? Or might they have opposite relationships with some outcomes and no relationship with others?

Burke (1999g) considered the question of whether the workaholism triad components had different consequences. A research model was developed to guide both variable selection and analysis strategy. There have been suggestions that both personal and work setting factors are antecedents of workaholic behaviors (Scott et al., 1997; Schaef and Fassel, 1988). Thus both individual difference characteristics and organizational factors were included for study. Five panels of predictor variables were considered. The first consisted of individual demographic characteristics (such as, age, gender, marital status). The second consisted of three measures of personal beliefs and fears (Lee et al., 1996). The third consisted of work situation demographic factors (for example, years with present employer, size of organization). The fourth included measures of perceived organizational values supporting work–life imbalance (Kofodimos, 1993). The fifth included the workaholism triad components (work involvement, feeling driven to work, work enjoyment). The important questions were whether the workaholism triad components would add significant increments in explained variance on particular work and personal well-being measures, and, if they did, which of the workaholism triad components accounted for these increments.

Outcome measures included job behaviors indicative of workaholism (for example, hours worked, job stress, perfectionism), aspects of work satisfaction (for example, job satisfaction, career satisfaction, future career prospects, intent to quit), psychological well-being (psychosomatic symptoms, emotional well-being, lifestyle behaviors) and elements of life satisfaction (such as family satisfaction, friends satisfaction, community satisfaction).

Though significantly inter-correlated, the three workaholism components had only moderate interrelationships, none of these correlations exceeding .25. The three workaholism components, considered together, almost always accounted for significant increments in explained variance on outcome measures, controlling for a number of personal and work-setting factors. The magnitude of these effects was larger on job behaviors and work outcomes likely to be evidenced by workaholics and smaller on psychological well-being and extra-work satisfactions. It is likely that the latter would be affected by a wider array of work and life experiences, workaholic behaviors being only one of them.

An examination of the relationships among specific workaholism components and the various types of outcome variables revealed an interesting, and complex, pattern of findings. First, work enjoyment and feeling driven to work were significantly related to every job behavior measure, while work involvement was significantly related to about half of them. Respondents scoring higher on the workaholism components also scored higher on job behaviors reflecting workaholism, with one exception – difficulty in delegating. In this instance, respondents scoring higher on work involvement and feeling driven to work and lower on work enjoyment reported greater difficulty in delegating.

Second, joy in work was the only workaholism component related to work outcomes. Respondents reporting greater work enjoyment also reported more job satisfaction, more optimistic future career prospects and more career satisfaction to date.

Third, both work enjoyment and feeling driven to work were related to indicators of psychological well-being but in opposite directions. Respondents reporting greater work enjoyment and lesser feelings of being driven to work indicated more positive psychological well-being.

Finally, workaholism components had a significant effect on only one of the three measures of extra-work satisfactions. Respondents reporting greater work involvement and lesser feelings of being driven to work reported greater community satisfaction.

Although work enjoyment and feeling driven to work had consistent and similar effects on job behaviors reflecting workaholism, these two workaholism components had different effects on work outcomes and psychological well-being. One, work enjoyment, was associated with positive outcomes; the other, feeling driven to work, was associated with negative outcomes. Finally, none of the workaholism components showed consistent relationships with measures of extra-work satisfactions.

ADDRESSING WORKAHOLISM

There is a large speculative literature suggesting ways to reduce levels of workaholism. One part of this work focuses on individual and family therapy (Robinson, 1992, 1997); a second part emphasizes organizational and managerial interventions.

Individual Counseling

Workaholics Anonymous chapters have sprung up in some North American cities. These groups, patterned on Alcoholics Anonymous self-help groups, endorse the twelve-step approach common to the treatment of a variety of addictions. Killinger (1991) and Robinson (1998) include chapters which outline actions an individual might pursue to reduce levels of workaholism.

It has been suggested that workaholics must examine their feelings (Minirth et al., 1981) as well as their thought patterns. Korn et al. (1987) encourage individuals to reduce impulses supporting workaholism and re-establish healthy priorities (see also Killinger, 1991; Klaft and Kleiner, 1988; Minirth et al., 1981). Other writers have advocated self-help programs for workaholics (Kiechel, 1989b; Oates, 1971, 1981; Klaft and

Kleiner, 1988; Franzmeier, 1988). These include identifying alternatives to work, exploring new hobbies and outside interests and enjoying doing nothing. Professional help may be useful, both individual and group counseling, for those interested in developing new patterns of behavior (Naughton, 1987; Seybold and Salomone, 1994).

Burwell and Chen (2002) apply rational emotive behavior therapy (REBT) to an analysis of the causes of workaholism and its treatment. Workaholism has, as one of its possible causes, low self-image and low self-esteem. One of the basic irrational beliefs in REBT is that one must impress others through accomplishments and outperform them.

The difficulty in treating workaholism is compounded by the societal acceptance of workaholism and denial of the problem. REBT addresses the irrational beliefs that drive workaholism. REBT tackles irrational beliefs, using cognitive reframing, practicing unconditional self-acceptance, and behaving in ways that are opposite to previously held beliefs. The last might involve, for example, delegating tasks to others, setting boundaries between work and home, attempting to balance work and life, and engaging in more leisure activities.

Family Therapy

Robinson and his colleagues, consistent with their clinical and consulting perspective, focus on treatment, both individual and family. This is not surprising given the central role they give to both family of origin and current family functioning in the development, maintenance and intergenerational transmission of workaholism. The treatment recommendations Robinson offers (1998) are similar to those offered to alcoholic families.

Thus denial is common among workaholics and their family members. Family members are reluctant to complain. Workaholics define their behavior and symptoms in a favorable light (Killinger, 1991; Porter, 1996). Parental expectations of children, often unrealistic, must be addressed. Family structures need to be identified. How do family members collude with the workaholic parent? Family members need help in expressing their negative feelings to the workaholic. Families need to learn to set boundaries around the amount they work together and talk about work. Family members can set goals to improve family dynamics (for example, communication, roles, expression of feelings). Families can also get a deeper understanding of the intergenerational transmission of addictions. Family involvement and counseling is another vehicle for assisting workaholics. These initiatives may uncover family dynamics which contribute to the workaholic pattern, make spending time with families more satisfying, and create rewards for workaholics for their family participation. Family counseling may also foster improved communication within the family, often including the expression of other family members' frustration, hurt and anger.

Workplace Interventions

How can employers help workaholics and workaholics help themselves? Schaef and Fassel (1988) offer the following ideas. Employers should pay attention to the performance and work habits of employees and be alert to warning signs of workaholism. They should not reward addictive behavior, but recognize those employees who are productive but also lead balanced lives. They should ensure that employees take vacation time away from work. Finally, job insecurity, work overload, limited career opportunities and lack of control can make employees feel compelled to work longer. If these factors exist, employers should try to minimize their impact on the atmosphere within the organization.

Haas (1991) also highlights the role that managers can play in assisting their workaholic employees to change. Workaholic employees should be referred to an employee assistance program or a recovery program to start treatment processes. Managers should help prioritize projects for employees as long-term and short-term assignments. Workaholics must be encouraged and helped to delegate their work. At the end of each day, the manager should meet with the employee to discuss what has been accomplished during that day and to plan (down to short intervals) for the following day. The employee should be given specific times to take breaks and to leave work so that positive terms may be acquired through training. It may also be possible to reduce the negative effects of workaholism, particularly well-being and health consequences, through stress management training.

The development of workplace values which promote new, more balanced priorities and healthier life-styles will support those workaholism types who want to change their behaviors.

CONCLUSIONS AND IMPLICATIONS

This chapter has compared the job behaviors, work and non-work outcomes, psychological well-being and personal values among three types of workaholics, all of whom work equally long hours. A generally consistent pattern of findings emerged. WAs reported job behaviors likely to be associated with reduced contribution (job stress, perfectionism, difficulty delegating) in comparison with WEs and EAs. WAs also indicated lower levels of psychological health than the two other types. And WAs indicated less non-work satisfaction.

Why would three types of managers working the same hours per week at the same organizational levels, having the same family structures, the same job and organizational tenure and earning the same incomes indicate such different work and life experiences?

The findings shed some light on this. First, WAs need values and beliefs indicative of greater needs to prove themselves, greater insecurity (lower self-esteem) and a less supportive and trusting environment in general. Second, WAs described their organizational values as less supportive of work–personal life balance. Third, they scored higher on feeling driven to work because of inner needs, probably related to their beliefs and values. Fourth, they worked in ways that created higher levels of work stress for themselves – perfectionistic (non-delegating). Thus it was not a question of how hard they worked but why (their motivations) and how (their behaviors) they worked hard that mattered.

Contrasting Motives for Long Hours at Work

Porter (2001) distinguishes two motivations for long hours at work. A person can work long hours because of joy in the work. This is a constructive, highly committed achievement oriented style of workaholism. This expenditure of time results in achievement. A person can also put in long hours in a compulsive, perfectionistic fashion, driven to achieve perfect standards. Such individuals react to criticism with hostility and resentment, experience frustration from failing to meet superhuman standards, and express anger and competition with colleagues in the workplace.

WAs are addicted to the process of work; outcomes are important only as they supply external rewards for temporarily enhancing self-esteem. WAs strive for increasing accomplishments to achieve self-worth. WAs are given to rigid thinking and perfectionism. They have difficulty delegating, which limits the development of others around them – WAs are not likely to be effective team contributors. They are striving to be in control, in control of their work activities and other people around them. As a consequence they increase the chances of ill health, poor relationships and diminished leadership contribution – theirs and others around them.

Porter (2004) explores reasons people feel compelled toward excess work when externally imposed demands are absent. There are several reasons why people work hard and each reason may have both desirable and undesirable consequences to the individual, the organization or both. She provides a description of the workaholic consistent with the addiction paradigm. She concludes with a plea for a healthier approach to hard work that includes a balance of non-work interests.

There is an old saying that 'hard work never killed anybody.' Our research bears this out. Hard work that provides feelings of accomplishment and joy undertaken for noble, not selfish, motives is likely to enrich a person's life.

NOTE

1. Preparation of this manuscript was supported in part by the Schulich School of Business, York University. I am grateful to Janet Spence for permission to use her workaholism measures. Several colleagues contributed to the research, including Zena Burgess, Lisa Fiksenbaum, Fay Oberklaid, Stig Matthiesen and Astrid Richardsen.

REFERENCES

Bonebright, C.A., Clay, D.L. and Ankenmann, R.D. (2000), 'The relationship of workaholism with work–life conflict, life satisfaction and purpose in life', *Journal of Counseling Psychology*, **47**, 476–7.

Buelens, M. and Poelmans, S.A.Y. (2004), 'Enriching the Spence and Robbins typology of workaholism: demographic, motivational and organizational correlates', *Journal of Organizational Change Management*, **17**, 446–58.

Burke, R.J. (1991), 'Early work and career experiences of female and male managers: reasons for optimism?', *Canadian Journal of Administrative Sciences*, **8**, 224–30.

Burke, R.J. (1999a), 'Workaholism in organizations: measurement validation and replication', *International Journal of Stress Management*, **6**, 45–55.

Burke, R.J. (1999b), 'Workaholism in organizations: the role of beliefs and fears', *Anxiety, Stress and Coping*, **12**, 1012.

Burke, R.J. (1999c), 'Workaholism in organizations: the role of organizational values', *Personnel Review*, **30**, 637–45.

Burke, R.J. (1999d), 'Are workaholics job satisfied and successful in their careers?', *Career Development International*, **26**, 149–58.

Burke, R.J. (1999e), 'Workaholism in organizations: psychological and physical well-being consequences', *Stress Medicine*, **16**, 11–16.

Burke, R.J. (1999f), 'Workaholism and extra-work satisfactions', *International Journal of Organizational Analysis*, **7**, 352–64.

Burke, R.J. (1999g), 'It's not how hard you work but how you work hard: evaluating workaholism components', *International Journal of Stress Management*, **6**, 225–39.

Burke, R.J., Burgess, Z. and Oberklaid, F. (2002), 'Workaholism job and career satisfaction among Australian psychologists', *International Journal of Management Literature*, **2**, 93–103.

Burke, R.J., Richardsen, A.R. and Mortinussen, M. (2004), 'Workaholism among Norwegian managers: work and well-being outcomes', *Journal of Organizational Change Management*, **17**, 459–70.

Burwell, R. and Chen, C.D.F. (2002), 'Applying REBT to workaholic clients', *Counseling Psychology Quarterly*, **15**, 219–28.

Cherrington, D.J. (1980), *The Work Ethic*, New York: American Management Association.

Doerfler, M.C. and Kammer, P.P. (1986), 'Workaholism: sex and sex role stereotyping among female professionals', *Sex Roles*, **14**, 551–60.

Elder, E.D. and Spence, J.T. (Unpublished manuscript), 'Workaholism in the business world: work addiction versus work-enthusiasm in MBAs', Department of Psychology, University of Texas at Austin.

Engstrom, T.W. and Juroe, D.J. (1979), *The Work Trap*, Old Tappan, N.J.: Fleming H. Revell Co.

Fassel, D. (1990), *Working Ourselves to Death: The High Costs of Workaholism, the Rewards of Recovery*, San Francisco, CA: HarperCollins.

Franzmeier, A. (1988), 'To your health', *Nations' Business*, **76**, 73.

Garfield, C.A. (1987), *Peak Performers: The New Heroes of American Business*, New York: William Morrow.

Greenhaus, J.H., Parasuraman, S. and Wormley, W. (1990), 'Organizational experiences and career success of black and white managers', *Academy of Management Journal*, **33**, 64–86.

Haas, R. (1991), 'Strategies to cope with a cultural phenomenon – workaholism', *Business and Health*, **36**, 4.

Kanai, A. and Wakabayashi, M. (2004), 'Effects of economic environmental changes on job demands and workaholism in Japan', *Journal of Organizational Change Management*, **17**, 537–48.

Kanai, A., Wakabayashi, M. and Fling, S. (1996), 'Workaholism among employees in Japanese corporations: an examination based on the Japanese version of the workaholism scales', *Japanese Psychological Research*, **38**, 192–203.

Kiechel, W. (1989a), 'The workaholic generation', *Fortune*, 10 April, 50–62.

Kiechel, W. (1989b), 'Workaholics anonymous', *Fortune*, 14 August, 117–18.

Killinger, B. (1991), *Workaholics: The Respectable Addicts*, New York: Simon & Schuster.

Klaft, R.P. and Kleiner, B.H. (1988), 'Understanding workaholics', *Business*, **33**, 37–40.

Kofodimos, J. (1993), *Balancing Act*, San Francisco: Jossey-Bass.

Korn, E.R., Pratt, G.J. and Lambrou, P.T. (1987), *Hyper-Performance: The A.I.M. Strategy for Releasing your Business Potential*, New York: John Wiley.

Lee, C., Jamieson, L.F. and Earley, P.C. (1996), 'Beliefs and fears and Type A behavior: implications for academic performance and psychiatric health disorder symptoms', *Journal of Organizational Behavior*, **17**, 151–78.

Machlowitz, M. (1980), *Workaholics: Living with Them, Working with Them*, Reading, MA: Addison-Wesley.

McMillan, L.H.W., O'Driscoll, M.P., Marsh, N.V. and Brady, E.C. (2001), 'Understanding workaholism: data synthesis, theoretical critique, and future design strategies', *International Journal of Stress Management*, **8**, 60–92.

McMillan, L.H.W., O'Driscoll, M.P. and Burke, R.J. (2003), 'Workaholism in organizations: a review of theory, research and future directions', in C.L. Cooper and I.T. Robertson (eds), *International Review of Industrial and Organizational Psychology*, New York: John Wiley, pp. 167–90.

Minirth, F., Meier, P., Wichern, F., Brewer, B. and Skipper, S. (1981), *The Workaholic and his Family*, Grand Rapids, MI: Baker Book House.

Mosier, S.K. (1983), 'Workaholics: an analysis of their stress, success and priorities', unpublished Masters Thesis, University of Texas at Austin.

Naughton, T.J. (1987), 'A conceptual view of workaholism and implications for career counseling and research', *The Career Development Quarterly*, **14**, 180–87.

Oates, W. (1971), *Confessions of a Workaholic: The Facts about Work Addiction*, New York: World.

Oates, W.F. (1981), 'Excessive work', in S.J. Mule (ed.), *Behavior in Excess: An Examination of the Volitional Disorders*, New York: Free Press, pp. 264–72.

Pietropinto, A. (1986), 'The workaholic spouse', *Medical Aspects of Human Sexuality*, **20**, 89–96.

Porter, G. (1996), 'Organizational impact of workaholism: suggestions for researching the negative outcomes of excessive work', *Journal of Occupational Health Psychology*, **1**, 70–84.

Porter, G. (2001), 'Workaholic tendencies and the high potential for stress among co-workers', *International Journal of Stress Management*, **18**, 147–64.

Porter, G. (2004), 'Work, work ethic, work excess', *Journal of Organizational Change Management*, **17**, 424–39.

Price, V.A. (1982), 'What is Type A behavior? A cognitive social learning model', *Journal of Occupational Behavior*, **3**, 109–30.

Quinn, R.P. and Shepard, L.J. (1974), *The 1972–73 Quality of Employment Survey*, Ann Arbor, Michigan: Institute for Social Research, University of Michigan.

Robbins, A.S. (1993), 'Patterns of workaholism in developmental psychologists', unpublished manuscript, Department of Psychology, University of Texas at Austin.

Robinson, B.E. (1990), 'Workaholic kids', *Adolescent Counselor*, **2**, 24–47.

Robinson, B.E. (1992), *Overdoing it: How to Slow Down and Take Care of Yourself*, Deerfield Beach, FL: Health Communications.

Robinson, B.E. (1996a), 'Concurrent validity of the Work Addiction Risk Test', *Psychological Reports*, **79**, 1313–14.

Robinson, B.E. (1996b), 'The psychosocial and familial dimensions of work addiction: preliminary perspectives and hypotheses', *Journal of Counseling and Development*, **74**, 447–52.

Robinson, B.E. (1997), 'Work addiction: implications for EAP counseling and research', *Employee Assistance Quarterly*, **12**, 1–13.

Robinson, B.E. (1998), *Chained to the Desk: A Guidebook for Workaholics, their Partners and Children and the Clinicians who Treat Them*, New York: NYU Press.

Robinson, B.E. (1999), 'The Work Addiction Risk Test: development of a tentative measure of workaholism', *Perceptual and Motor Skills*, **88**, 199–210.

Robinson, B.E. (2000), 'Adult children of workaholics: clinical and empirical research with implications for family therapists', *Journal of Family Psychotherapy*, **11**, 15–26.

Robinson, B.E. (2001), 'Workaholism and family functioning: a profile of familial relationships, psychological outcomes and research considerations', *Contemporary Family Therapy*, **23**, 123–35.

Robinson, B.E. and Kelley, L. (1998), 'Adult children of workaholics: self-concept, anxiety, depression, and locus of control', *American Journal of Family Therapy*, **26**, 35–50.

Robinson, B.E. and Post, P. (1995a), 'Split-half reliability of the Work Addiction Risk Test: development of a measure of workaholism', *Psychological Reports*, **76**, 1226.

Robinson, B.E. and Post, P. (1995b), 'Work addiction as a function of family of origin and its influence on current family functioning', *The Family Journal*, **3**, 200–06.

Robinson, B.E. and Post, P. (1997), 'Risk of work addiction to family functioning', *Psychological Reports*, **81**, 91–5.

Robinson, B.E. and Rhoden, L.(1998), W*orking with Children of Alcoholics: the Practitioner's Handbook* (2nd edn), Beverly Hills, CA: Sage Publications.

Robinson, B.E., Post, P. and Khakee, J.E. (1992), 'Test–test reliability of the Work Addiction Risk Test', *Perceptual and Motor Skills*, **74**, 9–26.

Schaef, A.W. and Fassel, D. (1988), *The Addictive Organization*, San Francisco, CA: Harper & Row.

Schor, J.B. (1991), *The Overworked American*, New York: Basic Books.

Scott, K.S., Moore, K.S. and Miceli, M.P. (1997), 'An exploration of the meaning and consequences of workaholism', *Human Relations*, **50**, 287–314.

Seybold, K.C., and Salomone, P.R. (1994), 'Understanding workaholism: a view of causes and counseling approaches', *Journal of Counseling and Development*, **73**, 4–9.

Spence, J.T. and Robbins, A.S. (1992), 'Workaholism: definition, measurement, and preliminary results', *Journal of Personality Assessment*, **58**, 160–78.

Sprankle, J.K. and Ebel, H. (1987), *The Workaholic Syndrome*, New York: Walker Publishing.

Spruel, G. (1987), 'Work fever', *Training and Development Journal*, **41**, 41–5.

Waddell, J.R. (1993), 'The grindstone', *Supervision*, **26**, 11–13.

9.   Dr Jekyll or Mr Hyde? On the differences between work engagement and workaholism

Wilmar B. Schaufeli, Toon W. Taris and Arnold B. Bakker

Although for the lay public workaholism is synonymous with working excessively hard, scholars have proposed several more elaborate definitions (for an overview see McMillan et al., 2003). However, to date, a generally accepted definition of workaholism is lacking. Moreover, there is still some controversy about its true nature: is workaholism good, bad, or maybe both? Ultimately, of course, the answer to this question depends on the way workaholism is defined. It is our contention that workaholism should be considered a negative psychological state akin to an addiction and that the recently introduced concept of work engagement is similar to 'good' workaholism. Thus, instead of distinguishing between 'bad' and 'good' forms of workaholism, we propose to differentiate between workaholism and work engagement. In order to provide an empirical basis for this distinction we assess in this article the discriminant validity of both concepts by: (a) analyzing the underlying factorial structure of the instruments that measure workaholism and work engagement; (b) assessing the relationships of both concepts with overwork; (c) investigating the associations of both concepts with employee well-being; (d) investigating the associations of both concepts with job performance.

THE CONCEPTS OF WORKAHOLISM AND WORK ENGAGEMENT

The term 'workaholic' was coined in 1971 by an American professor of religion, Wayne E. Oates. According to Oates (1971, p. 11), workaholism is 'the compulsion or the uncontrollable need to work incessantly'. For workaholics, the need to work is so exaggerated that it endangers their health, reduces their happiness, and deteriorates their interpersonal relations and social functioning. Many other scholars agree with this view of the founding father of the concept that workaholism is – by definition – 'bad' because it is an addiction akin to alcoholism (Cherrington, 1980; Killinger, 1991; Robinson, 1989; Schaef and Fassel, 1988). As Porter (1996, pp. 70–71) has put it: 'Whereas an alcoholic neglects other aspects of life for the indulgence in alcohol, the workaholic behaves the same for excessive indulgence in work.'

In contrast, others view workaholism as 'good'. For instance, in a qualitative interview study, Machlowitz (1980) found workaholics to be both satisfied and productive. In a similar vein, Korn et al. (1987) regard workaholism as positive, at least from an organizational perspective. Accordingly, they call workaholics 'hyper-performers'. For Cantarow (1979) the workaholic personality is positive because its hallmark is the joy of creativity and, according to her, workaholics seek passionate involvement and gratification through work. This agrees with Peiperl and Jones (2001, p. 388) who state: 'We see workaholics as hard workers who enjoy and get a lot out of their work.'

Finally, many authors view workaholism positively *and* negatively; that is, they distinguish between different types, some of which are 'good' whereas others are 'bad'. For instance, Keichel (1989) distinguished between happy and dysfunctional workaholics, and Naughton (1987) discriminates 'good' job-involved workaholics – who are high in work commitment and low in compulsion – from 'bad' compulsive workaholics – who are high in work commitment and high in compulsion. Furthermore, Scott et al. (1997) identified compulsive-dependent workaholics, perfectionist workaholics, and achievement-oriented workaholics, whom they referred to as hyper-performers (cf. Korn et al., 1987). The most widely empirically studied approach to workaholism assumes three underlying dimensions; the so-called *workaholic triad* consisting of work involvement (that is, being highly committed to work and devoting a good deal of time to it), drive (that is, feeling compelled to work because of inner pressures), and work enjoyment (that is, experiencing work to be pleasant and fulfilling) (Spence and Robbins, 1992). Different combinations of these three elements are assumed to produce different types of workaholics: (a) non-enthusiastic workaholics, who are high in involvement, high in drive, and low in enjoyment; (b) enthusiastic workaholics, who are high in involvement, high in drive, and high in enjoyment; and (c) work enthusiasts who are high in involvement and enjoyment and low in drive. Buelens and Poelmans (2004, p. 454) refer to this final group as the 'happy hard workers', who 'are enthusiastic, meet interesting people, love their jobs, and avoid conflict at home and in the workplace, possibly owing to their resulting positive attitude and a high level of social intelligence'.

This description of work enthusiasts – the 'good' workaholics – agrees with the recently introduced concept of work engagement, the positive opposite of job burnout (Maslach et al., 2001). Contrary to those who suffer from burnout, engaged employees have a sense of energetic and effective connection with their work activities and they see themselves as able to deal well with the demands of their job. More specifically, work engagement refers to a positive, fulfilling, work-related state of mind that is characterized by vigor, dedication and absorption (Schaufeli et al., 2002a). Vigor is characterized by high levels of energy and mental resilience while working, the willingness to invest effort in one's work, and persistence also in the face of difficulties. Dedication refers to being strongly involved in one's work, and experiencing a sense of significance, enthusiasm, inspiration, pride and challenge. Finally, absorption is characterized by being fully concentrated on and happily engrossed in one's work, whereby time passes quickly and one has difficulties with detaching oneself from work.

Engaged employees work hard (vigor), are involved (dedicated) and feel happily engrossed (absorbed) in their work. In this sense they seem similar to workaholics. However, in contrast to workaholics, engaged workers lack the typical compulsive drive. For them work is fun, not an addiction, as was concluded from a qualitative study among 15 engaged workers (Schaufeli et al., 2001). Engaged employees work hard because they like it and not because they are driven by a strong inner urge they cannot resist. Hence, for the sake of conceptual clarity, instead of discriminating between 'good' and 'bad' forms of workaholism, we propose to discriminate between workaholism (being intrinsically bad) and work engagement (being intrinsically good). In doing so we follow the recommendation of Porter (1996, p. 71), who calls on students of workaholism to 'return to the origin of the term as a starting point for future research'. And this origin is an addiction to work. Porter (ibid.) argues that, like alcoholism, workaholism is an addiction which is characterized by (1) excess work behavior implying the neglect of family, personal relationships and other responsibilities; (2) distorted self-concept (that is, striving through work for better feelings of self); (3) rigidity in thinking (that is, perfectionist about work details, non-delegation of tasks); (4) physical withdrawal into work and anxiety if away from work; (5) progressive nature (that is, needs increasingly to work more to boost self-esteem and block other feelings); (6) denial (that is, uses workplace affirmations to offset objections from others). By definition, this original 'bad' view of workaholism as an addiction – as first expressed by Oates (1971) – excludes perspectives that consider workaholism 'good' (for example, Cantarow, 1979; Keichel, 1989; Korn et al., 1987; Machlowitz, 1980; Peiperl and Jones, 2001; Scott et al., 1997).

In defining workaholism we follow the lead of Scott et al. (1997), who, after critically reviewing the literature, summarize three features of workaholism. First, workaholics spend a great deal of time in work activities when given the discretion to do so – they are excessively hard workers. Second, workaholics are reluctant to disengage from work and they persistently and frequently think about work when they are not at work. This suggests that workaholics are obsessed with their work – they are compulsive workers. The third element in Scott et al.'s (1997) definition is that workaholics work beyond what is reasonably expected from them to meet organizational or economic requirements. This is a specification of the first and second features, because it deals with the *motivation* for spending an excessive amount of time on work. That is, workaholics work harder than is required out of an inner compulsion, need or drive, and *not* because of external factors such as financial rewards, career perspectives, a poor marriage or organizational culture. In sum, we distinguish two aspects of workaholism: working excessively and working compulsively.

THE MEASUREMENT OF WORKAHOLISM AND ENGAGEMENT

In line with our conceptualization of workaholism, we operationalize it in terms of two scales, namely *Working Excessively* and *Working Compulsively*. These scales are taken from two frequently used workaholism inventories: the Work Addiction Risk Test (WART; Robinson, 1999) and the Workaholism Battery (WorkBat; Spence and Robbins, 1992), respectively. Unfortunately, the label of the scale of the WART that we use to assess excess work (Control Tendencies) is somewhat misleading because most of its items refer to working hard, without any reference to the underlying motivation, whereas the remaining items refer to the inability to relax and to feeling guilty when not working. For that reason we re-labeled the Control Tendencies scale as Working Excessively. A recent validity study, using three independent Dutch samples, showed that the Work Excess scale could be used as a short version of the full 25-item WART (Taris et al., 2005).

Studies on the factorial validity of the WorkBat failed to confirm Spence and Robbin's (1992) three-factor model of workaholism that included work involvement, work enjoyment and drive (Kanai et al., 1996; McMillan et al., 2002). Instead, the data suggest the elimination of the work involvement factor, leaving a two-factor model with enjoyment and drive as the core components of workaholism. In the current study only the drive component was included, because in our definition of workaholism we exclude 'good' forms of workaholism that are characterized by enjoyment. The

Drive scale of the WorkBat, that explicitly refers to the compulsive nature of the underlying motivation to work hard as well as to the compulsiveness of excessive work behavior, was relabeled as Working Compulsively so that it fits our definition of workaholism.

Work engagement is operationalized in the current study with the Utrecht Work Engagement Scale (UWES), a self-report instrument that includes the three dimensions mentioned above: vigor, dedication and absorption (Schaufeli et al., 2002a). Extensive psychometric research with the UWES showed encouraging results (for an overview, see Schaufeli and Salanova, forthcoming). For instance, the three subscales (vigor, dedication and absorption) are interrelated, internally consistent, and stable across time. Moreover, these favorable psychometric characteristics have been observed in different types of samples in different countries.

Correlates of Workaholism and Engagement

Three types of correlates are used for studying the discriminant validity of workaholism and work engagement.

Overwork

The most obvious characteristic of workaholics is that they work beyond what is required. Consequently, they devote much more time to their work than do others (for example, Brett and Stroh, 2003; Buelens and Poelmans, 2004; Mudrack and Naughton, 2001; Scott et al., 1997). For instance, North American workaholics work on average 50–60 hours per week (Burke, 1999; Peiperl and Jones, 2001; Spence and Robbins, 1992). Not surprisingly, positive correlations have been found between the time committed to the job (for example, working during weekends, taking work home) and workaholism (Burke, 1999; Kanai et al., 1996; Kanai and Wakabayashi, 2001; Spence and Robbins, 1992; Taris et al., 2005).

In a similar vein, it appears from a large representative sample of the Dutch full-time workforce that work engagement is associated with overwork (Beckers et al., 2004). However, results from in-depth interviews suggest that engaged employees work long hours but that they lack the obsession to work that is characteristic of workaholics (Schaufeli et al., 2001). Thus, it seems that engaged employees work hard but not compulsively so.

Well-being

Workaholics report relatively high levels of job strain and (mental) health complaints, particularly as far as the drive or compulsion component is concerned (Burke, 1999, 2000, 2001; Burke et al., 2004; Buelens and Poelmans, 2004; Kanai et al., 1996; McMillan and O'Driscoll, 2004; Mudrack and

Naughton, 2001; Spence and Robbins, 1992; Taris et al., 2005). Therefore, it is not surprising that McMillan and O'Driscoll (2004) suggest that 'drive may be the toxic (i.e. harmful) element in workaholism, while enjoyment may be a protective factor that buffers the influence of drive' (p. 517). Furthermore, it seems that, compared with non-workaholics, life satisfaction of workaholics is low (Bonebright et al., 2000). The latter study also shows that life satisfaction of work enthusiasts (in our terms: engaged workers) is significantly higher than that of both 'bad' workaholic groups (that is, the enthusiastic and non-enthusiastic workaholics). Similar results were obtained by Buelens and Poelmans (2004), who observed that 'bad' workaholics were dissatisfied with their salary, family, relationships at work, and relationships with their supervisor, whereas 'good' work enthusiasts were quite satisfied in these respects.

Work engagement is negatively related to burnout (Demerouti et al., 2001; Durán et al., 2004; Montgomery et al., 2003; Salanova et al., 2000; Schaufeli et al., 2002a, b) and psychosomatic health complaints (Demerouti et al., 2001; Schaufeli and Bakker, 2004). In addition, qualitative (Schaufeli et al., 2001) and quantitative evidence (Hallberg and Schaufeli, 2006; Schaufeli et al., 2005) suggests that engaged employees enjoy good mental health.

Job performance

Whereas some authors maintain that workaholics are extremely productive (for example, Korn et al., 1987; Machlowitz, 1980; Peiperl and Jones, 2001), others have claimed the opposite (Oates, 1971; Porter, 2001). The latter argue that workaholics work hard rather than smart. They create difficulties for their co-workers, suffer from perfectionism, are rigid and inflexible, and do not delegate. Unfortunately, virtually no empirical research has been carried out on the relationship between workaholism and job performance. Burke (2001) found some indirect evidence suggesting that workaholics do not perform particularly well: workaholic behaviors were *not* associated with salary increases. Because research is lacking, no firm prediction can be made about the nature of the relationship between workaholism and job performance. However, we expect that, given the long list of negative attitudes and behaviors that might interfere with job performance (Scott et al., 1997, p. 291), workaholics are not necessarily good and are perhaps even poor performers.

There is some preliminary evidence that engaged employees perform better than their less engaged colleagues. Recently, Salanova et al. (2005a) showed that levels of work engagement of contract employees in hotels and restaurants were positively related to service quality, as perceived by customers. In a similar vein, the more engaged students are with their studies, the more exams they pass during subsequent semesters (Schaufeli et al., 2002b) and the higher their next year's grade point average (Salanova et al., 2005b). Using a different measure of work engagement, Harter et al. (2002) demonstrated that employees' levels of engagement are positively related to business-unit performance (for example, customer loyalty, profit and productivity).

THE PRESENT RESEARCH

The purpose of the current study is to distinguish between 'good' and 'bad' workaholism, the former being re-phrased as work engagement. Basically, the WorkBat (Spence and Robbins, 1992) claims to make this distinction, namely between 'workaholics' and 'work enthusiasts', whereby the former score high on involvement and drive and low on enjoyment whereas the latter score high on involvement and enjoyment but low on drive. So why perform the current study then? There are two reasons for this, a methodological one and a conceptual one. First, Spence and Robbins (1992) have been criticized for clustering people (that is, workaholics and work enthusiasts) before validating the scales on which the profiles were based (McMillan et al., 2002). And, unfortunately, the assessment of this validity did yield negative results (Kanai et al., 1996; McMillan et al., 2002). In addition, on a more fundamental level, because for the assessment of different psychological phenomena ('good' and 'bad' workaholism) the same instrument was used, these assessments are not independent from each other. An analogy with positive and negative affect may illustrate this point. Research on the structure of affect demonstrated that a low score on sadness (negative affect) differs from a high score on happiness (positive affect), and vice versa (Lloret and Gonzalez-Romá, 2003). In other words, when people do not enjoy their work this does not mean that they hate their jobs, and when they do not hate their jobs this does not mean that they feel enthusiastic about them. Second, on a conceptual level, Spence and Robbins (1992) maintain that work enjoyment is part of their 'workaholic triad'. But if one agrees with the original view of workaholism as an addiction to work, that is, excessive and persistent work behavior with *harmful consequences*, this precludes any type of 'good' workaholism. We feel that the conceptual analysis of Porter (1996) convincingly showed that, in essence, workaholism is an addiction to work and thus inherently 'bad'. In short, we believe that, in order to study distinct psychological states, different labels and different assessment instruments should be used. Only in this way can the question whether or not these states are different be studied empirically.

More specifically, we assessed the discriminant validity of workaholism (working hard compulsively) and work engagement (vigor, dedication and absorption). We used an Internet survey to test our hypotheses which was completed by over 2000 Dutch employees. First, we investigated the factorial validity of the measurement instruments that were used to assess workaholism and work engagement. Can the items that are supposed to measure workaholism be distinguished from those that are intended to measure work engagement? For that purpose, the fit to the data of a one-factor model including *all* workaholism and *all* work engagement items was compared with that of a three-factor model that includes the two workaholism scales (Working Excessively and Working Compulsively) as well as work engagement. We expect (*Hypothesis 1*) that the fit of the latter model is superior to that of the former model, which would demonstrate the distinctiveness of both instruments.

To further examine the validity of the distinction between Working Excessively and Working Compulsively on the one hand and Work Engagement on the other, these scales will be related to concepts that are theoretically related to both workaholism and engagement but that are expected to show different patterns of relationships with these concepts. Three additional hypotheses are tested that specify different relationships of workaholism and work engagement with overwork, employee well-being, and performance, respectively.

Hypothesis 2: Like engagement, workaholism is associated with overwork, but this association is stronger for the work excess component than for the compulsion component of workaholism.

Hypothesis 3: Workaholism is negatively related to employee well-being, whereas associations with work engagement are positive.

Hypothesis 4: Workaholism is negatively related to job performance, whereas associations with work engagement are positive.

Method

Sample
Participants in this study were Dutch employees from a wide range of companies and occupations, who participated in a survey on the Internet ($N = 2, 164$). Table 9.1 compares some characteristics of the current sample with those of the Dutch workforce as a whole (Statistics Netherlands, 2005).

The chi-square tests reported in Table 9.1 show that males, younger workers and highly educated persons were significantly overrepresented in

Table 9.1   Sample characteristics compared with the Dutch workforce

Sample characteristic	Current sample (%) (N = 2164)	Dutch workforce (%)* (N = 7 444 000)
Gender[a]		
Men	64	58
Women	36	42
Age[b]		
15–24	12	15
25–44	55	52
45–65	33	33
Employment status[c]		
Company employed	88	87
Self-employed	12	13
Educational level[d]		
Low	12	27
Medium	31	43
High	57	30

Notes:
[a] = Chi-square with 1 df (N = 2164) = 32.00, $p < .001$;
[b] = Chi-square with 2 df (N = 2164) = 16.58, $p < .001$;
[c] = Chi-square with 1 df (N = 2164) = 1.86, ns;
[d] = Chi-square with 2 df (N = 2164) = 777.35, $p < .001$.

Source: Statistics Netherlands (2005).

our sample, compared with the Dutch workforce. This is a frequently recurring phenomenon in Internet surveys (for example, Bandilla et al., 2003), whereas the differences between the sample and the population categories are relatively small ($<$ 7 per cent), with the notable exception of the number of highly educated workers (57 per cent of our sample were highly educated workers, whereas only 30 per cent of the population are highly educated). There were no differences in employment status.

Procedure
Between September 2004 and April 2005 a survey was published on the website of the largest Dutch popular psychology magazine. Visitors to its homepage were invited to learn more about their work-related well-being – specifically workaholism and work engagement – by filling out a 60-item questionnaire that included socio-biographical background variables, questions about their job, and the questionnaires discussed below. The confidentiality and anonymity of the data was emphasized. After filling out the survey, participants were informed about their engagement and

workaholism scores, which were calculated on-line, and they received feedback that was automatically customized to their own workaholism and engagement scores. The data were automatically written to an external file. The data of 64 persons (3 per cent) were excluded from the analyses, because a closer look at the time of questionnaire completion, gender, age, profession, and the response pattern suggested that they had filled out the web survey more than once.

Instruments

Workaholism was measured with two scales: (1) the nine-item Dutch version (Taris et al., 2005) of the Compulsive Tendency scale proposed by Flowers and Robinson (2002), which was relabeled *Working Excessively* ($\alpha = .84$); (2) the eight-item Drive scale of Spence and Robbins' (1992) WorkBat, which was relabeled *Working Compulsively* ($\alpha = .86$). Both scales were scored on a 4-point rating, ranging from 1 ('totally disagree') to 4 ('totally agree') and correlate positively ($r = .66$, $p < .001$). Both workaholism scales are available on www.schaufeli.com.

Work engagement was assessed with the shortened, nine-item version of the Utrecht Work Engagement Scale (UWES; Schaufeli et al., 2006) ($\alpha = .93$). Example items are: 'At my job I feel strong and vigorous' and 'I am immersed in my work'. All items were scored on a seven-point rating scale ranging from 0 ('never') to 6 ('always').

Overwork was measured with two separate questions: 'How often do you take work home?' and 'How often do you work at weekends?' scored on a four-point rating scale ranging from 1 ('almost never') to 4 ('almost always'). The answers on both questions correlate strongly ($r = .54$, $p < .001$). In addition, an index was calculated of the *percentage of overtime* using the formula $[(a - c)/c]*100$, whereby a equals the number of actual work hours per week and c equals the number of contractual working hours per week. The mean percentage of overtime is 15.9 per cent ($SD = 16.1$), meaning that on average employees worked almost 16 per cent longer than was agreed upon in their labor contract. As expected, taking work home and working at weekends is correlated positively with the percentage of overwork ($r = .47$ and $r = .39$, respectively both $p < .001$).

Employee well-being was assessed with three indicators: (1) a rating of one's own level of *perceived health*: 'Generally speaking, how healthy do you feel?' (with a four-point rating scale ranging from 1 = 'almost never' to 4 = 'almost always'); (2) a rating of one's level of *overall life satisfaction*: 'Generally speaking, how satisfied are you with your life as a whole?' (with a four-point rating scale ranging from 1 = 'almost never' to 4 = 'almost always'); (3) the number of *sickness absence days* during the previous 12 months ($M = 7.68$; $SD = 27.02$). Perceived health and happiness are correlated positively ($r = .48$; $p < .001$) whereas both indicators are negatively related to sickness absence ($r = -.23$ and $r = -.12$, respectively both $p < .001$).

Job performance was assessed with three scales. *In-role performance*, which is defined as those officially required outcomes and behaviors that directly serve the goals of the organization (Motowidlo and Van Scotter, 1994), was measured by three items of Goodman and Svyantek's (1999) scale (for example, 'Achieves the objectives of the job'). Participants were asked to indicate the extent to which they found each statement characteristic of themselves (0 = not at all characteristic, 6 = totally characteristic) ($\alpha = .86$).

Extra-role performance, which is defined as discretionary behaviors that are believed to directly promote the effective functioning of an organization without necessarily directly influencing an employee's productivity (also termed *organizational citizenship behaviors*, McKenzie et al., 1991), was also measured by three items of Goodman and Svyantek's (1999) scale (for example, 'Willingly attends functions not required by the organization, but which help in its overall image'). The response format is similar to that used for in-role performance ($\alpha = .74$). Finally, the employee's level of *innovativeness* at work was measured by six items (for example, 'I invent new solutions for problems at work') based on Janssen (2003). A five-point response format was used, ranging from 1 ('never') to 5 ('very often') ($\alpha = .90$).

Results

The distinction between the measures of workaholism and work engagement (*Hypothesis 1*)

Structural equation modeling methods as implemented by AMOS (Arbuckle, 1997) were used to test the fit of two competing models: the one-factor model that includes *all* seventeen workaholism and *all* nine work engagement items (M1) versus the three-factor model that includes both workaholism dimensions (Working Excessively and Working Compulsively) and work-engagement (M2). Maximum likelihood estimation methods were used and the input for each analysis was the covariance matrix of the items. The goodness-of-fit of the models was evaluated using the χ^2 goodness-of-fit statistic. However, χ^2 is sensitive to sample size so that in a large sample – as in the present study – the probability of rejecting a hypothesized model is very high. To overcome this problem, the computation of relative goodness-of-fit indices is strongly recommended (Bentler, 1990). Two relative goodness-of-fit indices were computed: the Non-Normed Fit Index (NNFI) and the Comparative Fit Index (CFI). The latter is particularly recommended for model comparison purposes (Goffin, 1993). For both relative fit-indices, as a rule of thumb, values greater than .90 are considered as indicating a good fit (Byrne, 2001, pp. 79–88). In addition, the Root Mean Square Error of Approximation (RMSEA) is computed; for which values up to .08 indicate a reasonable fit of the model (Cudeck and Browne, 1983).

The fit to the data of M1 and M2 is displayed in Table 9.2. M1 fits poorly to the data, and thus – not surprisingly – the fit of M2 is clearly superior to that of M1: $\Delta\chi2$ $(df=4) = 9875.16$, $p<.001$. Inspection of the so-called Modification Indices for M2 revealed that the fit of the model could be increased by allowing two items tapping Working Excessively to load on the latent Working Compulsively factor. This makes sense because inspection of their contents revealed that rather than working excessively both items reflect work compulsion: 'I feel guilty when I am not working on something' and 'It is hard for me to relax when I am not working'. Therefore it was decided to change both workaholism scales accordingly: the revised work excess scale now contains seven items ($\alpha = .80$) and the revised Working Compulsively scale 10 items ($\alpha = .86$). The fit of M3 could be improved significantly by allowing four pairs of errors to correlate: $\Delta\chi2 (df=4) = 749.31, p<.001$. The rationale for this decision lies in the overlapping item content. For instance, the Working Compulsively items 'I feel obliged to work hard, even when it's not enjoyable' and 'It's important to me to work hard even when I don't enjoy what I'm doing' both refer to a strong need to work hard even when it is no fun. The fit of the final model M4 is superior to that of the one-factor model ($\Delta\chi2 (df=6) = 11130.38, p<.001$), with all fit-indices satisfying their respective criteria (see Table 9.2). Both latent factors, Working Excessively and Working Compulsively, are highly correlated ($r = .75; p<.001$), whereas the correlations of these two workaholism factors with engagement are substantially lower: $r = .33$ ($p<.001$) and $r = .05$ (*n.s.*), respectively. In conclusion: *Hypothesis 1* is confirmed: the two aspects of workaholism – working

Table 9.2   Fit of models specifying the relationship between workaholism and work engagement (N = 2164)

Model description		χ^2	df	AGFI	GFI	NFI	NNFI	CFI	RMSEA
M1	1-factor	14030.40	300	.35	.44	.49	.45	.50	.15
M2	Original 3-factor	4155.24	296	.83	.86	.85	.85	.86	.08
M3	Revised 3-factor	3649.33	296	.85	.88	.87	.88	.87	.07
M4	M3 plus correlated errors	2900.02	292	.88	.90	.90	.91	.91	.06

Note: For M1–M4 see text.

excessively and working compulsively – and work engagement can be distinguished from each other.

Relationships with overwork (*Hypothesis 2*)

Table 9.3 shows the relationships between the three indicators for overwork, and workaholism and work engagement. As hypothesized, *all* correlations displayed in Table 9.3 are positive, and *all* three indices of overwork are more strongly correlated with Working Excessively than with Working Compulsively: notably, work at weekends (t (2161) = 4.30, $p <$ .001), take work home (t (2161) = 9.12, $p < .001$) and overwork percentage (t (2161) = 12.88, $p < .001$). Consequently, the mean correlation across all three indicators of overwork also differs significantly (t (2161) = 11.35, $p <$ .001) between Working Excessively and Working Compulsively, with the former showing the strongest mean correlation ($r = .40$ *vs.* $r = 29$). This means that *Hypothesis 2* is confirmed. Additional analyses revealed that employees' *actual* work hours are more strongly related to all three measures than their contractual work hours: for Working Excessively, $r =$ .47 ($p < .001$) *vs.* $r = .26$ ($p < .001$); for Working Compulsively, $r = .29$ ($p <$ .001) *vs.* $r = .14$ ($p < .001$); and for Work Engagement, $r = .24$ ($p < .001$) *vs.* $r = .08$ ($p < .01$).

Relationships with employee well-being (*Hypothesis 3*)

In order to test *Hypothesis 3* on the relationship between workaholism and engagement on the one hand and employee well-being on the other hand, a path model was tested using AMOS (Arbuckle, 1997). That is, the model that was fitted to the data included exclusively observed variables. To correct for measurement error of the scale scores, the error variances of Working Excessively, Working Compulsively and Work Engagement were estimated using the formula $1 - \alpha$ (Var).

Table 9.3   *Correlations of overwork with working excessively (WE), working compulsively (WC) and work engagement (EN) (N = 2164)*

	WE	WC	EN
Work at weekends	.30	.25	.29
Take work home	.47	.36	.26
Overwork (%)	.42	.26	.25
Mean correlation	.40	.29	.27

Note: For all 'r's, $p < .001$.

The resulting model that is displayed in Figure 9.1 fits quite well to the data: χ^2 $(df=5)=33.31$ $(p<.001)$; AGFI$=.98$; GFI$=.99$; NFI$=.99$; NNFI$=.96$; CFI$=.99$. All estimated parameters in Figure 9.1 differ significantly from zero $(p<.001)$ and the model explains 19 per cent, 1 per cent and 16 per cent of the variance in health, sickness absenteeism and happiness, respectively. As predicted, workaholism is negatively related to perceived health and well-being, whereas associations with work engagement are positive (Figure 9.1). More particularly, Working Excessively and Working Compulsively are both negatively related to perceived health, but neither Working Excessively nor Working Compulsively is significantly related to sickness absence. In addition, Working Compulsively is negatively related to happiness, whereas Work Engagement is positively related to perceived health and happiness, and negatively related to sickness absence. Finally, the pattern of relationships between Working Excessively, Working Compulsively and Work Engagement is similar to M4 (see above) and – as to be expected – perceived health is negatively related to sickness absenteeism and positively to happiness. In sum, employees who work excessively hard report poor health and employees who work compulsively report that they feel less happy as well. Engaged employees, on the other hand, feel healthy and happy and they indicate that in the previous year they have been less frequently absent from work because of sickness. This

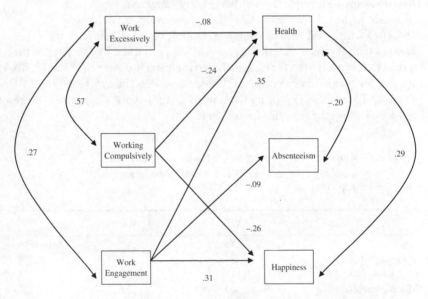

Figure 9.1   The relationships between workaholism, work engagement and employee well-being

means that *Hypothesis 3* is largely confirmed: six out of nine associations were significant and in the expected direction.

Relationships with job performance (*Hypothesis 4*)
In order to test *Hypothesis 4* on the relationship between workaholism and engagement on the one hand and performance on the other hand, a path model was tested using the same procedure as outlined above.

The model with three performance indicators displayed in Figure 9.2 only includes significant paths ($p < .001$) and fits quite well to the data: χ^2 ($df = 4$) = 6.19 ($p = .19$); AGFI = .99; GFI = 1.00; NFI = 1.00; NNFI = 1.00; CFI = 1.00. The model explains 14 per cent, 15 per cent and 23 per cent of the variance in in-role performance, extra-role performance and innovativeness, respectively. Contrary to expectations workaholism is also positively related to employee performance. More particularly, Working Excessively and Working Compulsively are related to extra-role performance but *not* to in-role performance. In addition, Working Excessively is positively related to innovativeness. Engagement is positively related to all three performance indicators. Finally, the pattern of relationships between Working Excessively, Working Compulsively and Work Engagement is similar to M4 and to the model displayed in Figure 9.1. In sum, employees who work excessively hard and who work compulsively exhibit greater

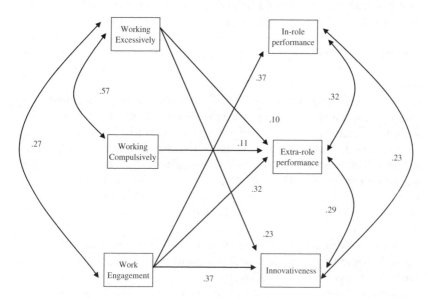

Figure 9.2   *The relationships between workaholism, work engagement and employee performance*

extra-role performance, whereas those who only work hard also show more innovativeness. Engaged employees, on the other hand, report more in-role and extra-role performance as well as more innovativeness. This means that *Hypothesis 4* was confirmed for engagement but *not* for workaholism.

Discussion

The aim of the present chapter is to contribute to the ongoing discussion about the 'good' or 'bad' nature of workaholism. The literature on workaholism is inconclusive on this issue; some authors consider workaholism as inherently 'bad', some consider it inherently 'good', whereas still others consider it 'good' or 'bad', depending on its form (see Snir and Harpaz, 2004, for an overview). We believe that it is wrong to subsume different psychological phenomena under the same rubric (for example, 'good' workaholism and 'bad' workaholism), not only because it obscures differences and creates conceptual confusion, but also because it hinders empirical research. This is even more salient when the phenomena are assessed by the same instrument, such as the WorkBat (Spence and Robbins, 1992).

The first contribution of our study is that we introduced the recently emerged notion of work engagement (Maslach et al., 2001; Schaufeli et al., 2002a) as the equivalent of what has been described in the literature as 'good' workaholism, denoted by such terms as hyper-performing workaholics (Korn et al., 1987), happy workaholics (Keichel, 1989), achievement-oriented workaholics (Naughton, 1987), work enthusiasts (Spence and Robbins, 1992) and happy hard workers (Buelens and Poelmans, 2004). So we refined and clarified the conceptual framework to study positive and negative forms of employee well-being.

Secondly, we operationalized 'good' workaholism or engagement using the Utrecht Work Engagement Scale (Schaufeli et al., 2002a), which includes items that refer to vigor (working hard), dedication (being involved) and absorption (feeling happily engrossed in one's work). 'Bad' workaholism was defined as a behavioral pattern that is characterized by working excessively hard out of an inner compulsion. This conceptualization is similar to its original meaning, as formulated by Oates (1971), who characterized workaholism as an addiction akin to alcoholism (see also Porter, 1996).

Third, we demonstrated the discriminant validity of workaholism (working hard compulsively) versus work engagement by showing that the instruments to assess workaholism and work engagement can be distinguished, and that both concepts relate differently to various sets of variables (that is, overwork, employee health and performance). Below, the results are discussed in greater detail.

The distinction between the measures of workaholism and work engagement (*Hypothesis 1*)

Using a large Internet survey that included over 2000 Dutch employees, we first studied the factorial validity of the questionnaires that were used to assess workaholism and work engagement. Confirmatory factor analyses showed that the fit to the data of the three-factor model including both workaholism scales (Working Excessively and Working Compulsively) and work engagement was superior to that of the undifferentiated one-factor model in which all items were lumped together. This means that *Hypothesis 1* was confirmed: both workaholism components can be differentiated for work engagement. As expected, these two workaholism components are strongly correlated, sharing more than half of their variances. The finding that the excess work component was positively correlated with work engagement, whereas the compulsion component was *not*, underscores that working compulsively, rather than working hard, lies at the core of workaholism. In other words, it is the strong inner drive – or the addiction component – that distinguishes 'good' from 'bad' workaholism and not the hard work per se. This agrees with Porter (1996), who argues that, in essence, workaholism is an addiction. She defines workaholism as 'excessive involvement with work evidenced by neglect in other areas of life and based on internal motives of behavior maintenance rather than requirements of the job or organization' (p. 71). So it seems that, indeed, with our operationalization of workaholism we returned to the origin of the concept: workaholism as work addiction.

In testing the factorial validity of both workaholism scales it appeared that two items loaded on the 'wrong' factor; instead of loading on Working Excessively, they loaded on Working Compulsively. Inspection of both items revealed that these were the only items that did *not* refer to working excessively hard, but referred to the inability to relax and to feeling guilty when not working, respectively. Thus, rather than being typical for working excessively, both items reflect the compulsive component of workaholism. It is interesting to note that originally five of the nine items of the Working Excessively scale were supposed to constitute a scale dubbed 'Overdoing', and that both wrongly loading items were supposed to be part of *another* scale labeled 'Self-worth' (Robinson and Post, 1994). So it seems that our relabeling, as well as our findings from the factor analyses, are in line with the original sub-scale structure of the WART.

In sum, our findings show that both workaholism scales – reflecting working excessively and working compulsively – are highly interrelated and can be discriminated from work engagement. Although at first glance two workaholism items loaded on the 'wrong' factor, subsequent inspection of their content showed that they had been misplaced. Finally, it appeared that working excessively was positively related to work engagement, indicating that working hard is characteristic of 'good' as well as for 'bad' workaholism. In contrast, working compulsively is *not* related to work engagement, indicating that it is typical for 'bad' workaholism.

Relationships with overwork (*Hypothesis 2*)

As expected (*Hypothesis 2*), working at weekends, taking work home, and working longer than one's regular contractual work hours is more strongly positively associated with the excess work component of workaholism than with its compulsive component. In fact, this result underscores the conceptual validity of the work excess component, because working excessively implies working more hours (outside the workplace). It is important to note that the positive correlations cannot be explained by item overlap, because none of the work excess items refers to working at weekends or taking work home, and only one item refers to making long work hours: 'I find myself continuing working after my co-workers have called it quits'. In fact, rather than working extra hours the Working Excessively scale reflects being busy and working hard at work; for instance, by racing against the clock, doing more things at one time, and keeping many irons in the fire. The positive correlations of the three indicators of overwork with both workaholism components concur with the prevailing view that workaholics work 'any time and anywhere' (McMillan et al., 2001, p. 71). If anything, students of workaholism agree that workaholics work, or think about work, in any circumstances. This is illustrated by Scott et al. (1997, p. 292), who concluded after their thorough review of the literature: 'Our analysis, like that of Spence and Robbins (1992), revealed clearly that the amount of time spent in work was the critical defining feature of workaholism.' However, our results indicate that engaged workers also often take work home, work at weekends and perform overwork. On balance, the size of the correlation is similar to that of the compulsive component. Using a large representative sample of the Dutch workforce, Beckers et al. (2004) found a comparable positive correlation between (self-reported) overwork and work engagement ($r = .21$). So, rather than being specific for workaholism in general, overwork seems to be related to the particular aspect of excess work, whilst 'good' workaholics – those who are engaged – also work beyond what is required by the job or by the organization.

Relationships with employee well-being (*Hypothesis 3*)

Although *Hypothesis 3*, which stated that workaholism is negatively related to employee well-being and work engagement is positively related to well-being, was largely confirmed, not *all* relationships were significant (see Figure 9.1). For instance, working excessively was only (weakly) negatively related to perceived health and neither to absenteeism nor to happiness. The fact that hard work is related to poor perceived health agrees with previous research that showed that working excessively long hours is associated with elevated levels of strain and ill health (for a review, see Van der Hulst, 2003). The second component of workaholism – working compulsively – is (more strongly) negatively related to perceived health and happiness. This is in line with observations from other studies that suggest that a strong inner drive may be the harmful element of workaholism (McMillan et al., 2001; McMillan and O'Driscoll, 2004). It can be speculated that, contrary to working compulsively, working excessively leads to rewards such as pay, recognition, career advancement and esteem (Peiperl and Jones, 2001) that may buffer negative effects on employee health and well-being.

Furthermore, it is interesting to note that *neither* working excessively *nor* working compulsively is significantly related to sickness absenteeism. Despite their high job involvement (Mudrack, 2004) and their strong work ethic (Porter, 2004), workaholics do *not* seem to be less absent from work than their less addicted colleagues. Conversely, engaged employees report fewer sickness absence days, and also better health and more happiness, than those who are less engaged. Generally speaking, compared with workaholism, relationships of engagement with well-being outcomes are also stronger. In sum, particularly working compulsively seems to be 'bad' for employees' well-being, whereas work engagement seems to be 'good' for employees' well-being.

Relationships with employee performance (*Hypothesis 4*)

Contrary to expectations (*Hypothesis 4*), instead of negatively workaholism was *positively* related to performance – at least as far as extra-role performance and innovativeness were concerned (see Figure 9.2). The fact that both workaholism components are positively related to extra-role performance but unrelated to in-role performance suggests that workaholics go beyond their job description. According to most authors, working beyond what is reasonably required by the job or by the organization is a hallmark of workaholism (Scott et al., 1997). And this is exactly what extra-role performance is all about: going the extra mile (Morrison, 1994). Innovativeness – by the way – may be considered a special type of extra-role performance because, for instance, inventing original solutions for work problems is usually not included in the employee's job description. In-role performance, on the other hand, refers to activities strictly required on the job and includes meeting organizational objectives and effective functioning (Behrman and Perreault, 1982). Obviously, contrary to 'extra-ordinary' extra-role performance, working excessively and working compulsively are not related to 'ordinary' in-role performance. An alternative explanation why workaholism is positively instead of negatively related to performance might be that we assessed *self-reported* performance. It cannot be ruled out that performance as assessed by colleagues, supervisors or company records would show the expected pattern, as by their very nature workaholics see themselves as driven, hard-working, successful and well-performing employees.

Hypothesis 4 is supported as far as work engagement is concerned – it is positively and significantly associated with all three performance indicators. As in the case of employee well-being, relationships with work engagement are stronger than with workaholism. In sum, both workaholism and work engagement seem to be 'good' for employees' performance, albeit that for workaholism this only applies for extra-role performance and not for in-role performance.

Limitations and suggestions for further research

All data in the current study are based on self-reports, which means that the magnitude of the effects that we reported may have been biased, owing to common method variance or the wish to answer consistently (Conway, 2002). Unfortunately, we cannot test the strength of this type of bias but several studies (for example, Semmer et al., 1996) have indicated that common method variance is not as troublesome as one might expect in studies such as the current one. Nevertheless, we believe that future research could greatly benefit from including more objectively measured variables, such as company records, for measuring absenteeism rates and work performance.

Another potential limitation is the nature of the sample, which was somewhat biased; compared with the Dutch workforce, slightly more men (6 per cent) and much more highly-educated employees (27 per cent) were included. Despite the popular belief that workaholism is particularly prevalent among those with higher occupational or educational levels, this is not supported by empirical evidence (Buelens and Poelmans, 2004; Snir and Harpaz, 2004). The same applies for age and gender but, compared with salaried employees, the self-employed have higher levels of workaholism (Snir and Harpaz, 2004). Fortunately our sample was representative for the Dutch workforce as far as type of employment is concerned (see Table 9.1). Hence, it seems unlikely that our results are distorted by sample bias.

Another limitation is the cross-sectional nature of our study that precludes cause–effect relationships from being uncovered. For at least two reasons, longitudinal research is important when it comes to discriminating workaholism from work engagement. First, both may be causally linked. For instance, one could speculate that work engagement might develop into workaholism when the employee becomes more and more 'drawn into' work, whereas the reverse – a workaholic stepping back from work – seems much less likely. Second, employee well-being and performance may be distinctively causally related to workaholism and work engagement. For instance, work engagement and well-being might be reciprocally related in such a way that an upward gain-spiral develops, resulting in higher engagement and greater well-being (Llorens et al., forthcoming). On the other hand, it can be speculated that the opposite might occur for workaholism (particularly working compulsively): the harder the employee works, the more his or her well-being is corroded and the more the capacity to work hard is undermined – a downward loss-spiral. Not surprisingly, it has been suggested that workaholism might lead to burnout (Maslach, 1986). However, this assumption still remains to be tested using a longitudinal design.

A unique feature of the current study was the use of the Internet as a research tool, which can be considered a weakness and strength. On the negative side, Internet surveys usually attract participants of higher socio-economic and educational status (Smith and Leigh, 1997) and thus suffer from selection bias. As we have seen, this is also the case in our study but it is not very likely that this has greatly influenced our results. On the positive side, the present research includes employees from a wide range of occupations and employment sectors, ranging from industry (6 per cent), commerce (7 per cent) and transportation (7 per cent) to education (12 per cent) and health care (23 per cent). The majority of the sample work with people (71 per cent), while the remaining employees work with data (22 per cent) or with things (7 per cent). Using traditional sampling techniques, it would have been very difficult to obtain such a large and heterogeneous sample.

Final remark

Our study suggests that 'bad' workaholism can be distinguished from 'good' workaholism. The latter was operationalized as work engagement because the description in the literature of 'good' workaholism comes very close to how this recently emerged concept is described. Overall, it seems that working excessively but particularly working compulsively is 'bad' for employees' well-being. However, in terms of self-reported performance, workaholism seems to be 'good'. Work engagement, on the other hand, is related much more strongly and positively to *all* indicators of employee well-being and performance. So, despite the fact that, like workaholics, engaged employees work hard, their work involvement is 'good'.

REFERENCES

Arbuckle, J.L. (1997), *AMOS Users' Guide Version 4.0*, Chicago, IL: Smallwaters Corporation.

Bandilla, W., Bosnjak, M. and Altdorfer, P. (2003), 'Survey administration effects? A comparison of web-based and traditional written self-administered surveys using the ISSP environment module', *Social Science Computer Review*, **2**, 235–43.

Beckers, D.G.J., Van der Linden, D., Smulders, P.G.W., Kompier, M.A.J., Van Veldhoven, J.P.M. and Van Yperen, N.W. (2004), 'Working overtime hours: relations with fatigue, work motivation, and the quality of work', *Journal of Occupational and Environmental Medicine*, **46**, 1282–9.

Behrman, D.N. and Perreault, W.D. (1982), 'Measuring performance of industrial persons', *Journal of Business Research*, **10**, 355–70.

Bentler, P.M. (1990), 'Comparative fit indexes in structural equation models', *Psychological Bulletin*, **107**, 238–46.

Bonebright, C.A., Clay, D.L. and Ankenmann, R.D. (2000), 'The relationship of workaholism with work–life conflict, life satisfaction, and purpose in life', *Journal of Counseling Psychology*, **47**, 469–77.

Brett, J.M. and Stroh, L.K. (2003), 'Working 61 plus hours per week: why do managers do it?', *Journal of Applied Psychology*, **88**, 67–78.

Buelens, M. and Poelmans, S.A.Y. (2004), 'Enriching the Spence and Robbins' typology of workaholism: demographic, motivational and organizational correlates', *Organizational Change Management*, **17**, 459–70.

Burke, R.J. (1999), 'It's not how hard you work but how you work hard: evaluating workaholism components', *International Journal of Stress Management*, **6**, 225–40.

Burke, R.J. (2000), 'Workaholism in organizations: psychological and physical well-being consequences', *Stress Medicine*, **16**, 11–16.

Burke, R.J. (2001), 'Workaholism components, job satisfaction, and career progress', *Journal of Applied Social Psychology*, **31**, 2339–56.

Burke, R.J., Richardsen, A.M. and Mortinussen, M. (2004), 'Workaholism among Norwegian managers: work and well-being outcomes', *Journal of Organizational Change Management*, **7**, 459–70.

Byrne, B.M. (2001), *Structural Equation Modeling with AMOS: Basic Concepts, Applications, and Programming*, Mahwah, NJ: Erlbaum.

Cantarow, E. (1979), 'Woman workaholics', *Mother Jones*, **6**, 56.

Cherrington, D.J. (1980), '*The Work Ethic*', New York: American Management Association.

Conway, J.M. (2002), 'Method variance and method bias in industrial and organizational psychology', in S.G. Rogelberg (ed.), *Handbook of Research Methods in Organizational and Industrial Psychology*, Malden, NJ: Blackwell Publishers, pp. 344–65.

Cudeck, R. and Browne, M.W. (1983), 'Alternative ways of assessing model fit', in K.A. Bollen and J. Scott Long (eds), *Testing Structural Equation Models*, Newbury Park, CA: Sage, pp. 1–9.

Demerouti, E., Bakker, A.B., De Jonge, J., Janssen, P.P.M. and Schaufeli, W.B. (2001), 'Burnout and engagement at work as a function of demands and control', *Scandinavian Journal of Work, Environment and Health*, **27**, 279–86.

Durán, A., Extremera, N. and Rey, L. (2004), 'Engagement and burnout: analyzing their association patterns', *Psychological Reports*, **94**, 1048–50.

Flowers, C. and Robinson, B.E. (2002), 'A structural and discriminant analysis of the Work Addiction Risk Test', *Educational and Psychological Measurement*, **62**, 517–26.

Goffin, R.D. (1993), 'A comparison of two new indices for the assessment of fit of structural equation models', *Multivariate Behavioral Research*, **28**, 205–14.

Goodman, S.A. and Svyantek, D.J. (1999), 'Person–organization fit and contextual performance: do shared values matter?', *Journal of Vocational Behavior*, **55**, 254–75.

Hallberg, U. and Schaufeli, W.B. (2006), '"Same same but different": can work engagement be discriminated from job involvement and organizational commitment?', *European Psychologist*, **11**, 119–27

Harter, J.K., Schmidt, F.L. and Hayes, T.L. (2002), 'Business-Unit-Level relationship between employee satisfaction, employee engagement, and business outcomes: a meta-analysis', *Journal of Applied Psychology*, **87**, 268–79.

Janssen, O. (2003), 'Innovative behavior and job involvement at the price of conflict and less satisfactory relations with co-workers', *Journal of Occupational and Organizational Psychology*, **76**, 347–64.

Kanai, A. and Wakabayashi, M. (2001), 'Workaholism among Japanese blue-collar employees', *International Journal of Stress Management*, **8**, 129–203.

Kanai, A., Wakabayashi, M. and Fling, S. (1996), 'Workaholism among employees in Japanese corporations: an examination based on the Japanese version of the Workaholism Scales', *Japanese Psychological Research*, **38**, 192–203.

Keichel, W. (1989), 'The workaholic generation', *Fortune*, **119**, 50–62.

Killinger, B. (1991), *Workaholics: The Respectable Addicts*, New York: Simon and Schuster.

Korn, E.R., Pratt, G.J. and Lambrou, P.T. (1987), *Hyper-performance: The A.I.M. Strategy for Releasing your Business Potential*, New York: John Wiley.

Llorens, S., Salanova, M., Bakker, A.B. and Schaufeli, W.B. (forthcomiong), 'Does a positive gain spiral of resources, efficacy beliefs and engagement exist?', *Computers in Human Behavior*.

Lloret, S. and González-Romá, V. (2003), 'How do respondents construe ambiguous response formats of affect items?', *Journal of Personality and Social Psychology*, **85**, 956–68.

Machlowitz, M. (1980), *Workaholics: Living with Them, Working with Them*, New York: Simon and Schuster.

Maslach, C. (1986), 'Stress, burnout and workaholism', in R.R. Killberg, P.E. Nathan and R.W. Thoreson (eds), *Professionals in Distress: Issues, Syndromes and Solutions in Psychology*, Washington, DC: American Psychological Association, pp. 53–73.

Maslach, C., Schaufeli, W.B. and Leiter, M.P. (2001), 'Job burnout', *Annual Review of Psychology*, **52**, 397–422.

McKenzie, S.B., Podsakoff, P.M. and Fetter, R. (1991), 'Organizational citizenship behavior and objective productivity as determinants of managerial evaluations of salespersons' performance', *Organizational Behavior and Human Decision Processes*, **50**, 123–50.

McMillan, L.H.W. and O'Driscoll, M.P. (2004), 'Workaholism and health: implications for organizations', *Organizational Change Management*, **17**, 509–19.

McMillan, L.H.W. O'Driscoll, M.P. and Burke, R.J. (2003), 'Workaholism: a review of theory, research, and future directions', in C.L. Cooper and I.T. Robertson (eds), *International Review of Industrial and Organizational Psychology, Vol. 18*, New York: Wiley, pp. 167–89.

McMillan, L.H.W., Brady, E.C., O'Driscoll, M.P. and Marsh, N.V. (2002), 'A multifaceted validation study of Spence and Robbin's (1992) Workaholism Battery', *Journal of Occupational and Organizational Psychology*, **75**, 357–68.

McMillan, L.H.W., O'Driscoll, M.P., Marsh, N.V. and Brady, E.C. (2001), 'Understanding workaholism: data synthesis, theoretical critique, and future design strategies', *International Journal of Stress Management*, **8**, 69–91.

Montgomery, A.J., Peeters, M.C.W., Schaufeli, W.B. and Den Ouden, M. (2003), 'Work–home interference among newspaper managers: its relationship with burnout and engagement', *Anxiety, Stress and Coping*, **16**, 195–211.

Morrison, E.W. (1994), 'Role definitions and organizational citizenship behavior: the importance of the employee's perspective', *Academy of Management Journal*, **37**, 1543–67.

Motowidlo, S.J. and Van Scotter, J.R. (1994), 'Evidence that task performance should be distinguished from contextual performance', *Journal of Applied Psychology*, **79**, 475–80.

Mudrack, P.E. (2004), 'Job involvement, obsessive-compulsive personality traits, and workaholic behavioral tendencies', *Journal of Organizational Change Management*, **17**, 490–508.

Mudrack, P.E. and Naughton, T.J. (2001), 'The assessment of workaholism as behavioral tendencies: scale development and preliminary testing', *International Journal of Stress Management*, **8**, 93–112.

Naughton, T.J. (1987), 'A conceptual view of workaholism and implications for career counseling and research', *Career Development Quarterly*, **35**, 180–87.

Oates, W. (1971), *Confessions of a Workaholic: The Facts about Work Addiction*, New York: World Publishing Co.

Peiperl, M. and Jones, B. (2001), 'Workaholics and overworkers: productivity or pathology?', *Group and Organization Management*, **26**, 369–93.

Porter, G. (1996), 'Organizational impact of workaholism: suggestions for research-ing the negative outcomes of excessive work', *Journal of Occupational Health Psychology*, **1**, 70–84.

Porter, G. (2001), 'Workaholic tendencies and the high potential for stress among co-workers', *International Journal of Stress Management*, **8**, 147–64.

Porter, G. (2004), 'Work, work ethic, work excess', *Journal of Organizational Change Management*, **17**, 424–39.

Robinson, B.E. (1989), *Work addiction*, Dearfield Beach, FL: Health Communi-cations.

Robinson, B.E. (1999), 'The Work Addiction Risk Test: development of a tentative measure of workaholism', *Perceptual and Motor Skills*, **88**, 199–210.

Robinson, B.E. and Post, P. (1994), 'Validity of the Work Addiction Risk Test', *Perceptual and Motor Skills*, **78**, 337–8.

Salanova, M., Agut, S. and Peiró, J.M. (2005a), 'Linking organizational resources and work engagement to employee performance and customer loyalty: the medi-ating role of service climate', *Journal of Applied Psychology*, **90**, 1217–27.

Salanova, M., Bresó, E. and Schaufeli, W.B. (2005b), 'Hacia un modelo espiral de la autoeficacia en el estudio del burnout y engagement [Towards a spiral model of self-efficacy in burnout and engagement research]', *Estress y Ansiedad*, **11**, 215–31.

Salanova, M., Schaufeli, W.B., Llorens, S., Peiró, J.M. and Grau, R. (2000), 'Desde el "burnout" al "engagement": una nueva perspectiva [From burnout to engage-ment: a new perspective]', *Revista de Psicología del Trabajo y de las Organizaciones*, **16**, 117–34.

Schaef, A.W. and Fassel, D. (1988), *The Addictive Organization*, San Francisco, CA: Harper and Row.

Schaufeli, W.B. and Bakker, A.B. (2004), 'Job demands, job resources and their relationship with burnout and engagement: a multi-sample study', *Journal of Organizational Behaviour*, **25**, 293–315.

Schaufeli, W.B. and Salanova, M. (forthcoming), 'Work engagement: an emerging psychological concept and its implications for organizations', in S.W. Gilliland, D.D. Steiner and D.P. Skarlicki (eds), *Research in Social Issues in Management*, Greenwich, CT: Information Age Publishers.

Schaufeli, W.B., Bakker, A.B. and Salanova, M. (2006), 'The measurement of work engagement with a short questionnaire: a cross-national study', *Educational and Psychological Measurement*, **66**, 701–16.

Schaufeli, W.B., Taris, T.W. and Van Rhenen, W. (2005), 'Workaholism, burnout and engagement: three of a kind or three different kinds of employee well-being?', manuscript submitted for publication.

Schaufeli, W.B., Salanova, M., González-Romá, V. and Bakker, A.B. (2002a), 'The measurement of engagement and burnout: a confirmatory factor analytic approach', *Journal of Happiness Studies*, **3**, 71–92.

Schaufeli, W.B., Martinez, I., Marques Pinto, A. Salanova, M. and Bakker, A.B. (2002b), 'Burnout and engagement in university students: a cross national study', *Journal of Cross-Cultural Psychology*, **33**, 464–81.

Schaufeli, W.B., Taris, T., Le Blanc, P., Peeters, M., Bakker, A.B. and De Jonge, J. (2001), 'Maakt arbeid gezond? Op zoek naar de bevlogen werknemer [Does work make one healthy? The quest for the engaged worker]', *De Psycholoog*, **36**, 422–8.

Scott, K.S., Moore, K.S. and Miceli, M.P. (1997), 'An exploration of the meaning and consequences of workaholism', *Human Relations*, **50**, 287–314.

Semmer, N., Zapf, D. and Greif, S. (1996), ' "Shared job strain": a new approach for assessing the validity of job stress managements', *Journal of Occupational and Organizational Psychology*, **69**, 293–310.

Smith, M.A. and Leigh, B. (1997), 'Virtual subjects: using internet as an alternative source of subjects and research environment', *Behavior, Research Methods, Instruments and Computers*, **29**, 496–505.

Snir, R. and Harpaz, I. (2004), 'Attitudinal and demographic antecedents of workaholism', *Journal of Organizational Change Management*, **17**, 520–36.

Spence, J.T. and Robbins, A.S. (1992), 'Workaholism: definition, measurement, and preliminary results', *Journal of Personality Assessment*, **58**, 160–78.

Statistics Netherlands (2005), *StatLine Databank*, retrieved 15 August 2005, from http://www.cbs.nl/nl/cijfers/statline/index.htm.

Taris, T.W., Schaufeli, W.B. and Verhoeven, L.C. (2005), 'Internal and external validation of the Dutch Work Addiction Risk Test: implications for jobs and non-work conflict', *Applied Psychology: An International Review*, **54**, 37–60.

Van der Hulst, M. (2003), 'Long work hours and health', *Scandinavian Journal of Work, Environment and Health*, **29**, 171–88.

PART IV

Addressing work hours and workaholism

10. 'Decent working time': balancing the needs of workers and employers

Jon C. Messenger*

BACKGROUND

Over the last several decades a number of broad socio-economic trends have emerged which have had an enormous impact on the hours that we work. These trends include globalization and the resulting intensification of competition, advances in information and communications technologies, and new patterns of consumer demand for goods and services in an emerging '24-hour economy'. There have also been profound demographic changes, particularly the increasing entry of women into the paid labour market, and the resulting shift from single-earner to dual-earner (or at least 'one-and-one-half earner') households. All of these changes are reflected in a variety of working time arrangements that differ from traditional full-time, permanent, weekday work in terms of their duration and/or timing. For example, some workers are working much longer hours, while others are working fewer hours as part-time work has expanded – especially in many of the old European Union (EU-15) member states, most notably the Netherlands.

In other words, the assumption of a relatively uniform or 'standard' working week for most (if not all) non-managerial workers is no longer valid; an increasing diversity in the paid workforce is being complemented by an increasing diversity in the hours being worked. And this growing diversity in hours worked is not limited to the *number* of hours worked. Other factors, including advances in information and communications technologies and new patterns in consumer demand for goods and services, have also been changing the *timing* of when workers need to be available for work. In response, enterprises have been demanding increasing flexibility to respond more rapidly to these fluctuations in demand,

---

* The author is Senior Research Officer at the International Labour Office (ILO) in Geneva, Switzerland. The responsibility for the opinions expressed in this chapter rests solely with the author, and do not necessarily reflect the policies or positions of the ILO.

including an increased use of temporal (working time) flexibility measures, such as working 'on call' as and when needed, and annualized hours schemes allowing for the averaging of working hours over periods of up to a year. All of these developments have contributed to a growing concern about conflicts between paid work and workers' personal responsibilities (including unpaid domestic and care work) and point to the importance of helping workers to achieve a better work–life balance.

THE CONCEPT OF 'DECENT WORKING TIME'

In response to these changing circumstances, the International Labour Organization (ILO) has sought to advance 'decent work', that is, to 'promote opportunities for women and men to obtain decent and product-ive work, in conditions of freedom, equity, security, and human dignity' (ILO, 1999, p. 3). Decent work includes four distinct but mutually re-inforcing components: creating employment; ensuring certain fundamen-tal principles and rights at work, such as freedom of association and the elimination of discrimination in the workplace; providing adequate social protection, such as the provision of health care and insurance against old age and disability; and promoting social dialogue, in order to ensure that different stakeholders have the opportunity to make their voices heard. That is, decent work is about both creating jobs and ensuring that those jobs meet certain minimum standards of quality.

A recent ILO publication (Messenger, 2004a) has analyzed the gaps between the working hours that individuals need or would prefer and the actual hours that they are required to work. This report found that there are several different types of 'gaps' between workers' actual and preferred hours of work that are particularly common. These include the following situa-tions: those workers who are working 'excessively' long hours and would prefer to work substantially fewer hours; those workers who are working part-time – and especially those in 'marginal' part-time jobs of less than 20 hours per week – who would prefer to work more hours; and finally, those workers for whom the primary concern was not the number of hours they are working, but rather the *arrangement* of those hours, particularly for those working at night, at weekends, or on irregular or rotating shift schedules.

From the perspective of decent work, these gaps which exist between people's aspirations regarding their work and their current work situations can be viewed as 'decent work deficits'. The ILO defines a decent work deficit as 'a gap between the world that we work in and the hopes that people have for a better life' (ILO, 2001, p. 8). Thus, the gaps that have been identified between workers' actual and preferred hours of work can be considered as one type of decent work deficit. By adopting this approach, we can establish a basis from which to consider how the goal of decent work can be advanced in the arena of working time – that is, 'decent working time'.

Based upon both the existing international labour standards in the area of working time and recent research on working time trends and developments focusing on industrialized countries,[1] the ILO's Conditions of Work and Employment Programme has proposed five significant dimensions of 'decent working time'. These five dimensions provide a broad policy framework by which the goal of decent work can be advanced in the arena of working time. The five dimensions are as follows: working time arrangements should be healthy; 'family-friendly'; promote gender equality; advance the productivity of enterprises; and facilitate worker choice and influence over their hours of work. Advancing each of these five dimensions requires a broad range of policies, which may be articulated at the national, sectoral and/or enterprise levels. Of course, the precise mix of policies that need to be pursued will vary substantially across countries (and perhaps even across states or regions within the same country), depending upon the socio-economic realities in each country.

DIMENSION ONE: HEALTHY WORKING TIME

The first of the five dimensions of decent working time is healthy working time. The need for working time to be both healthy and safe is a traditional concern – one that dates back to the very first international labour standard, the Hours of Work (Industry) Convention in 1919. Long working hours and 'unsocial' working hours, particularly night work, are neither preferred by workers nor healthy for them. Moreover, one must keep in mind that the effects of long hours and so-called unsocial working hours (that is, work in the evenings, at nights and at weekends) are not limited to individual workers, but also affect their families and society at large (see, for example, Spurgeon (2003) for a review of the effects of working time on health and safety).

The principle which underlies this dimension of decent working time is that hours of work which are unhealthy should not be a means of improving firms' profitability, a principle referred to in the international standards on working time, most significantly the Hours of Work (Industry) Convention, 1919 (No. 1) and the Hours of Work (Commerce and Offices) Convention, 1930 (No. 30). This principle is also a primary objective of the European Union (EU) Directive on Working Time (93/104/EC).

Nevertheless, as Golden (2004) points out, both employers and individual workers may not properly consider the potential negative effects on health and safety in determining working hours, which may result in the

overutilization of labour or 'overwork'. Golden (ibid., p. 6) defines overwork as the point 'when the length of work hours begins to adversely affect
the health and safety of individuals, families, organizations and the public,
even if workers themselves voluntarily work the excess hours'. He emphasizes that these negative externalities with regard to health and safety – that
is, the 'spillover costs of overwork' – justify the need for some type of regulation to provide a 'countervailing force' to restrain excessively long hours
(ibid., p. 16). Golden emphasizes that the need for such regulation holds
not only in those cases in which the long hours are involuntary, but even
when the long hours are worked 'voluntarily',[2] in order to protect the safety
and health of both the workers involved and the general public. A similar
justification can be applied to protective measures concerning night work
and other forms of 'unsocial' hours.

Appropriate public policies to protect workers against excessively long
and unsocial working hours are a necessary, but not sufficient, condition
for achieving the goal of healthy working time. Both Campbell (2004) and
Golden (2004) point to the relatively weak regulatory and institutional
frameworks regarding working time which exist in Australia and the
United States, respectively, as being important factors in the increasing
incidence of long or 'extended' hours in those countries (see also Lee,
2004). Noting that the move towards longer hours is the dominant trend
for full-time employees in Australia, Campbell (2004) stresses the importance of unpaid overtime, particularly among managers and different categories of salaried professionals, and a lack of paid annual leave due to an
increasing casualization of the Australian labour force. Obviously, these
factors relate directly to the regulatory framework in Australia, which
excludes most professionals and managers from overtime pay requirements, which might help limit the recourse to extended hours, and excludes
'casual workers'[3] from employee entitlements such as a minimum amount
of paid annual leave. Similarly, Golden notes that the only regulatory res-
traints on long working hours in the US are the overtime premium imposed
under the Fair Labor Standards Act (FLSA) and the weekly and daily limitations on hours of work that apply only to truck drivers. There is no
general limitation on maximum hours of work in the US, and a broad range
of managerial, professional and technical occupations are exempt from the
overtime pay requirements of the FLSA under regulations which are established by the US Department of Labor.[4]

Nonetheless, establishing a sound national framework for regulating
working time is not, in and of itself, sufficient to make healthy working
time a reality. Strong economic pressures or incentives towards long or
'extended' hours can reduce the effectiveness of any regulatory framework.
For example, it appears that the traditional link between low pay and long

hours continues to exist in many developing countries, as overtime payments provide an important source of additional income for some low-wage workers. This is particularly true for workers with low educational levels, especially in developing countries such as Brazil and China (Saboia, 2002; Zeng et al., 2005). Paid overtime, while increasing the earnings of these workers, can, however, become institutionalized, often as a cost-saving strategy for firms as compared with the increased fixed costs of hiring additional workers. When this occurs, workers may gradually come to accept long hours of work – in some cases, they may even come to be 'dependent' on the additional income generated by overtime working – adjusting their working hour preferences towards their current hours (as suggested by Golden, 2004) and becoming unwilling or (economically) unable to reduce their working hours. In this case, perhaps the most effective policy for encouraging reduced working hours is a minimum wage set at a level sufficient to allow workers to earn a 'decent' income during the standard or 'normal' workweek.

In addition, it is becoming more and more obvious that, at least in the industrialized world, those workers with the highest levels of remuneration, such as managers and professionals, exhibit the longest working hours. As Nätti et al. (2004) report in their study of working time in Finland, long working hours were best predicted by occupational status, with managers and professionals being substantially more likely to work long hours compared with other occupational categories. According to this study, '[a]mbiguity of working time is a reality for many knowledge workers in Finland: half of them had difficulties in defining their working hours, men more often compared to women' (ibid., p. 11). The most common reason that they found for such 'ambiguous' and 'stretching' working hours among managers and professionals was the 'nature of the work' (ibid.).

In other cases, however, it may be that corporate culture and management strategies, as well as intense competition among colleagues, induce workers to work long hours. For example, Haipeter (2004), working with Lehndorff on a series of case studies of German firms with innovative working time systems (see, for example, Lehndorff, 2002), emphasizes the 'financialization' of corporate decision-making, which focuses on increasing shareholder value (and often results in cutting staff levels to an absolute minimum), combined with the use of 'market-driven management systems' that require employees to achieve market-based objectives (such as specific performance targets) within a framework that allows individuals extensive discretion in organizing their work. This combination of high performance targets, or heavy workloads, and extensive autonomy in organizing work, including individual working hours, often results in hours of work that extend 'as necessary' to achieve the established performance targets or business objectives. As a result of this situation, there are now increasing concerns about the effects of excessively long hours on the health and safety of managerial and professional staff.

Combating the pressures for long and 'stretching' working hours among managers and professionals is not an easy task. Despite the effects of such long hours on the health, safety and personal lives of these workers, it is often difficult to address unhealthy working time among managers and professionals, and in fact most national working hour regulations exclude many workers in these occupations from their provisions. Extending regulations on working hours, such as those for overtime pay and maximum hour limits, would be an important step towards reducing the long hours among these workers. In France, for example, the working hour laws have been extended to cover most *cadres* (a category that includes both certain managerial and certain professional staff), by limiting the total number of days that they work (via extended paid holidays) rather than limiting total hours worked as for other employees (IDS, 2002). In some circumstances it can also be feasible to incorporate at least some of these types of workers into workplace collective agreements, but new mechanisms of regulation that centre on the volume of hours worked may also be necessary.

DIMENSION TWO: 'FAMILY-FRIENDLY' WORKING TIME

A second important dimension of decent working time is providing workers with family responsibilities engaged in paid employment with the time that they need to handle those responsibilities – in line with the principle established in the ILO's Workers with Family Responsibilities Convention, 1981 (No. 156). Such responsibilities include caring for family members (children, elderly relatives and so on) and performing other necessary household tasks (cooking, cleaning, shopping and so on). 'Family-friendly' working time allows individuals sufficient time to meet these essential domestic obligations, and therefore benefits not only workers but also society as a whole. In particular, family-friendly working time measures[5] are designed to help meet the needs of parents – both men and women – to have sufficient time to care for their families, particularly (although certainly not exclusively) *on a daily basis*, a reality that is often forgotten in so-called post-Fordist working time arrangements that often function by averaging hours over a period of weeks, months, or even an entire year.

According to studies of life-cycle working time (for example, Boulin and Hoffman, 1999), working time patterns and workers' preferences regarding their hours of work are highly influenced by variations across the life cycle of individual workers – variations which have become more dramatic as individuals' biographies have become more diverse. Such studies argue that the allocation of an individual's time among paid work, domestic tasks, care, leisure and other activities is highly sensitive to household composition (for example, the number and age of household members) and also their current phase in the life course. Indeed, in some countries, such as Japan, the entire social system is based on an individual's age – that is, their particular stage of life.

Family responsibilities and the precise nature of those responsibilities – for example, the presence of children and their age(s) – exerts a strong influence on households' time allocation and gender division of labour (see, for example, Anxo, 2004). However, these impacts vary substantially across countries and societal contexts, such that the ability to combine family commitments and work exhibits a large variation among countries. Some of these family responsibilities are already outsourced, at least in part (for example, childcare facilities, schools, and market-based services for domestic tasks). Nevertheless, not all such activities can reasonably be outsourced; thus, a significant portion of these activities remains the responsibility of the family or household. Both 'inflexible' working hours and limited childcare and other family-related support tend to reinforce the traditional 'male breadwinner–female homemaker' division of labour within households, and thus create or at least exacerbate difficulties in combining paid work and family duties.

However, successfully blending work with family responsibilities is also about *when* people are available, and the energy that they have available to devote to family activities (Fagan, 2004). 'Non-standard' working hours in the evenings, at night and at weekends, as well as unpredictable variations in working hours based on fluctuating market demands, tend to increase the likelihood that workers will report work–family conflicts (see Fagan, 2004; European Foundation for the Improvement of Living and Working Conditions, 2001). Of course, the inconveniences involved with working 'non-standard' hours are not equally shared by all groups of workers; for example, Zeytinoglu and Cooke (2004) demonstrate that, in Canada, those workers in part-time, temporary or seasonal jobs are more likely to work at weekends than full-time, permanent employees.

The possibility of using working time arrangements to facilitate the combination of work and family commitments may be achieved by different but complementary means. These 'family-friendly' working time measures include a variety of policy options, ranging from a collective reduction in full-time hours to an individual right to reduce (or adapt) working time for family reasons, such as has been recently introduced in the UK. In general, short working hours – that is, part-time work – appear to be a widely employed strategy for balancing paid employment with family responsibilities.

However, there are two main problems with this reliance on part-time work as a strategy for work–family reconciliation. The first problem is that part-time jobs are, on average, of lesser quality than comparable full-time jobs. This is the case in many countries, not only in terms of hourly wages but also with regard to non-wage benefits such as pensions (and health insurance in the US), social insurance coverage, training opportunities, and career development (see, for example, Polivka et al., 2000; O'Reilly and Fagan, 1998). In addition, 'substantial' part-time hours (20–34 hours a week) are much more popular than 'marginal' part-time hours of less than 20 hours per week (see, for example, Fagan, 2004). In fact, it appears that many full-timers would prefer to switch to part-time work if it were not for the significant workplace obstacles and career penalties that are currently associated with part-time work. The second problem is that part-time workers are overwhelmingly female,[6] meaning that part-time work is gender-segregated in nearly all the countries in which it exists (see the discussion in the next section).

These findings point to the importance of improving the quality of available part-time positions as a means of achieving family-friendly working time. This in turn suggests the need to 'normalize' part-time work vis-à-vis the full-time standard that exists in each country. As noted by Yerkes and Visser (2004), such a process of 'normalization' has already occurred in the Netherlands, and a movement in this direction has begun in Germany and the United Kingdom. Equal treatment regulations in employment, non-wage benefits and social protection systems help to improve the conditions of part-time work, and at the same time make a substantial contribution towards promoting gender equality, a subject to which we turn in the next section (McCann, 2004).

Certain types of 'flexible' working time arrangements can also contribute to work–family reconciliation, particularly those flexitime programmes and 'time-banking' schemes that permit workers to accumulate extra hours and then use them to take full or partial days of paid time off at a later date. If properly structured, such schemes can also allow workers to vary their hours of work according to their individual family situations. Finally, offering workers the possibility of 'telecommuting' to their jobs by working from home can also provide them with the ability to blend work and family responsibilities on a daily basis, although care must be taken that this does not lead to excessive hours owing to the inevitable blurring of the boundaries between paid work and personal life.

Maternity, paternity, parental and similar care-related leave can also advance family-friendly working time by providing longer-term working time adjustments for family responsibilities (and physical recovery for mothers in the case of maternity leave). For example, Sweden offers one model for using blocks of paid leave, including sabbaticals, to help individuals to better organize their working time over the life cycle. And although few countries have family leave entitlements as generous as those in Sweden, statutory entitlements to maternity, paternity and parental leave have been increased in almost all OECD countries in recent years (OECD, 2001).

A final point regarding work–family reconciliation measures is that take-up of working time adjustments or extended leave is often low – particularly for men – and so there is a substantial gap between policy and practice. Employees may feel that they cannot afford to take advantage of such opportunities, perhaps because their line manager is unwilling to agree to these arrangements, or because they may perceive that it will jeopardize their future promotion potential or even their job security. In particular, take-up rates for these measures are systematically much lower for men than women, and long weekly working hours are largely (though not exclusively) a male phenomenon. All of these factors suggest that, in general, men have insufficient time for family life. This phenomenon and the resulting gender inequality in the sharing of family responsibilities that it spawns are addressed in the next section.

DIMENSION THREE: GENDER EQUALITY THROUGH WORKING TIME

The third dimension of decent working time involves using working time as a tool for promoting gender equality. Equality of opportunity and treatment between women and men in the world of work is a principle established in a number of international labour standards, most notably the Discrimination in Employment and Occupation Convention, 1958 (No. 111). This ILO Convention enshrines the elimination of discrimination regarding employment and occupation as a fundamental principle – one which remains at the core of the ILO Decent Work agenda today (ILO, 2000). This means that the overall objective of advancing gender equality also needs to be applied in the area of working time – and integrated into the full range of working time policies – in order to ensure that policies designed to advance other 'decent work' objectives do not inadvertently have a negative impact on gender equality.

An important example in this respect is to distinguish between working-time measures that are family-friendly *per se* and those that are family-friendly and can *simultaneously* promote gender equality as well. For example, measures such as part-time work and parental leave provide parents with the opportunity to spend more time caring for their children or older relatives. However, if mothers are the only ones who make use of such leave, then, while these policies may help promote work–family balance, they may simultaneously reinforce gender inequality by relegating women to marginal forms of labour market participation – rather than paving the way for *true* equality in paid employment. To promote gender equality, working time policies must, first, enable women to be on an equal footing with men in employment (position levels, career advancement, and so on) and, second, enable '*both partners* [to] combine paid work, family responsibilities, and lifelong learning', as suggested by Bosch (2004, p. 18, emphasis added) in his proposed model for a new, more flexible standard employment relationship. Realizing such a model will obviously require a more equal division of domestic tasks between men and women, including care responsibilities – which can be promoted via working time policies that encourage men to adjust their working hours at different stages of the life course, such as when they have young children.

From this discussion, it is clear that the gender equality dimension of the decent working time policy framework has two important implications for working time policies. First, working time policies promote gender equality in employment through gender-neutral measures. Second, it is important to ensure that policies that advance other dimensions of decent working time do not negatively impact on gender equality.

As discussed in the ILO's recent book on working time in the industrialized countries, a coordinated combination or 'portfolio' of policies is required to promote gender equality, because the efficacy of one particular instrument is usually contingent upon other measures (Messenger, 2004a). First, policies are needed to close the 'gender gap' in the volume of hours of paid employment for men compared with those hours worked by women. This objective can be achieved both by limiting excessively long hours among full-time workers and by encouraging longer hours for part-timers. Changing the 'long hours culture' that is often associated with the self-determined working time patterns of many managers and so-called 'new economy' professionals is a particularly thorny problem, as these individuals are largely exempt from working time regulations. The long hours in such positions act as an (often invisible) barrier to the advancement of women who have family responsibilities, and hence reinforce the 'glass ceiling' that already exists in these occupations.

Second, with regard to the question of part-time work, the key issues are twofold. First, it is essential that the quality of part-time work be improved if it is to be made compatible with the objective of promoting gender equality (Fagan, 2004; OECD, 2001; O'Reilly and Fagan, 1998). As mentioned earlier in this chapter, one particularly important mechanism for improving the quality of part-time work – and thus helping promote gender equality, since (as noted above) the vast majority of part-time workers are women – is the use of equal treatment regulations in employment, non-wage benefits and social protection systems, which will help to improve the employment conditions of part-time workers. Promoting the equal treatment of part-time and full-time workers is a principle that was established in the ILO's Part-Time Work Convention, 1994 (No. 175), and has been extended to the laws of a number of countries, as well as to the European Union as a whole through the 1997 EU Part-time Work Directive (97/81/EC) (McCann, 2004). The equal treatment approach is clearly an essential step towards improving the quality of part-time work. Ultimately, this means embarking on a process, the objective of which is to make part-time positions equivalent to those of full-time ones in terms of their pay, benefits, and career development opportunities. As noted above, such a process is sometimes referred to as the 'normalization' of part-time work.

The occupational profile of part-time positions is also important. Policies designed to promote equal treatment between part-timers and full-timers require 'comparable' full-time positions with which comparisons regarding the equal treatment of part-time workers can be made. If part-time workers are concentrated into a narrow range of occupations, there may be few if any comparable positions. To address this situation, policies are needed to help 'desegregate' part-time work, such as making part-time positions available in a wider range of jobs and incentivizing employers to structure part-time positions around 'substantial' rather than 'marginal' part-time hours (which are typically defined as less than 20 hours per week) by, for example, removing provisions in social security regulations that favour the creation of marginal hours jobs (see, for example, McCann, 2004). With a wider range of part-time positions plus more substantial part-time hours, the underemployment (including earnings losses) associated with part-time work is reduced, as are the career advancement penalties; as a result, part-time workers become more fully integrated alongside full-timers in the workplace and the labour market as a whole (O'Reilly and Fagan, 1998). According to Yerkes and Visser (2004), such a broad profile of part-time positions already existed in the Netherlands by the end of the 1990s.

Beyond the question of part-time work, promoting gender equality involves overcoming the 'no-win' dilemma of work–family reconciliation measures: that is, policies designed to facilitate women's integration into the labour market may simultaneously reinforce gender inequality in the domestic division of labour and thus inadvertently undermine gender equity in employment (for example, Moss and Deven, 1999). In particular, managerial resistance and the negative attitudes of colleagues can create obstacles to men's use of reconciliation measures. To help overcome such obstacles, a broad range of policies (and not just working time policies) are needed to promote the involvement of fathers in domestic tasks and care activities. One possible approach would be to provide fathers with the right to take extended leave for family reasons or reduce their working hours when they have young children – rights that are already available to mothers in many industrialized countries. In addition, enterprise-level policies designed to reduce organizational resistance to men adapting their working hours according to family needs would also have positive 'ripple' effects for their female colleagues by 'normalizing' the use of a broad range of working time arrangements.

DIMENSION FOUR: PRODUCTIVE WORKING TIME

Obviously, it makes no sense to talk about decent working time without considering its effects on the productivity of enterprises. In that sense, 'decent working time' is also *productive working time*, in that more and more companies are recognizing that promoting a healthy 'work–life balance' for their employees is not just the 'right thing' to do, but that such an approach can also serve as an effective competitiveness strategy. Enterprise policies and practices that seek to promote decent working time can benefit businesses in a number of different ways, as will be discussed below.

Before considering the range of positive effects that have been shown from various aspects of decent working time policies and practices, however, a few words of caution are in order. In particular, those human resource management practices associated with 'post-Fordist' forms of work organization – such as the 'self-regulated' working time of many managerial and professional staff and the 'fragmented' time systems (for example, very short part-time hours) often used in the retailing industry – lead to flexible working hours that have the potential for a 'double-edged impact': that is, the end result can be either a positive or a negative one depending upon how the working time arrangement is implemented. Thus, as with many other employment practices, there is the potential for both a 'high road' and a 'low road' to achieving working time flexibility – and, as we will see, taking the 'high road' generally requires a proactive approach.

Having said that, there are nonetheless substantial business benefits that can be reaped from decent working time policies and practices. First, there is evidence that points to a link between reductions in working hours and increased hourly productivity, including the ILO's own research (see White (1987) for a review of the relevant literature). Such productivity gains result not only from physiological factors such as reduced fatigue (as in the case of workers who are working long hours on a regular basis) but also from an improvement in employee attitudes and morale. The largest potential productivity gains can be expected from reductions in 'excessive' hours of work – that is, more than 48 hours per week – which also helps to advance the other dimensions of decent working time as well.[7] There is substantial empirical evidence that reductions in 'excessively' long hours of work – typically linked with changes in work organization, methods of production, and similar factors – have resulted in substantial productivity gains over the years (see, for example, Bosch and Lehndorff, 2001; White, 1987).[8] Also, since long hours of work are positively related to absenteeism and staff turnover, reducing such long hours can provide firms with benefits in terms of reduced absenteeism and lower staff turnover (see, for example, Barmby et al., 2002).

A number of enterprise studies also show the business benefits of adopting company policies that promote various aspects of decent working time, such as working time arrangements that allow workers to adjust their work schedules in response to their individual needs. For example, a major study in the US found that flexitime and telecommuting had positive effects on productivity (Boston College Center for Work and Family, 2000). Flexible working time arrangements such as flexitime and compressed workweeks have also shown positive effects on employee attitudes and morale (see, for example, Hogarth et al., 2001; Gottlieb et al., 1998). These improvements in employee attitudes and morale can, in turn, translate into a better 'bottom line' – as demonstrated by a recent study that shows a statistically valid, positive relationship between employees' emotions regarding their work and firms' financial performance (Towers Perrin et al., 2003). A review of the literature on the effects of flexible working time arrangements (Avery and Zabel, 2001) also found benefits to firms from such arrangements due to decreased tardiness and absenteeism, as well as improved recruitment and retention of employees, particularly when labour markets are tight. Finally, some studies indicate that perhaps the most important factor is not the working time arrangement per se, but rather workers' *ability to choose* their arrangement – often referred to as 'time sovereignty' – that shows the strongest impact on employees' job performance, and hence on firms' productivity (for example, Gottlieb et al., 1998). Thus, there appears to be substantial evidence regarding at least the potential benefits of decent working time arrangements on enterprise productivity.

This is not to say, however, that these business benefits will *automatically* result from simply deploying working time arrangements that are consistent with decent working time. Realizing these benefits requires firms to implement innovative arrangements that *consciously* seek ways of combining business efficiency with increased worker influence over their working hours. Such an approach is demonstrated in the company cases studied by

Haipeter (2004), in which we see a number of different German firms experimenting with innovative forms of working time arrangements, including flexitime and various forms of 'working time accounts' (that is, 'time banking' schemes that allow workers to accumulate 'credits' in working hours for later use) that attempt to make just such a combination. Not surprisingly, Haipeter finds both successes and failures among his company case studies. For example, those flexitime arrangements that actively seek to balance the interests of workers with firms' operational requirements are a particular 'success story' that emerges from these case studies. On the other hand, Haipeter also finds that *long-term* working time accounts – designed to enable employees to take time off in extended blocks (that is, 'sabbaticals') – have not lived up to their promise, primarily because of practical difficulties with scheduling the withdrawal of large blocks of time credits from these accounts (in the form of sabbaticals) in an intensely competitive environment in which staffing levels are tight.

Ultimately, as Bosch (2004, p. 18) emphasizes, 'Any attempt to combine business efficiency with increased time sovereignty for employees inevitably raises the question of work organization.' Bosch goes on to cite Lehndorff's work on innovative forms of work organization (see, for example, Lehndorff, 2001), which, he says, 'show[s] that such a synthesis can be made to work successfully' (ibid., p. 40). In the ILO's recent book on working time in industrialized countries, Messenger (2004b), in his analysis of working time arrangements at the firm level, reaches a similar conclusion, but emphasizes that making such a synthesis work in practice requires firms to make a conscious attempt to align business objectives and strategies with workers' needs and preferences in ways that are mutually reinforcing.

DIMENSION FIVE: CHOICE AND INFLUENCE REGARDING WORKING TIME

The concept of 'decent work deficits' discussed at the beginning of this chapter – with its notion of 'gaps' between people's aspirations regarding their work and their current work situation – implies that increasing workers' ability to choose, or at least influence, the length of their working hours and their work schedules can help to advance decent working time. Increasing workers' choice and influence regarding their working hours is – as discussed in the ILO's recent book on the subject (Messenger, 2004a) – a matter of considering workers' *subjective* needs and preferences, with all the technical difficulties that this approach entails, rather than making the (often incorrect) assumption that actual working time arrangements reflect workers' preferences regarding their hours of work. Expanding this kind of choice means expanding the range of opportunities for workers to structure their work and personal activities, such that their working hours can more closely approximate their individual situations. This is the fifth and final dimension of decent working time: choice and influence regarding working time.

This objective can be advanced in two related ways. First, the number of working time options available to employees can be increased, such that workers can choose from a 'menu' of alternatives. Second, workers can be permitted to exercise a direct ongoing influence over the length and arrangement of their working hours. This latter approach (which is often referred to as an 'individual influence' approach) recognizes that decent working time should help to promote the outcomes that individual workers prefer.

Policy measures to advance worker choice and influence regarding working time can be adopted at the national, sectoral and enterprise levels. For example, national legislation has been introduced in a number of European countries that can enhance worker influence by allowing collective agreements to implement or modify working time standards (EIRO Online, 1998). Laws have also been enacted in a few countries, particularly the Netherlands, Germany and the UK, which provide individual workers with a right to request changes in their working hours. Although the specific provisions of these laws vary[9] – and both the working time regulatory frameworks and socio-economic circumstances in these three countries are quite different – such 'right to request' legislation has the potential to advance workers' ability to influence their working hours, as well as to address the existing dichotomy between full-time and part-time work. In fact, this 'right to request' approach favours a notion of the *modulation* of working hours, by promoting smoother transitions between different working time arrangements (see, for example, McCann, 2004).

At the firm level, flexitime programmes and 'time banking' accounts that allow workers to build up time 'credits' for later use are tools that have the *potential* to offer workers a substantial amount of influence over their working hours. As noted above, such approaches can combine business efficiency with increased worker influence over their working hours – for example, by creating working time accounts that combine time banking with aspects of hours averaging over multi-week periods. Indeed, any firm-level practice that provides workers with a choice among alternate work schedules or facilitates worker influence over scheduling would be of some benefit to individual workers and can be encouraged through a range of government incentives.

Mechanisms like a right to request changes in working hours law and time banking accounts do not always work as intended, however. For example, Fourage and Baaijens (2004) investigated Dutch workers' preferences regarding their working hours in the context of the pioneering legislation in

the Netherlands regarding the right to request working time changes
(including changes in both the number of hours worked and scheduling)
enacted in 2000. Their early findings[10] showed that, despite the law, changes
in working hours are still often associated with job mobility; this finding
indicates that certain 'rigidities' in how companies structure working hours
persist. Likewise, Haipeter (2004) discusses flexitime and other types of
working time accounts and identifies some problems with their use. In particular (as noted above), he finds problems with the withdrawal of time
credits in *long-term* time accounts (for example, for sabbaticals), often
leading to the forfeiture of working time.

One must also be cautious about a tendency to assume that providing
workers with greater choice and influence over their hours of work necessarily means a complete individualization of decisions regarding working
hours. A strong collective framework is essential to provide the social
support necessary for increasing the range of realistic working time options
from which individuals workers can choose. Such support can be provided
at various levels, including through laws that strengthen trade unions (for
example, those on independence, recognition and the right to strike).

Finally, it is important to consider how broader social objectives can
be realized in conjunction with the facilitation of individual choice. The
synchronization of working hours and social times, such as those times traditionally dedicated to community and family activities, becomes increasingly difficult in a context of individualized hours. Thus, working time
policies also need to explicitly address these concerns wherever possible.
For example, such policies need to consider the opening hours of public
and private services, including changing these hours when necessary to
accommodate changing lifestyles, in order to promote an improved quality
of life. The 'Times of the city' (*tempa della città*) initiative in Italy provides
a good illustration of how this concern regarding the synchronization of
working hours and social times might be addressed (see, for example,
Boulin and Mückenberger, 1999).

FUTURE DIRECTIONS

As we have seen, the five dimensions of decent working time provide a
broad policy framework by which the goal of decent work can be advanced
in the arena of working time. These five dimensions should be considered
as a set of *guiding principles* that point in a direction that leads towards
decent working time – at whatever stage a country may be in their process
of development. As principles, the five dimensions of decent working time
will of necessity vary substantially in their implementation (that is, the

specific mix of policies used to advance decent working time) from one country to another, according to variations in national, regional and perhaps even local circumstances.

The five dimensions of decent working time can also offer an overall structure for future research in the field of working time – in fact, each of these five dimensions constitutes an important theme for future research on working time. For example, from the perspective of healthy working time, it remains essential to focus on the traditional question of excessively long working hours – but this time not only in the industrialized world but also in newly emerging economies such as China and India. It will also be crucial to further explore the obvious tradeoffs between the dimensions of 'family-friendly' working time and gender equality through working time, such as in the area of part-time work – seeking policies and practices that can *simultaneously* promote work–family reconciliation and gender equality.

While it is hoped that all of these efforts will assist in advancing decent working time, ultimately any movement in this direction will depend on the *relative value* that both institutions and individual citizens place upon their quality of life compared with their material wealth. The economic imperatives driving societies towards the '24–7 model' of operating hours and greater diversification in working hours for individual workers appear unlikely to diminish, and may well continue to intensify. The question then becomes one of individual and societal values: what working hours do people want? And what are they willing to accept to get them – for example, lower earnings? Even in a country such as the US – where material incentives are strong and very long working hours are commonplace – a significant portion of workers are now saying that they would like to reduce their hours, even if that means some reduction in income (see, for example, Jacobs and Gerson, 2004; Golden, 2004). Perhaps not surprisingly, in the last few years a citizen movement dedicated to fighting 'time poverty' and promoting a more 'balanced life' has sprung up in that country.[11] Thus, as a greater focus on quality of life issues emerges among individuals and in institutions across the industrialized world, we might well expect to see an increased call for policies and approaches that offer the promise of moving towards decent working time.

NOTES

1. A similar research effort focusing on developing countries and countries in transition is now nearing completion, and the results of this project will be published in an ILO report on *Working Time around the World* (working title) in 2007.
2. Golden also notes that there is a tendency for workers to adjust their working time preferences in line with their current hours, so in such cases workers may actually be internalizing 'preferences' for long working hours according to the requirements of their jobs.

3. The category of 'casual workers' in Australia is quite broad.

   > There is no standard number of working hours that defines a casual worker . . . the main difference between a permanent and a casual worker is the notion that a permanent employee has an ongoing contract of employment of unspecified duration while a casual employee has not. The characteristics of casual employment that flow from this notion are:
   >
   > - Limited entitlements to benefits generally associated with continuity of employment such as annual and sick leave, and
   > - No entitlement to prior notification of retrenchment (no security of employment) and only a limited case for compensation or reinstatement. (Kryger, 2000)

4. See *Defining and Delimiting the Exemptions for Executive, Administrative, Professional, Outside Sales, and Computer Personnel; Final Rule*. US Department of Labor, Employment Standards Administration, Wage and Hour Division, Federal Register 69: 22122, 23 April 2004.
5. The entire range of 'family-friendly' measures can comprise a variety of different policies and practices, including not only those relating to hours of work but also a number of other measures such as maternity protection and affordable, accessible and high-quality child care services.
6. In industrialized countries, women hold nearly three-quarters of all part-time positions (OECD, 2004, p. 311), and part-time work is increasingly used in developing countries as well (for example, Taylor, 2004).
7. The ILO is in the process of developing 'decent work' indicators, which include as one indicator the proportion of the workforce with 'excessive hours of work', defined as having usual hours of work of over 48 hours per week in the main job. This 48-hour threshold is in line with the ILO Hours of Work (Industry) Convention (No. 1) (1919) and the ILO Hours of Work (Commerce and Offices) Convention (No. 30) (1930), both of which establish 48 hours as the maximum for weekly hours under normal circumstances.
8. It should be noted that the productivity gains connected with reductions in working time tend to decrease as the length of working time decreases. More recent empirical studies of the productivity effects of reductions in working time have focused on the reduction of hours of work from a lower baseline level (that is, 40 hours per week or less), and these studies generally show weak or no effects of working time reductions in countries in which hours of work are already relatively short (see, for example, Anxo and Bigsten, 1989).
9. For example, the British provision, which is included in the Employment Rights Act 1996, applies only to parents with children under the age of six or disabled children under the age of 18.
10. This study uses data from the OSA Labour Supply Panel through the year 2002, which is only two years after the Adjustment of Working Hours Act in the Netherlands came into effect (in July 2000). Therefore, it is probably too early for any significant impacts of the law to have materialized.
11. Take Back Your Time is a 'grass-roots' citizen movement whose stated objective is to fight 'time poverty' in the US. For more information about this organization, see www.simpleliving.net/timeday.

REFERENCES

Anxo, D. (2004), 'Working time in industrialized countries: a household perspective', in J. Messenger (ed.), *Working Time and Workers' Preferences in Industrialized Countries: Finding the Balance*, London and New York: Routledge.

Anxo, D. and Bigsten, A. (1989), 'Working hours and productivity in Swedish manufacturing', *Scandanavian Journal of Economics*, **91** (3), 613–19.

Avery, C. and Zabel, D. (2001), *The Flexible Workplace: A Sourcebook of Information and Research*, Westport, CT: Quorum Books.

Barmby, T., Ercolani, M. and Treble, J. (2002), 'Sickness absence: an international comparison', *The Economic Journal*, **112**, F315–31.

Bosch, G. (2004), 'Working time and the standard employment relationship', paper presented at the 9th Conference of the International Symposium on Working Time, Paris, 26–28 February.

Bosch, G. and Lehndorff, S. (2001), 'Working-time reduction and employment: experiences in Europe and economic policy recommendations', *Cambridge Journal of Economics*, **25**, 209–43.

Boston College Center for Work and Family (2000), *Measuring the Impact of Workplace Flexibility: Findings from the National Work/life Measurement Project*, Boston, MA: Boston College Center for Work and Family, Wallace E. Carroll School of Management, http://www.bc.edu/centers/cwf/research/highlights/meta-elements/pdf/flexexec-summ.pdf.

Boulin, J.-Y. and Hoffman, R. (1999), 'The conceptualisation of working time over the whole life cycle', in J-Y. Boulin and R. Hoffman (eds), *New Paths in Working Time Policy*, Brussels: European Trade Union Institute.

Boulin, J.-Y. and Mückenberger, U. (1999), *Times in the City and Quality of Life*, BEST European Studies on Times, Luxembourg: Office for Official Publications of the European Communities.

Campbell, I. (2004), *Employer Pressures and Overtime: Exploring the Causes of Extended Working Hours in Australia*, paper presented at the 9th Conference of the International Symposium on Working Time, Paris, 26–28 February.

European Foundation for the Improvement of Living and Working Conditions (2001), *European Union Survey on Working Conditions* [acceding and candidate countries], Luxembourg: Office for Official Publications of the European Community.

European Industrial Relations Observatory (EIRO) Online (1998), *Flexibility in Working Time in Europe*, Dublin: European Foundation for the Improvement of Living and Working Conditions, http://www.eiro.eurofound.ie/2001/11/study/TN0111143S.html.

Fagan, C. (2004), 'Gender and working time in industrialized countries', in Messenger, J.C. (ed.), *Working Time and Workers' Preferences in Industrialized Countries: Finding the Balance*, London and New York: Routledge.

Fourage, D. and Baaijens, C. (2004), 'Labour supply preferences and job mobility of Dutch employees', paper presented at the 9th Conference of the International Symposium on Working Time, Paris, 26–28 February.

Golden, L. (2004), 'Overemployment in the US: which workers are willing to reduce their work hours and income?', paper presented at the 9th Conference of the International Symposium on Working Time, Paris, 26–28 February.

Gottlieb, B., Kelloway, E.K. and Barham, E. (1998), *Flexible Work Arrangements: Managing the Work–Family Boundary*, Chichester, UK: John Wiley & Sons, Ltd.

Haipeter, T. (2004), 'Can norms survive market pressures? The practical effectiveness of new forms of working time regulation in a changing German economy', paper presented at the 9th Conference of the International Symposium on Working Time, Paris, 26–28 February.

Hogarth, T., Hasluck, C., Pierre, G., Winterbotham, M. and Vivian, D. (2001), *Work–life Balance 2000: Results from the Baseline Study*, Norwich, UK: Department for Education and Employment.

Incomes Data Service (IDS) (2002), 'France: managers' hours and the European Social Charter', *Employment Europe*, **483**, 5.

International Labour Office (ILO) (1999), *Decent Work*, Report of the Director-General to the International Labour Conference, 87th Session, Geneva.

International Labour Office (ILO) (2000), *Decent Work for Women: an ILO Proposal to Accelerate the Implementation of the Beijing Platform for Action*, Geneva: ILO.

International Labour Office (ILO) (2001), *Reducing the Decent Work Deficit*, Report of the Director-General to the International Labour Conference, 89th Session, Geneva.

Jacobs, J.A. and Gerson, K. (2004), *The Time Divide: Work, Family, and Gender Inequality*, Cambridge, MA: Harvard University Press.

Kryger, T. (2000), 'Casual employment: Research note 2, 1999–2000', Canberra: Parliament of Australia, Parliamentary Library, http://www.aph.gov.au/library/pubs/rn/1999–2000/2000rn02.html.

Lee, S. (2004), 'Working-hour gaps: trends and issues' in Messenger, J.C. (ed.), *Working Time and Workers' Preferences in Industrialized Countries: Finding the Balance*, London and New York: Routledge.

Lehndorff, S. (2001), *Weniger ist Mehr: Arbeitszeitverkürzung als Gesellschaftpolitik*, Hamburg: VSA-Verlag.

Lehndorff, S. (2002), 'The governance of service work – changes in work organization and new challenges for service-sector trade unions', *Transfer*, **8** (3), 415–34.

McCann, D. (2004), 'Regulating working time needs and preferences', in Messenger, J.C. (ed.), *Working Time and Workers' Preferences in Industrialized Countries: Finding the Balance*, London and New York: Routledge.

Messenger, J.C. (ed.) (2004a), *Working Time and Workers' Preferences in Industrialized Countries: Finding the Balance*, London and New York: Routledge.

Messenger, J.C. (2004b), 'Working time at the enterprise level: business objectives, firms' practices, and workers' preferences', in J.C. Messenger (ed.), *Working Time and Workers' Preferences in Industrialized Countries: Finding the Balance*, London and New York: Routledge.

Moss, P. and Deven, F. (eds) (1999), *Parental Leave: Progress or Pitfall?*, Brussels: CVBG-Centrum voor Bevolkings-en Gezinsstudie.

Nätti, J., Anttila, T. and Väisäsen, M. (2004), 'Managers and working time', paper presented at the 9th Conference of the International Symposium on Working Time, Paris, 26–28 February.

O'Reilly, J. and Fagan, C. (eds) (1998), *Part-time Prospects: An International Comparison of Part-time Work in Europe, North America, and the Pacific Rim*, London and New York: Routledge.

Organization for Economic Co-operation and Development (OECD) (2001), 'Work and family life: how do they balance out?', in *OECD Employment Outlook 2001*, Paris: OECD.

Organization for Economic Co-operation and Development (OECD) (2004), *OECD Employment Outlook 2004*, Paris: OECD.

Polivka, A., Cohany, S. and Hipple, S. (2000), 'Definition, composition, and economic consequences of the non-standard workforce', in F. Carré et al. (eds), *Nonstandard Work: the Nature and Challenges of Changing Employment Arrangements*, Champaign, IL: Industrial Relations Research Association.

Saboia, J. (2002), 'Survey report: working week and organization of labour in Brazil', Conditions of Work and Employment Programme, unpublished report.

Spurgeon, A. (2003), *Working Time: its Impacts on Safety and Health*, Seoul: ILO and Korea Occupational Safety and Health Research Institute.

Taylor, O. (2004), 'Working time and work organization in Jamaica', Conditions of Work and Employment Programme, unpublished report.

Towers Perrin and Gang and Gang (2003), *Working Today: Exploring Employees' Emotional Connections to their Jobs*, New York: Towers Perrin.

White, M. (1987), *Working Hours: Assessing the Potential for Reduction*, Geneva: ILO.

Yerkes, M. and Visser, J. (2004), 'Women's preferences or delineated policies? The development of part-time work in the Netherlands, Germany, and the United Kingdom', paper presented at the 9th Conference of the International Symposium on Working Time, Paris, 26–28 February.

Zeng, X., Liang, L. and Idris, S.U. (2005), *Working Time in Transition: the Dual Task of Standardization and Flexibilization in China*, Conditions of Work and Employment Programme Series No. 11, Geneva: ILO.

Zeytinoglu, I.U. and Cooke, G.B. (2004), 'Who is working when we are resting? Determinants of weekend work in Canada', paper presented at the 9th Conference of the International Symposium on Working Time, Paris, 26–28 February.

11. The unlikely referral of workaholics to an employee assistance program

Gayle Porter and Robert A. Herring III

INTRODUCTION TO THE POTENTIAL INTERSECTION OF EAPs AND WORKAHOLISM

Employee assistance programs (EAPs) were once defined as 'job-based strategies for the identification, motivation, and treatment of bio-medical conditions not limited to, but usually including, alcohol and drug addictions, mental health problems, and adjustment problems' (Sonnenstuhl and Trice, 1986). More recently, Oher et al. (1998) refer to EAPs as 'workplace-focused mechanisms designed to identify and aid employees with problems in living that frequently impair their job performance'. Research documents from the Society for Human Resource Management utilize the following broad definition of an EAP:

> a worksite-based program designed to assist organizations in addressing productivity issues and assist employee clients in identifying and resolving personal concerns, including, but not limited to, health, marital, family, financial, alcohol, drug, legal, emotional, stress or other personal issues that may affect job performance. (Lockwood, 2004)

EAPs have their roots in the occupational alcoholism programs begun by some large companies in the 1940s. In 1974 the National Institute on Alcoholism and Alcohol Abuse (NIAAA) adopted the term 'employee assistance program' to describe job-performance intervention programs in the workplace. The NIAAA noted that, while workplace job performance deterioration could most often be attributed to the effects of alcohol abuse, it could also be related to other personal problems. The concept of an EAP thus broadened the scope of employer concern and involvement. Since that time, EAPs have evolved into multi-service programs addressing a broad range of personal problems in addition to alcohol abuse, including drug abuse and a variety of mental health problems or family problems affecting worker performance (Hartwell et al., 1996).

A manager or supervisor can either require or suggest that an employee contact the EAP when problems arise with performance. Typically the trigger event is performance being something less than the manager deems it could be, usually by comparison with past performance. While managers have experience and tracking mechanisms to identify a drop in perform-ance, they seem less prepared to establish what constitutes 'good enough' ongoing performance. The question, 'Are these employees putting as much as they should into the work effort?' is all too often answered in terms of whether or not they are spending a lot of hours at the workplace. This con-tinues in spite of evidence that greater 'face time' is not predictive of greater productivity, and that too much time at work leads to distress, fatigue, errors and threats to safety (Barnett and Hall, 2001).

Programs to promote work/life (W/L) balance – which often encom-pass an EAP – are still having to prove their worth to organizations (Guglielmino, 2001). This industry as a whole faces the related challenges of gaining credibility and making a business case for the importance of W/L balance programs. Professionals in the field are, additionally, chal-lenged to educate and obtain buy-in from managers and to shift organiza-tional cultures toward balance as a success strategy (ibid.). In too many cases, employees still believe that working long hours is necessary for career advancement, even while they report high awareness of their own stress caused by work/life conflict (Hansen, 2002).

The culture of long work hours reflects organizational demands for doing more (work) with less (workforce). However, some researchers also believe that there are employees who would work to excess even if these demands were not so prevalent (Fassel, 1990; Porter, 1996; Robinson, 1998). These authors consider excess work – workaholism or work addic-tion – to follow the same addiction pattern as seen with drugs and alcohol, as well as other behavioral problems like gambling addiction. The parallel to other addictions includes the workaholic's unwillingness to stop work even when it is detrimental to personal well-being in terms of physical health and difficulty in relationships with family and friends (Robinson, 1989, 1998). In addition, the interpersonal difficulties carry into the work-place, causing a breakdown in trust (Porter, 1998), great stress among co-workers (Porter, 2001), and demand for others to either share the behav-ioral pattern or leave (Shaef and Fassel, 1988).

The organizational demands, therefore, are not the sole cause of excess work, but they do support the workaholic pattern. The tradition of EAPs in helping those with other addiction problems would suggest they could also be of great help in alleviating the personal and organizational difficulties resulting from workaholism. However, the manager's tendency to see hours at work as a sign of positive commitment to the job is incongruent with referring the workaholic to an EAP. An alternate route to accessing help is for the employee to self-refer, but denial of the problem is also a part of the addiction pattern (cf. Robinson, 1998), making this option seem remote as well.

Often there is a lack of realization that workaholism is a larger pattern of dysfunctional behavior that creates stress on interpersonal relationships through over-controlling behavior like information hoarding, perfectionist demands, focus on always having work to do rather than getting the work done, denial that there might be a better way to do things and actual distress (psychological and physical) with any attempt to ease back from these habits (cf. Porter, 1996; Robinson, 1998). In comparing two employees, the one working on Saturday seems more devoted when, actually, the one determined to spend weekends at home with family might have given much greater actual performance to the company in order to achieve that personal goal. At the same time that the general situation is being misinterpreted, the deeper level dynamics are ignored.

In spite of interpersonal issues as reason for organizational attention, the situation in most companies today includes high pressure to get more done with less and little time to look deeper than the surface appearance of working hard – hours on the job. Given these realities, it might seem unlikely that workaholic tendencies would ever result in the employee being referred or self-referring to an EAP. But, does that mean the workaholic employee would never obtain help?

THE GROWING SCOPE OF EMPLOYEE ASSISTANCE PROGRAMS

The magnitude of the problems that lead to utilization of EAPs is immense. Different figures are cited by different sources, depending on the way data are obtained and interpreted. However, recent federal data reports cite annual workplace losses from mental health problems at well over $100 billion (Challenger, 1997). Employers establish EAPs for a variety of reasons, including safety risk management, management of behavioral health benefits and cost containment, disability determinations, improving worker productivity, rehabilitating troubled employees, enhancement of labor/management relations, corporate social responsibility, drug-free workplace delivery, workplace violence interventions, work–life and wellness assistance, financial and legal consultations, and other specialty programs requested by employers (Challenger, 1997; Daniels et al., 2004).

Recent trends in EAP services include post-traumatic stress counseling evidenced by such incidents as the 11 September 2001 terrorist attack, problems faced by veterans and their families as a result of the ongoing war against terrorism in Afghanistan and Iraq, and the record devastation caused by hurricanes in August and September of 2005. A second area, related to the above, is the problem of the depressed employee. It is estimated that over 19 million adult Americans aged 18 and over will suffer from depressive disorder (major depression, bipolar disorder, or dysthymia) each year. One study stated that the economic costs from depression have been estimated at $44 billion annually, and another estimated that clinical depression costs American businesses around $30 billion per year in absenteeism and poor work performance (Chima, 2004).

A third growing area of emphasis is that of 'work–life effectiveness', the preferred term of the Alliance for Work–Life Progress. This term 'refers to a specific set of organizational practices, policies, programs, and a philosophy that recommends aggressive support for the efforts of everyone in the workforce to achieve success both at home and at work'. To meet the needs of the 'dual-focused worker' the work–life effectiveness concept 'is no mere repackaging of benefit offerings, but a major restructuring of the workplace "deal" in alignment with the new realities in the workplace' (Courtois et al., 2004).

In recent years events such as passage of the Drug Free Workplace Act, mandated DOT substance abuse testing for transportation industry workers, the increasing use of managed care in an attempt to cut health care costs, and the impact of corporate restructurings, downsizings and layoffs have each had a major impact on the workplace. Consequentially, the design of EAPs to serve organizations and their employees has also changed. While still maintaining their original roots in substance abuse problems, EAPs have become increasingly 'broad brush' in nature. Over the past 10–15 years or so, many EAPs have added services to deal with problems in the areas of marriage and family, mental health, stress, financial and other concerns.

Despite the lack of any direct reference to workaholism, the inclusion of family issues, mental and physical health, and stress could easily be considered as means to deal with the outcomes of workaholic behavior. Yet, 'Certain work environments encourage and enable workaholism' (Tyler, 1999). It seems a vicious cycle that the same organization encouraging the behavior then invests in means to help people deal with outcomes of that behavior. To what extent might people recognize the detrimental side of allowing the behavior earlier? The following commentary tracks a process of research in which we tried to refine this question and gather information from the professionals most directly charged with creating healthy work behavior to the benefit of both the employee and the organization. Further contextual comments regarding study of EAPs and of workaholism are inserted as pertinent to the development, implementation and interpretation of the research.

STUDYING THE POTENTIAL OF EAP REFERRALS FOR WORKAHOLISM

A Focus Group

Our research began with a presentation at a chapter meeting of the Employee Assistance Professionals Association (EAPA). These individuals all worked in some relationship to EAP operations. Our goal was to expose them to the addiction view of workaholism and then, through discussion, obtain their assessment of whether a person working in this pattern would ever be referred to an EAP. The extensive discussion portion of the program became a focus group from which we could formulate how to advance this research.

We framed our comments around the characteristics of workaholism as parallel to other addictions and as published in previous research (Porter, 1996). In this profile, there are two defining characteristics of workaholism or work addiction – that the individual (1) will sacrifice other aspects of life in favor of work (that is, work becomes the sole source of satisfaction) and (2) will work to excess whether or not there are external demands to do so.

Several other characteristics are part of this pattern. One is rigid thinking, which manifests in one of two ways: either as perfectionism or as high need for control. In either case, this places greater demands on self and others, thereby ensuring there is always more work to be done. The workaholic usually has a very high sense of responsibility, believing that no one else is willing or able to do the job as conscientiously (linked to perfectionism) unless they are watched over and guided (linked to control).

The attraction of excess work also results in the workaholic being attracted to crisis situations. A crisis requires extra work at the moment. Often, after the crisis is somewhat resolved, there is also a backlog of other work that has been temporarily set aside. In addition, being the person who is willing and able to handle a crisis brings praise and recognition. These are important to the workaholic, because another characteristic is an identity issue, such as weak self-esteem and a need for ever-greater external recognition of worth.

The appeal of a crisis is so great that a workaholic may not be as focused as one could be on avoiding the occurrence of crisis situations, or might even create the conditions that lead to crisis. The surface appearance is that this individual is the problem solver, but the deeper truth may be that he or she is a major contributor to the problem. Similarly, a person who appears to be the most conscientious employee, the one who works the hardest, might be an over-controlling perfectionist who blocks opportunities for others to perform or to further develop their own skills. These are organizational concerns that are frequently masked by the workaholic's long hours, which are taken as a positive contribution to the workplace. The ongoing social support helps the workaholic maintain denial of any problem, another addiction characteristic. Finally, there is withdrawal, in both physical symptoms and psychological distress, when a workaholic tries to separate from work.

The EAP professionals responded to our initial presentation with comments to indicate they did often see people who fit this general pattern but who had been referred to the EAP for only one specific symptom, which might match with our terminology or might be something entirely different. For example, a consultation with an employee who is having difficulties in interpersonal relations might be from a referral that directly mentioned perfectionist tendencies. In contrast, a controlling manager who insists on personally handling a new employee's training might be referred out of fear that, because it is a male manager demanding extensive one-on-one time with a new female employee, there is a potential for charges of sexual harassment.

The above are two sample stories related during the focus group. In each case, the subsequent counseling did reveal more aspects of the presenting problem to indicate this identified symptom was part of a larger pattern of workaholism. This suggests that a workaholic may be referred to the EAP, although *not* under a referral labeled workaholism. As the professionals talked about these specific cases and their multiple issues, they recognized a commonality with our description, but most had not previously considered it under a single term of workaholism or work addiction. They also acknowledged that many other people in similar situations were not being referred for help, exactly for the reason we referenced – the managers do not want to discourage their extra time and effort on the job and would rather discount problems that arise than consider that the extra work is symptomatic in itself.

According to the extant literature, the role of the EAP counselor is to prepare and catalyze clients for change. It is also the role of the counselor to work with a broad array of other professionals to find a solution to the client's problems. The other professionals or resources to which a client needing further intervention or treatment may be referred include psychotherapists, physicians, human resource managers, job counselors, educators, alcohol or drug rehabilitation programs, and community resources. A typical treatment plan for an EAP intervention involves the following steps: (1) problem selection, (2) problem definition, (3) goal development, (4) construction of objectives, (5) intervention creation, and (6) diagnosis determination (Oher et al., 1998). Our discussion with these EAP professionals culminated in general agreement that the more people who understood the workaholic pattern across the entire range of potentially involved professionals, the stronger the possibility of correctly identifying the deeper problem and setting goals for improvement that go beyond the most quickly recognized symptom.

The focus group participants agreed that every person with one symptom should not be assumed to have the entire pattern. Yet, they also believed more people would receive help if managers, counselors and others were educated to recognize the multiple characteristic, and they encouraged us to find ways to promote that increased awareness. We took their stories, altered only to remove or change any reference to a particular type of company or profession, and wrote eight short scenarios representing the employees' situations prior to referral to an EAP.

Manipulation Check

For a group of 38 students, we again presented the characteristics of workaholism as parallel to other addictions. This group consisted of 20 MBA students and 17 undergraduates. The average age was 31, and they averaged nine years of full-time work experience. After the presentation, we asked them to fill out a questionnaire containing the eight scenarios. They were asked to read each one and then identify the workaholic characteristics they saw in that person's behavior by checking one or more of the boxes labeled identity/self-esteem problems, need for high control, crisis attraction, perfectionism, withdrawal symptoms, denial that relationship to work is a problem, and 'I see no symptoms in this scenario'. If they checked more than one box, they were also asked to rank the most obviously evident as 1, the next most obvious as 2, and so on.

To summarize this information, we scored a single response or a top ranking as a score of five; when there were multiple responses, the one ranked second received a score of four, the one ranked third a score of three, fourth a score of two, fifth a score of one; items not marked at all received a zero. We then could create a composite score and examine the total ranking (with higher numbers being the stronger identification), the number of times ranked and the average ranking. Overall, they did accurately identify the intended representation in each scenario. More feedback from this group will be included as part of the discussion of the scenarios in the final large survey.

Pilot Study

Using the same eight scenarios, we mailed a survey instrument to 59 members of another regional EAPA chapter. They were asked, for each scenario, to rate the likelihood, first, that the focal individual would be referred to an EAP and, second, that he or she might self-refer to an EAP.

In practice, employees may be mandatorily referred to an EAP by a supervisor for workplace performance problems, or they may self-refer.

EAPs are generally classified in one of two ways. The traditional model is the internal ('in-house') program, in which the EAP is affiliated with a unit such as human resources or a medical department belonging to the company or work organization. The second type, a model that has gained increasing popularity in recent years, is the external ('contracted-out') EAP, in which the work organization contracts with an external provider of EAP services.

Some of these EAP providers are nationwide in scope and subcontract with individual professionals or clinics in various locations to provide local services. More recently, new integrated models of programs (sometimes referred to as 'combined programs'), which merge internal and external approaches, have become increasingly popular (Beidel, 2004).

The incidence of self-referral, whether completely self-initiated or from the gentle suggestion of a supervisor or colleague, is becoming more common in conjunction with the shift toward contracted-out programs. In this process, there is a greater assurance of confidentiality, as the employer may never know that a specific employee has been seen by an EAP; the referral may show up only as a number in a report sent to the employer. For this reason, we felt it important to explore both possibilities – referral and self-referral to an EAP. Each likelihood was marked on a four-option scale of: very likely, somewhat likely, not very likely, and highly unlikely. After indicating the likelihood of referral, subjects optionally wrote in how that referral might be labeled. After indicating the likelihood of self-referral, they could also write in how the person would describe his or her difficulty in that self-referral.

Eleven people mailed back the survey, making a response rate of 22 per cent. These subjects – average age of 48 – consisted of four men and seven women, and held titles ranging from executive director and EAP manager to therapist, consultant and clinical coordinator. Most represented either an external EAP (4) or a combination EAP (3); several indicated other organizations such as healthcare facilities. We learned from this group that the individuals described in the scenarios were, at best, only moderately likely to be referred to an EAP and even less likely to self-refer. Their descriptions of a referral label, if one should occur, often matched that of the original story on which it was based but usually showed no similarity to terminology used in the addiction description of a workaholic.

The Survey

To shorten the survey, we selected five of the original eight scenarios, based on information gathered through the manipulation check and the pilot survey. We targeted a sub-set that would include the best range of coverage on both sides of the issue, the recognized workaholic characteristics from the manipulation check and the types of referrals from the pilot study.

Other than shortening the survey, our only change was a shift to on-line data collection. Using a national listing of EAPA members, we sent an email asking recipients to use the included web link to access and complete a survey for 'research on the likelihood that a variety of employee tendencies might result in that individual either "being referred to" or "self-referring to" an Employee Assistance Program'. There was no reference in the instructions or the survey content to workaholism or workaholic tendencies. The instructions assured subjects anonymity and instructed them to email the authors separately to request summary results, if desired.

The original email contact list was a total of 1939 names. Of those, 166 contact attempts returned as 'non-deliverable'. An additional 68 resulted in 'out of office' type responses for people who were on vacation or otherwise unavailable during the data collection time window. This left a contact list of 1705. We received 195 completed on-line surveys, a response rate of 11.44 per cent. Demographics of the sample are reported in Table 11.1, and professional information appears in Table 11.2.

Survey instructions were: 'Please read each of the following descriptions, indicate the likelihood of a referral, and/or self-referral to an EAP, and

Table 11.1   Demographics of respondents (total sample = 195 subjects)

Item	Response categories	No. of responses
Age	Range 28–75; mean = 51	170;
	missing	25
Gender	male	67
	female	105
	missing	23
Race	White/Caucasian	162
	Asian/Asian-American	0
	Black/African-American	6
	Hispanic or Latino	1
	American Indian/Alaskan Native	1
	Other	2
	missing	23
Education	Associate's degree or comparable	6
	Bachelor's degree	7
	Master's degree	129
	Doctorate	24
	missing	29

Table 11.2 Employment information on respondents (total sample = 195)

Item	Response categories	No. of responses
Place of employment	Internal EAP	51
	External EAP	47
	Combination internal/external	32
	Treatment facility/hospital	7
	Individual practitioner	22
	Other	18
	missing	18
Job titles (only most	Consultant	30
frequent response	Owner / President / CEO	15
clusters shown; 174	Manager / EAP Manager	16
responses – 21 missing)	HR Manager	2
	Director or Executive Director	18
	Regional or National Director	5
	Program Dir./Mgr./Administrator	7
	EAP Coordinator/Program Coordin.	10
	Counselor	15
	Therapist	12
	Clinical Dir./Supr./Admin.	4
	Substance abuse/drug/alcohol specialty	5
Professions/licensures	Cert. Employee Assistance Professional	112
(individuals indicated		
multiple responses; 174	Addictions counselor	58
people responded – 21	Counselor/therapist	84
missing)	Nurse	3
	Pastoral/theological	7
	Physician	0
	Psychiatrist	0
	Psychologist	14
	Social worker	68
	Other	43
	Substance abuse professional	12
	Marriage and family therapy	7
	MBA	4

provide the terminology you believe would be used in that referral. Additional space is provided for any further comments you want to include.'

Some people read the 'label' request to be asking for designation of whether the referral would be mandatory or voluntary, formal or informal, or generated through the human resources department or from the manager. This comparison is interesting as a separate type of result. However, for this reporting, we are focusing on those respondents who applied specific, descriptive wording to the problem behind referral, rather than these referral categories. Therefore, in the following discussions, when there is reference to a number of people labeling the referral it should be understood to be the net number of those applying descriptive labels after setting aside those that are categorizations of formal/informal, and so on.

Scenario #1

Milt Bonner is head of the advertising department in a mid-size firm. Recently a female employee complained that Milt often requires she work individually with him in his office, and she is wary of the reason behind this focused attention on being alone with her. When asked about this, Milt explained that he feels he is the only one who can teach her the needed techniques properly. If he doesn't work with her individually, she will pick up too many bad habits and misunderstandings from other employees. A great deal of tension has developed, due to the differing interpretations of why Milt continues to require that this employee work alone with him.

How likely is it that Milt would be referred to the EAP?

Likelihood	Response total	Response per cent
very likely	20	10.4
somewhat likely	67	34.9
not very likely	**88**	**45.8**
highly unlikely	18	9.4
Total respondents	**192**	

If referred, how would this referral be labeled?   Of the 76 who put a specific problem label on the referral, nearly half (33) identified the issue as sexual harassment. Another eight people identified it as related to conflict management; seven thought Milt needed help with interpersonal skills. Fifteen

How likely is it that Milt would self-refer to an EAP?

Likelihood	Response total	Response per cent
very likely	1	0.5
somewhat likely	9	4.7
not very likely	76	40
highly unlikely	**104**	**55.3**
Total respondents	**190**	

respondents considered this a situation in which the individual would benefit from education, coaching or consultation, sometimes referencing general skills related to supervision of employees.

If he does self-refer, *how would he describe his difficulty?*   Ten people felt that Milt might self-refer for a reason related to stress; another three believed it might be in response to accusations of harassment. Six mentioned conflict as a basis, and six more mentioned communication difficulties. Nine people referenced interpersonal or relationship difficulties. Most notably, of the 112 people giving a response, 44 people specified in their answer that, if Milt did self-refer, the reason would be expressed in terms of having to deal with others' problems. For example:

- 'he would likely say he is unfairly targeted'
- [he] 'needs help dealing with a difficult employee'
- 'my guess is he sees her cooperation as a problem'
- 'I'd bet that Milt would see himself as her "victim", arguing that he's not done anything inappropriate'
- 'people not realizing the importance of how he has to train specific employees'
- 'issues with employees' "bad habits". Not his fault'
- 'his attempts to train a staff member are being misinterpreted, and he is being misunderstood'.

Additional comments   Further comments about this scenario predominantly followed the same theme of potential harassment, likely not to be realized by Milt. Most respondents approached it as an opportunity/need for more awareness on harassment; a few questioned the assumption that there was evidence of harassment. Sample comments follow:

- 'My assumption is that if Milt sought EAP services, that it would be to discuss the female employee as a problem, not because he self-identified that his behavior might be harassing.'
- 'In my experience, Milt would not be referred to the EAP because the primary problem would be seen by management as an HR matter, risk of sexual harassment suit, etc. Oftentimes management will only think to refer to EAP if the identified employee(s) self-report having personal difficulties or a history of behavioral health treatment.'
- 'Milt needs to be approached with his responsibility to inspire confidence and trust in his employees as a department head. If specific behaviors indicating misconduct are identified discipline and a formal EAP referral is appropriate.'

- 'There is nothing here that indicates that this could be harassment, e.g. there are no complaints about his touching her. No indication of how often he meets with her privately, etc.'
- 'It's Milt that's sick, either with power, self-importance, or need for dependence from the opposite sex. Inasmuch as he's boss, who's going to refer him to the EAP? And, unless there's a higher power to intervene, the female employee either needs to find help from the EAP in handling her sense of powerlessness or seek work in a less hostile climate.'

This scenario was written to suggest the rigid thinking pattern of a high need for control. The manipulation check revealed this as the most recognized characteristic but followed closely by interpretations of Milt's actions in the other rigid thinking variation, perfectionism. Consider the implications of this difference. If one could determine that the issue truly is lack of sensitivity to gender issues, greater awareness might make the needed difference. However, if the root of the issue is a high need for control, Milt might take in that information but then feel that the solution is to better 'control' related elements of the situation but continue to insist on direct, personal training. He would now be more aware of gender-based interpretations but just as controlling, and it would surface again in new situations.

In this scenario, the chance for a referral usually referenced a potential legal issue. Even with that organizationally relevant aspect, more than half the respondents thought a referral was unlikely. The even lower estimation that he would self-refer fits with considering this as a problem of rigid thinking. If Milt firmly believes he is the only one able and willing to do the job right and, therefore, he must take on this added responsibility, any suggestion to the contrary will be interpreted as others' inability to appreciate his higher standards. If Milt's issues are control and perfectionism, he will be genuinely surprised by any claims related to harassment and, possibly, even take those as further confirmation that others cannot even recognize higher standards when they see them.

A potential harassment complaint is definitely the most immediate problem to explore and deal with, as the employee has mentioned discomfort with what is happening. However, stopping at that problem identification might carry the risk of applying an off-the-shelf program or training on that information and topic and then wondering later why other employee complaints are coming in about this same manager.

Scenario #2
Vivonics Corporation has recently redesigned its production employees into self-directed work teams. All the new teams are struggling to some

extent. Team 'eagle', however, is having the most difficulty. Sharon, one of the team members, refuses to cross-train with other members. She blocks the potential of others learning her job by refusing to give them the necessary information to learn it fully. According to Sharon, no one else on the team has the background needed to handle her function.

How likely is it that Sharon would be referred to *the EAP?*

Likelihood	Response total	Response per cent
very likely	53	28.2
somewhat likely	**86**	**45.7**
not very likely	39	20.7
highly unlikely	10	5.3
Total respondents	**188**	

If referred, *how would this referral be labeled?* Among the 102 offering specific labels, 25 people mentioned the 'team' aspect of Sharon's situation, often clarifying that she needed training or help to understand her responsibilities and the expectations of being a team member. Thirteen people labeled the problem 'interpersonal' without specific reference to a team. Eleven respondents considered it a 'conflict' problem. Three specifically mentioned dealing with change or change management. Twenty-four respondents felt this was what might be considered a more traditional EAP referral for being ineffective on the job, calling it performance (17), job related (3), inappropriate behavior (2), or an uncooperative employee (3).

This scenario was written to relay the control aspect of a workaholic pattern. Sharon is controlling information and controlling people on the team by not allowing them access to it. One respondent said she was 'unwilling to move forward, inflexible' – a good description of rigid

How likely is it that Sharon would self-refer to *an EAP?*

Likelihood	Response total	Response per cent
very likely	1	0.5
somewhat likely	37	21.3
not very likely	**88**	**46.8**
highly unlikely	62	33.0
Total respondents	**188**	

thinking in general. In the manipulation check, slightly higher than the control factor, this was considered an identity or self-esteem problem for Sharon. Perhaps the shift in context from manager/employee relations to team member interactions highlighted an aspect of personal insecurity in this situation compared with the previous description of Milt. One respondent referred to it as fear of loss.

If she does self-refer, *how would she describe her difficulties?* Again, there were answers stating 'others' problems' – 'others not being cooperative', 'the other team members have a problem', 'being misunderstood'. The most frequently mentioned self-referral reason was stress (25 respondents). Conflict was mentioned ten times, several overlapping with stress as a result of the conflict. There were also frequent explanations (17) involving others' ineptitude or unwillingness to meet necessary standards, such as:

- 'she is the only one that can do the job'
- 'having to do all the work and carry the rest of the ignorant team'
- 'she works with incompetents'
- 'can't tolerate poor output, "loyal" to past company standards'
- 'not getting along because they don't know how to do the work, it's too hard to teach, unreasonable demands on her'
- 'she cannot train employees incapable of doing the work; that the project is doomed to fail, as people are being asked to do work they cannot do'
- 'she is being forced to work with incompetent people'.

Eighteen respondents felt her reasons would include complaints against the decisions and, sometimes, incompetence of the supervisor or manager. Six people mentioned dealing with change. Another six included fear of job loss as a reason to seek help from the EAP. When speculating from Sharon's side of the picture, rigid thinking displayed as perfectionism was still dominant in responses.

Additional comments   Many of the additional comments about Sharon's situation centered on the issue of job performance. As such, it might fall under the purview of HR or further handling by the manager or supervisor first. Also, the handling might vary according to the type of EAP and its integration into the organization's operations:

- 'Human Resources would typically handle this kind of problem.'
- 'I feel this might not be an EAP issue; this might turn out that way but HR should be contacted and to keep them in the loop.'

- 'Primarily an HR issue since the employee may need work related coaching or training or team building may be indicated for the department.'
- 'Manager needs to remove Sharon from the team in order to get the job done and put Sharon on another assignment.'
- 'Depending on the organization, the EAP might have been involved in the transition planning and processes. If that were the case, Sharon might be more likely to reach out for support.'
- 'It depends on the role EAP plays in the organization and whether Sharon would see EAP as a resource. If the EAP has marketed itself as a resource for work-related issues, there is a chance that both the manager as well as Sharon might use the EAP.'
- 'It depends on the nature, function, penetration, and focus of the EAP. An internal EAP that is well connected to the operation would likely be involved in assisting the team and Sharon. A disconnected external EAP would likely not get the referral until HR got involved.'

Five people mentioned that this would trigger activity with the full team:

- 'I would recommend interceding at the group level first since everyone is having difficulty adjusting – reminding everyone of the availability of the group and addressing individual issues in the workplace first. As others begin to have less difficulty, then it would be appropriate to identify individuals who are still not adjusting and to make a supervisory referral (non-mandated) to the EAP and begin the progressive disciplinary process.'
- 'We get referrals very similar to this and in most situations we are asked to come into the department, or in this case, the team, and conduct teambuilding classes to reduce the negativity and barriers and promote trust among the team members.'
- 'Our EAP is known for mediation, as well, so she may be referred individually at first, but most likely the entire team would be asked to meet with us to resolve this concern. We have about 12 departments we are working with right now with similar concerns.'
- 'This is really a performance problem and should be handled accordingly. EAP frequently gets these referrals to assess for pathology and to fix the employee and get her back into the fold. Team members need to be taught team dynamics and how to use the team to get her to act as a team member.'
- 'I would hope if management is referring they are smart enough to refer and/or consult re the entire team . . . it might also make a big

difference how integrated EAP is in this firm. Internal much more effective with corporate culture issues.'

Scenario #3

Andy Meyers is in charge of a small insurance claims office, typically staffed by clerical support people and himself. The head office acknowledges that he really needs another claims adjuster to help with the ever-increasing workload. Several times he has brought in a trainee. In each case the new hire has left within six months. Departing employees say Andy is simply too difficult, because he is never satisfied with anyone else's work. Andy tells a different story. He believes he has done everything possible to teach these people how to be effective in the job. He sighs and describes how it is still up to him to cover everything, no matter how many hours he must spend on the job, because he can't find a good enough person to help him.

How likely is it that Andy would be referred to *the EAP?*

Likelihood	Response total	Response per cent
very likely	23	12.4
somewhat likely	**90**	**48.3**
not very likely	61	32.8
highly unlikely	12	6.5
Total respondents	**186**	

Among the 92 contributions, 43 people recommended coaching/training/consultation for Andy, usually referencing leadership or management skills. Of these, five specifically mentioned needing better skill in delegation or needing to give up control and develop people. Twelve people identified this as a performance problem, several specifying issues of retention or turnover. An additional four people simply referred to the problem as Andy's 'perfectionism'. One individual suggested a depression assessment, another said anxiety disorder, and one said the performance problems might be related to personal issues.

This scenario involves the business issue of continuing turnover related to rigid thinking in both variations. The perfectionism aspect is strongly represented, but followed closely by observations of control. The majority (more than 60 per cent) of respondents felt that a referral was at least somewhat likely. Note that this is lower than the 74 per cent who thought Sharon was at least somewhat likely to be referred. The higher likelihood for Sharon's referral might be tied to Andy being in a management position, or that Sharon's situation had immediate, daily impact on such a large number of people in her team.

How likely is it that Andy would self-refer to an EAP?

Likelihood	Response total	Response per cent
very likely	1	0.5
somewhat likely	36	19.3
not very likely	**93**	**49.7**
highly unlikely	57	30.5
Total respondents	**187**	

If he does self-refer, how would he describe his difficulty?   Of 120 responses, 48 people said he would self-refer for stress. Six more did not specify stress but said he would claim to be overworked or overwhelmed with the work. Others referenced not being appreciated (8) or being misunderstood (6). Two more respondents specifically said burnout would be the reason given. A number of people mentioned Andy might recognize his own perfectionism (4) or attention to detail (1), or the contributing problems of his high standards (2) and others' inability to work up to what he defines as suitable performance (2).

In these responses on self-referral, we see the same tendency for outward blaming, but a slightly more common speculation that he might have some awareness of the perfectionism aspect. However, Andy's likelihood of self-referral was less than Sharon's. One respondent offered the insight that 'He may also have an unhealthy need to be at work', a very appropriate comment on the total picture of a workaholic but unusual to be mentioned under consideration of self-referral.

Additional comments   For the most part, the additional comments on Andy's situation re-iterated those made above. Andy is driving people away but is unlikely to self-refer unless the stress of his heavy workload begins to get the better of him. A few comments repeated the company/EAP relationship that might impact on how the involved parties view the EAP as a resource. A number of comments on this scenario stand out as directly pertinent to consideration of the workaholic profile from an addiction view:

- 'Andy needs to see a therapist to get evaluated to determine his problem and to perhaps be on meds.'
- 'I wonder if [Andy] has problems in other areas of his life as well.'
- 'A quality supervisor will recognize this problem of "co-dependent over-management" by Andy, and will ask the EAP counselor to address quality leadership-management competencies with Andy; as well as check out Andy's childhood/teenage years to determine if this "co-dependency" trait might result from a family dysfunction.'

- 'Andy apparently perceives himself as a high achiever, and who may also suffer from feelings of insecurity, and thus have difficulty trusting others to work at the same job he does, perhaps fearing they may do it better than he does, or maybe even replace him. This case is not likely to be solved in one or two sessions. After an assessment, I might well refer Andy to a skilled therapist for work on self-esteem and other related issues.'
- 'Andy is a perfectionist. There should be a 12-step program for these folks, but I don't know of one!'
- 'He's a perfectionist, must have things done his way or it's no good. Most likely condescending, judgmental, and controlling. Very difficult to work for.'

Scenario #4

Terry Leonard is a highly paid, although somewhat unpopular, employee of the ANX Electronics Company. Both his pay and his reputation are due to the company's tendency to send Terry in when there is a crisis situation to clean up. He takes charge in a way that may seem abrupt to the existing staff nearest to the crisis, but he works incredible hours and, somehow, always brings things under control in a relatively short time. Recently, Terry has been asked to stay at one site to manage ongoing operations, because this facility has shown a steady trend of one crisis after another. The problems still arise as often as before, but having Terry there gives the company directors a sense that each situation is being handled as quickly and as efficiently as can be expected.

How likely is it that Terry would be referred to the EAP?

Likelihood	Response total	Response per cent
very likely	1	0.5
somewhat likely	3	1.6
not very likely	45	24.4
highly unlikely	**136**	**73.5**
Total respondents	**185**	

If referred, how would this referral be labeled? Fourteen people felt the referral would be related to stress. Two more expressed it in terms of potential burnout. Other responses (25) seemed to cluster around the idea that Terry might now need to soften his management approach or style due to changing situations. These ranged from reference to 'work in teams post-crisis', 'inappropriate management style', 'abrasive manner', 'anger management', and 'sensitive training' to suggestions related more generally to 'interpersonal relations' and 'communication'. One respondent suggested there might be a request to the EAP for 'an organizational assessment'. Five people wrote comments to emphasize that Terry would not be referred to the EAP because 'he thinks he's doing the right thing', 'according to management there is no problem', and he 'produces positive results and there is no implication of wrong-doing'.

The crisis attraction aspect of this scenario was correctly identified as primary in the manipulation check. Although survey respondents recognized the potential need to change his style when moving from crisis to standard operations, at this point they referenced it most often as something he needed to think about but not necessarily something they thought he would compulsively cling to. Here we have the strongest result across all scenarios saying that Terry is highly unlikely to be referred to the EAP, supporting the appeal of a crisis situation if Terry is a workaholic – he has had reason to be heavily absorbed by work and receives positive recognition for that. This is not necessarily a problem for any employee in such a situation. The defining question lies in whether he can now, in the current position, shift to avoiding crises or whether he will perpetuate the situations that suit a workaholic's needs.

How likely is it that Terry would self-refer to *an EAP?*

Likelihood	Response total	Response per cent
very likely	1	0.6
somewhat likely	15	8.3
not very likely	40	22.0
highly unlikely	**125**	**69.1**
Total respondents	**181**	
skipped this question	**14**	

If he does self-refer, *how would he describe his difficulty?* As with the referral comments, most of the 88 commenting respondents felt that if Terry did self-refer it would be related to stress (49), burnout (3), overwork (2) or feeling overwhelmed (2). A new theme appearing with this scenario is the potential that he would seek EAP help owing to family/relationship problems linked to long work hours and lack of work/life balance (6 related comments). One explicitly wrote 'marital difficulty due to workaholism'. Another new reference was to feelings of isolation or loneliness (2 responses) along with the more familiar variation of being misunderstood and/or unappreciated (5 responses) by fellow employees or management. Several people mentioned he might be experiencing boredom or frustration at 'being stuck in one place to baby-sit', 'working at the same site'.

These comments are accurately recognizing the type of problems Terry might experience in this job change. However, they are responding to what he might describe IF he self-referred, and they have given less than a 10 per cent chance that a self-referral would occur.

Additional comments   Nineteen of the 40 comments were a restatement of the opinion there is no problem that would instigate either referral or self-referral to an EAP. Seven people expanded on the potential of his needing to change his style for the current assignment – samples are:

- 'Sometimes trouble shooters are effective because they come in and "fix" and then move on. I have seen such a scenario go sour because the trouble shooter is not effective as a day-by-day manager.'
- 'If he is to be successful in a long-term management position, he will have to build loyalty and respect among his new charges, which may require a different style.'
- 'He may be able to "fix a crisis situation" but can he manage?'
- 'In the past, Terry has not had to deal with the "fall-out" from employees resulting from decisions he has made. His past roles may have been stressful but he would get a break between assignments. His more permanent role may lead him to feeling overwhelmed and stressed out.'

Some respondents expressed the view that deeper issues might be involved and that Terry might not be as ideal an employee as the impression given by his success at crisis management:

- 'Many organizations would value his ability to clean up messes without attending to the fact that he does not do any proactive or preventative measures.'
- 'If the crises continue to arise with his prolonged presence, they may recognize that his ability to get them out of a crisis does not translate to his ability to mitigate a crisis.'
- 'Though Terry is good at getting things under control quickly, repeated difficulties at a particular unit suggest some type of internal problem. While Terry may get it under control, he may not see or address the triggers to the repetitious nature of the problems at the facility. ANX Electronics may not be willing to address deeper issues in the organization, but prefer to put fires out.'
- 'I would recommend the directors or other supervisors gather more information from Terry and staff and coach toward organizational change for cooperation. Is Terry the reason for all the crises, or does it go deeper?'

These comments seem to show great awareness of potential problems among our sample of EAP professionals, and problems that fit with consideration of an addictive pattern. Unfortunately, without the referral or self-referral happening, there is no opportunity for this depth of understanding to be applied to Terry's situation.

Scenario #5

Sue's mother is concerned, but she has stopped asking whether Sue has met or is dating anyone nice. The idea of ever seeing grandchildren is becoming more and more unlikely. Sue has explained repeatedly that she has no time for dating, until her career is more firmly established. Over the past eight years, Sue has lost touch with all her friends and rarely sees family. When asked about this Sue replied, 'Several times I thought I'd made new acquaintances with people having similar interests. Eventually, each one has drifted away after complaining that all I do is work. OK, so I put in a lot of hours and I don't take vacations. They just don't understand how competitive this industry is – especially for a woman. They don't realize what I'm up against, I guess. But, if this is what I choose to do, what's their problem? Real friends wouldn't give me a hard time about it.'

How likely is it that Sue would be referred to *the EAP?*

Likelihood	Response total	Response per cent
very likely	4	2.2
somewhat likely	19	10.3
not very likely	55	29.7
highly unlikely	**107**	**57.8**
Total respondents	**185**	

If referred, *how would this referral be labeled?*   Out of 72 comments, 32 related to life outside work – six made specific use of the terms workaholic or workaholism as a problem; eleven mentioned work/life balance issues

How likely is it that Sue would self-refer to *an EAP?*

Likelihood	Response total	Response per cent
very likely	8	4.4
somewhat likely	67	36.6
not very likely	**69**	**37.7**
highly unlikely	39	21.3
Total respondents	**183**	

(with six of the 11 even proposing family/friends' involvement in accomplishing a referral). Fifteen respondents indicated stress/anxiety, and seven more referred to burnout. Risk of depression was mentioned three times.

If she does self-refer, *how would she describe her difficulty?* One hundred and thirty people wrote in possible descriptions for a self-referral, most referencing difficulty with interpersonal relationships in general (13), problems stemming from pressure/stress by friends and family (especially mother) about her work habits (6), and the fact that friends and family 'don't understand' (14). Those comments seemed written as though the issue resided with those other people, but resulting in her having to deal with difficulties. In contrast, another 38 phrased the issue as that she might self-refer because of her own perception of lack of balance, need for more friendships or simply loneliness. Stress/anxiety was a prominent theme (mentioned 24 times), along with burnout (4 times) and depression (10 times).

While a small number of people thought she might self-identify as a workaholic (3) or as engaging in compulsive behavior (1), others thought even a self-referral would be qualified by her rationale for the exclusive focus on work:

- 'I work too much but have to, to compete.'
- 'I am not a workaholic, I am simply trying to get ahead.'
- 'Victimized by her job.'
- 'Not as successful as she would like; looking for a mentor.'

Additional comments Fifteen of 46 responses re-emphasized the low likelihood that Sue will ever find her way to the EAP, many adding that it would have to be self-referral, because she is a terrific employee from the company's viewpoint:

- 'Employers love people like Sue. Why would they want to stop her?'
- 'A perfect corporate employee! No personal life. Workaholic.'
- 'In today's economy and workplace realities, Sue's behavior is actually endorsed and condoned by many organizations.'

Ten individuals described Sue's situation as indicating that, although any referral or self-referral is unlikely at this time, she is on a path that may lead to new problems and then things could change. For example:

- 'more likely as burnout and emotional crises increase'
- 'Eventually Sue will wear herself out since there is no balance in her life. My guess is that a sense of depression or unhappiness might bring her to the EAP.'

- 'until or unless she becomes ill and starts missing deadlines or using her sick leave'
- 'Sue will eventually self-refer after some precipitating event, possibly a workplace disappointment.'
- 'until she becomes lonely enough that she will need to re-evaluate her life's mission. This could come as a crisis in which she will seek help or she will come to a point where she again needs to sit down with someone to re-focus'
- 'This is a woman that will end up with serious symptoms of burnout, depression, and possibly have to take a leave of absence if she continues to be a workaholic.'

One respondent stated that 'Sue needs to get to see a therapist to help her with her issues. It appears that she is a perfectionist and needs to help herself with her compulsive behavior.' Another described her as 'private person, has been hurt by relationships, tends to isolate and may be lonely'. Yet another speculated that Sue might be a lesbian and finds working all the time to be easier than 'to come to grips with this issue and inform her mother, family and co-workers of her true feelings'. One individual offered this very concrete suggestion for help: 'A talented, 45+-year-old female counselor who knows the "business world" would do wonders with Sue.'

This scenario describes the individual willing to sacrifice other relationships and other satisfactions in life for the sake of work. Sue is described as currently doing so, in spite of the messages from friends and family that her life has become too unbalanced. This is the rare case in which likelihood of self-referral was stronger than likelihood of referral. Those respondents who saw this as a pattern that is destined to lead to problems at some point seemed to feel that the problems will negatively affect Sue before there are work-related deficiencies that draw attention. In the manipulation check, there was moderate recognition of identity or self-esteem issues, but strong support for the idea that Sue was in denial that her relationship to work was a problem. As noted above in respondents' comments, that denial will break down only in the face of some emotional crisis, burnout, depression or physical illness.

CONCLUSIONS RELATING WORKAHOLISM AND EAP REFERRALS

EAP referrals are based on job performance problems. A workaholic is expert at managing to the standard performance metrics. The turmoil and atmosphere of frustration and distrust created by a workaholic may be affecting those figures, but not in a way that is easily recognized. If any awareness exists, the workaholic may be the last person suspected as being the eye of the storm. When organizations attempt to identify and document the *interpersonal* aspects of the work, they can better locate the dysfunction of workaholism. Examples include use of 360° performance reviews, wherein feedback comes from all levels and many sources. These processes can make a difference if the information is used well. Still, the majority of organizations continue to base performance judgments entirely on count-able features, one of which is the hours spent on the job, whether used efficiently or not.

Self-referral to an EAP by workaholics is unlikely, owing to denial that any existing problems are related to their working so hard. As mentioned earlier, the company, the business world in general and society at large support the workaholics' insistence that any complaints are due to lack of understanding or some selfish motive on the part of the people attacking their behavior. Results here confirm that only when there are direct perform-ance problems is a referral to an EAP considered likely. Even then, the per-centages are not overwhelming. From the organization's viewpoint this seems logical. Why create a problem when there is not evidence of one for which the company has any valid concern? However, this could be lack of understanding as to how performance might be enhanced if interpersonal difficulties and unhealthy patterns of excess work were eliminated earlier.

Through this study, we have reinforced our suspicion that few employees are referred to EAPs for workaholism, per se. However, it appears that in some cases employees are referred, or self-refer, for other presenting prob-lems that may be symptomatic of workaholism. Stress and related physical problems may prompt a referral, as might family difficulties such as divorce or children in trouble with either their schools or the legal system. Some people who admit to previous workaholic behavior will cite these types of issues as the eye-opener that caused them to look at their choices as a source of the problem. This anecdotal evidence provides some hope that EAPs can be beneficial in alleviating workaholism, but only if the individual work-aholic makes a decision to pursue recovery rather than temporarily addressing a single symptom.

Only some of the EAP professionals responded with comments that showed recognition of the broader pattern of workaholism, whether or not they directly applied that term. This suggests that, if they did have opportunity to meet with and design an intervention, some would be looking for the larger pattern and some would not. The compounding problem is that most of the time the EAP professionals will never have that opportunity.

CONTRIBUTIONS OF THE STUDY

This study contributes to research on workaholism and on EAPs, with the unique feature of combining the two.

The study of EAPs is an interesting one in its own right. The field is multidisciplinary, crossing such diverse disciplines as business, social work, counseling, psychology, criminology and others. All the various fields within the business discipline are involved as well.

EAPs have diffused broadly into the workplace, now reaching all types, sizes and varieties of organizations. A recent study determined that by 1991 over 45 per cent of the workforce was covered by EAPs. The study found that almost all large workplaces, and the majority of small workplaces, provide EAP services for their employees. However, coverage by EAPs was least likely in small worksites, where the majority of workers are employed (Blum et al., 1992). An EAP has become a component of the basic benefits package for over 90 per cent of Fortune 500 employers (Courtois et al., 2004). Recently it has been estimated that there are 65 million people in the US covered by EAPs and over 7000 professionals working in the EAP field (Daniels et al., 2004). Yet, opinions regarding the state and effectiveness of EAP research are somewhat mixed and contradictory.

In the current study, we have been able to show that a small problem description often alerts the EAP professional to a range of underlying issues on which treatment might focus for the benefit of both the individual and the organization. However, they are skeptical about whether or not they will be in a position to offer their expertise, owing to the unlikelihood of a referral. One area for valuable further research would be in line with frequent comments like 'it depends on the relationship between the EAP and the organization'. This reference was not targeting the internal/external situation but, rather, the culture of the organization and management's understanding of and belief in what an EAP has to offer.

Regarding the study of workaholism, our complete research process has shown that people inside the EAP profession and outside (as with our manipulation check) recognize symptoms of workaholism as problem areas, and they are often very accepting of the possibility that these symptoms can be either isolated characteristics or part of a larger pattern. Using the addiction view of workaholism helps relate the pieces into a whole that can be addressed comprehensively. We did not intend to suggest in this survey or its interpretation that one symptom automatically means the person will have the full profile of a workaholic – only that it is a possibility.

Our goal was to explore whether a workaholic would ever be referred to an EAP. The answer seems to be that it is not highly likely, but it is possible for there to be a referral or self-referral based on one or two symptoms. If the workaholic finds his or her way to the EAP, there is some chance the symptom will be interpreted as possibly part of a larger pattern. Overall, this means there is some good news for dealing with the problem of workaholism in organizations, although it is not strongly positive.

The current situation, then, is one in which EAPs have broadened their perspective on the range of issues pertinent to workplace performance, but expansion of services requires even greater cost justification than in the past. In this environment, it is difficult to promote the idea that a business organization should be concerned about some of the employees who *appear* to be their most conscientious workers. Some managers might welcome more knowledge about workaholic behavior and its detrimental impact in the workplace. Others might be highly resistant. Yet even those resistant to directly dealing with the issue of workaholism will increasingly be called upon to initiate EAP referrals for stress, depression and interpersonal difficulties that may be the outward signs. More comprehensive research is needed to determine how often a recovery process is initiated or helped along through use of EAP services.

Directly or indirectly, there is an intersection of EAP treatment and the organizational impact of workaholism. Although limited by a fairly low response rate, this study takes a step forward in exploring that intersection and, through feedback to survey respondents, helping to highlight the difference in comments among their own professional colleagues that might raise awareness of the total pattern of workaholism within an addiction framework.

REFERENCES

Barnett, R.C. and Hall, D.T. (2001), 'How to use reduced hours to win the war for talent', *Organizational Dynamics*, **29** (3), 192–210.

Beidel, B. (2004), 'A case for a common language in employee assistance programs', *Employee Assistance Quarterly*, **19** (4), 59–73.

Blum, T.C., Martin, J.K. and Roman, P.M. (1992), 'A research note on EAP prevalence, components, and utilization', *Journal of Employee Assistance Research*, **1** (1), 209–29.

Challenger, R. (1997), 'The need for employee assistance programs', in Hutchinson, W.S. and Enema, W.G. (eds), *Employee Assistance Programs: a Basic Text, 2nd edn*, Springfield IL: Charles C. Thomas.

Chima, F. (2004), 'Depression and the workplace: occupational and social work development and intervention', *Employee Assistance Quarterly*, **19** (4), 1–20.

Courtois, P., Dooley, R., Kennish, R., Paul, R. and Reddy, M. (2004), 'Employee assistance and work–life: lessons learned and future opportunities', *Employee Assistance Quarterly*, **19** (3), 75–97.

Daniels, A., Teems, L., Carroll, C. and Santiago-Fernandez, E. (2004), 'Crossing the quality chasm: opportunities for the employee assistance program field', *Employee Assistance Quarterly*, **19** (3), 27–43.

Fassel, D. (1990), *Working Ourselves to Death*, San Francisco: Harper.

Guglielmino, H.A. (2001), *2001 Career Survey of Work/Life Professionals*, McLean, VA: National Institute of Business Management.

Hansen, F. (2002), 'Truth and myths of work/life balance', *Workforce*, December, 34–9.

Hartwell, T.D., Steele, P., French, M.T., Potter, F.J., Rodman, N.F. and Zarkin, G.A. (1996), 'Aiding troubled employees: the prevalence, cost, and characteristics of employee assistance programs in the United States', *American Journal of Public Health*, **86** (6), 804–8.

Lockwood, N.R. (2004), 'Employee assistance programs: an HR tool to address top issues in today's workplace', in *SHRM Research*, available on-line at: http://www.shrm.org/research/briefly_published/

Oher, J.M., Conti, D.J. and Jongsma, A.E. (1998), *The Employee Assistance Treatment Planner*, New York: John Wiley and Sons.

Porter, G. (1996), 'Organizational impact of workaholism: suggestions for researching the negative outcomes of excessive work', *Journal of Occupational Health Psychology*, **1** (1), 70–84.

Porter, G. (2001), 'Workaholic tendencies and the high potential for stress among co-workers', *International Journal of Stress Management*, **8** (2), 147–64.

Robinson, B.E. (1989), *Work Addiction: Hidden Legacies of Adult Children*, Deerfield Beach, FK: Health Communications.

Robinson, B.E. (1998), *Chained to the Desk: a Guidebook for Workaholics, Their Partners and Children, and the Clinicians Who Treat Them*, New York: New York University Press.

Schaef, A.W. and Fassel, D. (1988), *Addictive Organization*, San Francisco: Harper and Row.

Sonnenstuhl, W.J. and Trice, H.M. (1986), *Strategies for Employee Assistance Programs: the Crucial Balance*, Ithaca, NY: ILR Press.

Tyler, K. (1999), 'Spinning wheels', *HR Magazine*, **44** (9), 34–7.

12. Career success and personal failure: a developing need to find balance[1]

Ronald J. Burke and Teal McAteer-Early

INTRODUCTION

> 'For all intents and purposes I'm a success! People think I've got it made. I don't know how many times this past year someone has told me I look and sound "just terrific". But how can someone who looks so good feel so bad? On the inside, I often waver between depression, feeling totally out of control, and feeling like I'm going to explode because I'm so full of pent-up emotions – confusion, anger, betrayal. I'm not productive at work. I don't feel particularly close to my wife.'

This personal statement expressed by a man in senior management captures a restlessness and anxiety in mid-life among successful careerists. The occurrence of career success and personal failure is identified as a phenomenon, or affliction as it may seem to those experiencing it, describing a set of conditions and experiences peculiar to certain individuals in their mid-life years. More generally, career success and personal failure refers to a situation where an individual has attained an unquestionable level of success according to the criteria set within society (high occupational status, prestige, power and responsibility, substantial income, relative material wealth, status in the community), but this success is to the detriment of personal fulfilment (Korman and Korman, 1980). According to Korman and Korman (ibid.), the ideals of career success and personal failure have been identified and challenged at various levels and settings. Moreover, in a contemporary context, the changing face of work itself challenges the principles underlying career success and personal failure.

A combination of current research and the environment of the contemporary economy has drastically altered the perception and interpretation of career success and personal failure as originally defined by Korman and Korman (ibid.). First it must be understood that the changing nature of work itself has inherently invited significant constructs as to what career success and personal failure really means (Jackson, 2005). The complex organizational framework of today takes into consideration the highly competitive global marketplace. Lowe (2000) suggests that there continues to be a pervasive and ongoing restructuring of the labour market and/or employment relationships, intended to promote productivity and competitiveness. These changes have increasingly created an underlying transition of work into personal life. Constructs such as technological advancement and a new innovative team-based organizational culture permit the homogenization of occupational culture and personal values, resulting in a new dimension of career success and personal failure. Therefore, the determinants of what constitutes career success are affected by how the individual employee experiences and interprets the meaning of success on both personal and professional levels. This paper will utilize the most basic concepts first established by Korman and Korman (1980) and furthered by Burke (1984) to examine career success and personal failure in a contemporary context with an emphasis on work–life balance and its effects on the professional/managerial category of employees.

Burke (1984) provides a comprehensive framework for understanding the determinants of career success and personal failure for an employee in a professional/managerial category of employment. Through the division of an identical labour market into two categories, Burke establishes straightforward criteria to define two coherent groups: those who appear to be more successful in advancing their careers and those who appear to be less successful in advancing their careers. The major distinction is accentuated through the latter group; those less successful in advancing their careers are more inclined to focus their energy on those aspects of life resting outside the organizational setting, such as their families, parents and relatives, leisure, recreation and social activities and spiritual and humanistic pursuits. On the other hand, those more successful in advancing their careers are more prone to direct their interests and ideologies towards the goals of the organization itself. The differentiation in attitudes can be explained by how the individual personally values rewards, and whether these rewards are intrinsic or extrinsic. Inevitably, it is the values themselves that play an intricate role in achieving career success, minimizing personal failure, and maintaining a healthy work/ non-work life balance.

In a contemporary context, career success and personal failure is a question of internal and external reward trappings and values. This extended analysis will examine those individuals in the professional/managerial category, and consider the existing deviation between individual and organizational values and, in turn, how this potential is actualized through venues of stress and disparity when attempting to achieve work/non-work life balance.

NATURE OF THE PROBLEM: CAREER SUCCESS AND PERSONAL FAILURE

Career Success

Career success has been a construct of significant interest to career schol-ars (Parsons, 1909; Hughes, 1958) and practitioners (for example, Robbins, 2003; Ziglar, 1997), as well as a multitude of individuals engaged in a career (Hall, 1976, 2002). The career literature describes theories (for example, Krumboltz, 1994), models (for example, Holland, 1997) and career inter-vention programs (for example, Chartrand and Rose, 1996) aimed at pre-dicting and facilitating career success.

Beyond addressing the constraints for those more or less successful in advancing their careers as proposed by Burke (1984), a definitive meaning of career success must first be established. Burke's previous analysis pro-vides a sound understanding of how career success and personal failure affected individuals in the late 1980s. The former views and attitudes devi-ate significantly from the contemporary context, thereby creating room for the contrasting ideals of today. Current studies have determined that success can have different meanings for different individuals and therefore different employees. Seibert et al. (1999) defined career success as positive psychological or work-related outcomes or achievements that individuals accumulate as a result of work experiences. Arthur et al. (2005) suggest that career success is an outcome of a person's career experiences and therefore defines outcomes at any point in a person's work experiences over time.

Perhaps one of the most useful definitions of career success came from the work of Hughes (1958), who was the first to identify the theoretical distinction between objective and subjective career success. Since then, career success research (Callanan, 2003; Heslin, 2003; Arthur et al., 2005) has increasingly assessed both objective and subjective career outcomes, therefore suggesting that many individuals define their career success largely in this way.

The objective career is publicly accessible and is concerned with social role and official position. As such, it reflects shared social understanding rather than distinctive individual understanding (Arthur et al., 2005). Objective career success refers to directly observable, measurable items, such as pay or promotion, that can be tangibly verified by an impartial third party. Objective career success equates to total compensation, number of promo-tions and other tangible trappings of accomplishment (Callanan, 2003).

Subjective career success is something that is experienced by the employee on a more personal and individual basis and is thereby measured relative to self-referent criteria such as the person's career goals and aspirations. People have very different career aspirations and place different values on such factors as income, employment security, the location of work, status, progression through different jobs, access to learning, the importance of work versus personal and family time, and so on (Arthur et al., 2005). Moreover, the subjective component of career success is viewed as a function of the individual's perception of satisfaction with the job and career progress (Callanan, 2003).

Overall, careers appear to unfold over time, and career success continues to have both objective and subjective career components. The duality and interdependence of both components make each relevant to the other, and likely to influence each other over time. Clearly, career success in the eyes of the organization can be and often is significantly different from the assessment of career success based on the individual's perception of achievement and/or satisfaction. The results of this disparity must be examined.

Personal Failure

According to Burke (1984), personal failure exists when an individual describes feelings of frustration, loneliness, alienation and despair, and is victim to pressing questions about the meaning and direction of his/her life. For many individuals, a primary determinant influencing their personal failure lies within the culture of the organizations in which they work. Heslin (2005) distinguishes two separate cultures: market culture and clan culture. For the purposes of this discussion, these two cultures are identified to establish a framework for analysing organizational culture in the context of work/non-work life balance, since both market and clan cultures include structural constraints contributing to an internalized feeling of personal failure.

Market culture is more often associated with a variation on how individuals conceptualize their career success. This potential dynamic can be illustrated by consideration of the prototypical organizational culture studied by Kerr and Slocum (1987), who argue that within market culture the relationship between the individual and the organization is contractual (meaning that mutual obligations are explicitly specified in return for some quantifiable performance) and therefore the employees are given an agreed-upon financial reward. Heslin (2005) determines that, within a market culture, there is little consideration given to the qualitative aspects of performance.

Clan culture depicts a situation wherein socialization and internalized values emphasize mutual interests and the tacit understanding that the required contributions of the organization may exceed contractual employee agreements (ibid.). Thus, the imposition of organizational citizenship to achieve success is required, accompanied by an internal drive for objective rewards. When compared with a market culture, financial bonuses are a small part of total compensation, while rituals and interaction that significantly cultivate a person's sense of belonging and status play a stronger role in the experience of work (ibid.). Market culture excludes those who require more subjective measures of success and acts as a barrier for achieving a work/ non-work life balance.

There has been an increasing emphasis on the desirability of achieving work/non-work life balance for individuals (Green and Skinner, 2005). According to Montgomery et al. (2005), in contemporary society, work and home represent the two most significant domains in the life of a working individual. When a balance is struck between these domains, an individual develops a sense of personal satisfaction, personal success. Unfortunately, achieving this balance has become increasingly difficult owing to a number of factors. In contemporary society, changes in family structures and technological changes (such as mobile phones and portable computers) that enable job tasks to be performed in a variety of locations have blurred the boundaries between work and home, making it more difficult to achieve balance. In addition, owing to an increasingly competitive business environment, organizations seeking to increase productivity and reduce costs have higher expectations of their employees. Individuals must work 'smarter' rather than harder and need to develop the ability to manage their time more effectively (Green and Skinner, 2005).

Outcomes

Burke (1984) highlights the discrepancy between the career identity of the individual, with its external trappings and rewards, and the idea that the individual's more personal sense of self forces itself into their own consciousness, creating varying degrees of psychosocial distress and demanding resolution of some sort. Current research suggests that this discrepancy has resulted in three disturbing outcomes: conflict of values; workaholism; and psychological, physiological and behavioural stress symptoms.

Conflict of values

Corporate values and culture, as established by senior organizational leaders, have become crucial predictors of the values and rewards which rest within the confines of the organization and which establish the basis for the very origins of career success and personal failure (Callanan, 2003). In fact, according to Callanan, individuals who fail to abide by the culture rules are likely to face a career plateau at best and outright dismissal at worst. Existence of these corporate values and culture undoubtedly have the potential to feed into the probability of an individual employee achieving career success but at the cost of pursuing goals based on personal values. Jackall (1983) speaks about a weeding out process and once completed, organizational decisions as to who achieves further career advancement to middle and senior executive ranks, hinge on factors beyond mere competence. These factors take into account whether the individual is willing to adhere to the demands of the organizational culture and meet the expectations of senior organizational leaders.

Schneider (1987) and Giberson et al. (2005) examine individual values and the organization. They agree that organizational homogeneity exists, in terms of personal values of members within an organizational unit. This in itself can harness the probability of achieving a healthy work/non-work life balance.

Schneider (1987) highlights the importance of interpersonal similarity in organizational behaviour and suggests that, over the course of time, organizations tend to become homogeneous in terms of the personality, values and interests of their members. Giberson et al. (2005) provide a conceptual replication of Schneider (1987) by suggesting that the organizational homogeneity phenomenon, in terms of values, occurs across organizational levels.

There is a definite congruence between the unique individual value-based profiles and the profiles of top organizational leaders, which suggests that ideals at the strategic level play a critical role in shaping the environments of their organizations (Giberson et al., 2005). Organizational homogeneity exists through the measurement of personality traits (extraversion, agreeableness, conscientiousness, emotional stability and intellect or openness to experience and values through aesthetics, affiliation, benevolence, materialism, hedonism, power, security, status). In order for leaders to embed their personality traits (which are reflective of their needs for both subjective and objective rewards) into the organizations, they lead by surrounding themselves with individuals who are similar to themselves. Within and across industries, organizations tend to retain managers with similar personality types, leading to the emergence of an organizational modal personality.

Therefore, organizational personality and value profiles developed within organizations are not random; rather they are reflective of the characteristics of leaders and founders who transmit their personality values through goal setting and recruitment and selection processes (Giberson et al., 2005).

Those who identify best with the organizational values have the ability to realize corporate culture and therefore put forth the additional organizational citizenship needed to gain quantifiable rewards. In a 'more or less successful in terms of advancing career' context, success is real because the 'more successful' individual strives for career success through identifying, understanding and taking an innovative approach to the existing ideologies established by the organization founder. This is not problematic as long as there is a true meshing of values. However, an individual who is successful in terms of advancing career and who is simply 'playing the part' may also be trapped between the corporate value system and his/her individual value system (career identity versus personal identity). Tarnowieski (1973) examines how people want a happy home life and good health (personal values) yet, when influenced by corporate values and culture, they deviate significantly and actually pursue upward mobility and materialism, a path said to deteriorate the capacity to achieve what they supposedly 'really want'.

In examining the pursuit of career rewards, Giberson et al. (2005) provides the framework for understanding why various negative responses exist among this group of individuals. While career success may be experienced by those who choose to identify with the organizational values and corporate culture, the questions remains: at what cost? A true conflict of values can be extremely costly to the individual and the organization.

Workaholism
Oates (1971) coined the term 'workaholic', referring to people whose need to work has become so exaggerated that it may constitute a danger to their health, personal happiness, interpersonal relations and social functioning. Over time, workaholism has become a popular term and has received great attention in terms of research as it continues to grow as a problem in organizations.

There are many reasons for the rise in workaholism, including the increasing complexity of professions, constant pressure to be more efficient, and the increased use of technology (Griffiths, 2005). There is a distinctive need to address workaholism as a unique and identifiable pattern, for, when this behaviour becomes prominent in an individual or within a team, it becomes extremely difficult for the individual to find reason to veer away from career based objectives and goals and even find reason to derive satisfaction from non-work goals, whether they be objective or subjective.

The organization should be concerned about the direct repercussions of having employees who are workaholics. Porter (1996) examined addictive patterns of excessive work and how this impairs functioning in the workplace and the negative outcome is both immediate and ongoing. She determined that workaholism affects interpersonal relationships and shapes the beliefs of individuals and their reactions to how they perceive everyday life. Eventually, this attitude permeates every aspect of the work setting, later extending itself into non-work related activities. Porter's research found that workaholics have an internal drive to maintain work involvement to the extent that they are willing to sacrifice other interests.

Porter (ibid.) determined that a workaholic might conveniently use non-demands as an excuse for excessive involvement. This type of addictive behavioural pattern is something that comes from within. The workaholic may feel that they are more necessary to the organization than is actually the case. Griffiths (2005) suggests that on a psychological level there appears to have been an increased desire to achieve, accomplish and succeed as a way of enhancing a person's self-esteem, all of which points to a perceived need to overwork and overextend.

According to the argument presented by Giberson et al. (2005), a work-aholic attitude is inherent within the managerial function of an organization. Realistically, workaholism should be seen as an assertion, and those who lack this obsessive behaviour may lack the ability to fully identify with the ideals of the chief executives, those creating the mission and vision of the organization. According to Griffiths (2005), workaholism is often viewed as a positive attribute by employers.

McAteer-Early (2005) focuses on the relationship between thinking styles and behaviours as originally proposed by Lafferty (1973, 1989). In a study of 114 upper-level managers, those measuring high on the perfectionist thinking style can be likened to the workaholic. Although perfectionism may be seen by some as a contributing factor in attaining excellent results, perfectionists typically work unceasingly on tasks and set unrealistically high performance standards. These individuals tend to remain dissatisfied with even their best work and that of others. In terms of managing, perfectionist thinkers need to oversee all aspects of a project and tend to get so absorbed in details that they often lose sight of the bigger picture. Perfectionist thinkers behave in ways that are costly to themselves and to others around them.

Thus, the general theme of the workaholism and stress literature is that workaholics reportedly focus on work at the expense of their personal relationships, which parallels the phenomenon of career success and personal failure. The most obvious sign that someone is a workaholic is when work and work-related concerns preoccupy their life to the neglect of everything else in it. What starts as love of work can often end up with the person developing perfectionist, then obsessional, traits. McMillan et al. (2004) determined that workaholism is bound to have increasingly harmful side effects for personal health and relationships. This research tested the proposition that workaholics deny their workaholism and experience greater disturbances in close relationships outside the work environment than do non-workaholics.

McMillan et al. (2004) characterize workaholism in terms of addiction, which is distinguished by the denial of relationship distress. Overall, findings determined that the workaholics appeared to possess a reasonably accurate perception of their levels of workaholic behaviour. As individuals, they overestimated the time spent communicating with their partners, which is a further demonstration of how this type of behaviour and set of attitudes has the potential to permit personal failure while maintaining career success.

Psychological, physiological and behavioural stress symptoms

Research has established strong links from unemployment and precarious employment to poor health outcomes, as well as from poor employment conditions to problematic physical and mental health. While poor employment conditions are often associated with exposure to harmful substances and the related physical health risks, such conditions can also mean jobs that are stressful by virtue of the pace or demands, jobs that are stressful because of an unequal balance of power; jobs that are stressful because they do not meet human development needs, and jobs that are stressful because they conflict with an individual's ability to experience work/non-work life balance.

Wilkens and Beaudet (1998) studied high job strain – an accumulation of high psychological demands at work combined with a low degree of control of the work process, as well as other sources of workplace stress. All were linked to an increased risk of physical injuries at work, high blood pressure, cardiovascular disease, depression and other mental health conditions, and increased lifestyle risks to health.

Jackson (2005) states that the quality of employment involves much more than pay. Work is better seen as a potential sphere for the development of individual human capacities and potentials. Therefore, in terms of the career success and personal failure relationship, those experiencing this phenomenon are prone to any combination of psychological, physiological and behavioural symptoms of stress.

McAteer-Early (2005), in focusing on the relationship between thinking styles and behaviours, found positive correlations between high defensive thinking (oppositional, power, competitive, perfectionist) and salary as well as organizational level within the hierarchy. However, this same group produced negative correlations between high defensive thinking and quality of interpersonal relations, psychological/physiological health and problem-solving effectiveness. During interviews, sample participants admitted full awareness of the costs involved in terms of relationships and health as they experienced career success.

RESOLVING THE CAREER SUCCESS AND PERSONAL FAILURE EXPERIENCE

Korman and Korman (1980) concluded that one has the ability to achieve a suitable work/non-work life balance by maintaining one's current position within established objectives while simultaneously dedicating energy towards non-work related areas. Perhaps in the past this statement was true. Today, maintaining a work/non-work life balance, while attempting to achieve and sustain the goals and values of the organization, is a concept that consistently challenges those in the professional/managerial category of the workforce. The intrusion of wireless internet, GPS cellular phone and mobile email makes creating the distinction between work and non-work time more difficult. The influence of technology has unconsciously merged the corporate responsibilities of the individual into the personal lives of these professionals.

Motivation to resolve the career success and personal failure phenomenon exists for both the organization and the individual. Measures for the alleviation of the driving force of challenge are available and can be classified into three categories: stress and time management strategies; embracing change techniques; and organizational flexibility measures.

Stress and Time Management Strategies

Inability to effectively manage stress and time ultimately lowers quality of life for the individual employee and can impact on the bottom line for corporations. While improved stress and time management skills will aid the individual employee to resolve the conflict of values, workaholism and stress symptoms previously discussed, according to Cullen and Turnbull (2005) organizations can also gain a competitive advantage by improving management capability in these areas. Their research examines the contemporary workplace and how organizations are choosing to focus on management development through learning better coping and adaptation techniques.

McAteer-Early (2005) suggests that the use of such techniques will allow individuals to be driven by personal values rather than the sense of urgency and materialistic trappings suggested by the corporation. A healthier career success can be achieved while still enjoying a work/non-work life balance and thus without compromising personal identity and integrity.

Embracing Change Techniques

Inability to embrace change and chaos will undoubtedly contribute to the career success and personal failure phenomenon. At the base of this inability is fear. Jeffers (1987) speaks of fear as keeping individuals from experiencing life the way they want to experience it. Grall (2004) examines personal and professional renewal by focusing on the principle that 'nothing changes until someone changes'. According to Grall, the cost of not making the change is often the largest cost of all. Deciding not to make a change can decrease life expectancy and affect self-esteem and sense of accomplishment.

In the contemporary workplace, learning to embrace change rather than simply meeting or managing it will allow individuals to achieve their desired work/non-work life balance while at the same time improving management skills necessary to work within their organization as it embraces change. Thus, there are advantages for both the individual and the organization in focusing on this type of managerial learning.

Permanently altering behaviour requires a shift in thinking (McAteer-Early, 2005). Albert Einstein said that an individual could not solve a problem with the same mindset that created it. To change what one feels and does requires that the individual must first understand what is in the mind – specifically, what is the driving belief/value system. Again, all too often it is competing agendas that affect whose value system takes precedence. Learning to conquer the fear of embracing change and related chaos will ultimately allow the individual to resolve the career success and personal failure problem and to reach a more healthy balance between work and non-work life.

An individual's honest examination of self is a necessary first step towards gaining a better perspective on his/her career achievement mentality and its limitations. This in turn may prepare the individual for the required commitment of time, energy and will to identify a new configuration of needs, goals, values which are relevant to the kind of person he is now, and which can guide him into a more satisfactory life space (Burke, 1984).

Organizational Flexibility Measures

The final recommendation is to implement an element of organizational flexibility in terms of human resource (HR) processes, systems as well as organizational structure. Bhattacharya et al. (2005) found measures of HR flexibility to be positively associated with return on sales, operating profit per employee and sales per employee. They also noted that skill flexibility plays a large role in reducing costs, because greater skill variety and its application lower the requirement for actual buffers against uncertainty. Increased HR skill flexibility implies a speedier response to changing environmental conditions – having employee skills as part of an HR inventory suggests that the firm will be able to respond more rapidly than if the firm had to enter the open market and acquire skills. Hall and Chandler (2005) suggest that the organization should allow increased specialization in direct managerial fields as well as implement a more flexible and adaptable structure to alleviate the stress of not achieving career objectives – of being an organizational member who is less successful in advancing his/her career.

Keene and Reynolds (2005) view the ability of individuals to make necessary adjustments at work because of family demands as another adaptive strategy that married workers use to manage competing obligations. Overall, research shows that flexibility in occupational and job characteristics is important to men and women's job experiences and their perceived work–family life balance. Working in demanding jobs with little autonomy and scheduling inflexibility is associated with negative family-to-work spillover effects. Such results encourage researchers and practitioners to focus on a broader range of subjective criteria when striving to assess what career success and personal failure means to individuals and populations under consideration (Heslin, 2005).

CONCLUSION

The career success and personal failure phenomenon continues to exist for the mid-life professional/managerial category of employees. Despite the corporate value system at the strategic level, corporate executives must recognize that one is not a true success if they are also a personal failure. The self-actualization of this affect can be detrimental to the organization and to the individual at a variety of levels. Costs to the individual suffering this affliction as well as the costs to organizations encouraging such, are substantial. By implementing practical measures to resolve the career success and personal failure dilemma, individuals and their organizations will also experience a resolution in terms of true value recognition, lower workaholism rates and decreased symptoms of distress. Ultimately a balance will be struck between individuals' work and non-work lives.

NOTE

1. Preparation of this chapter was supported by the Schulich School of Business, York University, and the Michael G. DeGroote School of Business, McMaster University.

REFERENCES

Arthur, M.B., Khapova, S.N. and Wilderom, C.P.M. (2005), 'Career success in a boundaryless world', *Journal of Organizational Behavior*, **26**, 177–202.

Bhattacharya, M., Gibson, D. and Doty, H. (2005), 'The effects of flexibility in employee skills, employee behaviors, and human resource practices on firm performance', *Journal of Management*, **31** (4), 622–40.

Burke, R.J. (1984), 'Career success and personal failure: nature of the problem and some possible solutions', in R.J. Burke (ed.), *Current Issues in Occupational Stress: Research and Intervention*, Toronto: Faculty of Administrative Studies, York University.

Callanan, G.A. (2003), 'What price career success?', *Career Development International*, **8** (3), 126–33.

Chartrand, J.M. and Rose, M.L. (1996), 'Career interventions for at-risk populations: incorporating social cognitive influences', *Career Development Quarterly*, **44**, 341–54.

Cullen, J. and Turnbull, S. (2005), 'A meta review of the management development literature', *Human Resources Development Review*, **4** (3), 335–55.

Giberson, T.R., Resick, C.J. and Dickson, M.W. (2005), 'Embedding leadership characteristics: an examination of homogeneity of personality and values in organizations', *Journal of Applied Psychology*, **90** (5), 1002–10.

Grall, P. (2004), *Just Change It!*, Toronto, Canada: Art Bookbindery.

Green, P. and Skinner, D. (2005), 'Does time management training work? An evaluation', *International Journal of Training and Development*, **9** (2), 124–39.

Griffiths, M. (2005), 'Workaholisim is still a useful construct', *Addiction and Research Theory*, **13** (2), 97–100.

Hall, D.T. (1976), *Careers in Organizations*, Pacific Palisades, CA: Goodyear.

Hall, D.T. (2002), *Careers in and out of Organizations*, San Francisco: Jossey-Bass.

Hall, D.T. and Chandler, D.E. (2005), 'Psychological success: when the career is calling', *Journal of Organizational Behavior*, **26**, 155–76.

Heslin, P. (2003), 'Self and other referent criteria of career success', *Journal of Career Assessment*, **11** (3), 262–86.

Heslin, P.A. (2005), 'Conceptualizing and evaluating career success', *Journal of Organizational Behavior*, **26**, 113–36.

Holland, J.L. (1997), 'Making vocational choices: a theory of vocational personalities and work environments', Odessa, FL: *Psychological Assessment Resources*.

Hughes, E.C. (1958), *Men and their Work*, Glencoe: Free Press.

Jackall, R. (1983), 'Moral mazes: bureaucracy and managerial work', *Harvard Business Review*, September–October, 118–30.

Jackson, A. (2005), *Work and Labour in Canada*, Toronto: Canadian Scholars' Press.

Jeffers, S. (1987), *Feel the Fear and Do it Anyway*, New York: Random House.

Keene, J.R. and Reynolds, J.R. (2005), 'The costs of family demands: gender differences in negative family to work spillover', *Journal of Family Issues*, **26** (3), 275–99.

Kerr, J. and Slocum, J. (1987), 'Managing corporate cultures through reward systems', *Academy of Management Executive*, **1**, 99–108.

Korman, A. and Korman, R. (1980), *Career Success and Personal Failure*, New York: Prentice Hall.

Krumboltz, J.D. (1994), 'Innovative career development theory from a social learning perspective', in M.L. Savikas and R.W. Lent (eds), *Congruence in Career Development Theories: Implications for Science and Practice*, Palo Alto, CA: CPP Books, pp. 9–31.

Lafferty, J.C. (1973, 1989), *Life Styles Inventory (LSI)*, St. Mary's, Ontario: Human Synergistics.

Lowe, G. (2000), *The Quality of Work: a People Centred Agenda*, Oxford: Oxford University Press.

McAteer-Early, T. (2005), 'The relationship between emotional intelligence and the Human Synergistics' Circumplex model for corporate Directors/CEOS', submission to the Canadian Psychological Association, 2006 Conference, Banff, Alberta, Canada.

McMillan, L.H.W., O'Driscoll, M.P. and Brady, E.C. (2004), 'The impact of workaholisim on personal relationships', *British Journal of Guidance & Counselling*, **32** (2), 171–86.

Montgomery, A., Panagopoulou, E.P., Peeters, M.C.W. and Schaufeli, W.B. (2005), 'The meaning of work and home', *Community, Work and Family*, **8** (2), 141–61.

Oates, W. (1971), *Confessions of a Workaholic: the Facts about Work Addiction*, New York: World Publishing.

Parsons, F. (1909), *Choosing a Vocation*, Boston, MA: Houghton Mifflin.

Porter, G. (1996), 'Organizational impacts of workaholisim: suggestions for researching the negative outcomes of excessive work', *Journal of Occupational Health Psychology*, **1** (1), 70–84.

Robbins, A. (2003), *Giant Steps*, New York: Simon & Schuster.

Schneider, B. (1987), 'The people make the place', *Personnel Psychology*, **40**, 437–53.

Seibert, S.E., Crant, J.M. and Kraimer, M.L. (1999), 'Proactive personality and career success', *Journal of Applied Psychology*, **84** (30), 416–27.

Tarnowieski, D. (1973), *The Changing Success Ethic*, New York: American Management Association.

Wilkins, K. and Beaudet, M.P. (1998), 'Work stress and health', *Health Reports*, **10** (3), 47–62.

Ziglar, Z. (1997), *Over the Top*, Atlanta, CA: Thomas Nelson.

13. Exploring career and personal outcomes and the meaning of career success among part-time professionals in organizations

Mary Dean Lee, Pamela Lirio, Fahri Karakas, Shelley M. MacDermid, Michelle L. Buck and Ellen Ernst Kossek

Over recent decades, the professional workforce and family structures have dramatically changed. For example, the dual-earner family is now the modal American family (Barnett, 2001). Only 17 per cent of families comprise a male breadwinner and a stay-at-home wife (US Department of Labor, 2004). According to the most recent National Survey of the Changing Workforce (NSCW) (Bond et al., 2002), the demographic occupational profile of the professional and managerial workforce in the US has also dramatically changed. In 2002 women held 39 per cent of professional and managerial jobs, compared with 24 per cent in 1977.

Work hours and demands are rising on the job and there is less time to devote to family or other personal life commitments. Over the 25 years between 1977 and 2002, the total work hours of all dual-earner couples with children under 18 years at home increased by an average of ten hours per week – from 81 to 91 hours (Bond et al., 2002). A recent national survey on overwork in America indicates that nearly half (44 per cent) of the US workforce experienced being overworked in their jobs in the past month (Galinsky et al., 2005). Another recent report based on the NSCW survey found that two-thirds (67 per cent) of employed parents believe they do not have enough time with their children (Galinsky et al., 2004). Over half of all employees participating in the NSCW survey said they do not have enough time for their spouses (63 per cent) or themselves (55 per cent).

Although these trends are important for all employee groups, professionals are a key labor market group that faces unique challenges in managing work and personal life demands. Many professionals encounter growing organizational pressures to increase workload and work hours

(Gerson and Jacobs, 2004). For most professionals, full-time work does not mean 40 hours a week. More typically, a full-time professional is expected to work 50, 60, or even 70 hours per week. For individuals who seek to advance in their careers, the hours they work can be seen as a symbol of career commitment. Some may fear that placing limits on work hours or workloads is likely to be negatively construed by customers, bosses or co-workers. Many professionals are also in dual-career households, where it is hard to be a parent or an elder caregiver or 'have a life' when work involves such long hours. Yet growing numbers of professionals are taking actions to create or adapt jobs in order to achieve the kind of work and family lives they want over their careers. They are negotiating to work less, to reduce their workloads with a proportionate reduction in pay.

In recent years there has been considerable attention given to examining this fairly new phenomenon among professionals, and it has been called reduced-load, part-time, 'new concept part-time' and customized work by different authors (Barnett and Gareis, 2000; Corwin et al., 2001; Epstein et al., 1998; Lee et al., 2000, 2002; Hill et al., 2004; MacDermid et al., 2001; Meiksins and Whalley, 2002). A body of research is developing that begins to explain why these new work forms are emerging, how they are working out and under what circumstances they result in positive outcomes for the individuals, work units and organizations concerned. However, little research has explicitly focused on how choosing to work less actually affects individuals, their careers and their lives over time. And there has been no attention paid to changing conceptions of career success which we would expect to accompany new ways of working among professionals wanting to work less for periods of time in their careers. The purpose of this chapter is to contribute to filling this gap by examining the personal, career and family outcomes of part-time professionals and by exploring their concep-tions of career success in the context of working on a part-time basis to accommodate personal or family commitments.

Of course there is a well-established stream of research on the inter-relationships between work and non-work life in general. However, empir-ical studies have tended to focus on one of the following issues: (1) determining the direction and type of influence of one domain on the other, for example, compensation, spillover, independence (Lee and Kanungo, 1984); (2) examination of predictors and outcomes of work–family conflict (for example, Greenhaus and Beutell, 1985); (3) identifying implications of participation in multiple roles based on a scarcity or expansionist perspec-tive (Marks, 1977; Rothbard, 2001). Although the theoretical literature has also suggested viable constructs for investigation such as work–life inte-gration (Kossek et al., 1999), work–family balance or facilitation (Frone, 2003), and a balanced life (Gallos, 1989), to date there has been little testing of the validity of such formulations (Aryee et al., 2005). Furthermore, there has been little exploratory qualitative research to surface individuals' actual conceptions of career success (Greenhaus, 2003; Heslin, 2005).

Yet one of the weaknesses of career theory in general, according to Sturges (1999), is the lack of an adequate and holistic conceptualization of career success from the perspective of the individual. A deeper understanding and a more complete picture of career success can be provided by a qualitative exploration of what individuals themselves define as salient or prevalent in their own conceptions of career success. The literature suggests that personal conceptions of career success for some individuals may be simultaneously associated with both internal and external criteria (Poole et al., 1993).

There has long been a distinction in the career success literature between objective and subjective career success, dating back to the initial theoretical distinction provided by Hughes (1937, 1958). On the basis of Hughes' framework, objective career success has been defined by observable and measurable criteria, such as pay, promotion and status. Subjective career success, on the other hand, has been defined by an individual's reactions to unfolding career experiences.

In the literature, traditional conceptions of career success were premised on the notion of linear hierarchical career progression in a competitive environment. In more than two-thirds of career studies published in major journals between 1980 and 1994, career success was measured by objective measures such as salary, rank and promotion (Arthur and Rousseau, 1996). On the other hand, a number of studies (Kofodimos, 1993; Powell, 1999; Sturges, 1999) have found that defining career success in terms of purely external and objective terms such as pay and position is not congruent with what many managers and professionals (especially women) feel about their own career success. Therefore, it is clear that there is a need for more holistic and multidimensional conceptions and definitions of career success, where the interplay between work, family, life, significant others and various life stages is acknowledged.

OVERVIEW OF RESEARCH STUDIES

The research findings reported here are based on two qualitative studies focused on the experiences of professionals and managers in reduced-load work arrangements conducted in 1996–98 and 2002–03. In Study 1 83 cases of reduced-load work were examined in a variety of kinds of jobs in 43 companies in the US and Canada. As four of these cases involved job sharing, there were actually 87 participants interviewed about their work arrangements and their careers, family and personal lives. Approximately six years later, in Study 2, we were able to do a follow-up interview with 81 of the original 87 participants in order to find out how their careers and lives had evolved over time. In the original study participants were recruited using personal contacts with human resources and work–life managers, cold calls to employers and direct mail solicitations to members of professional organizations (such as the Association of Part-Time Professionals). As this was an exploratory study of a new phenomenon, we were seeking a heterogeneous sample to support theory generation as opposed to hypothesis testing. We did not pursue more than three cases in any one company, and we tried to include cases that represented individuals pursuing working less for a variety of different reasons and in many different industries. We also sought and achieved having men comprise at least 10 per cent of the sample, given estimates of their representing 10–20 per cent of all professionals/managers in organizations working voluntarily on a reduced-load basis (Catalyst, 1997). The aim was to include individuals in a wide range of types of jobs and family situations, as well as those with a variety of experiences negotiating and maintaining part-time arrangements. In Study 2, conducted in 2002–03, we contacted the original participants through our records of their personal coordinates collected for purposes of providing an Executive Feedback Report on findings after Study 1. Eighty-one agreed to be interviewed approximately six years after the original interview.

In Study 1 working on a reduced-load basis was defined as working less than full-time and being paid proportionately. The lowest percentage of full-time being worked in the sample was 50 per cent and the highest was 90 per cent. The most typical percentage was either 60 per cent or 80 per cent, the equivalent of three or four days a week. The sample consisted of 87 professionals and managers in a variety of different kinds of companies (for example, financial, manufacturing, natural resources and telecommunications) in 43 different corporations in the US and Canada. Forty-five per cent (45 per cent) worked in individual contributor roles and are referred to here as 'professionals'; and 55 per cent were managers with at least three direct reports. Professionals were most likely to work in the areas of Finance, Human Resources and Corporate Communications, or Research and Development. However, 25 per cent were in Information Systems, Production/Operations, and Marketing. Although some of them had the title of 'Manager' and might supervise a secretary or administrative assistant, they did not have responsibility for a group of direct reports. Some examples of job titles were:

Project Director   Product Development Chemist
Director of Contracts   Organizational Effectiveness Manager

Principal Research Scientist   Vice President, Information Systems
Software Engineer   Manager, International Business Development
Vice President, Finance

There were three types of managerial jobs in the sample. Almost half (48 per cent) were managing professionals in a support function. Their direct reports were competent, seasoned professionals needing little direct supervision or coaching (for example, Director of Finance, or Vice President, Human Resources). Thirty-nine per cent of the managers were considered 'line' managers in that they were in functional areas linked directly to production and operations, or delivery of product/services to customers (for example, Manager, Export Operations; Sales Manager; Branch Manager). These managers described their jobs primarily as managing their direct reports, who were the ones actually doing the work. More than half and sometimes virtually all of their time was spent selecting, training, coaching, mentoring, monitoring and assessing those they were responsible for, as well as organizing and coordinating the work itself. They were also held accountable for financial or other deliverables on a monthly or quarterly basis, and they regularly operated under critical time deadlines. The final kind of management position involved project managers (13 per cent), who operated typically as matrix managers rather than traditional hierarchical managers (for example, Software Development). The members of their project teams were all professionals and needed minimal guidance and direction. Their work involved a great deal of lateral interface across different areas, seeking consultation and gaining cooperation on the basis of their expertise and interpersonal skills rather than their rank.

In Study 2, of the 81 participants interviewed, 47 per cent were still working on a reduced-load basis, although 13.5 per cent were self-employed; 38 per cent were working full-time; and 15 per cent were staying at home temporarily or retired. Of those employed in organizations, 65 per cent were with the same employers as in Study 1, and 55 per cent of them were in managerial roles with supervisory responsibilities. In Study 1 10 per cent of the sample were male, and in Study 2 11 per cent were male, because one of the six participants not willing to be interviewed the second time was male. Table 13.1 provides demographic information about the samples at the two different points in time.

In Study 1 confidential, semi-structured interviews, which were audiotaped and then transcribed verbatim, focused on learning about how reduced-load arrangements were negotiated and sustained and on what terms, as well as how they were working out from a personal, family and organizational perspective. For each case of reduced-load work, interviews were conducted not only with the target individual working less but

Table 13.1   Demographic information on sample of part-time professionals and managers, Times 1 and 2

	Time 1 mean	Time 2 mean
Age	39	45
Per cent female	89	89
Full-time equivalent salary	$80 454	$111 127
Spouse/partner salary	$86 982	$114 696
No. yrs. on reduced load	4.3	8.0
Per cent load reduction	72	66 (RL only)[a]
Hrs./wk. current		
Full-time		47.4
Part-time	31.8	29.9
Age of youngest child	4.9	8.4

Note: [a] Number of hours worked per week, on average, by those still working on a reduced load (RL) basis (not including the whole sample).

also with four other stakeholders (boss, co-worker, HR representative and spouse/partner), which enabled the interviewers to get a sense of the success of the arrangements from multiple perspectives. After reviewing all interviews completed in a case, the interviewers gave each case a 'global success' rating on a scale of 1 to 9, with 7–9 indicating a high level of success, 5–6 a moderate level of success and 1–4 a low level of success.

In Study 2 only target individuals who had worked on a reduced-load basis in the earlier study were interviewed. The focus was on what had happened in the intervening period of time and what changes and/or life events had occurred, as well as the current status of their careers and personal and family lives. In addition, each participant was asked to complete a Timeline on three dimensions (career, family and personal) from the time of the first interview to the time of the second, indicating 'how well things were working' with 7 indicating 'Things working very well' and 1 indicating 'Things not working well'. These charts yielded self-assessments of outcomes on each of the three dimensions at the time of Study 1 and Study 2: Career Self-assessment, Time 1 and Time 2; Family Self-assessment, Time 1 and Time 2; and Personal Life assessment, Time 1 and Time 2. Finally, in Study 2 each interviewer gave an overall Congruence rating of the individual he or she interviewed after an in-depth analysis of the interview data. This Congruence rating is meant to capture to what extent the participant was living the life he or she desired. So, on a scale of 1 to 7, those rated highest (7) were judged by the interviewers as having the greatest consistency between their dreams or ideals and their actual lives;

that is, how they orchestrated and calibrated their involvement in work, family and other domains.

CAREER AND PERSONAL LIFE OUTCOMES

Given that working less than full-time is a deviant pattern for professionals and managers in North America, we were curious about just how successful our sample would be in their careers and how satisfied they would be with the time gained and what they did with it. First we examine what we learned from our data in Study 1 about the career and personal life outcomes of these individuals, by using conventional measures of success and listening to bosses' assessments of 'potential'. Secondly, we look at participants' views of the outcomes, in terms of their own personal lives as well as their relationships with children and/or other family members. Finally, we look at interviewers' assessments of the 'global success' of the reduced-load arrangements, which are based on the views of all stakeholders interviewed in each case. At Time 2 we consider how participants' careers fared according to traditional objective criteria like salary and number of promotions received, as well as participants' self-assessments of how well things were going in their careers at Time 2, and in comparison with Time 1. We also examine their self-assessments of how things were going in their family and personal lives at Time 1 and Time 2. Finally we look at the Time 2 interviewers' assessments of the Congruence of participants' actual lives with their desired lives, in terms of their level of involvement in career, family and other life domains.

Time 1 Outcomes

Using conventional measures of career success, we were surprised to find in our interviews from 1996 to 1998 that 35 per cent of the sample had already been promoted while working on a reduced-load basis, even though the mean number of years working reduced load was 4.3. In addition, another third of the sample were expected by their bosses to be promoted within the next year. Reduced-load work arrangements were not necessarily a barrier to career advancement. Furthermore, an anonymous survey of the direct reports of the managerial participants (55 per cent of the sample) indicated that they rated their reduced-load managers' effectiveness on average at 7.2 on a scale from 1 to 9.

From a personal perspective participants reported gaining an average of 18 hours per week to spend on their family or other priorities as a result of working on a reduced-load basis. Ninety per cent reported positive effects of working less on their children – better relationships and more time to be together. Ninety-one per cent said they were happier and more satisfied with the balance between home and work.

As for the interviewers' global rating of the success of the reduced-load arrangements, our criteria were multifaceted and stringent, given that we had data from five different stakeholders per case, as mentioned above. First and foremost we looked at how happy the participants were with working less from a personal point of view – how they felt about their careers and the price they were paying for the time gained and whether they felt they were getting the extra time they wanted for their personal and family lives. Second, we looked at the outcomes from an organizational perspective. Were there costs in performance or productivity in the work unit? Did others in the group have to 'pick up the slack', creating an unfair overload situation? Third, we looked at how the family was faring to see whether there were positive outcomes for the overall quality of family life, for children, or for the couple relationship. Then we looked for consistency across stakeholder interviews in reporting positive consequences of the reduced-load arrangements. Interviewers rated each case, taking into consideration all accumulated data from different sources. On a scale of 1 to 9, 1 indicated consistently negative outcomes reported across stakeholders, and 9 indicated consistently positive outcomes. Each success rating was checked for validity by another member of the research team. After the ratings were completed, three groups were created: high, moderate and low. Most of the cases (62 per cent) were in the high success group, 31 per cent in the moderate success group, and 7 per cent in the low success group.

Time 2 Outcomes

At Time 2 the 81 participants were no longer all in reduced-load positions. Forty-seven per cent were still working less than full-time, whereas 38 per cent had returned to full-time work. Fifteen per cent were staying home, mostly to spend time with their children, but two had retired and one was temporarily unemployed. Participants experienced many changes and challenges during the period between the two interviews; some were work-related and some had to do with family and personal life. Certain changes came about as a result of events totally out of their control, such as a company being acquired or going through downsizing, or an illness in the family. Others were self-initiated, or came about because of a spouse's decision, for example, to change jobs. Major life events experienced by at least a third of the sample included birth or adoption of a child, serious illness or death of a close friend or relative, organizational downsizing, and either a child with a serious illness or learning problem or personal serious illness. In examining how successful participants were in all aspects of their lives, we looked at their own subjective point

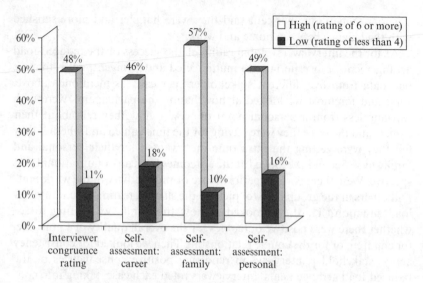

Figure 13.1   Percentages of sample with high and low ratings on subjective measures

of view, according to their personal goals, as well as at conventional objective measures of career success, such as upward mobility and salary increases.

Overall we found that, despite experiencing many changes and challenges over six years, most of the participants were doing quite well, as assessed by both subjective and objective measures of outcomes. Employed participants as a whole had an average rate of increase in full-time equivalent salary of 38 per cent over six years, and the mean salaries of the full-time versus part-time participants were virtually the same (US$111 725 and 111 927 respectively) after adjusting the latter for the degree of reduced load. Over six years the group overall had received 65 promotions or clear increases in responsibility or status through a career move outside their former organization, with 44 individuals receiving at least one and 17 receiving two or more. These gains were made in spite of the fact that the average number of years the participants had spent working on a reduced-load basis was eight.

Subjective measures of success provided by the interviewer and self-assessment ratings were also quite positive, as shown in Figure 13.1. The interviewers rated participants on the basis of how congruent their current lives were with their desired lives, on a scale of 1 to 7, with 7 indicating the greatest congruence or consistency. Overall, the average rating was 5.3, with a minimum of 2 and a maximum of 7. Half of the sample received a rating greater than 6, and only 11 per cent received a rating less than 4. The self-assessment ratings were calculated on the basis of a timeline exercise on three

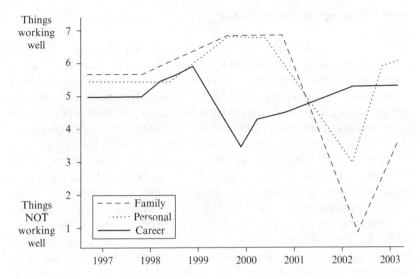

Figure 13.2   Example of timeline

dimensions (career, family, personal) covering the time from the first interview to the second.

Participants were asked to draw a line to indicate how their career, personal and family lives were working out, as shown in Figure 13.2. The horizontal axis was time, and the vertical axis was how well things were working. The point where each line (career, family or personal) ended at the time of the second interview was interpreted as the individual's assessment of how things were going on a scale of 1 to 7. Close to 50 per cent of the sample indicated things were going very well (>6) in each of the three domains, and less than 20 per cent of the sample indicated things were not going well (< 4) in each of the domains.

CONCEPTIONS OF CAREER SUCCESS

In order to study participants' conceptions of career success, we asked specific questions about what career success meant to them and what they saw ahead in their future, at both Time 1 and Time 2. We then used a content analysis approach to the transcribed interview material and through an iterative process identified recurrent themes that captured the predominant meanings associated with career success in the sample. As most participants mentioned several ideas or definitions of career success, all were recorded and included in the analysis.

Time 1 Meanings of Career Success

Table 13.2 shows the eight recurrent themes in respondent conceptions of career success. The most frequently occurring themes, with over half of respondents mentioning them, were: (1) being able to have a life outside work (74 per cent); (2) performing well (63 per cent); and (3) doing challenging work and continuing to grow professionally (62 per cent). The eight conceptions of career success fell into three categories: (a) those related to organizational perceptions, judgments and actions; (b) those involving individual respondents' perceptions and personal experiences, more or less independent of the objective work context; and (c) those involving individuals' perceptions of outcomes rooted in objective organizational reality. Those related to organizational perceptions and judgments included peer respect, upward mobility and recognition/appreciation and were labeled 'organization-based'. Although these themes appeared to be 'objective', 'external' criteria of success, only upward mobility was clearly observable. Themes which represented more subjective criteria of success, in that they were based on the individual's reactions, were labeled 'personal' themes and included: able to have a life outside work, being challenged at work and continuing to learn and grow professionally, and enjoying work. The final category of emergent themes, labeled 'personal and organizational inter-linked', included performing well and having an impact. These themes represented conceptualizations of career

Table 13.2   Meaning of career success, Times 1 and 2 (percentages)

Career success theme	Interview 1	Interview 2		
	Total sample	Total sample	Reduced-load	Full-time	Staying at home
Organization-based themes					
Peer respect	47	28	24	29	42
Upward mobility	37	14	b13	16	8
Appreciation/recognition	14	28	32	29	17
Personal themes					
Having a life outside work	74	75	66	84	75
Learning, growing and being challenged	62	53	61	58	17
Fun and enjoyment/doing interesting work	12	31	24	48	8
Personal and organizational inter-linked					
Performing well	63	32	37	26	33
Having an impact/making a contribution	44	62	58	68	58

success that suggest individuals evaluate their effectiveness at work using feed-back generated through actually doing their jobs, as well as through informal feedback from clients, co-workers and other stakeholders.

Organization-based themes

Respondents talked about career success having to do with three distinct organization-dependent outcomes: peer respect, upward mobility and recognition/appreciation. Although less than half the sample mentioned each of these conceptions of career success, 76 per cent of respondents mentioned at least one of them. So clearly some kind of external confirmation of value added is important to these part-time professionals.

Peer respect   The most frequently mentioned theme was peer respect, or being perceived as adding value to the organization. Forty-one of the 87 individuals (47 per cent) talked about the importance of how others view them or having a good reputation, being seen as responsible, dedicated and successful. This theme was more frequently mentioned by professionals (54 per cent) than managers (40 per cent). Perhaps those who are in managerial positions receive affirmation of their value by virtue of their positions of authority, so that they are less concerned about how others view them.

> I don't ever want my reputation to be tarnished. I want my colleagues to think of me as someone who is responsible and has a lot of integrity about my job and getting things done.

> I give importance to the issue of how I am perceived at work . . . I value high quality relationships and networking at work. Sometimes I care too much about what people think of me; and this causes peer pressure.

Upward mobility   The second most frequently occurring meaning of career success that was organization-based was upward mobility or career advancement through promotions and increased salary and other financial enhancements. Thirty-three of the 87 participants (34 per cent) mentioned these more traditional and objective aspects of career success, which are clearly observable and measurable. More managers (46 per cent) than professionals (28 per cent) indicated this was an important aspect of career success for them. They valued tangible monetary rewards and visible increases in status.

> Visible criteria for success are still important for me. I sometimes feel angry why I cannot move upward to executive positions working part-time . . . I made concessions on my career working reduced-load. It is difficult for career, real career advancement.

> . . . promotion will be the ultimate test of my career performance.

Appreciation/recognition The other organization-based meaning of career success that emerged was recognition or appreciation, not necessarily linked to promotions and financial incentives. About 14 per cent of managers and professionals brought up this aspect of career success. The focus here was on getting approval and support from the organization or from specific leaders in the organization.

> I mean, career success is doing the best job that I feel I can do and then having it appreciated and valued by the organization.

> Selling issues and convincing top management is always a prevalent issue, in my view of success. Because you like to have a sense of being important, you want your results to be recognized and appreciated.

Personal themes
Although 76 per cent of participants made clear that their conceptions of career success included having the organization or its members as a key point of reference, recurrent themes in definitions or conceptions of career success that were most popular and found in virtually all respondent comments (99 per cent) were those related to individuals' reactions to their work experiences. The personal themes most frequently found included: being able to have a life outside work, opportunities for professional growth and development, and doing interesting, enjoyable work.

Having a life outside work By far the most frequently mentioned criterion of career success was being able to have a life outside work. For 74 per cent of the sample the concept of career success overlapped with their overall life goals and dreams. They insisted that feeling successful in their careers meant being able to devote time and energy to the other important things in their lives, whether family or other personal pursuits. These individuals valued having enough personal space, flexibility and freedom in their careers. Balance and well-being were the prevalent and crucial issues for these people.

> To me success has changed over the course of my career. But I would say at this point in my life, it is achieving a certain amount of flexibility . . . I have a great life. I have taken up horseback riding lessons. I have more friends. I have excellent relationships with my children and their teachers. The balance is because what you give up there you take on the other side. Because I focused my energy and rechanneled energy. But the success piece of it, I do not need the prestige and the power.

> I am actually religious about keeping part-time – 3 days. I almost do not care what I do, as long as it is part-time and I can make a contribution. The arrangement

is wildly successful. The balance issue is really important for me, and my life is in the direction I want . . . And this is what allows me to keep that balance. So that is definitely the positive piece. I still get the money and professional interaction, but I get four days with my kids, which is great.

Challenge/learning/growth   A second common personal aspect of career success was feeling challenged and intellectually stimulated in their work and feeling that they were continuing to grow and develop professionally, mentioned by 63 per cent of the managers and professionals. These individuals valued developing their skills, expanding their knowledge, and enlarging their visions. Many respondents indicated that they felt this was the most important criterion of career success for them, now that they had chosen to work less and were likely to receive fewer promotional opportunities. They often expressed the sentiment that they had come to terms with watching peers move beyond them on the company ladder. They felt good about their choice to be able to spend the time they wanted at home, and they felt they had not had to sacrifice continuing to be challenged and stimulated at work.

> As long as I am learning something new, I really do not care all that much what I am doing . . . I have a job that I like, I am learning something, I feel challenged – that is what I need out of a job.

> I just realized that it is just me, that I have to continue to take on new challenges. Status quo is not the way I operate. So as long as I am feeling that I am continuing to grow and learn things, you know, in my profession and am pleased with that.

> I can get the intellectual stimulation I need by working . . . And I want to continue to do some new, innovative, exciting things outside of my company and yet still have my involvement with my company.

Fun/enjoyment   The final self-referent meaning of career success found was having fun, enjoying work. Twelve per cent of the managers and professionals said that they felt successful in their careers only if they were truly enjoying their work, getting a kick out of what they did on a regular basis. These individuals gave importance to personal satisfaction, excitement and creativity.

> I'd like to do some work just for personal satisfaction . . . The person's satisfaction is what it is all about. There is a need to earn income, obviously, but what attracts me to this business and kept me in this business is working with a variety of clients and professional colleagues over the years . . . I certainly enjoyed every aspect of my career here. I think I was certainly given great freedom to manage the group. Our partners . . . gave me a wonderful opportunity and if I had to

describe what my job was I would say I was a general manager. I was involved in marketing, sales, direct client service, administration, personnel . . . And not all that many people get that opportunity, to do all those things. So I found it extremely rewarding and fun.

Personal and organizational inter-linked themes

The final two emergent themes in respondent characterizations of what career success meant to them involved a mix of self-perceptions and organizational feedback. Those mentioning these two themes clearly saw career success as not just being an objective phenomenon, indicated by specific measurable achievements, nor as just a subjective experience that can be determined by individuals' reactions to personal experiences. Rather, career success to them meant a combination of objective evidence and subjective perception, or the intersection of the two.

Performing well   Sixty-three per cent of respondents talked about the importance of doing a good job and fulfilling their commitments. To these individuals career success meant maintaining high quality work and having a strong sense of responsibility and discipline at work. They talked about being able to focus, concentrate, work intensely and prioritize to get things done. This theme involved individuals essentially evaluating their own effectiveness from an organizational perspective. It was a subjective judgment, but based on objective information and communication received as they went about their work.

> And then there is a personal element of it too, which is that I do it in a way that is really very honorable. That I keep my word, that I am a person of commitment, you know what I mean. That I fulfill my commitments.

> I define myself successful, because they don't have to worry about me. I'm a real independent operator. I'm a real good communicator. They don't have to wonder about me . . . I don't feel like I've created a problem. I think I know if I'm not cutting with somebody's expectations . . .I feel like I have satisfied customers.

Impact/contribution   The final theme emerging in respondents' conceptions of career success was having an impact and making a contribution. This theme was often found in formulations by those respondents who contrasted this kind of outcome with the outcome of upward mobility, climbing the corporate ladder. They often expressed the sentiment that they were very comfortable with not progressing in the traditional manner and gaining that kind of recognition, as long as they felt they were still able to make a contribution to or have some tangible influence on organizational outcomes. Forty-four per cent of respondents discussed this aspect of career success. One of the sub-themes noted here was the importance of helping or mentoring others, and even opening doors for others by being successful at pursuing reduced-load work arrangements. This conception of career success was also a mix of individual perceptions mediated by organizational realities. The respondents talked about 'feeling they were making a contribution' as being critical to their being successful in their careers. Clearly, it is possible for someone to 'feel' they are making a contribution when there is no objective evidence of impact. But the ways these professionals and managers talked about this theme made it evident that what they meant was *actually* having an influence and seeing the ways they added value.

> I define career success as making a contribution to my organization. Having the freedom to move and to make change and to make progress. Changing the way we do business, whatever, in my own way, making some sort of change.

> It has got to do with making a contribution to the organization that I am in and the company at large, really having an impact, feeling that something I'm doing isn't just pushing a pencil but that I contributed towards making them what they are.

> I, I love doing this, the work, I love contributing, I love seeing the effort, the results of my efforts.

Conceptions of Career Success – Time 2

At Time 2 we found the same eight emergent themes in participants' commentary about what career success meant to them, and there were similarities in the predominance of certain themes. At Time 1 and Time 2 three-quarters of the sample talked about career success meaning having a life outside work. Secondly, at both times over half of the participants said that career success to them meant learning, growing and being challenged. These are both personal themes, and they are clearly very important to this particular group of professionals and managers, as shown by the fact that they were among the most frequently mentioned aspects of career success at two different points in time.

Although the similarities in articulated conceptions of career success were striking, there were also some notable shifts in frequency of themes mentioned. Most notable was that the 'performing well' theme, which was about doing a good job and fulfilling commitments, was mentioned by only 32 per cent of the sample at Time 2, compared with 63 per cent at Time 1. At the same time, there was an increase in participants' mention of career success being about 'having an impact, making a contribution', from 44 per cent to 62 per cent. Both of these themes involve a mix of self-perceptions and organizational feedback. One possible explanation for these changes is that at Time 1 these professionals and managers, when interviewed about their reduced-load work arrangements, were still relatively new in their positions and understandably concerned about their ability to perform well and deliver results as well as any other professional or manager. Six years later, with more experience in their organizations and in many cases having received promotions and/or salary increases, presumably the 'performing well' dimension of career success was less salient. Perhaps the increase in participants mentioning wanting to have an impact represents their 'raising the bar' as a result of success and thus wanting not just to fulfill commitments and perform well but to actually make a contribution, to see results or evidence of their value added.

As for the organization-based themes, at Time 2 both 'upward mobility' and 'peer respect' were less important to the sample as a whole; yet 'appreciation/recognition' were mentioned by twice as many participants as in Time 1. Perhaps upward mobility and peer respect were less salient in Time 2 simply because they had actually been achieved or accomplished over the intervening years. It is interesting that more participants mentioned appreciation or recognition as an important aspect of career success. They were clearly looking for this from their managers or other senior management in the company. It was seen as an important source of affirmation, even if career advancement through promotions was not proceeding apace. As for personal themes, the only change was a dramatic increase in the percentage of the sample talking about career success being about having fun, enjoying one's work, doing interesting things, from 12 to 31 per cent.

DISCUSSION

The findings reviewed above have theoretical implications, as they provide unexpected insights as well as challenges to state of the art knowledge in the field. The strongly held views of career success articulated by this sample also suggest the need for further research to examine contemporary views of career success from the perspective of other sub-groups of the new diverse workforce. If some of the themes and findings found here are replicated with other samples, there could also be practical implications in that organizations might benefit from adapting existing reward systems and advancement structures to be more appealing to the changing workforce of the twenty-first century.

Theoretical Implications

From a theoretical perspective one of the most provocative findings is that the emergent themes did not conform to current distinctions made in the literature between 'objective' and 'subjective' career success. Instead of there being clear objective and subjective aspects of career success, only four of the eight themes generated clearly fell into either of these two categories. This suggests that the theoretical duality between objective and subjective criteria may be less clear in individuals' minds than in the heads of career scholars. The findings also support Heslin's (2005) contention that we need to pay more attention to career success conceptions that involve others as the key referent. The predominance of themes that fit subjective criteria of career success supports several authors' propositions that, under the conditions of the new economy and more people being in boundaryless careers, the traditional objective criteria are simply not very meaningful (Arthur et al., 2005). And the fact that the subjective career success themes found here were quite different from those most often measured by career researchers supports suggestions made by others (Arthur et al., 2005; Heslin, 2005) that the construct of career success is more complex and multi-dimensional today than it was earlier, because of demographic changes in the workforce and changing organizational structures. Finally, our findings suggest that some people think of their careers and career success in a broader life context, rather than a separate domain where they operate independently of their family and personal life. Career theory has tended to ignore the broader life context of individuals' careers.

Objective vs. subjective career success

Of eight emergent definitions of career success, only four fit well the presumed duality of objective and subjective aspects of the phenomenon. Upward mobility is clearly an objective, outwardly visible manifestation of success; but garnering respect from peers and getting appreciation or recognition for one's work may or may not be visible to anyone other than the job incumbent. In fact, these dimensions of career success are clearly other-referent but not necessarily objective. And they are not other-referent in the sense that the individual is comparing outcomes against others, which is how the term is most often used in the literature (Heslin, 2005). These dimensions of career success are other-referent in the sense that the individual is dependent upon other members of the organization to achieve these aspects of success. Yet there may be no evidence clearly discernible by others of when these manifestations of career success happen.

Another observation about the dimensions of career success that emerged from this study is that the most dominant organization-based conception was *not* upward mobility – career advancement, increased responsibility, high salary and so on. Rather, the more prominent organization-based aspect of career success mentioned was respect from peers – being perceived as adding value, and so on. This aspect of career success also raises questions about the relevance of distinctions between the 'objective' and 'subjective' criteria. On the one hand, others' perceptions are not easy to assess and require the individual professional working reduced-load to make a calculation, draw inferences, make a judgment about whether others respect him or her, which might argue for 'peer respect' being treated as a subjective career outcome. On the other hand, presumably there are also data – objective, observable evidence – that could be gathered to assess how any given person is viewed or treated in a work unit. So peer respect seems not to qualify as strictly a subjective or an objective criterion of career success. We grouped 'peer respect' along with 'upward mobility' and 'recognition/appreciation' in the category of organization-based themes, because the source is organizational rather than personal. The individual professional working part-time does not have direct control over these career outcomes. For example, that individual could be performing at the very highest level according to his or her manager, yet a co-worker could still perceive him or her as not equally competent or committed because of a bias against part-time work in general. We wondered also whether this aspect of career success was important partly because some of these professionals and managers had accepted that they had made tradeoffs and might experience career plateauing or slower upward mobility, yet they realized that they must do something to maintain their 'career capital' while they were opting to invest more in their lives outside work. As long as their peers still viewed them as having valued expertise and being responsible and committed, these part-time professionals and managers could keep their options open for the future.

There were three clearly subjective career success themes – being able to have a life outside work, opportunities to do challenging work and continue to grow professionally, and enjoying work. However, none really matches the notion of intrinsic satisfaction or psychological success usually associated with subjective career outcomes (Hall and Chandler, 2005). The theme closest to psychological success or intrinsic satisfaction was 'performing well'. But this was categorized as a personal and organizational inter-linked theme, rather than personal, because participants clearly expressed that they wanted evidence that they were performing well. It was not sufficient for them to carry out an internal assessment and feel that they were doing well. There had to be a confirmation externally.

Performing well and having an impact, which were categorized as personal and organizational inter-linked themes, clearly could not be categorized as either objective or subjective, because they represented a synthesis of the two, or a sort of incorporation of the objective into the subjective. Performing well and having an impact or making a contribution can be viewed as both self-referent and other- (organizational-) referent. To feel that one is performing well requires some external verification or confirmation but is not necessarily a matter of a visible designation. Having an impact or making a contribution is of the same order in that it is clearly the individual's reaction ('feeling' that one is having an impact) and yet seems to require some visible evidence, even if there is no tangible attribution made by any organizational member.

So four of the eight themes that emerged from respondents' reflections on the meaning of career success suggest that the boundary between objective and subjective career success is ambiguous. Peer respect, Recognition/ appreciation, Performing well, and Having an impact are all conceptualizations that demand, in fact, a synthesis of the objective and the subjective. These themes also suggest that career success research could be enhanced by approaches that gather information from multiple sources and that, in fact, offer the opportunity to compare the individuals' perceptions with those of key stakeholders in the organization.

What is subjective career success?
The part-timers studied here appeared to be similar to knowledge workers labeled by Arthur and Rousseau (1996) as having boundaryless careers in that they had a tendency to put more weight on subjective aspects of career success (such as continuing to learn and grow). This focus may be because they see fewer promotional opportunities in any one given employer, or it may be because they prefer the independence to determine their own career movement. But knowledge workers in the new economy are generally portrayed as having little loyalty to employers and as thinking of their careers in a broader industry context. Part-time professionals and managers in our study, however, were quite loyal and committed to their employers, and they believed that, given their desire to work on a reduced-load basis, their career capital was greater staying in an organization where they had built up credibility and a good reputation based on past history, as well as a set of strong networks and relationships.

Of the three self-referent dimensions of success found, all did seem to fit the subjective category – able to have a life outside work, feeling that one is doing challenging work and continuing to grow and learn professionally, and having fun, enjoying work. However, none approximated the subjective criterion which is most often measured in the empirical literature – career satisfaction – which raises questions about what this construct actually means. The term suggests that individuals maintain a long-term perspective on their sequence of work-related experiences over time and indeed can articulate a coherent reaction or attitude toward that sequence at a given point in time. Only one of the emergent themes in this study included a longitudinal view (upward mobility), and the rest were clearly grounded in the present. Perhaps the idea of people feeling a sense of satisfaction or dissatisfaction with their careers is a social construction of academic researchers rather than a reflection of something professionals and managers actually think about.

Career in a life context

The most novel and yet not surprising finding in this study was the high percentage of participants who talked about career success simply meaning being able to have a life beyond the workplace. To suggest that career success consists of something outside the career domain, or even that it is determined by something outside, may seem outlandish or paradoxical. However, for individuals who have chosen to work less in order to create more space for other things in their lives, this concept seems almost commonsensical.

The emergent theme of career success as being able to have a life outside work may also have to do with the predominantly female sample. Career success for men has traditionally been assumed to be associated with career-related achievements and accomplishments and the concomitant recognition received. The meanings of career success to women may well turn out to be somewhat different, as a function of the different roles they play and the salience of various identities at different times in their lives. Lee et al. (2004) have proposed a model of Identity Transformation which suggests that, after professionals become parents, they go through a gradual process of socialization into parenthood, while also enacting changes in their work and family patterns, leading to a new overall identity as professional and parent. If they are correct, it would clearly follow that the meaning of career success would change through this process. Of course, more research is needed to investigate women's definitions of career success and their career conceptions at different points in time, and how career fits into their overall lives. Hall (1976, 2002) and Hall et al. (2003) are in the process of developing an instrument that measures career and life orientation in a manner that recognizes the embeddedness of individuals' careers in a broader life context. It may help us to identify more precisely how professionals working reduced-load differ from professionals working full-time in their conceptions of career success and their career thinking in general.

Eaton and Bailyn (2000) point out that the conventional view of career has been that professionals act as individuals and are always seeking to maximize their own outcomes independent of other elements in their lives. Yet men and women are embedded in a set of relationships, and in a context much larger and broader than a single employing organization, or even several over time. They suggest thinking of 'career' as life path, as a trajectory that unfolds as a function not only of workplace events, accomplishments, relationships (and industry characteristics and so on), but also as a function of individual, family, partner (and partner's employer) and community events, accomplishments, relationships. This way of thinking may be helpful, but it still puts the individual career as the central focus. One thing we learned from this study is that some professionals conceive of their careers in a context rather than as a separate pursuit or domain inhabited solely by the individual and the implicated organizations that employ them. Perhaps, if we thought about careers as embedded in a larger context, we could gain more insight into the different meanings they have for people, because we would pay more attention to the different contexts of different individuals and study more of the interactions and changes that occur over time.

Practical Implications

Among part-time professionals and managers studied here, the three most prevalent definitions of career success at Time 1 were: being able to have a life beyond work; performing well; and doing challenging work and continuing to grow professionally. At Time 2 'performing well' was replaced by 'having an impact'. These conceptualizations of career success suggest that organizations have a lot to learn about the shifting priorities and values of their professional and managerial employees, and that they may need to redesign their reward systems and career paths if they want to stay competitive in attracting and retaining the best knowledge workers and leaders of people. Not surprisingly, this research with non-traditional professionals who have chosen to work part-time simply confirms what other writers have suggested: that there has been a shift from the prominence of a more traditional definition of career success (meaning regular promotions and increasing responsibility, compensation and status over time) to the emergence of a more individualized and idiosyncratic definition of career success (Arthur et al., 2005; Cleveland, 2004; Heslin, 2005; Moen and Roehling, 2004). At first glance employers might be concerned about this change, because it suggests that they lose some leverage to motivate, to relocate, to redeploy their valuable people if these employees value highly goals other than upward mobility in the corporation. However, this shift in employee goals can be viewed as felicitous given the widespread flattening of corporations and the dramatically reduced opportunities for vertical movement up the ladder.

It should also be noted that two of the top three definitions of career success in our sample at both points in time suggest that these part-time professionals are still highly committed to their careers and able to deliver added value to their organizations. They wanted either to perform well or to have an impact, and they want to be challenged and continue to learn. This bodes well for organizations, and they would be well-advised to experiment with ways of supporting their part-time professionals and managers. One of the biggest barriers to successful part-time work is the challenge of constituting or redesigning professional and managerial jobs in such a way that they can truly be done on a reduced schedule. Yet, given the importance of performing well or having an impact to these employees, it is clearly in the best interests of the organization *and* the individual to succeed in constituting reduced work loads so that there is a win–win situation.

The importance of doing challenging work and continuing to learn to part-time professionals and managers also represents a great opportunity for employers to benefit from the changing values and priorities of their employees. These highly committed knowledge workers are saying that they are more motivated by being challenged and stimulated to develop professionally than by being enticed by the carrot of upward mobility. Organizations can ill afford not to pay attention to this, even as they face the reality that there is always a risk of investing in and developing your best and brightest and then losing them to the competition. This does not mean just sending people to training courses or workshops, of course. It means making sure that part-time professionals and managers are not accommodated by just being given low-challenge assignments or 'put on hold' in marginal positions until they are willing to return to full-time work. It means really grappling with how to constitute jobs with different workloads and how to be creative in deploying talent. It means making sure that there is high-quality mentoring going on with people choosing to work less for a while.

The prevalence of respondents viewing career success as meaning having a life outside work should be taken as a call to action for any employers who have up to now been trying to dismiss work–life initiatives as a passing fad or trend. This finding is especially significant given this is a sample of professional and managerial employees. The fact that this theme was most common among our sample suggests that, if organizations want to retain this new generation of professionals who are in dual-career families, they simply must find ways to support and facilitate employees in continuing to progress in their careers while also committing the time and energy they want to family or other personal life commitments. Because of the greater diversity in the workforce, this support will not be forthcoming from developing one or two policies with standard parameters, or launching a single initiative designed to 'solve the problem'. It will mean that organizations must develop a capacity for responding flexibly and constructively to individual requests and must develop a culture that promotes acceptance of a wide variety of career paths and means of making a contribution.

REFERENCES

Arthur, M.B. and Rousseau, D.M. (eds) (1996), *The Boundaryless Career*, New York: Oxford University Press.

Arthur, M.B., Khapova, S.N. and Wilderom, C.P.M. (2005), 'Career success in a boundaryless career world', *Journal of Organizational Behavior*, **26**, 177–202.

Aryee, S., Srinivas, E.S. and Tan, H.H. (2005), 'Rhythms of life: antecedents and outcomes of work–family balance in employed parents', *Journal of Applied Psychology*, **90** (1), 132–46.

Barnett, R.C. (2001), 'Women, men, work and family: an expansionist theory', *American Psychologist*, **56**, 781–96.

Barnett, R.C. and Gareis, K.C. (2000), 'Reduced-hours employment', *Work and Occupations* **27** (2), 168–87.

Bond, J., Thompson, C., Galinsky, E. and Prottas, D. (2002), *Highlights of the National Study of the Changing Workforce*, New York: Families and Work Institute.

Catalyst (1997), 'A new approach to flexibility: managing the work/time equation', New York: Catalyst.

Cleveland, J.N. (2004), 'What is success? Who defines it? Perspectives on the criterion problem as it relates to work and family', in E.E. Kossek and S.J. Lambert (eds), *Work and Life Integration*, Mahwah, NJ: Lawrence Erlbaum Associates, pp. 319–46.

Corwin, V., Lawrence, T.B. and Frost, P.J. (2001), 'Individual strategies of successful part-time work', *Harvard Business Review*, July–August, 120–27.

Eaton, S. and Bailyn, L. (2000), 'Career as life path: tracing work and life strategies of biotech professionals', in M. Peiperl, M. Arthur, R. Goffee and T. Morris (eds), *Career Frontiers*, New York: Oxford University Press, pp. 177–98.

Epstein, C.F., Seron, C., Oglensky, B. and Saute, R. (1998), *The Part-time Paradox: Time Norms, Professional Life, Family and Gender*, Boston: Routledge.

Frone, M.R. (2003), 'Work–family balance', in J.C. Quick and L.E. Tetrick (eds), *Handbook of Occupational Health Psychology*, Washington, DC: American Psychological Association, pp. 143–62.

Galinsky, E., Bond, J. and Hill, J. (2004), *When Work Works: a Status Report on Workplace Flexibility. Who Has it? Who Wants it? What Difference Does it Make?*, New York: Families and Work Institute.

Galinsky, E., Bond, J., Kim, S., Backon, L., Brownfield, E. and Sakai, K. (2005), *Overwork in America: When the Way we Work Becomes Too Much*, New York: Families and Work Institute.

Gallos, J.V. (1989), 'Exploring women's development', in M.B. Arthur, D.T. Hall and B.S. Lawrence (eds), *Handbook of Career Theory*, New York: Cambridge University Press, pp. 110–32.

Gerson, K. and Jacobs, J. (2004), *The Time Divide: Work, Family, and Gender Inequality*, Cambridge, MA: Harvard University Press.

Greenhaus, J.H. (2003), 'Career dynamics', in W.C. Borman, D.R. Ilgen and R.J.

Klimoski (eds), *Comprehensive Handbook of Psychology: Industrial and Organizational Psychology*, Vol. 12, New York: Wiley, pp. 519–40.

Greenhaus, J.H. and Beutell, N.J. (1985), 'Sources of conflict between work and family roles', *Academy of Management Review*, **10**, 76–88.

Hall, D.T. (1976), *Careers in Organizations*, Santa Monica, CA: Goodyear.

Hall, D.T. (2002), *Careers In and Out of Organizations*, Thousand Oaks, CA: Sage.

Hall, D.T. and Chandler, D.E. (2005), 'Psychological success: when the career is a calling', *Journal of Organizational Behavior*, **26**, 155–76.

Hall, D.T., Briscoe, J.M., Kossek, E.E. and Lee, M.D. (2003), personal communication.

Heslin, P.A. (2005), 'Conceptualizing and evaluating career success', *Journal of Organizational Behavior*, **26**, 113–36.

Hill, E.J., Martinson, A., Ferris, M. and Baker, R. (2004), 'Beyond the mommy track: the influence of new-concept part-time work for professional women on work and family', *Journal of Family and Economic Issues*, **25** (1), 121–36.

Hughes, E.C. (1937), 'Institutional office and the person', *American Journal of Sociology*, **43**, 404–13.

Hughes, E.C. (1958), *Men and Their Work*, Glencoe: Free Press.

Kofodimos, J. (1993), *Balancing Act: How Managers Can Integrate Successful Careers and Fulfilling Personal Lives*, San Francisco: Jossey-Bass.

Kossek, E.E., Noe, R. and DeMarr, B. (1999), 'Work–family role synthesis: individual, family and organizational determinants', *International Journal of Conflict Resolution*, **10** (2), 102–29.

Lee, M.D. and Kanungo, R.H. (eds) (1984), *Management of Work and Personal Life*, New York: Praeger.

Lee, M.D., MacDermid, S.M. and Buck, M.L. (2000), 'Organizational paradigms of reduced-load work: accommodation, elaboration, transformation', *Academy of Management Journal*, **43** (6), 1211–26.

Lee, M.D., Engler, L. and Wright, L. (2002), 'Exploring the boundaries in professional careers: reduced load work arrangements in law, medicine and accounting', in R.J. Burke and D.L. Nelson (eds), *Advancing Women's Careers*, Oxford: Blackwell, pp. 174–205.

Lee, M.D., MacDermid, S.M., Dohring, P.L. and Kossek, E.E. (2004), 'Professionals becoming parents: socialization, adaptation, and identity transformation', in E.E. Kossek and S.J. Lambert (eds), *Work and Life Integration*, Mahwah, NJ: Lawrence Erlbaum Associates, pp. 287–318.

MacDermid, S.M., Lee, M.D., Buck, M.L. and Williams, M.L. (2001), 'Alternative work arrangements among professionals and managers: rethinking career development and success', *Journal of Management Development*, **20** (4), 305–17.

Marks, S.R. (1977), 'Multiple roles and role strain', *American Sociological Review*, **42**, 921–36.

Meiksins, P. and Whalley, P. (2002), *Putting Work in its Place*, Ithaca, NY: Cornell University Press.

Moen, P. and Roehling, P. (2004), *The Career Mystique: Cracks in the American Dream*, Boulder, CO: Rowman and Littlefield.

Poole, M.E., Langan-Fox, J. and Omodei, M. (1993), 'Contrasting subjective and objective criteria as determinants of perceived career success: a longitudinal study', *Journal of Occupational and Organizational Psychology*, **66**, 39–54.

Powell, G.N. (1999), 'Reflections on the glass ceiling: recent trends and future prospects', *Handbook of Gender and Work*, Thousand Oaks, CA: Sage, pp. 325–46.

Rothbard, N.P. (2001), 'Enriching or depleting? The dynamics of engagement in work and family roles', *Administrative Science Quarterly*, **46**, 655–84.

Sturges, J. (1999), 'What it means to succeed: personal conceptions of career success held by male and female managers at different ages', *British Journal of Management*, **10**, 239–52.

US Department of Labor (2004), 'Women in the labor force: a databook', Report 973, Table 6, http://www.bls.gov/cps/wlf-databook.pdf, accessed 30 May 2005.

14.   Improving work–life balance: REBT for workaholic treatment

Charles P. Chen

Developed by renowned psychologist and scholar Albert Ellis (1962, 1994, 1995, 1997), rational emotive behavior therapy (REBT) has been one of the most recognized contemporary humanistic approaches for counseling and psychotherapy, along with ample support of empirical research evidence for its effectiveness and efficiency in clinical interventions (Corey, 2001; Dryden, 1989). Through its formation and evolution in the last five decades, REBT has been utilized in various therapeutic contexts, helping clients cope with a variety of psychological difficulties they encounter in their lives (Bernard, 1991; Ellis, 1973, 1998, 1999, 2000; Ellis and Bernard, 1985; Ellis and Dryden, 1997). This chapter considers the pertinence and application of REBT in working with clients who suffer from the workaholic syndrome.

Workaholism has become one of the most serious psychological detriments to human health as the world of work continues its fast evolution in a post-industrial era in Western society (Burke, 2001; Burke et al., 2004; McMillan and O'Driscoll, 2004; Porter, 1996, 2004). The workaholic syndrome can seriously weaken or even destroy individuals' work–life balance, incapacitating all aspects of an individual's wellbeing – personal, social and vocational alike. Thus, caring professionals are called upon to use effective treatment strategies in aiding workaholic clients to overcome their unhealthy lifestyle and to make a successful transition toward a constructive work–life balance (Burwell and Chen, 2002; Chen, 2003; Naughton, 1987; Seybold and Salomone, 1994).

With this purpose in mind, this chapter takes a close look at some of the essential theoretical tenets and therapeutic strategies of REBT that seem to present promise for effective intervention with workaholic clients. The chapter first reviews the key concepts and orientation of REBT. In doing so, it provides an overview of the REBT framework that can help to tackle the issue of workaholism. This is followed by a brief description of the symptoms of workaholism. On the basis of the review of REBT and the workaholic phenomenon, the chapter finally proposes some considerations for intervention. It illustrates how the REBT principles can guide a set of effective counseling and therapeutic techniques that will help workaholic clients make positive change. As a result, these clients will be directed to take ownership of a healthy lifestyle that will enhance their personal and vocational wellbeing.

REBT: KEY THEORETICAL FRAMEWORK AND THERAPEUTIC ORIENTATION

Rational and Irrational Thinking

A basic assumption of REBT is that people are born neutral, and they exhibit a natural tendency to possess both rational and irrational thinking. In accordance with this human nature, people positively think and verbalize about themselves, communicate with others, and act towards the environment they are in. But they are not immune to mistakes in thinking. When this happens, people think and act negatively toward themselves and the environment. In particular, they tend to blame themselves as the cause for failure or undesirable situations, and they create misperceptions that become barriers for their personal growth (Ellis, 1962, 1971, 1973). According to the theoretical frame of REBT (Ellis, 2000; Ellis and Dryden, 1997; Ellis and Harper, 1997; Ellis and MacLaren, 1998), several related key points can be drawn from this assumption: (a) human irrationality, which originates unnecessary disturbing perceptions for oneself, is biologically and culturally oriented; (b) disturbance is not generated by environmental conditions but rather by the individual's self-conditioning through misbeliefs; (c) the individual not only creates disturbing beliefs but also tends to keep him/herself continually engaged in the disturbances; and (d) in spite of human limitations of irrationality, humans are capable of building correct and rational thinking patterns in their life, and they can change their way of thinking, feeling and doing, and become more self-actualized.

The basis for rational and irrational thinking, as Ellis (2000) has pointed out, is the psychological uniqueness of human nature in that we are self-talking, self-evaluating and self-sustaining. Emotional and behavioral difficulties happen when people consciously or unconsciously direct their thinking process into an 'only-option' or 'only-choice' impasse, and do not know how or even do not want to get out of this deadlock. Personal growth unfolds a struggle between the positive-self and the negative-self. That is, the distorted (or crooked) side of thinking, such as self-devaluing and self-defeating patterns, always tries to interfere, hinder and detriment the innate potential and disposition toward positiveness, moving ahead and growth.

Emotional Disturbance

REBT postulates that false beliefs that people indoctrinate in their irrational thinking frame are primarily learned experiences which come from the encounter with significant others, especially during early childhood. The repetition of these misperceptions strengthens the formation of a pattern of irrational attitudes and behaviors in one's life. Consequently, emotional disturbances are generated. The core of most emotional disturbances is 'blame'. People tend to blame themselves as well as others for existing problems in life. Meanwhile, people are strongly inclined to intensify their preferences into dogmatic and absolutistic notions such as 'shoulds', 'musts' and 'oughts' to push themselves or others to take unnecessary blames and responsibilities. According to Ellis (1973, 1994, 1998), people are basically disturbed by the unrealistic and illogical demands they set for themselves. Thus, disruptive feelings and anxieties emerge.

It becomes apparent that people create disturbed thoughts and feelings based on their innate absolutistic dogmas such as 'musts' and 'shoulds'. However, since humans are capable of self-awareness and they can learn to think differently, they can change their irrational cognition (Ellis, 1998, 1999). The key point is to replace the internalized emotional disturbances, such as a self-defeating tendency, with appropriate emotions that derive from realistic and logical thoughts.

A-B-C Theory of Psychological Functioning

The essence of REBT is its A-B-C theory of personality. To illustrate human personality in REBT practice, Ellis (1973, 1991) proposed the well-known A-B-C model (Corey, 2001; Ellis, 1991, 1994, 2000). A is the activating event that can be a fact, a situation, the behaviour or attitude of a person. C, known as the emotional and behavioral consequence, is the reaction (either appropriate or inappropriate) of the person. C is not yielded by A. The element between A and C is B (the person's belief about A), and B causes C to happen. Ellis suggests that the central part in human personality depends on how a person's belief system is formed and functioning. In other words, B (belief) can be much more important than the meaning of A (event) itself. This shows how strong human influence can be in creating emotional reactions and disturbances in people's cognition. Therefore, REBT contends that it is essential to focus on changing people's irrational natural tendency that leads to their disturbed emotional aftermath. In order to make the change, D (disputing) is needed to follow A and B. By adopting logical and scientific methods into the thinking process, the person will be able to restore rational effect

(E) and generate healthy new feelings (F) toward self and others (Ellis, 1973, 1991, 1994).

THE WORKAHOLIC PHENOMENON

What is Workaholism?

The notion of workaholism was initially introduced in 1971 by Oates to define an emerging attitudinal and behavioral trend in individuals' work-life. In combining the words *work* and *alcoholic* into one term, the concept of workaholism depicts vividly a phenomenon of human obsession and impulsive tendency toward one's vocational life, in which work becomes almost the sole purpose for one's living (Killinger, 1991). When a person is preoccupied by and dependent on his or her worklife in such an excessive manner, the meaning of work changes drastically to represent a twisted psychological functioning in its relationship to other aspects of life. As a result, workaholism, like alcoholism, manifests an addiction (Killinger, 1991). As a serious hazard affecting individuals' mental health, the workaholic syndrome has received increasing attention during the last three decades from an array of interdisciplinary research in health promotion. While the negative impact of workaholism on individuals' personal and vocational wellbeing is conspicuous, the number of working people who are under the shadow of this psychological difficulty is also alarming. Research evidence estimates that up to 25 per cent of the current workforce are suffering from workaholic effects (Robinson, 1998). Workaholism has become one of the main health risks to ordinary working people, eroding their mental health and quality of life, while debilitating their effective functioning in vocational and personal/social lives (Burke, 2001).

The first academic definition of the term *workaholic* came from Spence and Robbins (1992, p. 162), who defined the workaholic as a person who 'is highly work involved, feels compelled or driven to work because of inner pressures, and is low in enjoyment of work'. Spence and Robbins differentiate a workaholic from a work enthusiast, that is, a person who is also highly involved in his or her work but does not experience the same internal drive to work or the same dissatisfaction with work. Work enthusiasts are individuals who work to live, enjoying and valuing rich experiences from other aspects of life while being actively and productively engaged in their professional and vocational lives. In contrast, workaholics live to work, having little or no sense of how to live a normal and multifaceted personal and social life other than their worklife (Robinson, 2000).

What Do Workaholics Look Like?

As previously defined, workaholics solely focus on and are excessively obsessed with their work while paying little or no attention to other areas of their lives (Porter, 1996, 2004). Most workaholics work consistently long hours, including evenings and weekends (Tyler, 1999), and when a workaholic can be persuaded to take a holiday, they will feel very uncomfortable or even a sense of guilt if they do not bring work along (Porter, 1996). Having a total and more direct control of worklife is the priority for workaholics, who believe that their participation and responsibility is of vital importance to the successful completion of a task in which they are involved. Thus, they often find it very difficult to delegate work to others (Spence and Robbins, 1992), pushing themselves to shoulder more work responsibilities than necessary. Consequently, they have to put more time and energy into their work. Notwithstanding the long work hours and excessive attention to their work, workaholics are not necessarily highly productive performers in the workplace. In fact, many could be quite inefficient, owing to the fact that they exhibit higher levels of perfectionism on the job than others (Spence and Robbins, 1992).

The more obsessed workaholics are with their worklife, the more convinced they become about their lifestyle depending on work as a means of survival. This one-sided attitude and behavior dominates not only how they conceive of life satisfaction, but also their relationship and interaction with others in life. For a workaholic, satisfaction derived from work is more important than the satisfaction derived from family life (Seybold and Salomone, 1994). Not surprisingly, a study conducted by Bonebright et al. (2000) showed that the workaholic has more work–life conflict than a non-workaholic. Similar conflicts may also constrain workaholics' relationships with others in other social and professional contexts, including effective and smooth communication and interactions with peers in the workplace (Taris et al., 2005). The continuing long work hours and excessive concentration on work also increase the risks for psychological and physiological welfare; workaholics are more vulnerable to a range of health problems such as stress-induced illnesses (Bonebright et al., 2000), chronic fatigue (Tyler, 1999), increased levels of anxiety (Burke, 1999) and substance abuse (Killinger, 1991).

Why Does Workaholism Occur?

Like most mental health issues, workaholism is a complex psychological difficulty originated and influenced by a range of internal and external factors. Seybold and Salomone (1994) postulated several contributing and related intra-personal causes of the workaholic problem. These include variables such as an uncontrollable obsession with work, using worklife as an excuse to escape issues in other aspects of one's personal and social life, a desperate need to maintain a sense of control, a highly competitive personality, influence from parents who are workaholics, and a negative self-concept and low self-esteem. Although one of these variables can be the root of workaholism, very often the causes of the workaholic problem are a collective interaction between several or all of these factors. Notwithstanding the dynamic complicity of such causes, it appears evident that a negative self-concept and its related self-perceptions, such as lack of self-confidence and low sense of self-worth, are the essential sources that trigger and moderate the workaholic symptom (Seybold and Salomone, 1994; Porter, 1996). Empirical evidence suggests that workaholics have a higher need to prove themselves than work enthusiasts, and 'workaholism thus emerges as work behaviors in response to feelings of low self-worth and insecurity' (Burke, 1999, p. 527).

An external environment that condones and reinforces the existence of workaholism further complicates these intra-personal factors. Society in general accepts the workaholic phenomenon as a normal way of life, or even a virtue demonstrating one's work ethics. Rather than the problematic nature of this distorted personality tendency being acknowledged, workaholism is normalized as an acceptable practice. Very often it is a worklife style that is encouraged and rewarded. As a workaholic is often considered an extremely hard-working individual who is committed to their work whole-heartedly, he or she is the ideal candidate for promotions and higher levels of salary – rewards that serve to perpetuate the problem. Also, workaholics may be in high demand in a highly competitive and unstable global economy, owing to their devotion to longer work hours for the same amount of salary. Employers' attitudes and organizational culture as such, intentionally or unintentionally, nurture and exacerbate the workaholic problem. This working environment validates workaholics' anxiety about job security and work merits, intensifying their belief that working long hours is the only way to ensure job security and to accomplish and sustain satisfactory performance.

As the internal and external factors interact, individuals who suffer from workaholism are drawn deeper into the trap of their addictive perception of and behavior in worklife. The more rationalization workaholics make about their addiction to work, the deeper they become swamped in this irrational and addictive lifestyle. This vicious cycle serves to validate a combination of irrational and distorted cognitive, emotive and behavioral patterns, making it extremely difficult for workaholics to recognize their problematic lifestyle. Consequently, the existence of the workaholic problem is very often denied as a lived experience by many workaholics themselves, along with much societal ignorance and condonation. According to Porter (1996, p. 78), 'denial of the problem may be the greatest hindrance to corrective action'. The state of denial may further intensify and worsen the workaholic problem before it is dealt with. Thus, a pivotal challenge for tackling workaholism is to raise public awareness of the common existence of this mental health hazard in individuals' vocational life, as well as its negative impact on other aspects of one's life experience (Caproni, 1997). Moreover, a similar effort is of paramount importance to the counseling and therapeutic intervention process that helps workaholic clients become aware of and understand the nature of the workaholic problem. Positive changes will occur only after the sense of denial is replaced by a sense of awareness, leading to a desire to acquire and practice an alternative healthy lifestyle of work–life balance.

REBT IN THE TREATMENT OF WORKAHOLISM

The foregoing overview of REBT and the workaholic phenomenon aims to provide a central rationale for the therapeutic approach to dealing with the psychological problem in an effective helping context. As described above, what lies at the core of workaholism is a vulnerable inner self entangled with much insecurity and negativity. Dealing with this kind of weakened and twisted sense of self-worth is a main therapeutic goal of REBT. According to Ellis (1994, 2000), much of the psychological difficulty a person encounters derives from irrational beliefs and emotions concerning his or her perceived self-image and self-worth in the eyes of others. Being trapped in this kind of irrational thinking, the person believes that he or she must 'impress, live up to the expectations of, and outdo the performances of other people' (Ellis, 2000, p. 176). This obsession with perfectionism and approval from others exemplifies the typical mindset of individuals who suffer from workaholism. Therefore, by treating workaholism as a form of irrational disturbance, REBT can help workaholic clients to understand the sources and maladaptive nature of this psychological difficulty, gaining insights and constructive behavior to cope with the workaholic tendency.

As indicated in the previous discussion, workaholism is a type of individual psychological problem that is reinforced and perpetuated by external and environmental factors. It is beyond the scope of this chapter to address ways to deal with these social and societal reinforcers and facilitators of the workaholic phenomenon. The following section only considers the utilization of key principles from one approach in counseling and psychotherapy, namely REBT, in helping workaholic clients tackle the issue of workaholism in the context of individual psychological intervention. While acknowledging the fact that different causes of workaholism may require different specific and focused therapeutic interventions (Bonebright et al., 2000), the following REBT intervention considerations deal with workaholism in a more general sense, with a central focus on helping clients build a positive and confident inner self. It is also assumed that in this context clients feel the need to seek help from a counselor and/or therapist, whether they are self-referred or referred by others. The term 'client' or 'clients' in the following discussion refers only to workaholic client(s) who intend to overcome the workaholic problem through the counseling intervention process. Likewise, the terms 'counselor' and 'therapist', 'counseling' and 'therapy' are used interchangeably to define the professional helper and the mode of clinical intervention in a more general and inclusive manner.

The Didactic and Educational Counseling Process

REBT adopts the principle of full acceptance or tolerance of the client. However, the notion of 'acceptance' here differs from the similar terms used by some other therapeutic approaches, especially those approaches that have an emphasis on relationship building. REBT takes the view that too much focus on warmth and understanding in the helping process may not be conducive to the healthy growth of the client. What lies at the heart of this working relationship is that the counselor accepts the client as a student who needs clear guidance for positive change. In the role of a teacher, the counselor does not intend to help the client explore feelings, but rather he or she shows the client the right direction and effective coping mechanisms that will lead to rational thinking and productive behaviors (Ellis, 1994, 1995, 2000).

This educational and didactic orientation may be of particular relevance to workaholic clients who need to correct their self-destructive thinking patterns, emotions and behaviors surrounding their addiction to work (Trimpey, 1993). The more explicitly the client is advised about the hazardous nature of the workaholic lifestyle and about the ways to cope with it, the sooner he or she will become capable of finding solutions to the problem. As indicated in the previous discussion, workaholics are very often obsessed with their false presuppositions about their worklife. To make matters worse, these misperceptions are taken for granted as a normal way of life, and thus have never been challenged. While the REBT process fully accepts the client as a person, it does not condone the client's irrational beliefs and their related behavioral deficiency. On the contrary, the REBT counselor is willing to take a clear stand, confronting the client's problem in an honest and direct manner. Obviously, the meaningfulness of the counseling process here is about educating the client to understand the problem and to take action to deal with the problem. Instead of comforting the client, the REBT counselor is open and straightforward in sharing her views and values with the client. This means that the counselor does not hesitate to challenge and debate the erroneous workaholic presuppositions unveiled in the therapeutic process. Guided in this mode of proactive teaching and modeling, a series of intervention strategies will then follow to implement the counseling intervention.

Intervention Considerations and Strategies

To illustrate how the intervention works, this section addresses the general applicability of REBT principles and their related strategies to workaholism. These treatment considerations follow the A-B-C theory, which is the basis of the REBT perspective on human functioning. These intervention proposals are drawn from a synthesis of some of the basic REBT strategies and techniques (Bernard, 1991; Burwell and Chen, 2002; Corey, 2001; Dryden, 1995; Ellis, 1998, 1999, 2000; Ellis and Bernard, 1985; Ellis and Dryden, 1997; Ellis and Harper, 1997; Ellis and MacLaren, 1998; Neenan and Dryden, 2000; Walen et al., 1992).

Note that the cognitive, emotive and behavioral strategies are always intertwined closely, and they work collectively to help clients understand and combat irrational beliefs, emotions and their associated behaviors, generating productive and logical action for positive changes in achieving and managing a work–life balance.

Cognitive intervention strategies
Cognitive intervention lies at the core of the REBT treatment for workaholism. This is because the workaholic problem, examined from the standpoint of the A-B-C principle of REBT, is essentially caused by irrational thoughts that are accompanied by inappropriate emotions and behaviors (Ellis, 1991, 1994). Therefore, to understand and correct the untenable and illogical thoughts and ideas stands out as the priority for the treatment task. Here are a few of the most commonly applicable cognitive strategies for consideration.

Debate irrational beliefs   To help clients debate their irrational beliefs is the most commonly used strategy for intervention (Dryden, 1983; Ellis, 1994; Ellis and Dryden, 1997). The counselor tells clients in a quick and direct manner the problematic nature of the workaholic mentality. Workaholic clients are preoccupied with a series of misperceptions toward their worklife. Some common examples of this kind of irrational beliefs are the following statements:

- 'I must complete the work by myself, as no one else can do it properly.'
- 'I must work extra hours to get the work done.'
- 'I ought to work long hours so I can maintain the quality of my performance and win the respect of my colleagues.'
- 'I ought to be a model worker in the eyes of my boss and co-workers, so I have to work even harder, and the proof of hard-working is to devote longer time to my work every day.'
- 'I should work long hours so I will always be competitive in keeping my job secure.'
- 'I should carry work assignments with me every weekend and in my holidays so I will not get behind and feel guilty about it.'

These 'must', 'ought' and 'should' statements, manifested in either an overt or a covert way by clients, represent typical irrational beliefs that keep clients trapped in their workaholic obsessions. According to REBT conceptualization, it is these irrational thoughts that are blocking clients' capacity to see the reality of their vocational life. Thus, the counselor forcefully teaches and encourages clients to learn how to deal with their irrational thinking, which is reflected in these excessively self-focused statements. To do so, the counselor actively disputes these irrational beliefs while teaching clients to challenge their own false presuppositions. 'Why must I do all the work and cannot trust that others will do it properly?' 'How do I maintain my quality of job performance if I do not put in extra long hours every day?' 'Why should I always work long hours to get things done?' 'Is it really true that working extra hours will provide me with more job security?' 'What will happen if I am not consumed by work during my family and leisure times?' As clients learn to ask themselves these questions, they become engaged in a self-education process that unveils the flawed and fallacious nature of these 'must', 'ought' and 'should' statements in their mind. This debating approach can be an effective intervention to empower clients to combat the very roots of the workaholic beliefs, shedding light on the need for rational and healthy perspectives in clients' worklife.

Transform language   From a REBT standpoint, workaholic clients are troubled by the incorrect language they use in their self-statements regarding their vocational life, as illustrated in the earlier discussion. These 'musts', 'oughts' and 'shoulds' are the causes of distorted assumptions underlying workaholism. Thus, the absolutistic language needs to be corrected in order to make constructive changes in clients' worklife. The counselor helps clients understand that they have options to change their language, that is, they can and may replace the absolutistic expressions with logical preferences. For example, instead of saying 'I must complete the work by myself, as no one else can do it properly', clients can learn to say 'I do not have to complete everything by myself, as there are many capable people around me and I can ask for and accept their help to finish the task.' Clients are taught to make such language changes in the therapeutic intervention process. With the direct teaching from the counselor, clients practice this language transformation exercise during an individual counseling session – a main intervention method reflecting the typical didactic approach for workaholic clients. It is even more important that clients are asked to make a deliberate and serious effort to correct their distorted expressions, whether conscious or unconscious, and transform such expressions into rational and open statements that fit with the reality.

It is essential that practicing this language transformation exercise becomes part of the REBT homework for clients. In doing this, clients pay attention to their language pattern in their daily routine, and use new and very different expressions to reverse the absolutistic and excessively self-obsessed language that has been one of the main reasons for workaholic clients' indulgence in excessively self-demanding and self-destructing beliefs and behaviors. Through the means of correcting and transforming language, clients come to realize that their misperceptions do not hold real truth because there are alternative, perhaps more importantly, effective ways to think and behave when they are in search of an improved balance between work and life. To illustrate, it is relevant to use the same example as in the previous paragraph. That is, alternative language transformation here is that clients practice the self-talk of 'feeling normal and fine to let other people help me in completing my work assignments'. Obviously, to teach and encourage clients to transform their language is not the ultimate purpose. Rather, through this purposeful exercise in their daily routine, clients can learn to think and express themselves differently and effectively, moving away from the irrational and distorted workaholic thinking patterns.

Emotive intervention strategies
With the goal of helping clients dispute, minimize and eventually overcome irrational workaholic thinking patterns, REBT utilizes emotive strategies in the counseling process. Unlike several other therapeutic models, REBT does not attempt to address all the specifics with regard to the presenting problem of workaholism. Rather than focusing on expressing feelings surrounding the problem, the emotive intervention strategies

aim to help clients cope with their problem-related emotions in the light of changing irrational thinking, feelings and behaviors here and now. Thus, positive change can occur in a timely, effective and efficient manner. Similarly to what has been described in the previous section, clients learn and practice emotive strategies both during their therapeutic encounters with the counselor and as homework exercises in their everyday life experiences.

Use rational–emotive imagery   The rational–emotive (RE) imagery strategy differentiates itself from the imagery interventions used in other therapeutic approaches in that the RE imagery work puts its focus on intense mental effort towards forming new emotional patterns (Ellis, 1998, 1999). Clients imagine a worst-case scenario that could occur in their vocational life, making them feel miserable and inadequate. They are asked to experience how they feel about these emotions. On this basis, clients are guided to ways of changing the negative emotions into relevant feelings. The attainment of this feeling transformation makes clients aware of their capacity and potential for positive change, which in turn will enhance their ability to correct and overcome irrational thoughts and adopt productive and effective behaviors in their worklife.

During the RE imagery intervention, workaholic clients imagine that, if they did not work longer hours, the quality of their job performance would suffer, and they might lose their jobs. When asked to experience their emotions associated with these 'could-be' situations, clients report that they would feel that they were losing face in the eyes of their colleagues if they saw others regarding their job performance as low. They would feel a paramount sense of distress or even depression if they lost their jobs. Not only would this involuntary job loss mean a huge blow to their sense of self-worth and their career identity, but also it would pose a real threat to their personal and/or familial wellbeing owing to worries about financial survival and related hardships ahead. The RE imagery then teaches clients to feel these 'could-be' and 'would-be' situations in different ways. Clients learn to feel appropriate and logical ways of managing their emotions that go with a rational flow of thinking. They come to realize that they can choose to feel less obsessed with their perceived image in the eyes of others, and not to be worried about an unreal scenario of job loss. While job loss can happen for various reasons and often with warning signs, it is useless to live with emotions of anxiety and fear that provide an excuse for total addiction to worklife. As clients transform their irrelevant feelings into normal and relevant feelings, they feel less disturbed by these inappropriate emotions related to workaholism. Clients are taught to practice RE imagery on a regular basis. The more such practice they are engaged in, the more skillful they become to live with relevant feelings in their vocational life.

Rehearse role-playing Role-playing combines emotional and behavioral aspects in the counseling intervention. The counselor constantly points out to clients the way they create emotional disturbances for themselves and things they can do to change their irrational feelings into relevant emotions. With the help of the counselor, clients rehearse the behaviors that reflect how they feel in a certain situation. While the role-playing exercise provides clients with the opportunity to experience unpleasant feelings, the purpose here is to examine the irrational thoughts that have caused the inappropriate emotional arousal in the first place. For example, a workaholic client may persist in working long hours because of the worry of not doing a perfect job to impress others. This excessive focus on self-perfection and concern with self-image in others' perception manifests the client's feelings of a fragile inner self that is obsessed with a sense of low self-confidence and insecurity. The client role-plays a scenario of communicating with her supervisor and her peers in the workplace in the case that she does not complete the work assignments as she has expected of herself.

Through the role-playing with the counselor, the client sees all the irrational beliefs and emotions that have caused the arousal of her anxiety. To use the role-playing as a here-and-now encounter, the client is taught and encouraged to challenge the misperception that working long hours is the only way to keep her performance quality and gain attention and respect from others. The counselor can actively interact with the client in the role-playing and interrupt whenever necessary to pinpoint the irrational gaps in the client's thoughts and emotions demonstrated in this exercise of therapeutic immediacy. As a result, clients can gain considerable understanding of their irrational thinking and feeling process, which in turn will lead to a first-hand educative experience for developing insights.

Practice the shame-attacking exercise Irrational shame, according to Ellis (1998,1999), is a major emotional disturbance that has to be dealt with if rational thinking and appropriate feelings are to function in clients' lives. The shame-attacking exercise is to intentionally participate in activities that will evoke disapproval from others (Neenan and Dryden, 2000). Ellis (1999, 2000) contends that individuals can firmly choose not to feel ashamed by telling themselves that it is not inauspicious if they are disapproved of or perceived by others as absurd and stupid. To combat the shame emotion is to help clients eliminate the feeling of shame regardless of others' disapproval. Workaholic clients are asked to take the risk of taking actions that they would usually avoid taking because of their concerns about others' perceptions and reactions. Clients are asked to cut down their usual long work hours, to say 'no' to extra work assignments that they have always accepted unquestioningly and to forcefully refuse to bring unfinished tasks home during the weekends.

There is no doubt that clients may feel the shame arousal when they are initially engaged in such actions that are contrary to their excessive protection of a perfectionist self-image in the eyes of others. Clients then notice that others' reactions are far less dramatic than imagined. Very often, there is hardly any reaction at all to clients' changing behavior toward the work assignments. Clients come to realize that they do not have to feel ashamed or humiliated by their behavioral change, as their sense of shame is actually a self-imposed false belief that is unfounded and groundless. Thus, even if they do not behave in their vocational life as perfectly as they have hoped for, life goes on as it is. Clients do not have to always gain others' approval and favorable reactions in order to maintain a positive self-perception. In this sense, the shame-attacking exercise is about attacking clients' self-created and self-imposed shame emotions that are part of the causes for the workaholic mindset and syndrome. The more strongly the shame-attacking is exercised, the weaker the foundation for the workaholism to be sustained, and the more insights are gained for positive change.

Behavioral intervention strategies
Like REBT interventions for other types of psychological difficulties, behavioral modification is always an integral part of enhancing workaholic clients' effort toward optimal rational and emotive functioning in their vocational life. Not only does behavioral intervention assist clients to acquire logical and effective skills in performance enhancement, but it also helps clients use the enhanced behavioral functioning to achieve constructive and productive rational-emotive outcomes. REBT utilizes a range of regular behavior therapy and counseling strategies in this helping context, including operant conditioning, self-management training, systematic desensitization, relaxation exercises, and modeling (Corey, 2001; Dryden, 1995; Ellis, 2000; Ellis and MacLaren, 1998; Walen, DiGiuseppe and Dryden, 1992).

While these behavioral modification techniques are taught during counseling sessions, clients are required to practice the behavioral strategies on a regular and continuing basis in their daily life. Behavioral change is not going to happen if clients are not committed to these homework assignments. Here are a few examples of how some of the behavioral strategies may work for clients in coping with their real-life situations.

Practice relaxation A basic technique in the behavioral therapeutic approach, relaxation exercise is an important component of the REBT treatment for workaholic clients. While the typical relaxation training may take several hours, the counselor can be flexible in teaching clients how to do the exercise in a gradual manner. Clients are taught to follow a set of instructions to relax. Posing in a passive and relaxed position in a quiet environment, clients are engaged in a series of very mild activities such as to contract and relax muscles, take deep and regular breaths, meditate on a tranquil scene, and imagine and focus on pleasant thoughts and moods. A critical aspect of this intervention is that clients need to maintain a 20-minute daily exercise routine to experience and practice relaxation. The commitment to this homework assignment itself can be a challenging yet powerful learning experience for workaholic clients. They come to realize that spending some time on aspects of personal life other than their work-life is appropriate and necessary, and they do not need to feel guilty about it. In the meantime, clients can experience the workaholic-symptom-engendered psychological and physiological tension such as arousal of anxiety emotions and muscle tension during the exercise. They learn to tell the difference between a tense and a relaxed state, transforming the former into the latter. When the more relaxed behavior is routinely practiced, it helps clients get accustomed to more easy-going behavior in dealing with their thinking and feeling on issues related to their vocational life, which is preoccupied with and dependent on a workaholic schema.

Desensitize anxiety arousal Closely connected to relaxation training, systematic desensitization is a commonly used behavioral modification technique. It helps workaholic clients increase or decrease an activity on a gradual basis, so that they can learn to get used to a more desirable situation or behavior in their worklife. Clients are taught to engage in behaviors that compete with their work-obsessed anxiety. For example, clients feel very anxious if they do not complete a task in hand, and this becomes their self-imposed excuse to prolong their work hours. To encounter their anxiety in this context, they are asked to finish their REBT desensitization homework of reducing their work time every day. This work time reduction can begin with 10 minutes per day for the first week, and then the length of this 'leaving-early' time can be gradually increased in the subsequent weeks and months. Parallel efforts can be made to gradually decrease the work assignments that clients feel obliged to take on.

Similarly, the immediate demand to have a work-free day-off can be an unimaginable and unrealistic expectation for a workaholic. Instead, clients can be asked to spend a few hours on their personal and/or familial life activities and leisure during the weekends of the first month of the therapy.

From there, the work-free time can be gradually extended in the coming months. This deliberate practice of the gradual increase or decrease of certain types of workaholic behaviors can lead to a systematic change in clients' habits. Clients become less sensitive or desensitized to the work-obsessed thoughts, emotions and behaviors. The key rationale for behavior change here is taking one small step at a time, ensuring the normalization and stabilization of the small progress made before proceeding to the next, larger step for minimizing and eliminating the irrational behaviors. Of central importance in this therapeutic process is that clients are required to expose themselves to the continuing action that encounters the anxiety arousal, and then reduce this arousal by persistence and commitment in the practice of appropriate and productive behaviors.

Improve self-management   To engage clients in self-management training can be a very useful approach for correcting workaholic behaviors. Self-management in this treatment process focuses on helping clients acquire and utilize a combination of effective coping mechanisms that will facilitate and maintain a healthy work–life balance, leading to an optimal state of mental and physical wellbeing in clients' life experiences – personal, social and vocational alike. Following Burwell and Chen (2002), clients can come to learn and implement self-management techniques as follows.

Reorganizing workload   Workaholic clients need to re-examine and rearrange their work responsibility in a logical and reasonable manner. In dong so, they learn to entrust other people with tasks. This means that clients have to disengage themselves from the overload work assignments that they have self-imposed under the impulsivity of workaholism. The counselor can help clients prioritize their objectives and expectations in the reorganization effort, so that a concrete and attainable workload can be planned and implemented.

Establishing boundaries   Setting boundaries to confine the timeline and workload is advisable (Burke, 1999). This refers to assuming the realistic and attainable work duties within an eight-hour workday. It is of vital importance that this routine practice is observed in a serious manner, and workaholic clients should not give a self-serving excuse to break the boundaries. Clients tell themselves: 'I have to stop and leave my work because my work time is up for today.' They may need to adjust and reallocate their tasks if they find repeatedly that they cannot successfully complete them within the planned timelines. This might be an indication that their objectives are not optimal, and a reassessment and more attainable work plan are required. A general rule to keep in mind is that clients should not accept and overburden themselves with a substantial number of new tasks when they are still busily working to fulfill their ongoing work commitment(s).

<u>Engaging in various life activities</u>   To participate in and enrich other activities in life can be an effective way to approach a more optimal work–life balance. Clients come to learn that they need to allocate their time and energy to various aspects of personal, interpersonal, familial and social life experiences. For example, they need to include social and leisure activities as necessary components in their lives in order to maintain their psychological and physiological wellbeing, which in turn will enhance their vocational wellbeing. Workaholic clients often have little or no knowledge of how to take these non-worklife-related activities, especially leisure activities, into their total life structure. With the didactic teaching and guidance from counseling sessions, clients are vigorously encouraged and facilitated to pursue various meaningful life projects such as to renew a long-time leisure interest, develop interests and hobbies for new and unknown leisure and health-enhancing activities and other familial, communal and socialization activities. For example, a client may be surprised by the enrichment of being involved in a few volunteer hours he or she has contributed to serving a needy group. Similarly, workaholic clients may find a substantial improvement in their relationships with their loved ones when some fixed weekends and holiday times are devoted to their families without worrying about their ongoing duties and assignments at the workplace.

CONCLUSION

Workaholism is a mental health hazard that has negative impact on all aspects of an individual's life. Professional therapists are called upon to help workaholic clients deal with this problem, improving their quality of life by achieving a work–life balance. The foregoing analysis has proposed the use of REBT as a therapeutic alternative for the treatment of the workaholic syndrome. It argues that the theoretical framework of REBT appears to provide some promise for the intervention process for workaholic clients. Following the central principle of the A-B-C theory of human psychological functioning, REBT provides a range of cognitive, emotive and behavioral strategies that can be quite applicable to minimizing and correcting the negative influences of workaholism in individuals' life-career pursuits.

A point worth noting is that, while the current analytical discussion has explored the applicability of REBT in the therapeutic context for workaholism in a general and synthesized manner, workaholic clients often struggle with their irrational and inappropriate lifestyle for various reasons. In this sense, each workaholic client carries his or her unique background experiences that have to be taken into serious consideration during the treatment process. This requires that counselors and therapists be sensitive to the specific needs of each client and be situational in utilizing REBT concepts and techniques in the helping process. It is expected that not all REBT strategies will work effectively for each individual workaholic case. Also, REBT may work more effectively with some workaholic clients if techniques from other therapeutic approaches are integrated into the helping intervention. With such awareness and openness in mind, helping practitioners, as well as clients, can appreciate the clinical value of REBT in tackling the workaholic problem and similar psychological difficulties. It is this clinical value that can contribute to improving the pivotal work–life balance in individuals' personal and vocational wellbeing.

REFERENCES

Bernard, M.E. (ed.) (1991), *Using Rational-emotive Therapy Effectively*, New York: Plenum.

Bonebright, C.A., Clay, D.L. and Ankenmann, R.D. (2000), 'The relationship of workaholism with work–life conflict, life satisfaction, and purpose in life', *Journal of Counseling Psychology*, **47**, 469–77.

Burke, R.J. (1999), 'Workaholism among women managers: personal and workplace correlates', *Journal of Managerial Psychology*, **15**, 520–34.

Burke, R.J. (2001), 'Workaholism in organizations', *International Journal of Stress Management*, **8** (2), 65–8.

Burke, R.J., Richardsen, A.R. and Martinussen, M. (2004), 'Workaholism among Norwegian managers: work and well-being outcomes', *Journal of Organizational Change Management*, **17**, 459–70.

Burwell, R. and Chen, C.P. (2002), 'Applying REBT to workaholic clients', *Counselling Psychology Quarterly*, **15** (3), 219–28.

Caproni, P.J. (1997), 'Work/life balance: you can't get there from here', *The Journal of Applied Behavioral Science*, **33**, 46–56.

Chen, C.P. (2003), 'Workaholism and its coping strategies', paper presented at the 64th Annual Convention of Canadian Psychology Association, Hamilton, Ontario, *Canadian Psychology*, **44** (2a), 106.

Corey, G. (2001), *Theory and Practice of Counseling and Psychology*, 6th edn, Belmont, CA: Wadsworth/Thomson Learning.

Dryden, W. (1983), 'Vivid RET II: disputing methods', *Journal of Rational-EmotiveTherapy*, **1** (1), 9–13.

Dryden, W. (1989), 'Albert Ellis: an efficient and passionate life', *Journal of Counseling and Development*, **67**, 539–46.

Dryden, W. (1995), *Brief Rational Emotive Behaviour Therapy*, London: Wiley.

Ellis, A. (1962), *Reason and Emotion in Psychotherapy*, New York: Lyle Stuart.

Ellis, A. (1971), *Growth Through Reason*, Hollywood, CA: Wilshire Books.

Ellis, A. (1973), *Humanistic Psychotherapy: the Rational-emotive Approach*, New York: Julian Press.

Ellis, A. (1991), 'The revised ABC's of rational-emotive therapy', in J. Zeig (ed.), *The Evolution of Psychotherapy: the Second Conference*, New York: Brunner/Mazel. (Expanded version: *Journal of Rational-Emotive and Cognitive-Behavior Therapy*, **9**, 139–72).

Ellis, A. (1994), *Reason and Emotion in Psychotherapy Revised*, Secaucus, NJ: Birch Lane.

Ellis, A. (1995), 'Changing Rational-Emotive Therapy (RET) to Rational Emotive Behavior Therapy (REBT)', *Journal of Rational-Emotive and Cognitive-Behavior Therapy*, **13**, 85–90.

Ellis, A. (1997), 'The evolution of Albert Ellis and rational-emotive behavior therapy', in J.K. Zeig (ed.), *The Evolution of Psychotherapy: the Third Conference*, New York: Brunner/Mazel, pp. 69–82.

Ellis, A. (1998), *How to Control Your Anxiety Before it Controls You*, Secaucus, NJ: Carol Publishing Group.

Ellis, A. (1999), *How to Make Yourself Happy and Remarkably Less Disturbable*, San Luis Ohispo, CA: Impact.

Ellis, A. (2000), 'Rational emotive behavior therapy', in R.J. Corsini and D. Wedding (eds), *Current Psychotherapies*, Itasca, IL: F.E. Peacock Publishers, pp. 168–204.

Ellis, A. and Bernard, M.E. (1985), *Clinical Applications of Rational-emotive Therapy*, New York: Plenum Publishing Corporation.

Ellis, A. and Dryden, W. (1997), *The Practice of Rational-emotive Therapy*, rev. edn, New York: Springer.

Ellis, A. and Harper, R.A. (1997), *A Guide to Rational Living*, 3rd edn, Hollywood, CA: Wilshire.

Ellis, A. and MacLaren, C. (1998), *Rational Emotive Behavior Therapy: a Therapist's Guide*, San Luis Obispo, CA: Impact.

Killinger, B. (1991), *Workaholics: the Respectable Addicts*, Toronto: Key Porter Books.

McMillan, L.H.W. and O'Driscoll, M.P. (2004), 'Workaholism and health: implications for organizations', *Journal of Organizational Change Management*, **17**, 509–19.

Naughton, T.J. (1987), 'A conceptual view of workaholism and implications for career counseling and research', *The Career Development Quarterly*, **35**, 180–87.

Neenan, M. and Dryden, W. (2000), *Essential Rational Emotive Behavior Therapy*, London: Whurr Publishers.

Porter, G. (1996), 'Organizational impact of workaholism: suggestions for researching the negative outcomes of excessive work', *Journal of Occupational Health Psychology*, **70**, 70–83.

Porter, G. (2004), 'Work, work ethic, work excess', Journal of Organizational Change Management, **17**, 424–39.

Robinson, B. (1998), *Chained to the Desk: a Guidebook for Workaholics, Their Partners and Children, and the Clinicians Who Treat Them*, New York: University Press.

Robinson, B.E. (2000), 'Workaholism: bridging the gap between workplace, socio-cultural, and family research', *Journal of Employment Counseling*, **37**, 31–47.

Seybold, K.C. and Salomone, P.R. (1994), 'Understanding workaholism: a review of causes and counseling approaches', *Journal of Counseling and Development*, **73**, 4–9.

Spence, J.T. and Robbins, A.S. (1992), 'Workaholism: definition, measurement and preliminary results', *Journal of Personality Assessment*, **58**, 160–78.

Taris, T.W., Schaufeli, W.B. and Verhoeven, L.C. (2005), 'Workaholism in the Netherlands: measurement and implications for job strain and work–nonwork conflict', *Applied Psychoplogy: An International Review*, **54**, 37–60.
Trimpey, J. (1993), 'Rational recovery from addictions', in W. Dryden and L.K. Hill (eds), *Innovations in Rational-Emotive Therapy*, Newbury Park, CA: Sage Publications, pp. 253–71.
Tyler, K. (1999), 'Spinning wheels', *HR Magazine*, **44**, 34–40.
Walen, S.R., DiGiuseppe, R. and Dryden, W. (1992), *A Practitioner's Guide to Rational-Emotive Therapy*, 2nd edn, New York: Oxford University Press.

15. Spiritual leadership theory as a source for future theory, research, and recovery from workaholism

Louis W. Fry, Laura L. Matherly and Steve Vitucci

INTRODUCTION

Since Oates (1971, p. 1) first coined the term workaholism as 'addiction to work, the compulsion or the uncontrollable need to work incessantly', researchers have defined workaholism in different ways, with both positive and negative consequences to the individual and the organization (Bonebright et al., 2000; Burke, 2001a; Burke and Matthiesen, 2004; Naughton, 1987; Porter, 1996; Scott et al., 1997; Spence and Robbins, 1992). Although the term is now widely used, there is little consensus about its meaning beyond that of its core element: a substantial investment in work that includes a personal reluctance to disengage from work and a tendency to think about work incessantly (McMillan and O'Driscoll, 2004; Snir and Harpaz, 2004). However, there is an emerging consensus that workaholism is likely to be a central concept in understanding the relationship of workplace experiences and a variety of personal and organizational outcomes, and that, after over 30 years of research, workaholism is still a useful construct (Burke, 2001a, 2004; Griffiths, 2005).

Workaholism seems to be increasing (Burke, 2001a; Fassel, 1990; Griffiths, 2005; Schor, 1991). Reasons for this include increasing complexity of professions, constant pressure to be more efficient, the increased use of technology, and an apparently increased desire for individual achievement, accomplishment and success as a way of enhancing one's self-esteem. Workaholism can be an acceptable addiction that is valued in a society where many, including the sages of corporate America, are quick to claim its influence (Bonebright et al., 2000). Similarly, workaholism is viewed as a positive attribute by employers, who may even recruit workaholics. However, there is evidence that workaholism can make either a positive or a negative contribution to the satisfaction and well-being of organizational members.

Numerous researchers have posited that there are different types of workaholics (Burke, 2000; Fassel, 1990; Naughton, 1987; Oates, 1971; Robinson, 1998; Scott et al., 1997; Spence and Robbins, 1992). In this study, the two types of workaholics identified by Spence and Robbins (1992) and further researched by Bonebright et al. (2000) – the enthusiastic workaholic and the nonenthusiastic workaholic – are examined. Although both types are defined as persons exhibiting high work involvement and a high drive to work, the enthusiastic workaholic reports high enjoyment of work while the nonenthusiastic workaholic reports low enjoyment (Spence and Robbins, 1992). The enthusiastic workaholic's reason for excessive work is attributed to the immense fulfillment and enjoyment derived from work. These workaholics seem to experience relatively high levels of positive human health and psychological well-being. Nonenthusiastic workaholics engage in excessive work owing to an uncontrollable urge or need to work, even when little or only momentary satisfaction is derived, and have been found to have significantly higher work–life conflict and lower levels of life satisfaction and purpose in life than enthusiastic workaholics (Bonebright et al., 2000).

This chapter draws from the emerging spiritual leadership paradigm (Fry, 2005b) to integrate the dispersed theory and research on workaholism. Drawing from previous theory and research, workaholism is defined as substantial investment in work that includes a personal reluctance to disengage from work and a tendency to think about work incessantly. We first review theories of extrinsic and intrinsic motivation and argue that enthusiastic workaholism is rooted in intrinsic motivation and is positively related to personal and organizational outcomes, while nonenthusiastic workaholism is based on extrinsic motivation and is negatively related to personal and organizational outcomes. Next, spiritual leadership theory is reviewed and used to explain these differences in positive human health and psychological well-being for enthusiastic and nonenthusiastic workaholics. Then, drawing on the recovery literature, we propose that workaholism is actually a continuum that can result in various degrees or levels of positive human health and psychological and spiritual well-being. Finally we discuss implications for future research and HRM practice in addressing the recovery and development of nonenthusiastic workaholics and the organizations which nurture them.

WORKAHOLISM AND MOTIVATION THEORY

Motivation includes the forces, either external or internal, on a person that arouse enthusiasm and persistence to pursue a certain course of action.

Motivation is primarily concerned with what energizes human behavior, what directs or channels such behavior, and how this behavior is maintained or sustained. The basic building blocks of a generalized model of the motivation process are needs or expectations, behavior, goals or performance, rewards and some form of feedback (Galbraith, 1977; Steers and Porter, 1983). Most contemporary theorists assume that people initiate and persist in behaviors to the extent that they believe the behaviors will lead to desired outcomes or goals (Deci and Ryan, 2000). Positive motivation in the workplace results when leaders create an environment that brings out the best in people as they achieve and receive individual, group and system-wide rewards. It refers to those desires that, coupled with the expectation of rewards contingent on performance, cause the individual to exert effort above minimum levels, be spontaneous and exhibit exploratory/cooperative behaviors (Galbraith, 1977).

There are two basic types of motivation: extrinsic and intrinsic. Figure 15.1 illustrates the distinction between them. Extrinsic motivation consists of behaviors that are motivated by factors external to the individual. Extrinsic rewards are given by others and may be individual, group-based or system-wide (Galbraith, 1977). Examples include promotions, pay increases, bonus payments, pressure to perform, supervisory behavior, insurance benefits and vacation time. Extrinsic rewards originate externally and require meeting or exceeding the expectations of others. Under extrinsic motivation individuals feel compelled to engage in task behavior for an outside source to satisfy lower-order needs, that is, to provide what they need (for example, money) to survive.

Intrinsic motivation is most basically defined as interest in and enjoyment of an activity for its own sake and is associated with active engagement in tasks that people find interesting and that, in turn, promote growth and satisfy higher-order needs. Intrinsic motivation has been shown to be associated with better learning, performance and well-being (Benware and Deci, 1984; Deci and Ryan, 1985; Valas and Sovik, 1993). It is believed to result from an individual's basic needs for competence, autonomy and relatedness.

Competence is a feeling or sense of craftsmanship or artistry in task accomplishment, that one is responding well to task situations, has mastery of the task or its activities, and is confident about handling similar tasks in the future. Autonomy tends to increase intrinsic motivation to the extent that there is an internally perceived locus of causality, task accomplishment is under one's control, and one feels free to exert extra effort in following one's inner interests. Moreover, intrinsic motivation will be more likely to flourish in contexts characterized by a sense of secure relatedness, especially when significant others in the task environment are experienced as

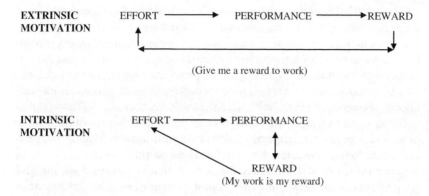

Figure 15.1   Extrinsic versus intrinsic motivation

warm and caring (Ryan and Grolnick, 1986; Ryan and La Guardia, 2000; Ryan et al., 1994).

Intrinsic rewards involving task performance are internal and under the control of the individual, to satisfy higher-order needs for competency, self-determination and self-fulfillment. These rewards result from the internal experience one has in performing a task that gives satisfaction through its performance. Solving a problem at work that benefits others or that may fulfill a personal mission or purpose, being part of a 'winning' team, or completing a complex task that gives a pleasant feeling of accomplishment are examples. For individuals experiencing intrinsic motivation the performance of the task becomes the reward. In this sense performance and rewards are fused, indistinguishable, or become one and the same (See Figure 15.1).

Enthusiastic Workaholism and Intrinsic Motivation

Enthusiastic workaholics experience immense enjoyment and fulfillment from work (Snir and Harpaz, 2004; Sprankel and Ebel, 1987; Warr, 1999). Hence, their impulse to work incessantly may be based on intrinsic motivation that leads to a sense of self-worth and produces positive personal and organizational outcomes. They seem to love their work and have a desire to work long and hard (Canatrow, 1979; Machlowitz, 1980). These workaholics seek passionate involvement, gratification and the 'joy of creativity' through their work. Enthusiastic workaholics strive for achievement and success, are stimulated by competition, are able to delay gratification and can focus on distant goals.

However, unlike nonworkaholics who possess these achievement-oriented qualities, enthusiastic workaholics spend a great deal of discretionary time on work activities, constantly think about work, work beyond employer and economic requirements, and describe their work as satisfying, fun, creative and stimulating. In addition, they are, compared with nonworkaholics, hypothesized to experience higher organizational commitment and performance and be more likely to engage in prosocial organizational behavior, which may enhance the organizational contributions of enthusiastic workaholics (Bonebright et al., 2000; Kiechel, 1989; Scott et al., 1997).

Intrinsic motivation in the workplace requires some degree of autonomy or self-management. Intrinsically motivated enthusiastic workaholics experience autonomy, competence and relatedness working either alone or in empowered teams that are directing their activities toward a meaningful purpose and doing something they regard as significant. They take pride in their work and are excited at having a sense of progress and seeing the results of their efforts (Conger and Kanungo, 1988; Spreitzer; 1996; Thomas, 2000).

Enthusiastic workaholics can also be intrinsically motivated at work through goal identification. Goal identification occurs to the extent that individuals have internalized into their own value systems the vision and values of the organization and the goals or sub-goals the organization is pursuing (Galbraith, 1977). The goals have value to the individual because they acquired them through a long process of socialization in the organization or because they participated in developing the organization's vision, values and goals and therefore have high acceptance of and are highly committed to them. The achievement of these goals then is instrumental in satisfying one's higher-order (spiritual) needs for self-esteem, relatedness and growth. It is through this process that behaviors perceived to be instrumental to goal attainment acquire value and become intrinsically rewarding.

Furthermore, high work and life satisfaction for the enthusiastic workaholic is also hypothesized to be dependent on the extent to which they are able to meet their work aspirations. Factors which could lead to lower personal and organizational outcomes include (Scott et al., 1997):

1.   restriction of job autonomy or flexibility to meet personal goals;
2.   inability to experience feelings of high achievement;
3.   pressure to accept family responsibilities or spend time in nonworking activities.

Interestingly, it appears that enthusiastic workaholics are not dependent on or obsessed with work and have the ability to disengage from working without harmful effects. But, unlike nonenthusiastic workaholics, even though they may choose to continue working to pursue personal achievement, enthusiastic workaholics are able to more effectively use stress management techniques, have little expressed anger, demonstrate more adaptability and creativity at work, and experience fewer physical and psychological problems (ibid.).

Nonenthusiastic Workaholism and Extrinsic Motivation

Extrinsic motivation is manifested by behaviors that are motivated by factors or forces that are external to the individual. The individual looks for rewards that are given by individuals, groups, the organization or the system (Galbraith, 1977). The rewards originate externally and require that a person meet or exceed the expectations of others. People are compelled to complete tasks to receive an external benefit provided by others in order to survive within the organization (Fry, 2003).

The traditional centralized, standardized and formalized models for bureaucratic organizations based on extrinsic motivation were highly successful during the industrial and machine age. The primary motivation used within these organizations was the external reward systems. These reward systems ensured minimum levels of effort, organizational compliance and performance (Daft, 2005; Fry, 2003). The rewards came from promotions, pay increases, bonus payments, pressure to perform and close supervision of the workforce. The organizations and methods of rewards prevented the individual from feeling good about their work. People within these organizations often found themselves feeling powerless and with little confidence. Behaviors within these organizations were compliance, little enthusiasm and almost no opportunity to be creative and innovative within the workplace (Ryan and Oestrich, 1991; Fry, 2003). Extrinsic motivation also leads to reduced trust, reduced communications and job dissatisfaction.

We propose that the nonenthusiastic workaholic's impulse to work incessantly may be based on extrinsic motivation, which results in a sense of negative self-worth and negative personal and organizational outcomes. It is also hypothesized that nonenthusiastic workaholics have an obsessive-compulsive personality that is manifested through a pervasive pattern of preoccupation with orderliness, perfectionism and mental and interpersonal control that reduces flexibility, openness, creativity and efficiency (Mudrack, 2004). At the extreme, nonenthusiastic workaholism can be an addiction rooted in the desire for the emotional 'rush' from receiving the extrinsic rewards of hard work that can crowd out family and almost all other activities (Bonebright et al., 2000; Griffiths, 2005; Kiechel, 1989).

This type of workaholism is both a negative and a complex process that eventually affects a person's ability to function and perform effectively (Griffiths, 2005; Killinger, 1992). At its heart is a compulsive-dependent drive to gain external approval from others and the trappings of success. It is hypothesized that, compared with enthusiastic workaholics and non-workaholics, nonenthusiastic workaholics experience higher levels of pessimism, impaired judgment, stress and burnout and have more personality breakdowns and health-related problems (for example, exhaustion, insomnia, agitation/enervation, substance abuse, cardiovascular complaints, depression, anger, apathy and secondary addictions such as drugs or alcohol) and lower life satisfaction. They also experience limited pleasure, satisfaction or enjoyment from their work and are perfectionists who engage in inflexible and controlling work activities because of their desire for personal control. Often, they impose unreasonable work standards, have more hostile interpersonal relationships, resist compromise and are less likely to delegate work to others, as compared with enthusiastic workaholics and nonworkaholics (Bonebright et al., 2000; Porter, 1996; Scott et al., 1997). These are characteristics that employers do not desire, because they slow progress and reduce flexibility and efficiency, thereby creating performance problems for the organization.

SPIRITUAL LEADERSHIP THEORY AND WORKAHOLISM

Attracting, keeping and motivating high-performers continues to be an important issue in contemporary organizations. The dramatic globalization of economic activity during the last twenty years and the subsequent 'flattening of the world' (Friedman, 2005) have exacerbated this challenge. Lawler (2000) identifies four major changes that will contribute to this increasingly complex environment: a boundaryless economy, worldwide labor markets, instantly linked information and agile new organizations. While the challenge was formerly faced only in advanced economies such as the United States, Japan and Europe, these factors have extended the challenge of attracting and motivating high-performers to emerging economies as well. Thus, the creation of work environments that provide a sense of challenge and meaningfulness for employees has become a priority. In fact, creating such a work environment may very well be the strategic imperative of the new century. This perspective has been articulated by Whetten and Cameron (1998) who concluded that 'good people management' is more important than all other factors in predicting profitability.

The practices suggested by Lawler (2000) are consistent with the perspectives of the organization transformation (OT) extension of organization development. OT seeks to create massive changes in an organization's orientation towards its environment, vision, goals and strategies, structures, processes and organizational culture. Its purpose is to effect large-scale, paradigm-shifting change. The overall goal of OT is to simultaneously improve organizational effectiveness and individual well-being (French et al., 2000, p. vii).

The organizational transformation that will respond most effectively to these forces for change will require a major shift to a learning mindset that is radically different from the traditional centralized, standardized and formalized bureaucratic organizational form based on fear that has dominated organizations since the beginning of the industrial revolution (Ancona et al., 1999; Fry, 2003; Gini, 1998). A learning organization is one in which expansive patterns of thinking are nurtured and collective aspiration is set free. People in learning organizations are intrinsically motivated and empowered to achieve a clearly articulated organizational vision. They are continually learning to learn together to expand their capacity to create desired results (Senge, 1990). This new networked or learning organizational paradigm is radically different from what has gone before: it is love-led, customer/client-obsessed, intrinsically motivated, empowered, team-based, flat (in structure), flexible (in capabilities), diverse (in personnel make-up) and networked (working with many other organizations in a symbiotic relationship) in alliances with suppliers, customers/clients and even competitors, and innovative and global (Ancona et al., 1999).

Leaders attempting to initiate and implement organizational transformations face daunting challenges, especially in gaining widespread acceptance of a new and challenging vision and the need for often drastic and abrupt change in the organization's culture (Cummins and Worley, 2005; Harvey and Brown, 2001). The two streams of thought emerging within the field of organizational studies that have important implications for organizational transformation are positive organizational scholarship and workplace spirituality. The foundations of these studies have been presented in three handbooks (Cameron et al., 2003; Giacalone and Jurkiewicz, 2003; Snyder and Lopez, 2001).

Spiritual leadership theory is an emerging paradigm for organization development and transformation that draws from these two areas and has the potential to guide the evolution of positive organizations where human well-being and organization-level performance can not only coexist but can also be optimized. Fry (2003, 2005a) and Fry and Matherly (2005) have developed a causal theory of spiritual leadership and performance excellence which discusses in some detail the implementation process using an intrinsic motivation model that incorporates vision, hope/faith and altruistic love, theories of workplace spirituality, and spiritual survival/well-being.

Spiritual leadership taps into the fundamental needs of both leader and follower for spiritual survival through calling and membership. It seeks to create vision and value congruence across the individual, empowered team and organization levels and, ultimately, to foster higher levels of organizational commitment and productivity. A major proposition of spiritual leadership theory is that spiritual leadership is necessary for the transformation to and continued success of learning organizations.

Operationally, spiritual leadership comprises the values, attitudes and behaviors that are necessary to intrinsically motivate oneself and others so that they have a sense of spiritual well-being through calling and membership (Figures 15.2 and 15.3). This entails (Fry 2003, 2005b):

1. creating a vision wherein leaders and followers experience a sense of calling in that their life has meaning and makes a difference;
2. establishing a social/organizational culture based on the values of altruistic love whereby leaders and followers have a sense of membership, feel understood and appreciated, and have genuine care, concern and appreciation for *both* self and others.

Fry (2005a) extended spiritual leadership theory by exploring the concept of positive human health and well-being through recent developments in workplace spirituality, character ethics, positive psychology and spiritual leadership. These areas provide a consensus on the values, attitudes and behaviors necessary for positive human health and well-being. Ethical well-being is defined as authentically living one's values, attitudes and behavior from the inside out in creating a principled center congruent with the universal, consensus values inherent in spiritual leadership theory (Cashman, 1998; Covey, 1991; Fry, 2005a).

Ethical well-being is then seen as necessary but not sufficient for spiritual well-being, which, in addition to ethical well-being, incorporates transcendence of self in pursuit of a vision/purpose/mission in service to key stakeholders to satisfy one's need for spiritual survival through calling and membership. Individuals practicing spiritual leadership at the personal level will score high on both life satisfaction in terms of joy, peace and serenity and the Ryff and Singer (2001) dimensions of well-being. In other words, they will:

1. experience greater psychological well-being
2. have fewer problems related to physical health in terms of allostatic load (cardiovascular disease, cognitive impairment, declines in physical functioning, and mortality).

More specifically, they will have a high regard for themselves and their past life, good-quality relationships with others, a sense that life is purposeful

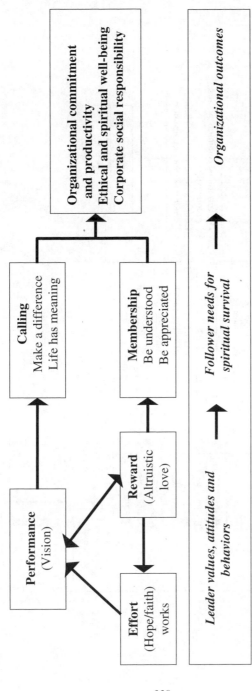

Source: Fry (2003).

Figure 15.2 Causal model of spiritual leadership

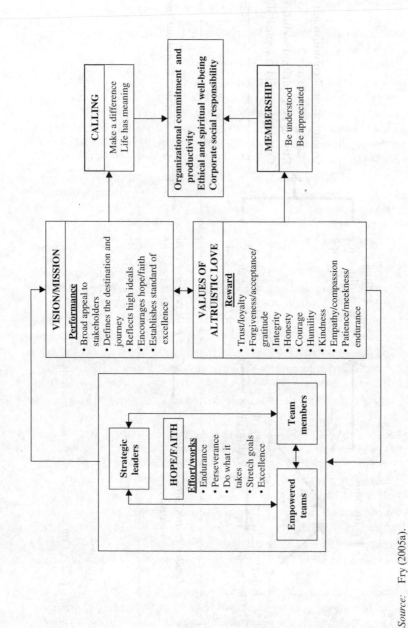

Source: Fry (2005a).

Figure 15.3 Spiritual leadership as a source of ethical and spiritual well-being and corporate social responsibility

and meaningful, the capacity to effectively manage their surrounding world, the ability to follow inner convictions, and a sense of continuing growth and self-realization.

Spiritual Leadership Theory and Enthusiastic Workaholism

Spiritual leadership theory may be used to explain the apparent contradictory condition wherein one can seem to be obsessed with work yet have high levels of psychological well-being, positive human health and organizational commitment and productivity. The enthusiastic workaholic will be energized by a job that is intrinsically motivating. To the extent that the spiritual leadership paradigm is implemented (Fry, 2003; Fry, 2005b; Fry et al., 2005; Malone and Fry, 2003), enthusiastic workaholics will be intrinsically motivated and will experience competence, autonomy, relatedness and spiritual well-being; ultimately, they may literally feel they have found 'heaven on earth'.

Spiritual Leadership Theory and Nonenthusiastic Workaholism

Spiritual leadership theory can also be used to explain the low levels of psychological well-being and positive human health and the dysfunctional organizational behavior of nonenthusiastic workaholics. Conventional organizational approaches rely on extrinsic motivation to appeal to individuals' lower, basic needs and rely on extrinsic rewards and punishments – carrot-and-stick methods – to motivate people to behave in ways that may be preferred organizationally but not be personally satisfying. Under these organizational conditions, the nonenthusiastic workaholic may perform adequately to receive the 'carrot' or avoid the 'stick', but they will not necessarily derive satisfaction from their work (Bonebright et al., 2000; Daft, 2005; Spence and Robbins, 1992).

However, although extrinsic rewards can appear to be quite effective, they are neither adequate nor productive motivators and may even be, for several reasons, detrimental to organizational performance over the long run (Daft, 2005). First, extrinsic rewards assume people are driven by lower needs and act to diminish intrinsic rewards, since the motivation to seek an extrinsic reward, whether a bonus or approval, leads people to focus on the reward rather on the nature of the work they do to achieve it. This type of reward-seeking behavior necessarily diminishes the focus and satisfaction people receive from the process of working. In addition, extrinsic rewards are temporary and targeted to short-term success but often at the expense of long-term quality. Thus, giving people extrinsic rewards undermines their interest in the work itself to the point that, if there is a lack of intrinsic rewards, performance levels out or stays barely adequate to reach the reward. This situation can also cause dysfunctional organizational behaviors to the extent that people will do what it takes to get the reward even if it ultimately hurts the organization's effectiveness (for example, unethical and/or hazardous activities).

Most importantly from a personal spiritual leadership perspective (Fry, 2005a), the focus on extrinsic rewards by the nonenthusiastic workaholic prevents them from satisfying their fundamental spiritual needs for calling and membership owing to an ego-driven, obsessive-compulsive need for self-gratification. The frustrations inherent in the relentless pursuit of self-gratification lead to negative thinking that creates negative emotions, which then unleash biochemical enzymes in the body that create destructive physical side effects. Continued high levels of stress cause the release of adrenaline, which destroys the immune system and leads to elevated amounts of dangerous cholesterol that clogs arteries. Anger, hostility and hurry release adrenaline, which causes high heart rate and blood pressure, which ultimately leads to damaged arteries and heart attack (Robinson, 1998). When taken to the extreme, this leads to the sort of spiritual death inherent in addiction that is the major target of 12-step recovery programs. Thus, a nonenthusiastic workaholic addict would have a preoccupation with the external rewards received from work that would lead to mood modification (either an arousing 'high' or, paradoxically, a tranquilizing feeling of 'escape' or 'numbing'). This activates a chemical (adrenaline) in the body whereby increasing extrinsic rewards are required to achieve the mood-altering effects. Eventually, there are withdrawal symptoms or unpleasant feelings or physical effects if the work cycle is interrupted. As the obsession escalates into compulsion, the person begins to experience increasing internal and external conflict with other activities and those around them. Finally there will be recurring reversions to earlier patterns of excessive work after periods of attempts at control (Griffiths, 2005).

SPIRITUAL LEADERSHIP THEORY AS A SOURCE FOR FUTURE THEORY, RESEARCH, AND RECOVERY FROM WORKAHOLISM

The trend in recent years in most industries and organizations is that every change increases demands on people to do more with less and then with less again (Porter, 2004). Work hour inflation is growing, not just in the United States but globally. While about 17 per cent of managers worked more than 60 hours a week in 2004, the 45–55-hour workweek is now the norm (Mandel, 2005). There is even an emerging class of extreme jobs requiring

80–100-hour weeks that are considered to be a dream for a group of elite workers who thrive on their challenge (Tisehler, 2005).

Why is it that some individuals seem to feel stretched to the limit while others thrive under the pressure? Applying the intrinsic/extrinsic theory of motivation can reconcile conflicting observations and conclusions about the existence of different types of workaholic behavior patterns and their impact on individual and organizational outcomes, such as performance, commitment and physical and psychological well-being.

We propose that the type of motivation that some people use to drive themselves to workaholic levels is directly related to their level of positive human health, psychological well-being and performance at work. Enthusiastic workaholics seek intrinsic rewards and, to the extent they can achieve them, are able to satisfy the higher-order needs, which is necessary for spiritual and psychological well-being and positive human health.

It may be that enthusiastic workaholism is a lifestyle choice rather than an addiction. Today's management literature is filled with the notion that workers can achieve work–life balance (Mandel, 2005; Farrell, 2005). Leaders whose values, attitudes and behaviors can intrinsically motivate their workers by meeting their spiritual needs will achieve organizational commitment and productivity as well as ethical and spiritual well-being and, ultimately, positive human health and psychological well-being (Fry, 2005a). These leaders are able to assist workers in realizing their calling and help them to see that their contributions make a difference both to the organization and to society in general. These leaders help their workers to feel appreciated for their contributions. The key to well-being is for the leaders to meet the spiritual needs of the individual and the workgroup through intrinsic motivation. It is also possible for some people to initially engage in enthusiastic workaholic behaviors and later opt to satisfy their higher-order needs for spiritual well-being through other outlets such as family or community service (Tisehler, 2005). Others may choose to make their work the primary means of satisfying these needs and forgo marriage, family and other outside commitments.

Nonenthusiastic Workaholic Recovery

Spiritual leadership theory has been offered as an emerging paradigm necessary for the transformation to the learning organization paradigm that has the potential to guide the evolution of positive organizations where human well-being and organization-level performance can not only coexist but can also be optimized. Spiritual leadership theory may also be considered a general model that can be used to guide the development of more specific models (Fry, 2003, 2005a; Fry and Whittington, 2005; Matherly et al., 2005).

Nonenthusiastic workaholics are motivated by extrinsic rewards that appeal to the lower needs of individuals, such as material comfort and possessions, safety and security. They also seem to have a high need for external approval and recognition from others. Through this egoistic, obsessive-compulsive focus on satisfying external, lower-order needs at the expense of higher-order needs, nonenthusiastic workaholics may find themselves slipping into or entrapped in a deadly addictive cycle (Robinson, 1998).

We propose the 12-step recovery process as a specific model of spiritual leadership for personal transformation of nonenthusiastic workaholics. At the heart of all 12-step programs is a fellowship based in unconditional or altruistic love where the person in recovery can find people who share their particular obsession-compulsion (for example, alcohol, drugs, gambling, nicotine, overeating, shopping, work) and have worked the 12-step program. Through their program workaholics have found a purpose in life based in intrinsic motivation and now have a sense of calling, membership and spiritual well-being. In addition, they have become productive and committed members of their organizations, family and society who must give to other suffering workaholics what they have been freely given or else lose what they have (Workaholics Anonymous, 2005).

To illustrate this process we refer to Figure 15.3 and offer Figure 15.4. We propose that workaholism is actually a continuum that, depending on the basis of motivation (extrinsic or intrinsic), can result in various degrees or levels of positive human health and psychological and spiritual well-being. Figure 15.4 also has as its base the proposition that, if spiritual leadership is used as a paradigm with the 12-step program of recovery as a specific model for personal recovery and development, the negative outcomes of workaholism can be transformed to positive. Once this point is reached on the continuum, it is hypothesized that the enthusiastic workaholic will move from an extrinsic to an intrinsic motivation base. They may

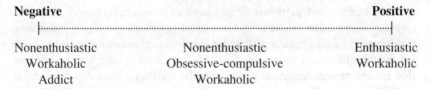

Positive human heath
Psychological well-being
Spiritual well-being

Negative		**Positive**
Nonenthusiastic	Nonenthusiastic	Enthusiastic
Workaholic	Obsessive-compulsive	Workaholic
Addict	Workaholic	

Figure 15.4   Continuum of workaholism

also develop the ability to choose other sources of intrinsic motivation (for example, family, community service) if a more balanced work-life is desired. In any case, even if they choose to remain enthusiastic workaholics, these people should have high levels of positive human health and psychological and spiritual well-being.

It is also proposed that, if nonenthusiastic workaholics experience enough negative consequences of their obsessive-compulsive need to work, are identified and are then given the opportunity by the organization, they will become honest, open-minded and willing enough to join a recovery program such as Workaholics Anonymous. This would follow a similar HRM process to that followed by organizations once they identify people who have drug and/or alcohol problems that are affecting their work. Upon joining the fellowship of Workaholics Anonymous, the nonenthusiastic workaholic freely experiences a sense of being understood and appreciated in a culture based on the values of altruistic love. He/she is also introduced to the vision and purpose of the program – to reach out to fellow workaholics who still suffer. By working the steps, the person in recovery develops hope/faith in the program. This initiates the intrinsic motivation cycle that satisfies the person's needs for calling and membership and ultimately produces positive organizational outcomes such as:

1. increased organizational commitment – people with a sense of calling and membership will do what it takes, become attached to, loyal to, and want to stay in the organization (fellowship);
2. increased productivity and continuous improvement – people who have hope/faith in the organization's vision and who experience calling and membership will 'do what it takes' to continuously improve and be more productive to help the organization (Workaholics Anonymous) achieve its purpose.

Ultimately, the individual experiences a heightened level of spiritual well-being that translates into higher levels of positive human health and psychological well-being.

Nonenthusiastic Workaholic Team and Organizational Recovery

Over time, the processes of employer recruitment and selection, employee self-selection, cultural socialization and reward systems in conventional, fear-based organizations could work to create an organizational culture which would reinforce nonenthusiastic workaholism. We propose that a similar transformation based on the spiritual leadership paradigm is needed for teams and organizations that are led by nonenthusiastic workaholics and/or have cultures that reinforce the nonenthusiastic workaholic's values, attitudes and behaviors.

Spiritual leadership theory's major purpose is to tap into the fundamental needs of both the leader and the follower for spiritual survival/well-being through calling and membership, to create vision and value congruence across the organization, empowered team and individual levels. While a discussion of the process for implementing spiritual leadership is beyond the scope of this chapter and is outlined in some detail elsewhere (Fry, 2003, 2005b; Fry et al., 2005; Fry and Matherly, 2005; Malone and Fry, 2003), spiritual leadership is proposed as a paradigm for organization development and transformation that has the potential to guide the evolution of positive organizations where human well-being and organization-level performance can not only coexist but can also be optimized (Matherly et al., 2005).

Referring to Figure 15.3, leaders who practice spiritual leadership through communicating a transcendent vision and organizational values based in altruistic love will encourage the manifestation of positive performance outcomes for both the individual and the organization (Fry, 2005b). When leaders personify the values, attitudes and behaviors of altruistic love that result in both the leader and employees feeling understood and appreciated, as well as a sense of calling, that their job makes a difference, they will tap into the intrinsic motivation cycle that results in high levels of human well-being and organizational performance (Fry and Matherly, 2005).

Schaef and Fassel (1988) argue that typical organizations in our society reproduce the characteristics which exemplify the substance-addicted individual. Organizations are often 'infected' with paranoid, obsessive-compulsive and depressive neurosis by their chief executives and leaders, and the impact from this unfolds throughout all levels of the organization. As in individuals, self-centeredness, over-control, dogmatism and obstinacy make participation an exercise in rhetoric to protect the position and power of the organization's leaders. This continues despite evidence of the destructive results and lack of ethics in the organization's behavior and prevents attention to the dysfunctional impact of the organization on its employees and its environment.

As on the individual level, there have been calls to apply the 12-step program of recovery to dysfunctional organizations (Mitroff et al., 1994; Robinson, 1998). Mitroff et al. (1994) argue that the vast majority of organizational development training and change techniques that have been developed – team building, sexual harassment, drug abuse, empowerment, motivational uplifting – not only fail to address and solve the problems but may actually help maintain the dysfunctionality of the system. Basically, the organizations that succeed with these techniques do not need them and those that do need them often have leaders who are adept at convincing organizations that are attempting fundamental change when they are not. Mitroff et al. argue that it is no longer sufficient for organizations to hire specialists in these areas. Until this is acknowledged and until programs are developed and adopted that are based on the principles of treating dysfunctional systems as systems, there will be little success in helping these leaders and their organizations to change.

Mitroff et al. (ibid.) envision the recovery and development center as a necessary aspect in the design of modern organizations. It would be implemented using a 12-step recovery model and institutionalized to the point that executives and leaders would see participation in programs of assessment, recovery and development as just as critical and important as learning the new knowledge skills that are necessary for leading and managing global organizations in the Internet age. At the heart of this process is the organization recognizing the need for and then adopting a higher set of ethical principles and values. These are essentially the same values of altruistic love in spiritual leadership theory (Fry, 2005a). So again, we propose a specific model of spiritual leadership theory as a general model that can incorporate the recovery model for team and organizational transformation of nonenthusiastic workaholics and the organizations that have cultures that support them.

CONCLUSION

This chapter has focused on the enthusiastic and the nonenthusiastic workaholic as developed from typologies from previous research. For example, Spence and Robbins (1992) defined two types of workaholics – enthusiastic workaholics, who exhibit high work involvement, a high drive to work and high enjoyment of work, and nonenthusiastic workaholics who also exhibit high work involvement and a high drive to work, but have low enjoyment. We have adopted this distinction between enjoyment and nonenjoyment of work and argued that different types of workaholics can be distinguished by whether they are based on an intrinsic or an extrinsic motivation model.

Scott et al. (1997) provide us with three types of workaholic behavior patterns. They are the compulsive-dependent, the perfectionist and the achievement-oriented workaholics. The first two types are more closely associated with nonenthusiastic workers (Bonebright et al., 2000). These types of workers are often found within the centralized bureaucratic organizations. The compulsive-dependent workaholic will display high levels of anxiety, stress, physical and psychological problems, poor job performance and low job satisfaction. These individuals find little meaning and purpose in life (Scott et al., 1997; Fry, 2003). The perfectionist workaholic is more apt to be identified with higher levels of stress, anxiety, physical and psychological problems, hostile or negative interpersonal relationships, low job satisfaction, poor job performance, high turnover rates and high absenteeism (Scott et al., 1997; Fry, 2003). Finally, the achievement-oriented workaholic is viewed by many as more positive and less likely to be problematic within the organization.

The main problem with the previous research in this area is that constructs such as enjoyment have been used as both dependent and independent variables. In addition, while specific workaholism dimensions may be empirically tested within some models, there is no generally accepted theoretical model that incorporates and explicates specific cultural, follower or effectiveness theoretical dimensions. This lack of specificity is an example of unrationalized categorization at the theoretical level (Stanfield, 1976) and has resulted in a hodgepodge of empirical studies, which, even if reliable and valid, have diffused rather than focused theory building in this area.

Our proposed continuum of workaholism overcomes these shortcomings. It is based on a causal model of spiritual leadership grounded in motivation theory that specifies Dubin's four components that provide the necessary and sufficient conditions for the development of any theoretical model: (1) the units or variables of interest to the researcher, (2) congruence as defined by the laws of relationship among units of the model that specify how they are associated, (3) boundaries within which the laws of relationship are expected to operate, and (4) contingency effects that specify system states within which the units of the theory take on characteristic values that are deterministic and have a persistence through time (Dubin, 1978; Fry and Smith, 1987).

Further research is needed on the beliefs and fears (for example, must constantly prove oneself or else be judged worthless; no moral principles exist so fear that good may not prevail; must strive against others to win or gain) investigated by Burke (2001a) that were the most consistent predictors of negative personal and work outcomes. At the heart of these beliefs and fears are egoistic values that are the antithesis of the values of altruistic love. 'They see the world in "dog-eat-dog" terms, all too often believing that "Nice guys finish last." ' (Burke, 2001a, p. 2355). They seem to lack purpose or a sense of calling that could provide meaning for their own and others' actions. These could be antecedents of nonenthusiastic workaholism that could be used to identify and target potential workaholics for recovery and training. They also could be used to screen job applicants.

When leaders personify these values and lead through fear, they use control strategies that emphasize compliance behavior that relies on the social exchange of valued resources that they can draw from their reward, coercive and legal power base. However, this compliance often leads to self-denial, the loss of self-worth and near destruction of followers' self-esteem for the benefit of the leader. This prevents people from feeling good about their work and leads to dysfunctional avoidance behavior. It can also reduce trust and communication, so that important problems and issues are hidden and suppressed (Daft, 2005; Kanungo and Mendonca, 1996). We have also proposed the 12-step recovery process as a specific model of spiritual leadership for team and organizational transformation of nonenthusiastic workaholics and the organizations that have cultures that support them.

Leaders may also be of assistance to nonproductive workaholics by identifying, coaching and mentoring these individuals and by helping them to find recovery programs such as Workaholics Anonymous. Although these programs are not yet widespread, there are some that exist and may be of great value in helping these individuals move from the negative nonproductive workaholic portion of the continuum to the positive enthusiastic workaholic side. Organizational counselors and healthcare professionals should encourage the formation of WA groups and refer their workaholic employees to them much as they would refer people with alcohol problems to Alcoholics Anonymous. This would require institutionalizing a process targeted at initiating a transformation in the individual that enables him or her to experience higher levels of spiritual well-being. In all instances the goal of the leader is to help the individual to find spiritual and psychological well-being and positive human health while becoming a more positive contributor to the organization and to society.

REFERENCES

Ancona, D., Kochan, T., Scully, M., Van Maanen, J. and Westney, D.E. (1999), *Organizational Behavior and Processes*, Boston: South-Western College Publishing.

Benware, C. and Deci, E.L. (1984), 'Quality of learning with an active and passive motivational set', *American Educational Research Journal*, **21**, 755–65.

Bonebright, C., Clay, D. and Ankenmann, R. (2000), 'The relationship of workaholism with work–life conflict, life satisfaction, and purpose in life', *Journal of Counseling Psychology*, **47** (4), 469–77.

Burke, R.J. (2000), 'Workaholism in organizations: concepts, results and future research directions', *International Journal of Management Reviews*, **2** (1), 1–16.

Burke, R.J. (2001a), 'Workaholism components, job satisfaction, and career progress', *Journal of Applied Social Psychology*, **31** (11), 2339–56.

Burke, R.J. (2001b), 'Workaholism in organizations: the role of organizational values', *Personnel Review*, **30** (6), 637–45.

Burke, R.J. (2004), 'Workaholism in organizations', *Journal of Organizational Change Management*, **17** (5), 420–23.

Burke, R. and Matthiesen, S. (2004), 'Short communication: workaholism among Norwegian journalists: antecedents and consequences', *Stress and Health*, **20**, 301–8.

Cameron, K., Dutton, J. and Quinn, R. (2003), *Positive Organizational Scholarship: Foundations of a New Discipline*, San Francisco: Berrett-Koehler.

Canatrow, E. (1979), 'Woman workaholics', *Mother Jones*, **6**, 56.

Cashman, K. (1998), *Leadership from the Inside Out*, Provo, UT: Executive Excellence Publishing.

Conger, J.A. and Kanungo, R.N. (1988), 'The empowerment process: integrating theory and practice', *Academy of Management Review*, **13**, 471–82.

Covey, S.R. (1991), *Principle-centered Leadership*, New York: Fireside/Simon and Schuster.

Cummins, T.G. and Worley, C.G. (2005), *Organization Development and Change*, 8th edn, Mason, OH: South-Western College Publishing.

Daft, R.L. (2005), 'The leadership experience', Fort Worth, TX: Harcourt College Publishers.

Deci, E.L. and Ryan, R.M. (1985), *Intrinsic Motivation and Self-determination in Human Behavior*, New York: Plenum.

Deci, E.L. and Ryan, R.M. (2000), 'The "what" and "why" of goal pursuits: human needs and self-determination of behavior', *Psychological Inquiry*, **11** (4), 227–68.

Dubin, R. (1978), *Theory Building*, New York: Free Press.

Farrell, C. (2005), 'The overworked, networked family', *Business Week*, 3 October, 68–73.

Fassel, D. (1990), *Working Ourselves to Death: the High Costs of Workaholism, the Rewards of Recovery*, San Francisco, CA: HarperCollins.

French, W.L., Bell, C.H. and Zawacki, R.A. (2000), *Organization Development and Transformation Managing Effective Change*, 5th edn, Burr Ridge, IL: Irwin-McGraw-Hill.

Friedman, T. (2005), *The World is Flat: a Brief History of the Twenty-first Century*, New York: Farrar, Straus, Giroux.

Fry, L.W. (2003), 'Toward a theory of spiritual leadership', *The Leadership Quarterly*, **14**, 693–727.

Fry, L.W. (2005a), 'Toward a theory of ethical and spiritual well-being and corporate social responsibility through spiritual leadership', in Giacalone, R.A. and Jurkiewicz, C.L. (eds), *Positive Psychology in Business Ethics and Corporate Responsibility*, Greenwich, CT: Information Age Publishing.

Fry, L.W. (2005b), 'Toward a paradigm of spiritual leadership', *The Leadership Quarterly*, **16** (5), 619–21.

Fry, L. and Matherly, L. (2005), 'Workplace spirituality, spiritual leadership, and performance excellence', in S. Roglberg and C. Reeve (eds), *The Encyclopedia of Industrial and Organizational Psychology*, San Francisco: Sage Publishing.

Fry, L.W. and Smith, D.A. (1987), 'Congruence, contingency, and theory building', *Academy of Management Review*, **12** (1), 117–32.

Fry, L.W. and Whittington, J.L. (2005), 'In search of authenticity: spiritual leadership theory as a source for future theory, research, and practice on authentic leadership', in B. Avolio, W. Gardner and F. Walumbwa (eds), *Authentic Leadership Theory and Practice: Origins, Development, and Effects* Monographs in Leadership and Management, Vol. 3, New York: Elsevier, pp. 183–200.

Fry, L.W., Vitucci, S. and Cedillo, M. (2005), 'Transforming the army through spiritual leadership: measurement and establishing a baseline', *The Leadership Quarterly*, **16** (5), 835–62.

Galbraith, J.R. (1977), *Organization Design*, Reading, MA: Addison-Wesley.

Giacalone, R.A. and Jurkiewicz, C.L. (2003), 'Toward a science of workplace spirituality', in R.A. Giacalone and C.L. Jurkiewicz (eds), *Handbook of Workplace Spirituality and Organizational Performance*, New York: M.E. Sharp, pp. 3–28.

Gini, A. (1998), 'Working ourselves to death: workaholism, stress, and fatigue', *Business and Society Review*, **100** (1), 45–6.

Griffiths, Mark (2005), 'Workaholism is still a useful construct', *Addiction Research and Theory*, **13** (2), 97–100.

Harvey, D. and Brown, D. (2001), *An Experimental Approach to Organization Development*, 6th edn, Upper Saddle River, NJ: Prentice Hall.

Kanungo, R.N. and Mendonca, M. (1996), *Ethical Dimensions of Leadership*, Thousand Oaks: Sage Publications.

Kiechel, W. (1989), 'The workaholic generation', *Fortune*, **119** (April), 50–62.

Killinger, B. (1992), *Workaholics, the Respectable Addicts*, East Roseville: Simon and Schuster.

Lawler, E. (2000), *From the Ground Up: Six Principles for Building the New Logic Corporation*, San Francisco: Jossey-Bass.

Machlowitz, M. (1980), 'Workaholism: what is it?', *Saturday Evening Post*, **252** (5), 78–87.

Malone, P.F. and Fry, L.W. (2003), 'Transforming schools through spiritual leadership: a field experiment', paper presented at the Academy of Management, Seattle, WA.

Mandel, M. (2005), 'The real reasons you're working so hard . . . and what you can do about it', *Business Week*, 3 October 63–7.

Matherly, L.L., Fry, L.W. and Ouimret, R. (2005), 'A strategic scorecard model of performance excellence through spiritual leadership', paper presented at the national meeting of the Academy of Management, Honolulu, Hawaii.

McMillan, L. and O'Driscoll, M. (2004), 'Workaholism and health', *Journal of Organizational Change Management*, **17** (5), 509–19.

Mitroff, I.I., Pearson, C.M. and Mason, R.O. (1994), *Framebreak: the Radical Redesign of American Business*, Edison, NJ: Jossey-Bass.

Mudrack, P. (2004), 'Job involvement, obsessive-compulsive personality traits, and workaholic behavioral tendencies', *Journal of Organizational Change Management*, **17** (5), 490–507.

Naughton, T.J. (1987), 'A conceptual view of workaholism and implications for career counseling and research', *Career Development Quarterly*, **6**, 180–87.

Oates, W. (1971), *Confessions of a Workaholic: the Facts about Work Addiction*, New York: World.

Porter, G. (1996), 'Organizational impact of workaholism: suggestions for researching the negative outcomes of excessive work', *Journal of Occupational Health Psychology*, **1**, 70–84.

Porter, G. (2004), 'Work, work ethic, work excess', *Journal of Organizational Change Management*, **17** (5), 424–39.

Robinson, B.E. (1998), *Chained to the Desk: a Guidebook for Workaholics, Their Partners and Children, and the Clinicians Who Treat Them*, New York: New York University Press.

Ryan, K.D. and Grolnick, W.S. (1986), 'Origins and pawns in the classroom: self-report and projective assessments of individual differences in children's perceptions', *Journal of Personality and Social Psychology*, **50**, 550–58.

Ryan, K.D. and La Guardia, J.G. (2000), 'What is being optimized over development? A self-determination theory perspective on basic psychological needs across the life span', in S. Qualls and R. Ables (eds), *Dialogues on Psychology and Aging*, Washington, DC: American Psychological Association, pp. 145–72.

Ryan, R.M. and Oestreich, D. (1991), *Driving Fear Out of the Workplace: How to Overcome the Invisible Barriers to Quality, Productivity, and Innovation*, San Francisco: Jossey-Bass.

Ryan, R.M., Stiller, J. and Lynch, J.H. (1994), 'Representations of relationships to teachers, parents, and friends as predictors of academic motivation and self-esteem', *Journal of Early Adolescence*, **14**, 226–49.

Ryff, C.D. and Singer, B. (2001), 'From social structure to biology: integrative science in pursuit of human health and well-being', in C.R. Snyder and S.J. Lopez (eds), *Handbook of Positive Psychology*, Oxford and New York: Oxford University Press.

Schaef, A.W. and Fassel, D. (1988), *The Addictive Organization*, San Francisco, CA: Harper & Row.

Schor, J.B. (1991), *The Overworked American*, New York: Basic Books.

Scott, K., Moore, K. and Miceli, M. (1997), 'An exploration of the meaning and consequences of workaholism', *Human Relations*, **50** (3), 287–314.

Senge, P. (1990), *The Fifth Discipline*, New York: Doubleday.

Snir, R. and Harpaz, I. (2004), 'Attitudinal and demographic antecedents of work-aholism', *Journal of Organizational Change Management*, **17** (5), 520–36.

Snyder, C.R. and Lopez, S.J. (eds) (2001), *Handbook of Positive Psychology*, Oxford and New York: Oxford University Press.

Spence, J. and Robbins, A. (1992) 'Workaholism: definition, measurement, and preliminary Results', *Journal of Personality Assessment*, **58** (1), 160.

Sprankel, J.K. and Ebel, H. (1987), *The Workaholic Syndrome*, New York: Walker.

Spreitzer, G. (1996), 'Social structural characteristics of psychological empowerment', *Academy of Management Journal*, **39** (2), 483–504.

Stanfield, G. (1976), 'Technology and structure as theoretical categories', *Administrative Science Quarterly*, **21**, 489–93.

Steers, R.M. and Porter, L.W. (eds) (1983), *Motivation and Work Behavior*, 3rd edn, New York: McGraw-Hill.

Thomas, K. (2000), *Intrinsic Motivation at Work: Building Energy and Commitment*, San Francisco, CA: Berrett-Koehler.

Tisehler, L. (2005), 'Extreme jobs (and the people who love them)', *Fast Company*, **93** (April), 54–60.

Valas, H. and Sovik, N. (1993), 'Variables affecting students' intrinsic motivation for school mathematics: two empirical studies based on Deci's and Ryan's theory of motivation', *Learning and Instruction*, **3**, 281–98.

Warr, P. (1999), 'Well-being and the workplace', in D. Kahnerman and N. Schwarz (eds), *Well-Being: the Foundation of Hedonic Psychology*, New York: Russell Sage Foundation.

Whetten, D. and Cameron, K. (1998), *Developing Management Skills*, 4th edn, Reading, MA: Addison-Wesley.

Workaholics Anonymous (2005), http://www.workaholics-anonymous.org/.

Index